I0818813

ALEXANDRA FULLERTON

THE ULTIMATE GUIDE TO HERMÈS BAGS

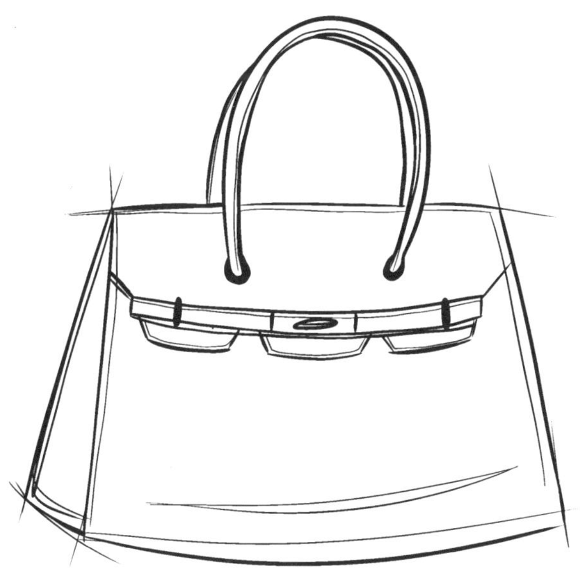

teNeues

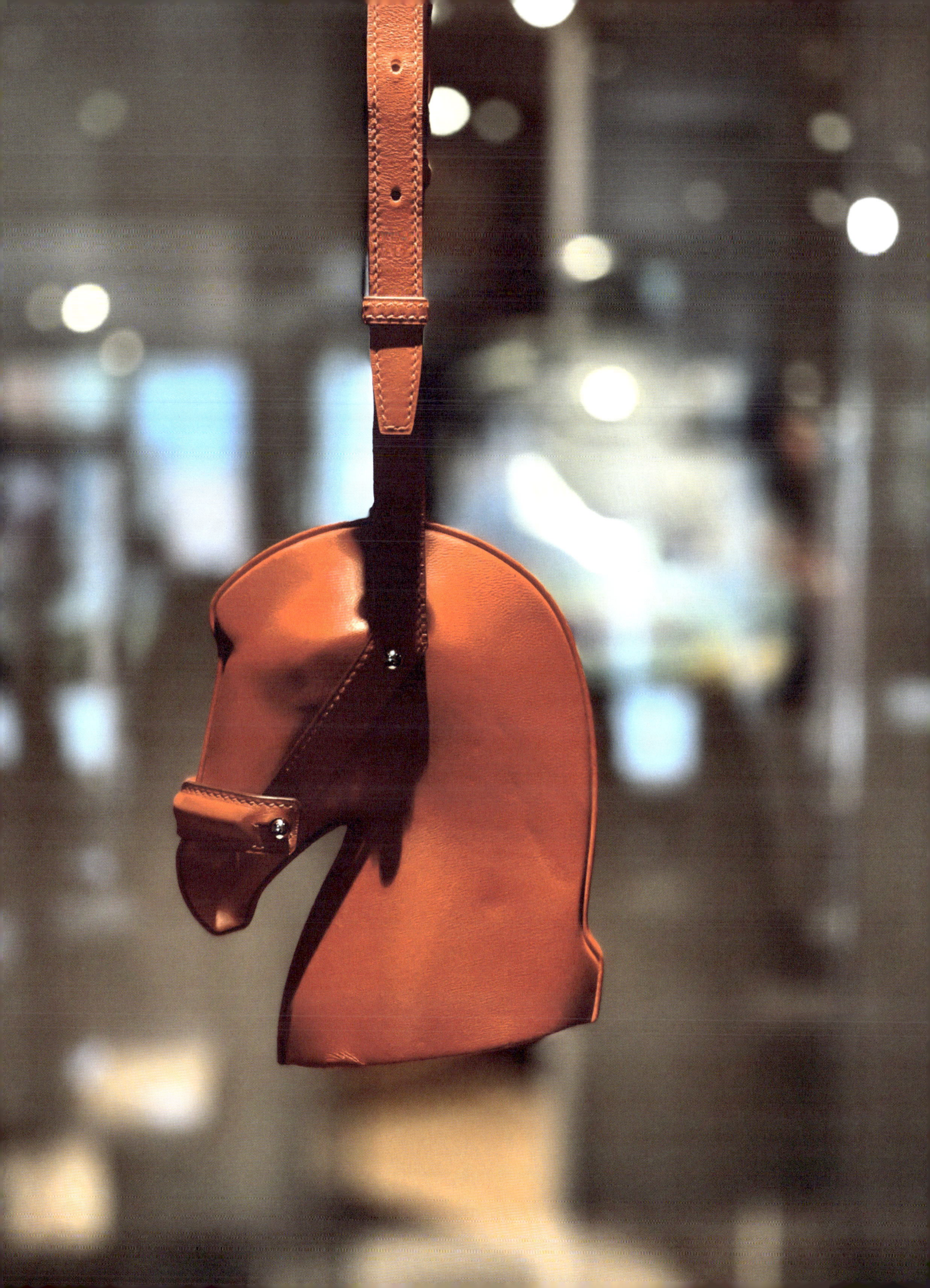

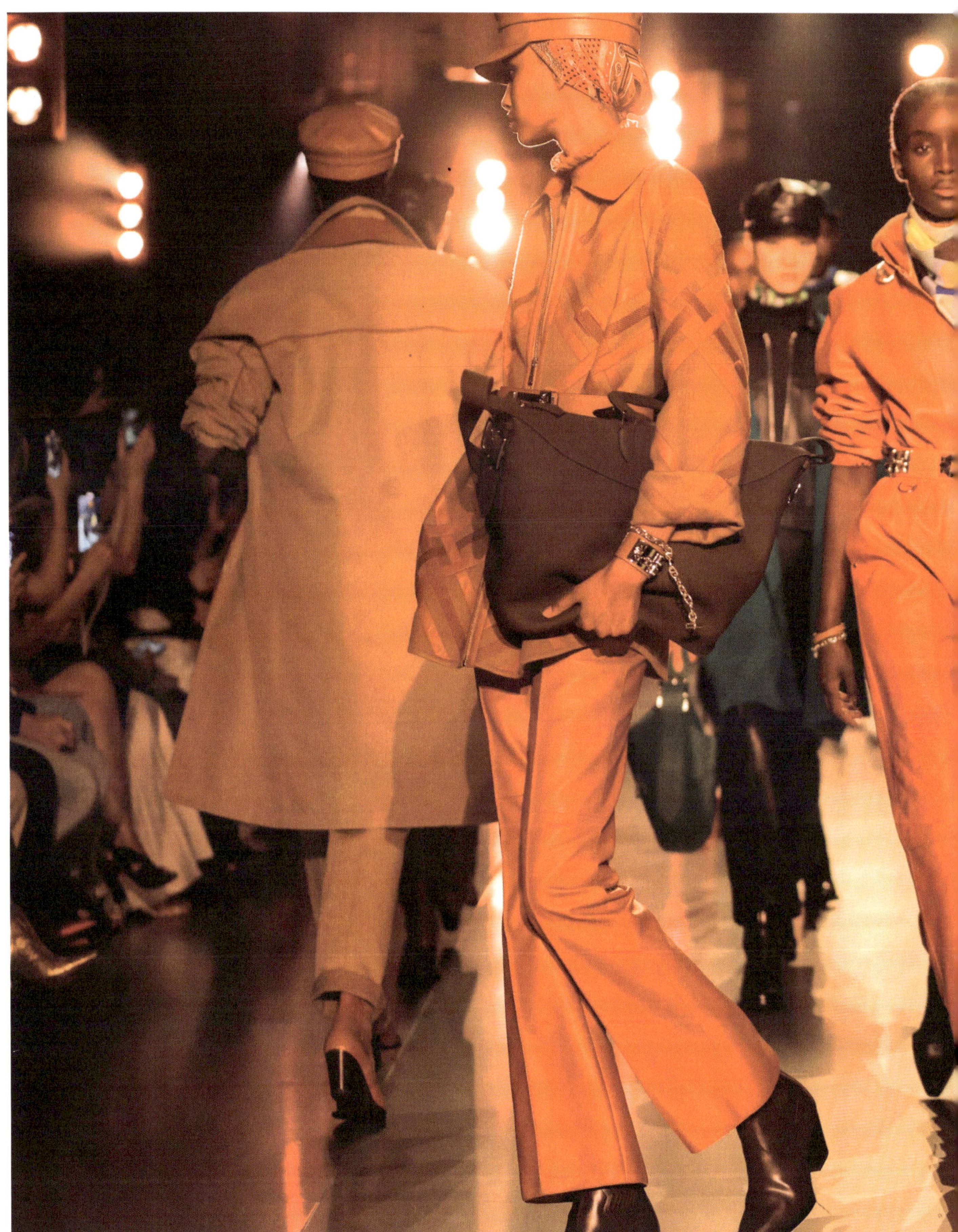

Fall/Winter 2024 Hermès women's runway show, New York City, 2024

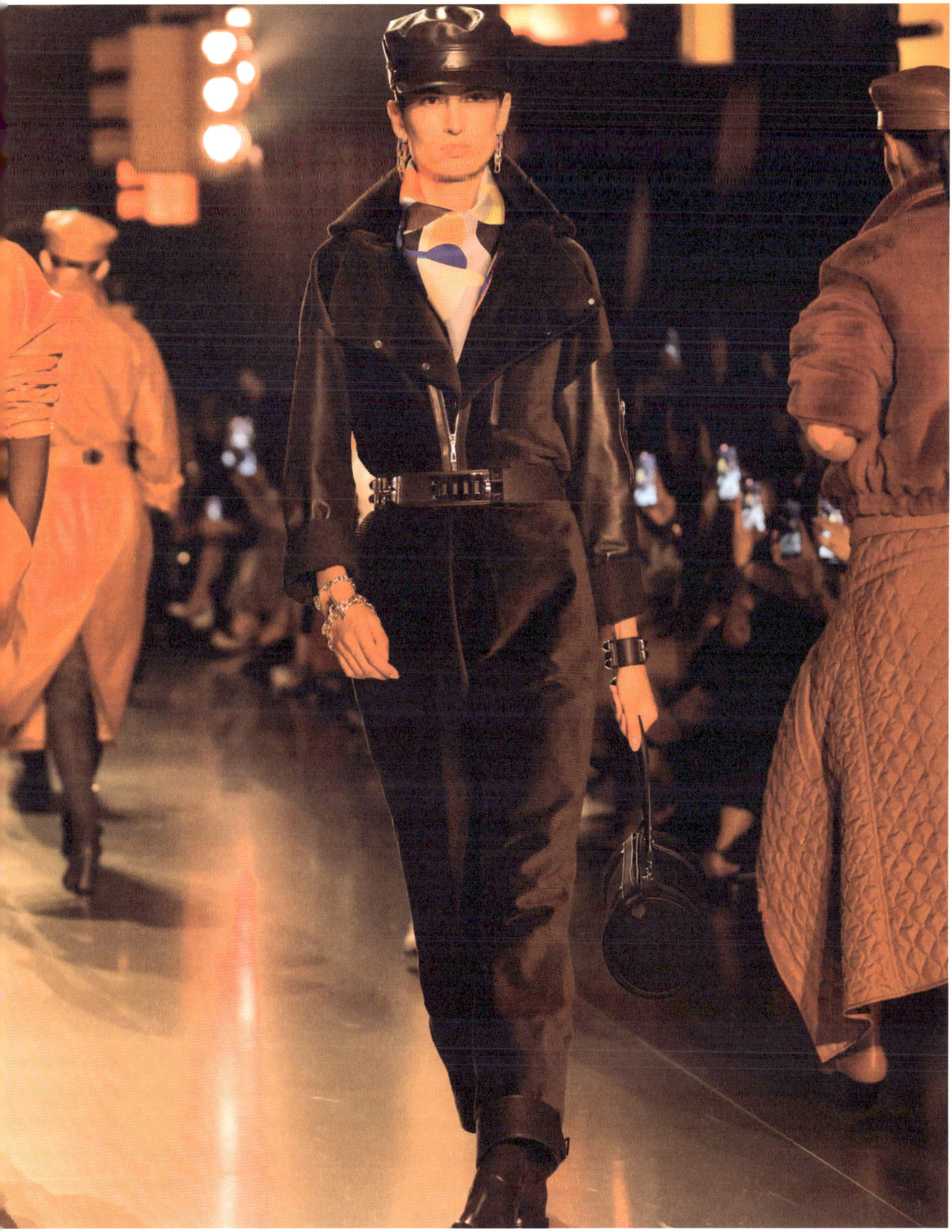

For those that dream of orange boxes, this book will become the ultimate guide to the rarified world of the Hermès handbag. Charting the history of the oldest luxury fashion maison in the world, we unpick the legacy of the Kelly bag and investigate the Birkin's status as the most desired bag in the world.

Highlighting the rarest Hermès bags and the most expensive models to be sold at auction, this book pays tribute to the incredible savoir faire and unique manufacturing methods that have created accessory icons.

In the pages of this book, you'll meet a glittering cast of film, fashion, music and TV legends, all enraptured with the heritage French house. As you discover the bags that are the very definition of the word luxury, you too will understand the world's obsession with the totes, clutches and handbags of Hermès.

Next page: Magazine advertisement for Birkin bags, 2004

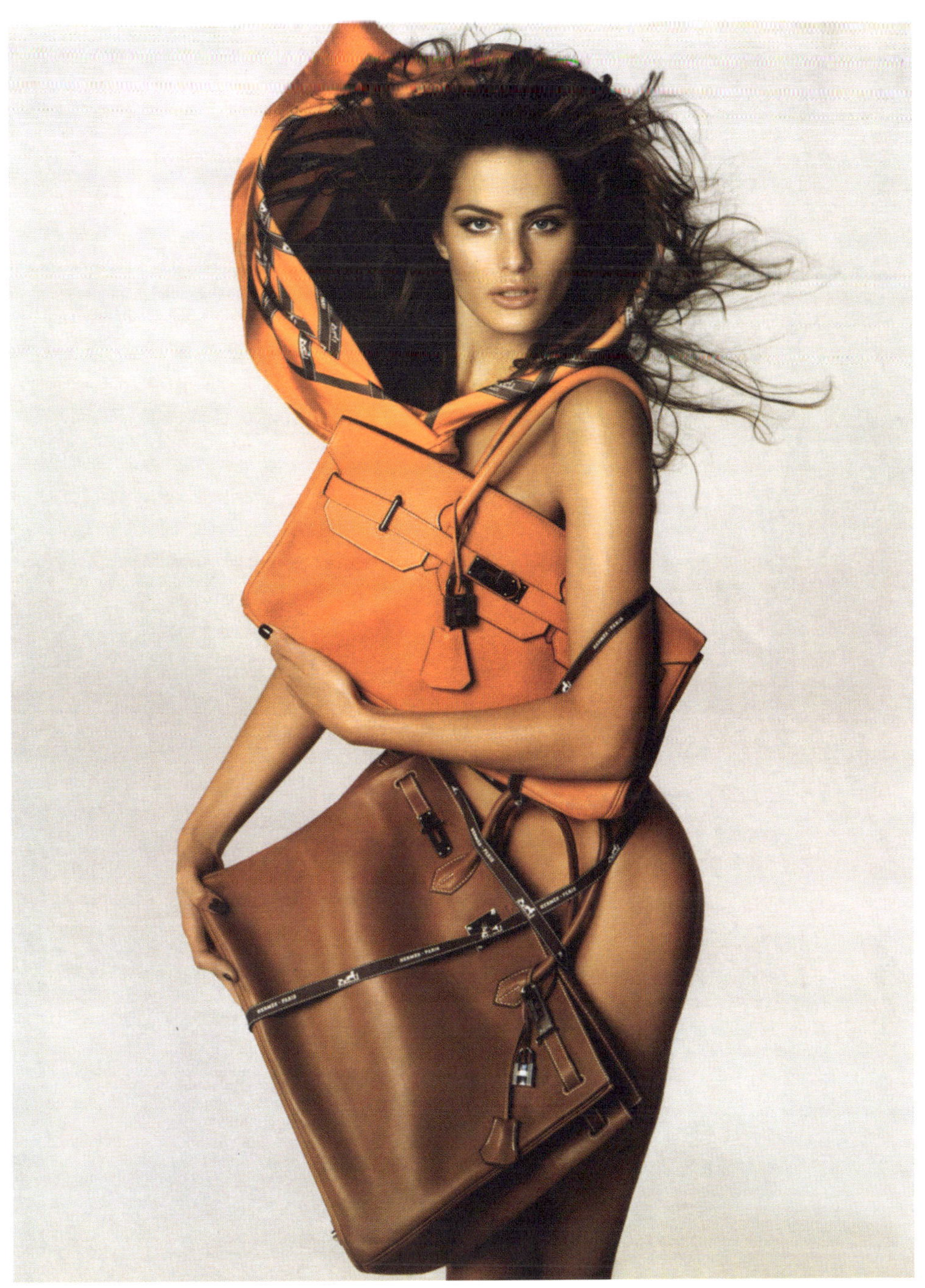
HERMES · PARIS

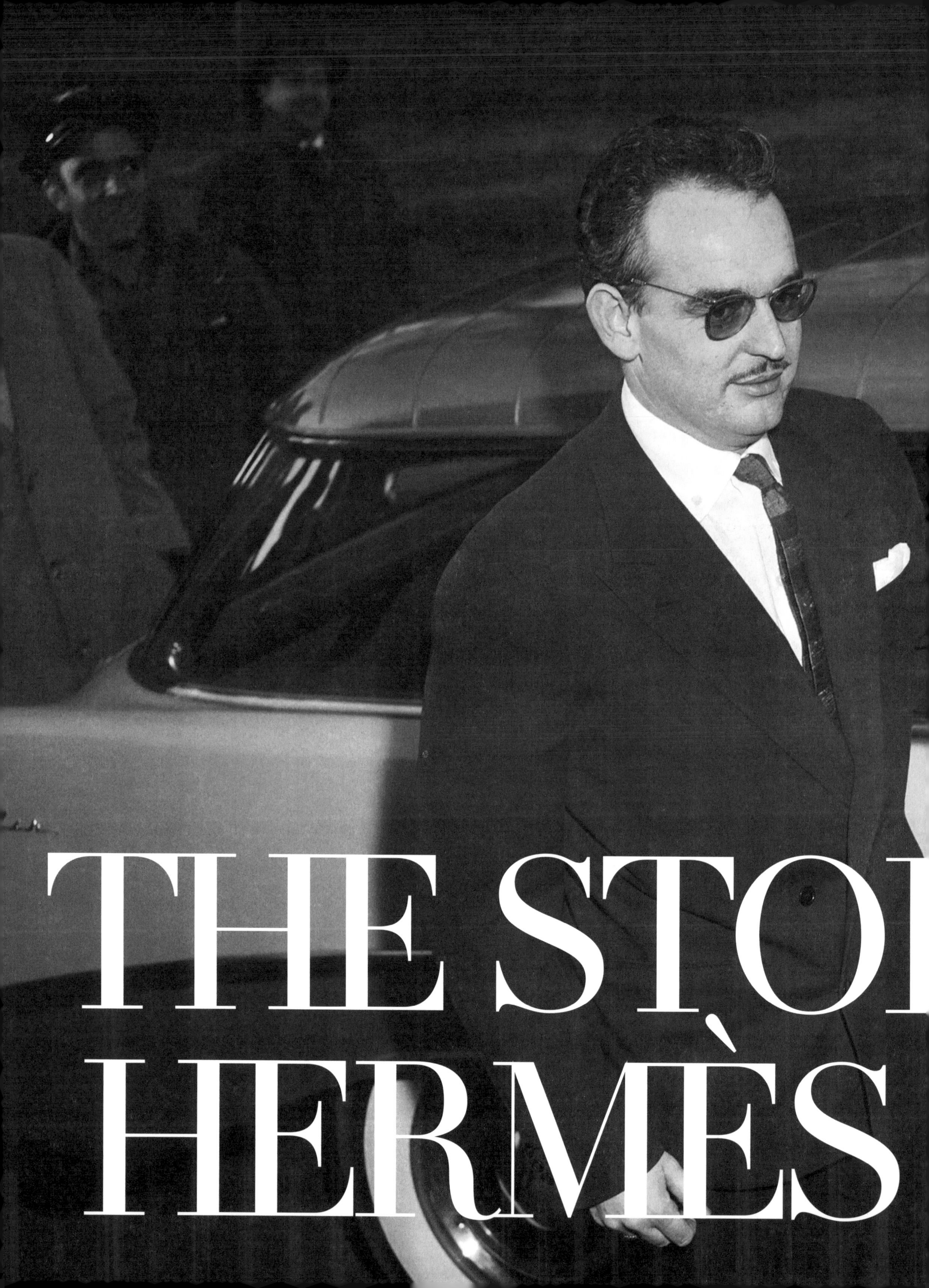

THE STO
HERMÈS

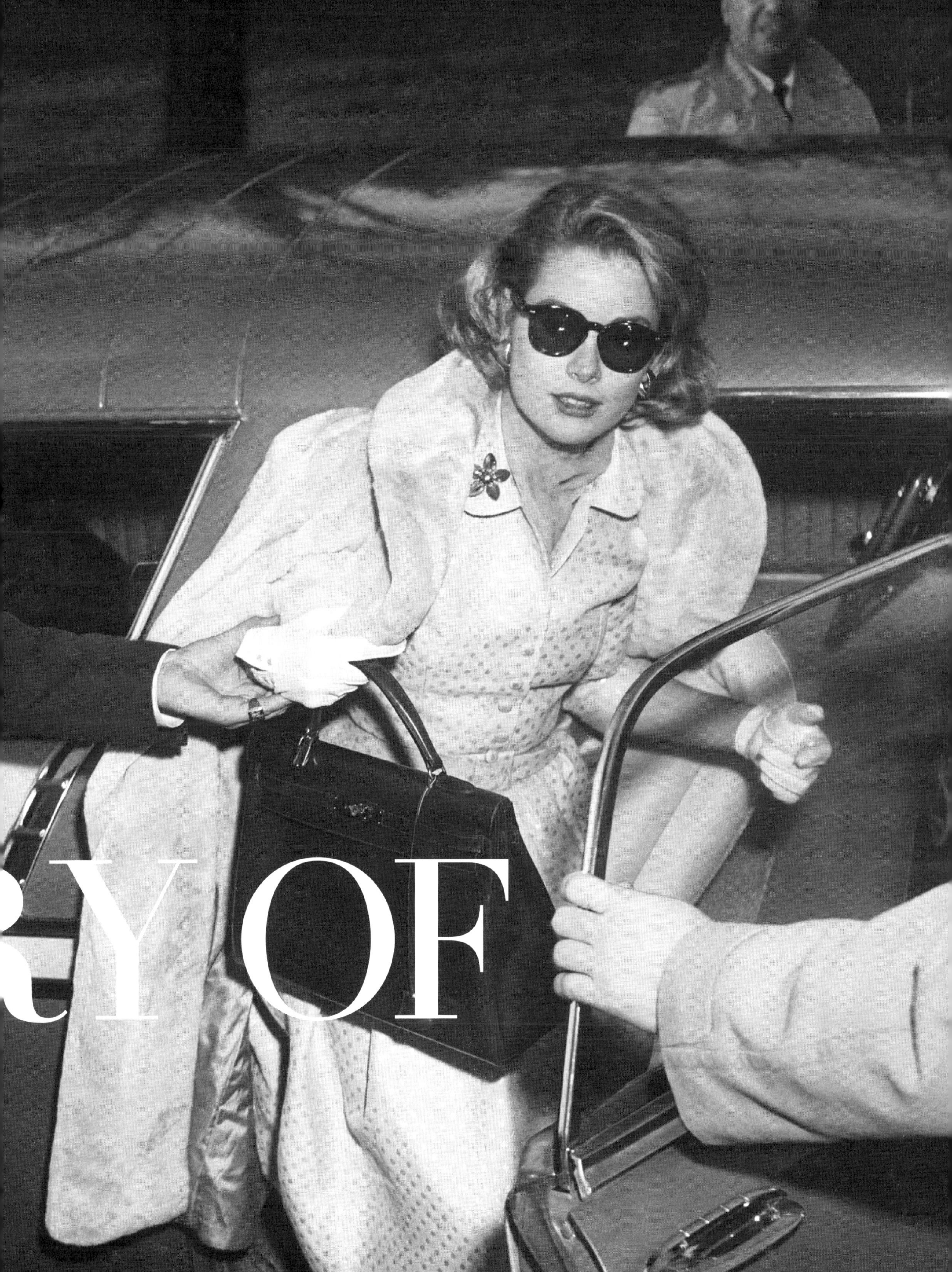
Y OF

HOW IT ALL BEGAN

As the oldest luxury *maison* still in operation today, Hermès has set itself apart from the fripperies of fashion for almost 200 years. Beyond the trends and one-season wonders, the house of Hermès has been synonymous with the very highest quality of leather goods and immaculate design since 1837. Today Hermès bags are the most sought-after—and expensive—on the planet. However, the *maison's* origins lay in a completely different field...

The man who started the story was Thierry Hermès. Born on January 10, 1801, he was the seventh child of Agnes Kuenen and Diederich Hermes (without the accent), in the city of Krefeld. Now situated in Germany, at the time, Krefeld was a French territory following Napoleon Bonaparte's Revolutionary Wars, thus the young Diederich (named after his father) was a French citizen by birth. His (and his father's) first name was Frenchified to Thierry in the birth certificate.

According to the latest research, the Hermes family had its roots in Krefeld and had been living in the region for some time. The details of Hermès' immediate family member's professions are hazy. Some sources suggest Hermes senior was an innkeeper, or that he ran a hotel or a silk business. The city of Krefeld was indeed known for its rich textile manufacturing businesses. However, regardless of their roles, both Agnes and Thierry senior died of tuberculosis in 1813 and 1814, and Hermès emigrated to France in 1921.

Settling in the town of Pont Audemar in Normandy, in northwestern France, Hermès started to learn leatherworking in the region believed to be his forefathers'. Water was essential to the leather industry, and since the town was situated on a river, with many canals weaving their way between timbered buildings, it was the ideal spot for tanneries and workshops. Hermès became an apprentice to Monsieur Pleumer, who operated a harness production company in the town. He excelled in all the skills and methods used to create exceptional leather goods.

While learning his trade, Hermès resided on Rue de la Brasserie in the town. In 1828 he married Christine Pierrat. Being both a brilliant artisan and an astute businessman, Hermès moved his family (with son Charles-Émile) to Paris in 1837. At the time, the French capital was powered by horses. With around 70,000 horses in Paris, each needing harnesses, carriage fittings and other tack, Hermès spotted a gap in the market for his beautifully crafted equestrian gear. The first Hermès workshops were situated at 59 Rue Basse-du-Rempart (now in the 9th *arrondissement.)* Targeting the nobility in the city, a cultural and commercial hotspot, Hermès' clients included Eugenie, wife of Napoleon III, whose influence encouraged other members of high society to patronize Hermès, too.

Previous pages: Prince Rainier III of Monaco and his fiancée Grace Kelly

Next page: Hermès building at 24 Rue du Faubourg Saint-Honoré in Paris, January 28, 1988, pictured on the company's 150th anniversary celebration.

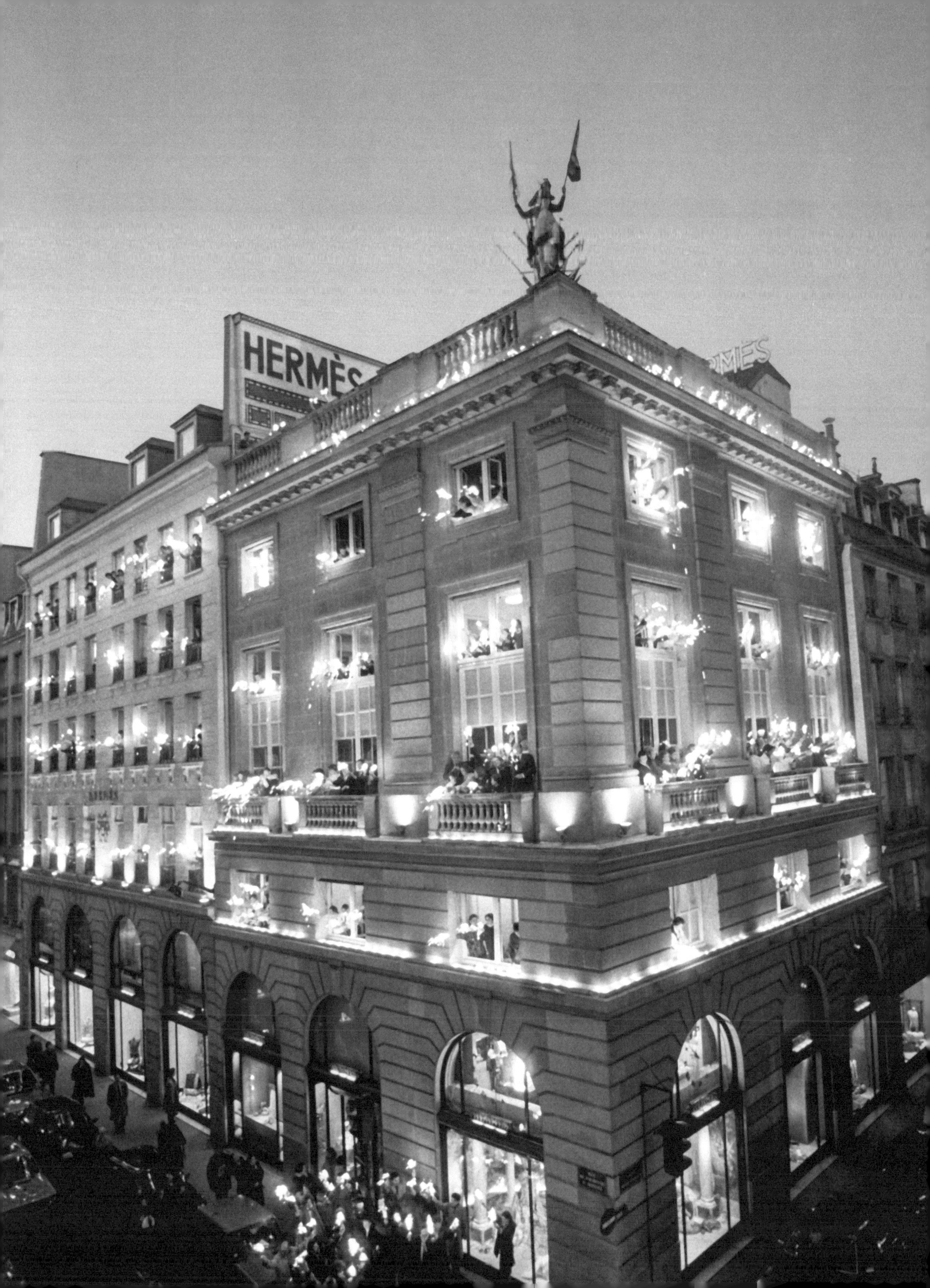
HERMÈS

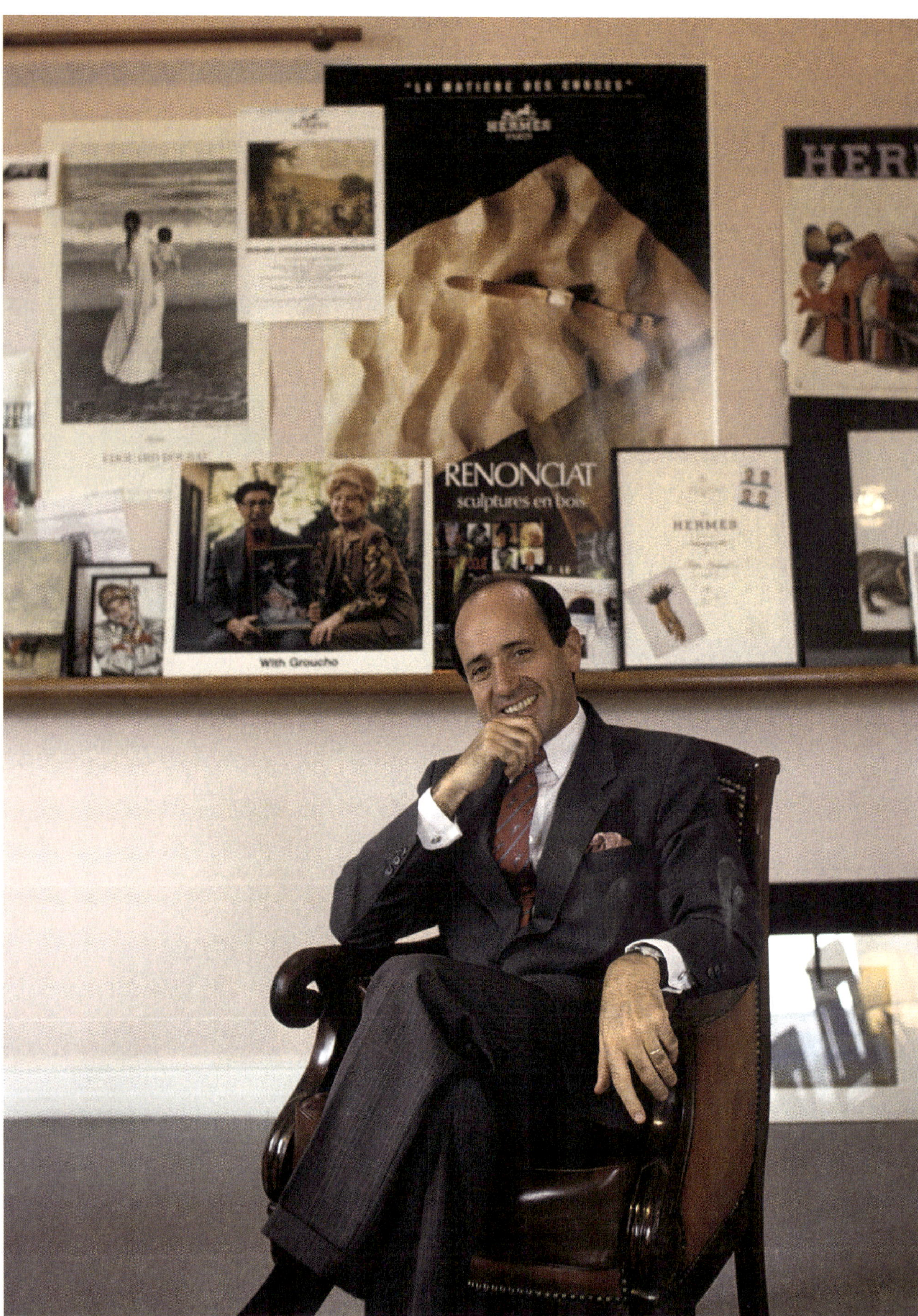

Jean-Louis Dumas, Paris, 1989

HERMÈS HAS BEEN SYNONYMOUS WITH THE VERY HIGHEST QUALITY SINCE 1837

The technical finesse in Hermès' harness work won an award at the *Exposition Universelle* in 1855; a prize for outstanding technical ability, craftsmanship and design followed in 1867 at the Paris World's Fair. Hermès created—and became famous for—a particular style of double saddle stitch. Using two needles and strong waxed linen threads, the stitches are created by sewing in opposite directions, so even if one row frays, there will always be a sturdy back-up. This unique stitch is still used today for every bag made by Hermès.

The growth of France's economy following Napoleon III's election as president in 1848 (and subsequent promotion to Emperor in 1852) coincided with a concerted effort to beautify Paris and create the architectural aesthetic we recognize today. A grand plan was undertaken to replace the smaller streets and alleys (such as Rue Basse-du-Rempart) with wide avenues. Hermés had to move and found a new workshop location on Place de la Madeleine. While it may have been an inconvenience to relocate, the economy was booming, which undoubtedly helped Hermés. Apparently, the relocation was partially funded by an eviction payment from the Prefect de Seine, the local government body, and the Rue Basse-du-Rempart buildings were demolished to make way for new, wider streets.

In 1859, Thierry decided it was time to step down from the business, and his son Charles-Émile began managing Hermès' workshops. Thierry died on his birthday in 1878, aged 77, but thanks to his years of experience, Charles-Émile was in a good position to help his father's *maison* grow and evolve.

Charles-Émile moved the retail shop to 24 Rue du Faubourg Saint-Honoré, where a store is still located today. In 1900, Charles-Émile introduced innovative new products: saddles and a clever bag to carry them in (the *Haut à Courroies)*. Meanwhile, his sons Adolphe and Émile-Maurice were learning the ropes. Legend has it that on Émile-Maurice's first business trip to Russia in 1897, he took a notepad with the addresses of influential people to meet. He returned to Paris with so many orders that the workshop took months to complete them all. It seems that waiting for a piece of Hermès magic has been stitched into the company's DNA for centuries.

Adolphe and Émile-Maurice took charge of the family business in 1902 following Charles-Émile's retirement. With the brothers in charge, Hermès was renamed to Hermès Frères, and sales expanded beyond Paris to North African, Asian and American clients, along with Czar Nicholas II of Russia. Hermès' fame was growing both internationally and at home in France. French workshops now employed 80 craftsmen, and new boutiques opened in Chantilly, famed for its horse racing and equestrian heritage, as well as Fontainebleau, Pau St Cyr, Samar, Le Touquet and La Baule. However, the rise of the motorcar made Adolphe nervous about the business's prospects. He sold his share of the family firm to Émile-Maurice in 1919 because he didn't believe a saddlery manufacturer could survive in an increasingly motorized world. Émile-Maurice disagreed. He proceeded to launch accessories for cars and secured exclusive rights to zippered fastenings, a revolutionary piece of innovative engineering at the time. Inspired by the 'close-all' device on the roofs of military cars, which Émile-Maurice had seen on a trip to Canada, Hermès launched the first zippered jacket in 1918. The bespoke jacket in question was a leather golf jacket made for Edward, Prince of Wales, the future Duke of Windsor—and the zipper became known in France as a *fermeture Hermès* (Hermès fastener).

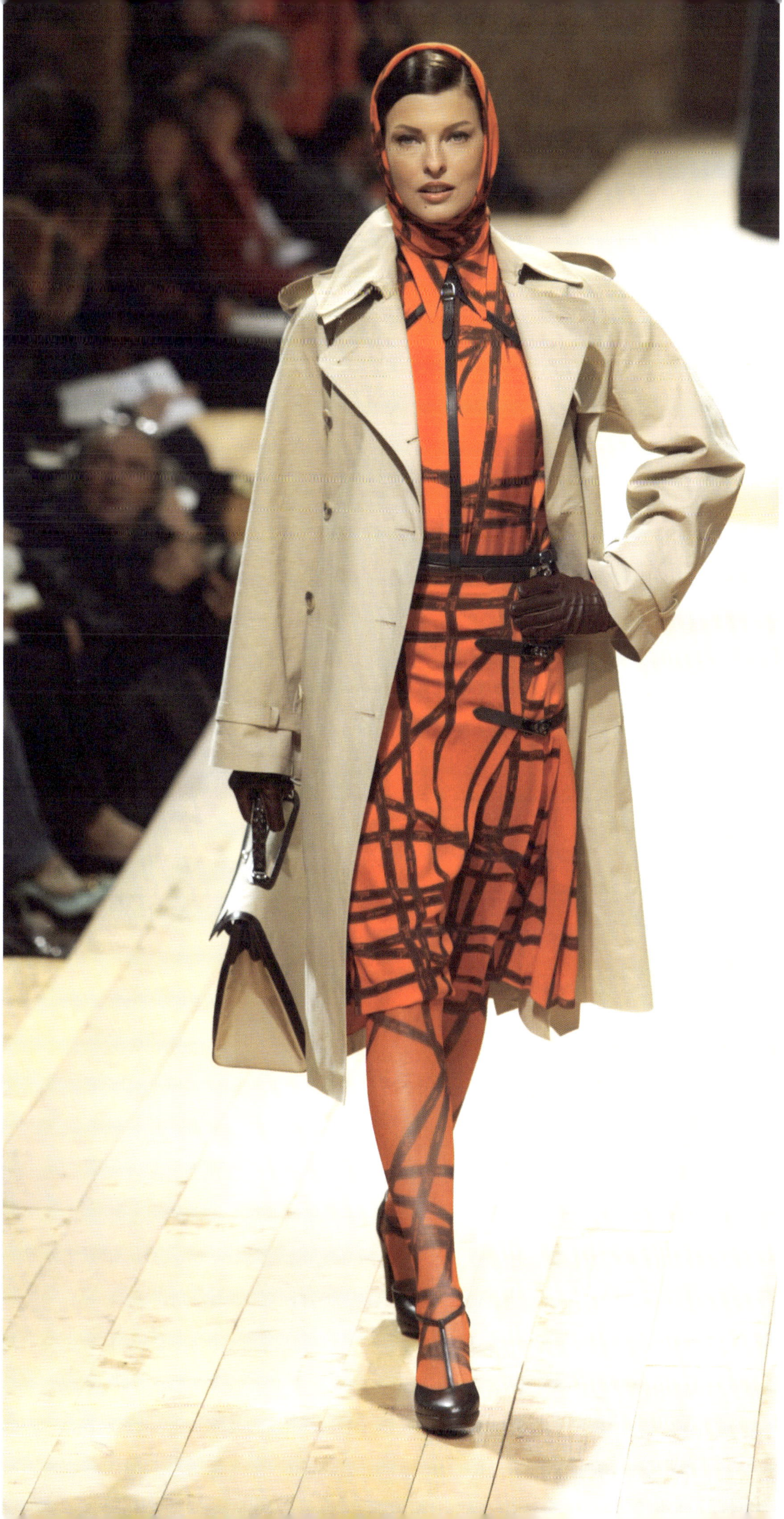

Previous page: Linda Evangelista walking down the runway at the Fall/Winter 2004 Hermès show in Paris

This page: The Duchess of Windsor wearing a Hermès bag, aboard the S.S. United States as she and the Duke of Windsor arrive in New York for one of their regular visits to the States

Next page: Prince Rainier III and Grace Kelly arriving at Rome Airport. Kelly is carrying the Hermès bag that was later named after her.

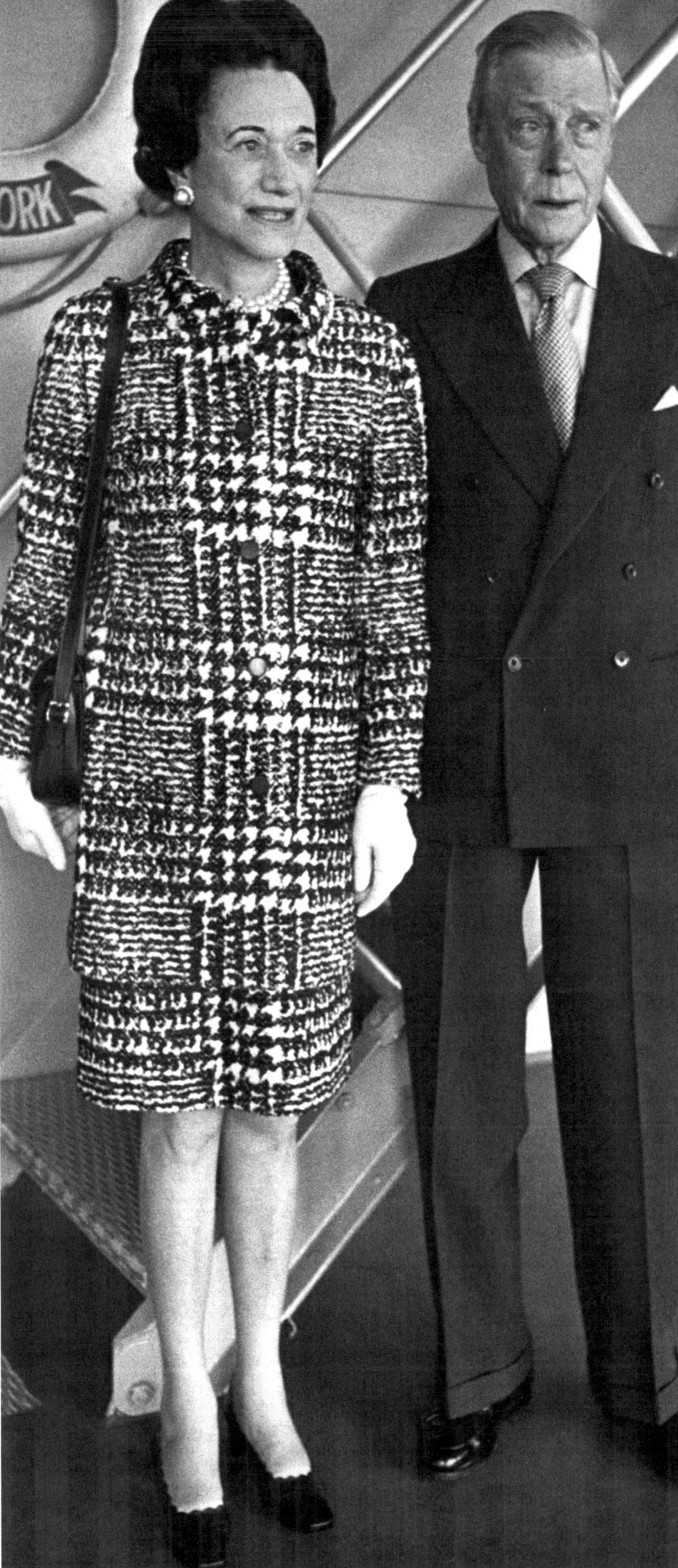

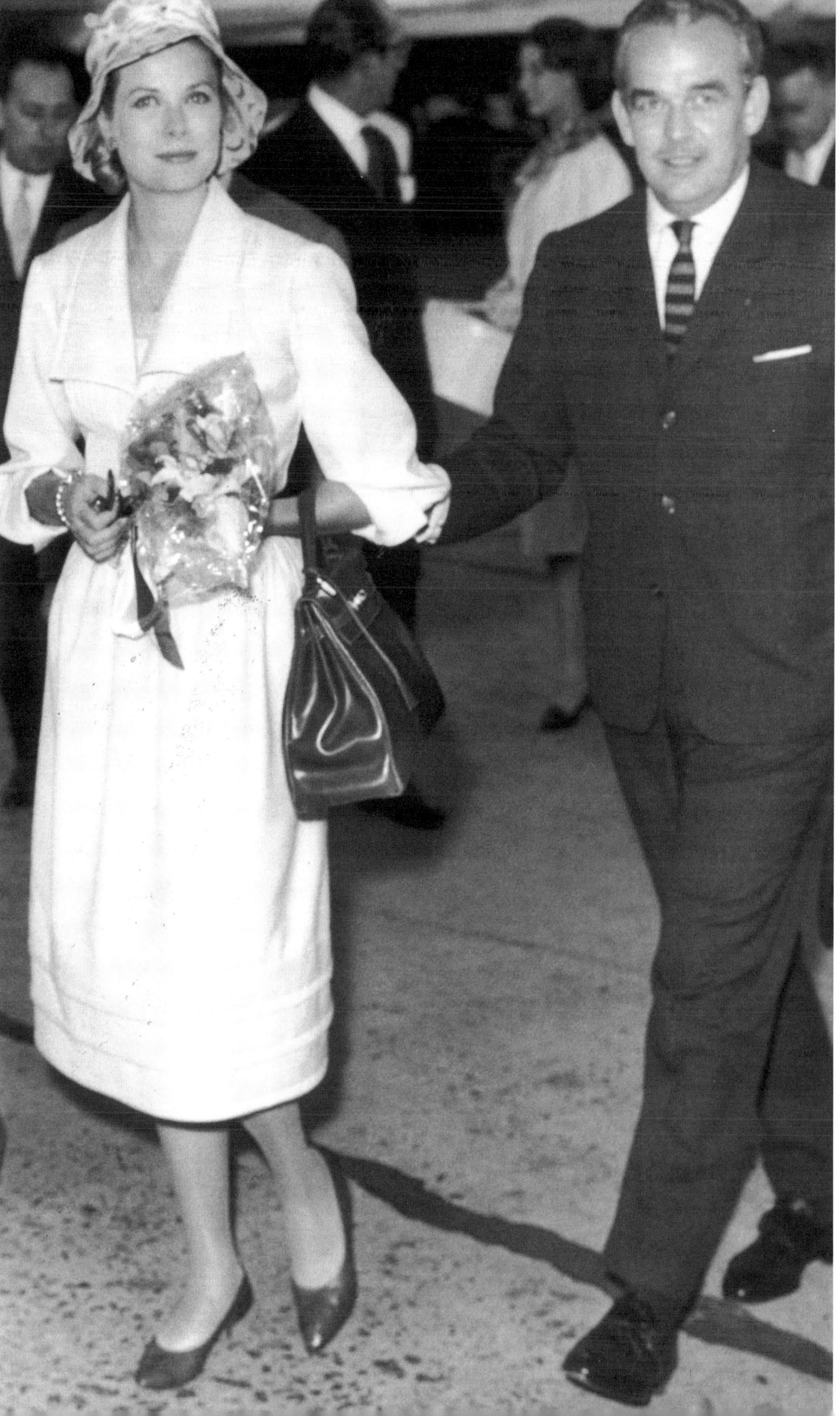

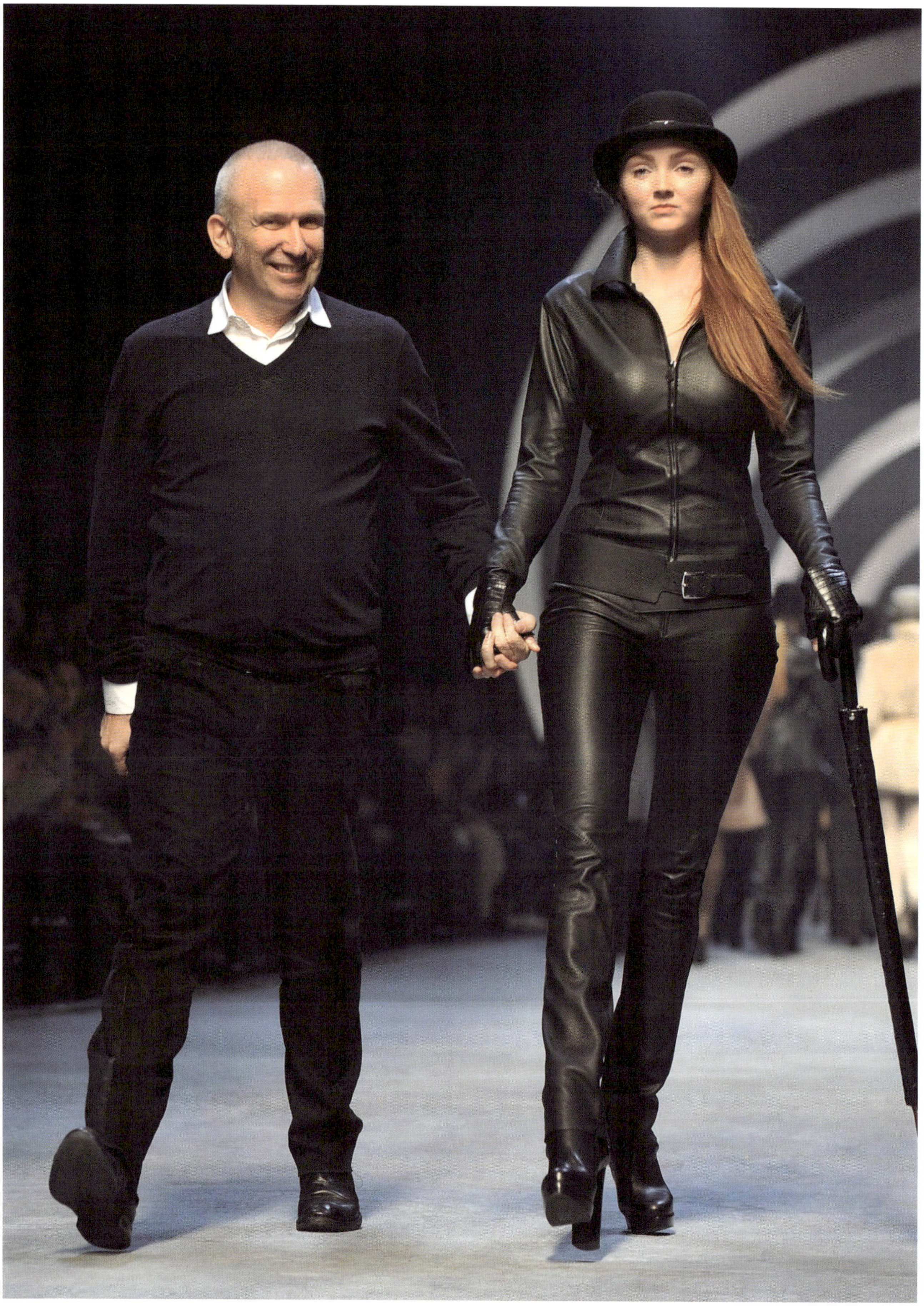

It was also poised to become a useful closure for luggage collections as international travel became more commonplace through the 1920s and beyond.

The Roaring Twenties was the decade when Hermès made a splash in womenswear, and it was also the decade when Hermès bags (beyond the saddle carrier) were launched. Émile-Maurice's wife, Julie, couldn't find a bag she wanted to carry. At the time, most bags for upper-class women were boxy and restrictive, while working women used satchel style bags. Undaunted, Émile-Maurice created the perfect bag for his wife, and the first collection of Hermès bags for women was launched in 1922. The focus continued to shift from horses to women: in 1929, Lola Prousac designed Hermés' first couture womenswear line, which previewed in Paris and included bathing suits. Today Hermès makes regular seasonal appearances at Paris Fashion Week.

Émile-Maurice and Julie had four daughters. Simone, their third child, sadly passed away at 15, but the other daughters went on to marry husbands who all joined Hermès as business partners. Yvonne married Francis Puech, Jacqueline married Robert Dumas and Aline married perfumer Jean René Guerrand. These men would all play significant roles in the company's next stages. Today it seems surprising that Émile-Maurice's daughters didn't join in the family business, but in the early 20th century, it was still very much a man's world, and working women would have been frowned upon.

During his tenure, Dumas was responsible for creating the *sac a dépeches*—a chic bag launched in 1935 which came to be known as the Kelly bag—and the signature square *carrés* scarves, first sold in 1937. Robert also changed his name to Dumas-Hermès, as he was the first family member not directly descended from Thierry to lead the *maison,* succeeding Émile-Maurice after his death in 1951.

World War II had a notable impact on Hermès' visual history. After Paris's liberation from German occupation in 1945, cream-coloured cardboard was scarce because of the war, and the supplier for Hermès packaging could only provide orange. Although it wasn't an intentional choice, the distinctive orange boxes accompanied every purchase and have become synonymous with the *maison* ever since. By contrast, *Le Duc Attelé,* the illustration of a two-horse carriage printed on every Hermès box, *was* a conscious branding choice and was registered as an official trademark around the same time.

Hermès' customers now included the Duke and Duchess of Windsor, Humphrey Bogart, Lauren Bacall and Jean Cocteau. The reputation of the *maison* was growing as the ultimate destination for bespoke luxury. Today, the brand is as strong as ever, with celebrity fans including the late Queen Elizabeth II, who had a vast collection of Hermès scarves; Meghan Markle (who owns everything from sandals to puffer jackets from the *maison);* and Kim Kardashian, who has a seemingly infinite collection of Birkin bags.

Throughout the fifties and sixties, watches, ties, jewelry, belts, perfumes and other exquisite *objets*, including a portable liquor cabinet commissioned by Sammy Davis, Jr. joined the Hermès catalog. New stores opened worldwide. However, sales slowed in the late 1960s, and in 1971, Robert and Jacqueline's son Jean-Louis was appointed CEO and tasked with reinvigorating Hermès design strategy. With experience from the buyer-training program at American department store Bloomingdales, Jean-Louis brought innovation and ideas to the *maison*. Following Robert's death in 1978, Jean-Louis was named chairman; during his tenure, sales grew from $50 million in 1978 to $460 million by 1990.

Some of Jean-Louis's strategies were met with surprise at the time. He introduced ostrich-skin jeans and python-skin biker jackets, appointed 19 year-old designer Eric Bergère as artistic director and commissioned a shocking ad campaign in 1979 featuring cool young Parisiennes wearing Hermès scarves *and* jeans. His colleagues were reportedly outraged, but it was actually a clever way to introduce the brand to a younger clientele and reinvigorate demand for all things Hermès for a new generation.

While Hermès family members took the helm in the earlier part of the *maison's* history and continue to lead on business matters, a significant number of external designers and creative directors have come on board over the years to create Hermès' distinctive quiet luxury look. Véronique Nichanian has been responsible for the men's collections since 1988, taking the role of artistic director for all men's products. While many describe Hermès as a luxury designer, in 2020 Nichanian told the Financial Times, "For many years, I hate this word of luxury, because it does not mean anything." In an interview with writer Alexander Fury, she continued, "Everybody does luxury. Small leather [goods], it's luxury. They put a logo, it's luxury." Explaining the Hermès approach, her thoughts become clearer. "We are doing quality things and beautiful things. What is luxury today? It is just to be deeply honest in what you're doing."

Between 1997 and 2003, Martin Margiela was Hermès' creative director and combined his own wildly avant-garde aesthetic with the *maison's* inherent classicism.

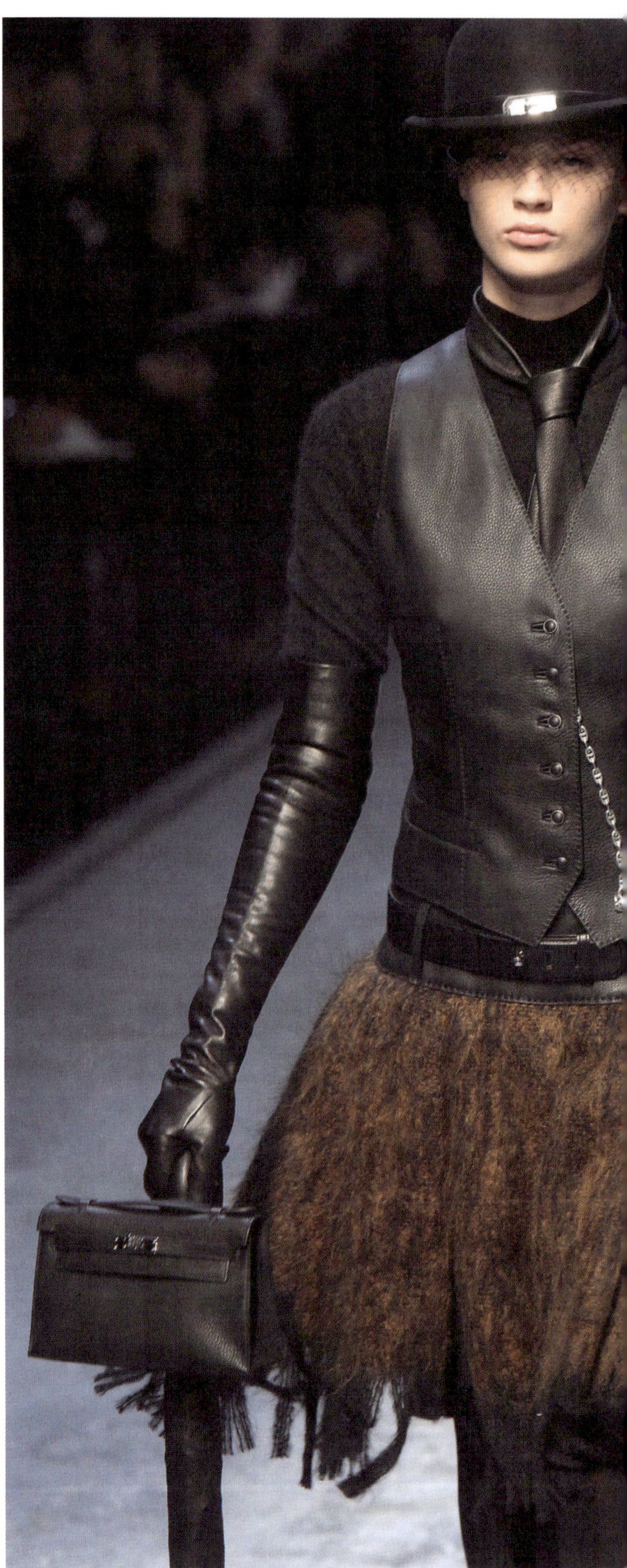

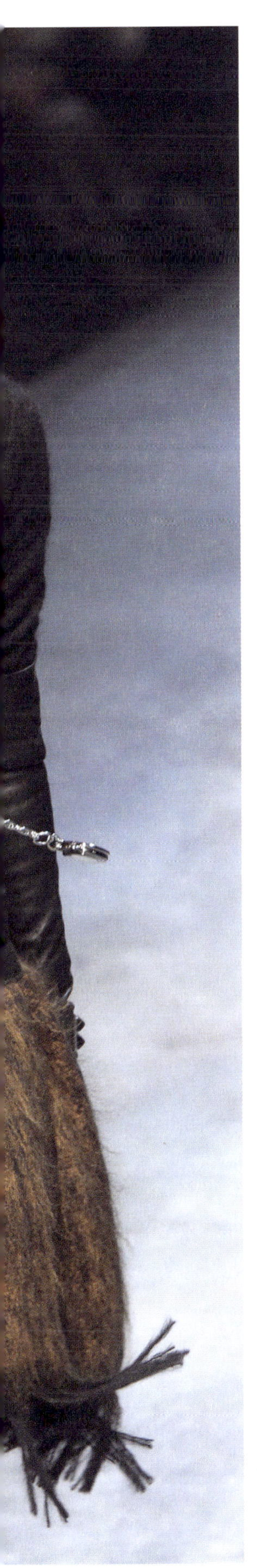

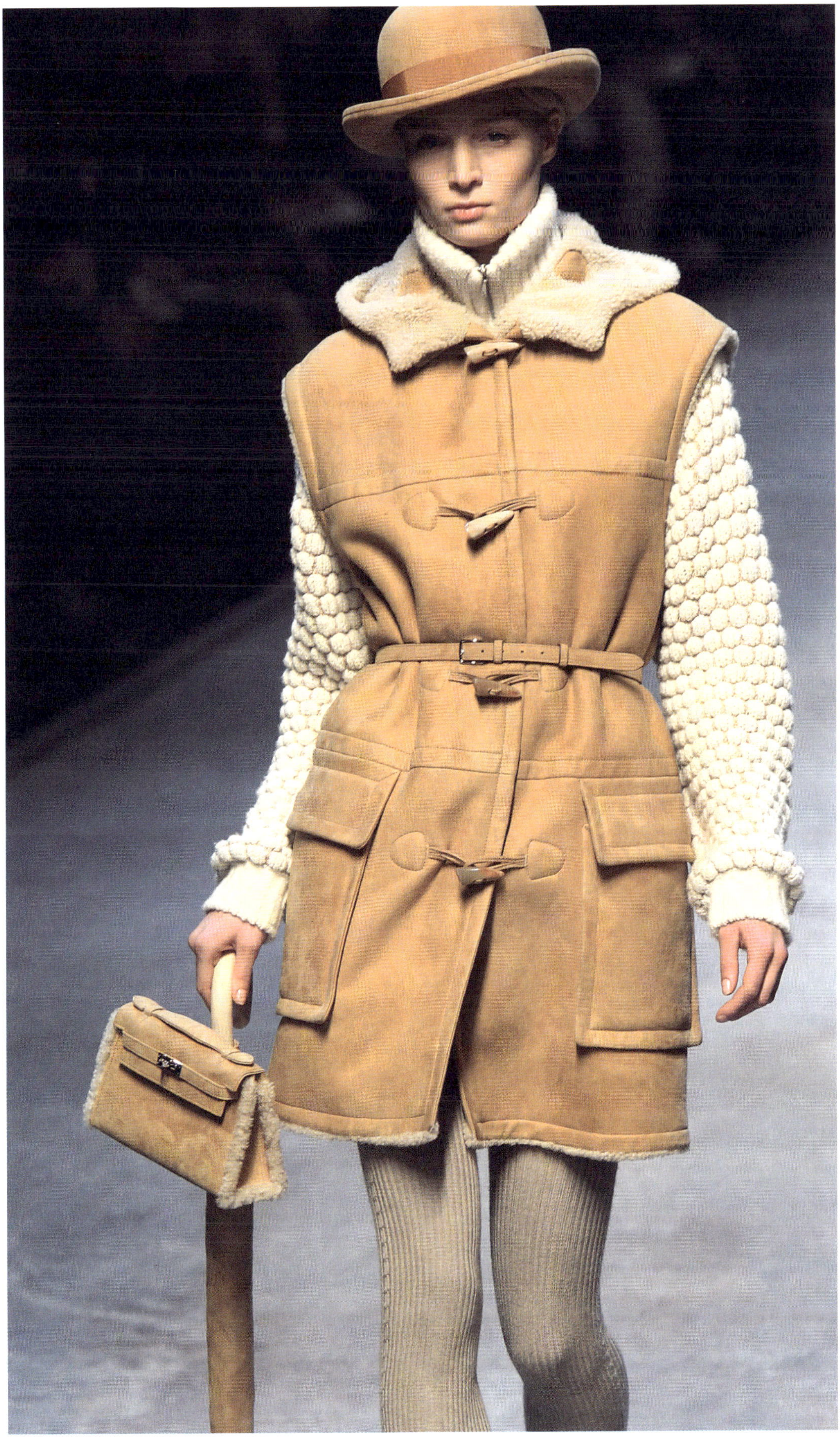

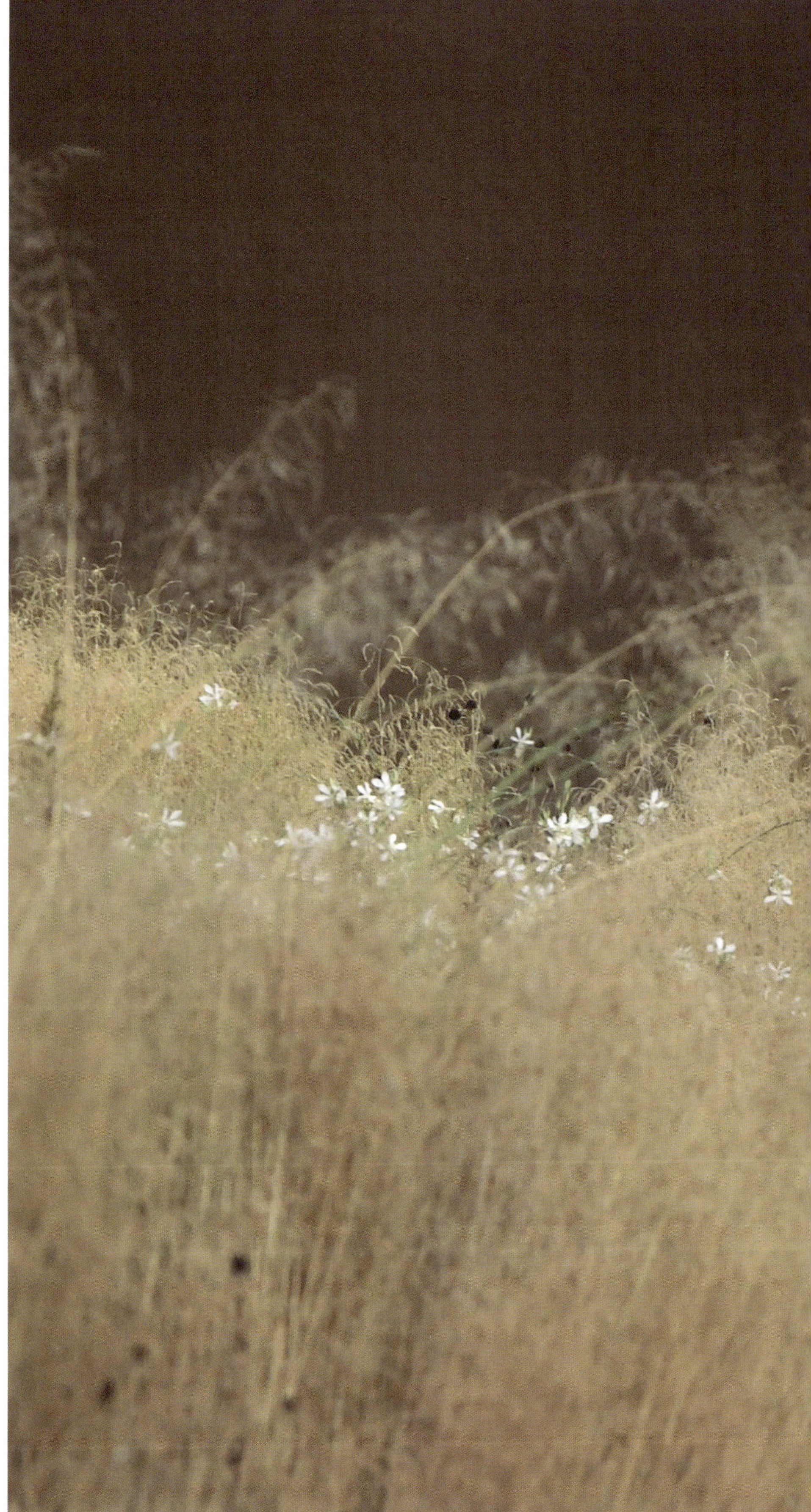

Page 18: Designer Jean Paul Gaultier and Model Lily Cole walk the runway at the end of the Hermès Fall/Winter 2011 ready-to-wear show in Paris, March 2010

Pages 20/21: Models present Mini Kelly bags created by Jean Paul Gaultier at the Fall/ Winter 2011 ready-to-wear show, Paris 2010

This page: Nadège Vanhee-Cybulski on the runway at the Hermès Spring/Summer 2024 ready-to-wear show held at Garde Républicaine, Paris, September 30, 2023

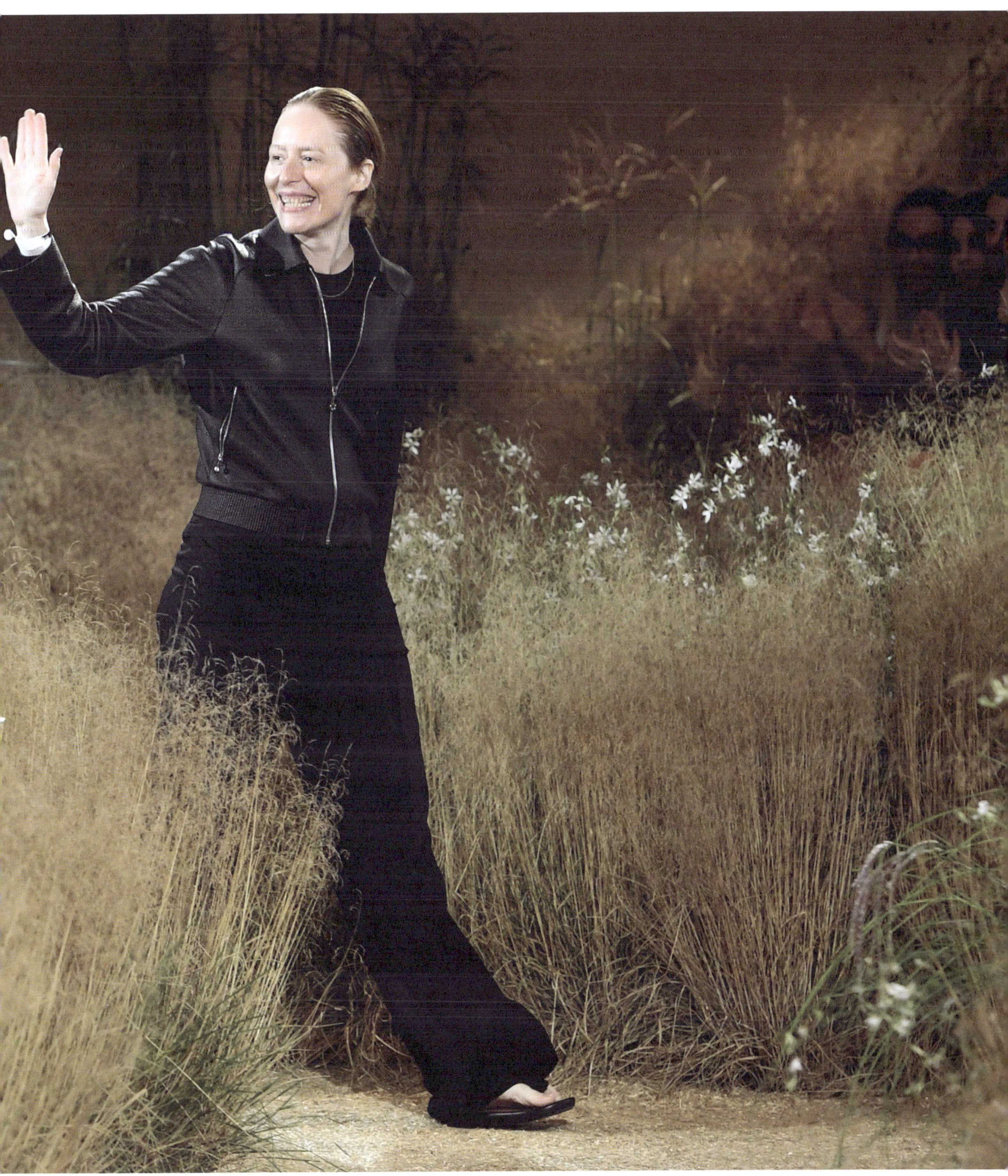

While the Belgian-born designer's own collections included clothes designed to be worn back-to-front, the cult split-toe Tabi shoe and conceptual *trompe l'oeil* motifs, his designs for Hermès were far subtler. Famously eschewing interviews and remaining anonymous, he was responsible for the best-selling *losange* scarf, the *double tour* strap of the Cape Cod watch, and buttons with six holes (allowing the thread to make the letter H) at Hermès.

Equally edgy, French designer Jean Paul Gaultier became Hermès' creative director in 2003 and brought his reputation for groundbreaking fashion statements to the house. Previously, he created skirts for men, dressed Madonna in a cone bra and designed a collection of dresses from rubbish bags. Before joining the house, Hermès had taken a 35% stake in Gaultier's label, in a deal worth $23 million. Gaultier's collections for the *maison* were theatrically charged but still reverential to Hermès' house codes, while his reworkings of the iconic bags are still wildly coveted by collectors today. He remained in the role until 2010.

Currently Nadège Vanhée-Cybulski is Hermès' creative director, following stints at The Row, Celine and Maison Martin Margiela. Having joined the house in 2014, CEO Axel Dumas told the *Financial Times* in 2021, "I wanted to work with her as she had three important qualities: a real appreciation and understanding for craftsmanship... she had a modern and empowering vision for women... and she was able to work in a collaborative creative environment." In the same *Financial Times* feature, Vanhée-Cybulski described an element of her role as, "(taking) codes and try to make them pertinent for the day." Her debut collection for Fall/Winter 2015 had an equestrian theme. Vanhée-Cybulski's love of color along with her pragmatic consideration of how women wear clothes has ensured a long-lasting relationship that continues today.

In 2024, Hermès employed 25,000 people, operating 294 stores across the globe with revenues of nearly €16 billion. After six generations, it's still family-owned and fiercely independent. Currently Axel Dumas, nephew of Jean-Louis, holds the reins as CEO, a position he assumed in 2014.

Next page: Hermès CEO Axel Dumas and Rosie Huntington-Whiteley (carrying a Maximors bag) attend the Hermès Fall/Winter 2023 women's runway show in Paris

Pages 26/27: Willabelle Ong carries a neon green leather Mini Kelly bag, during Paris Fashion Week, March 2025

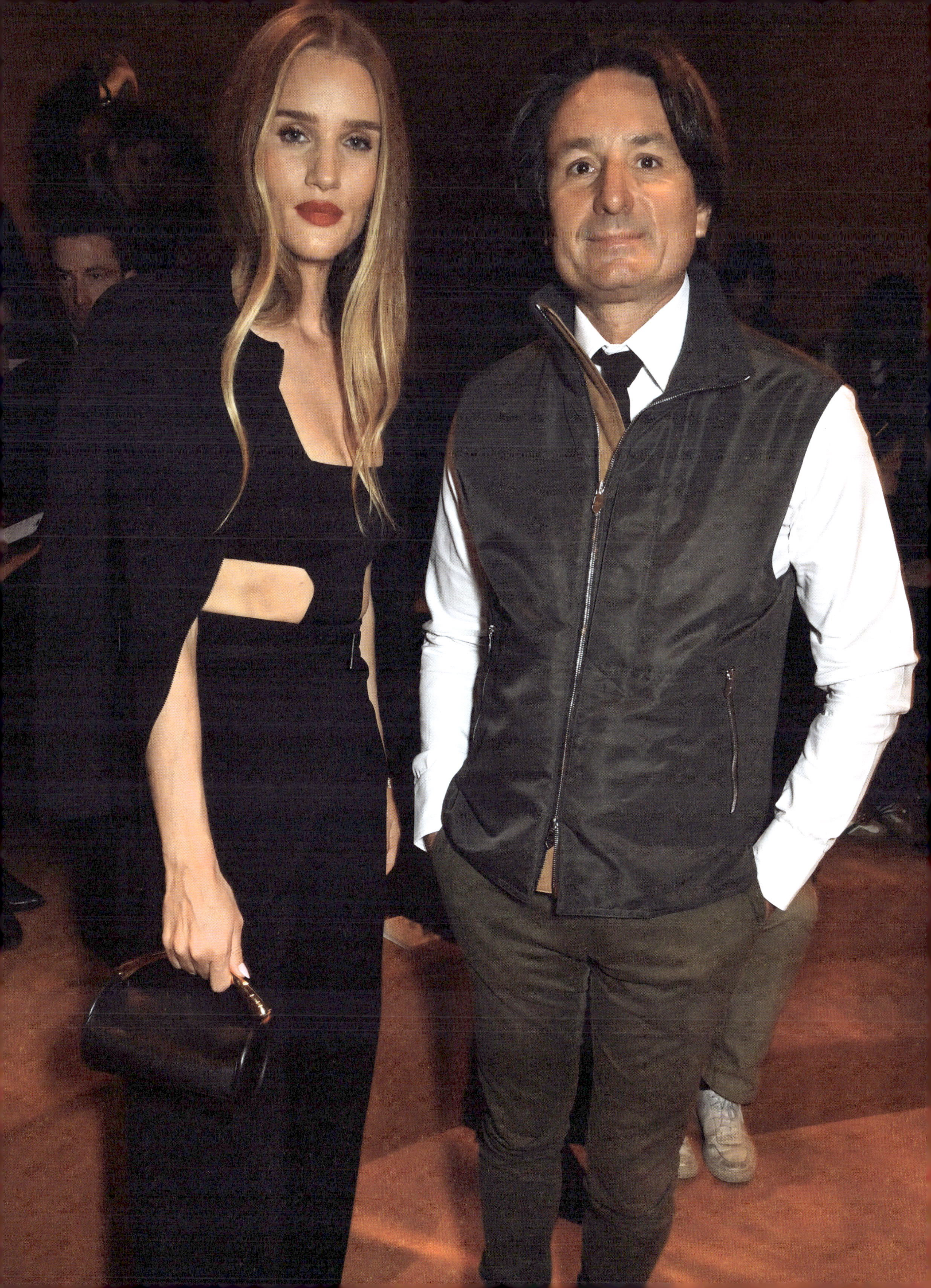

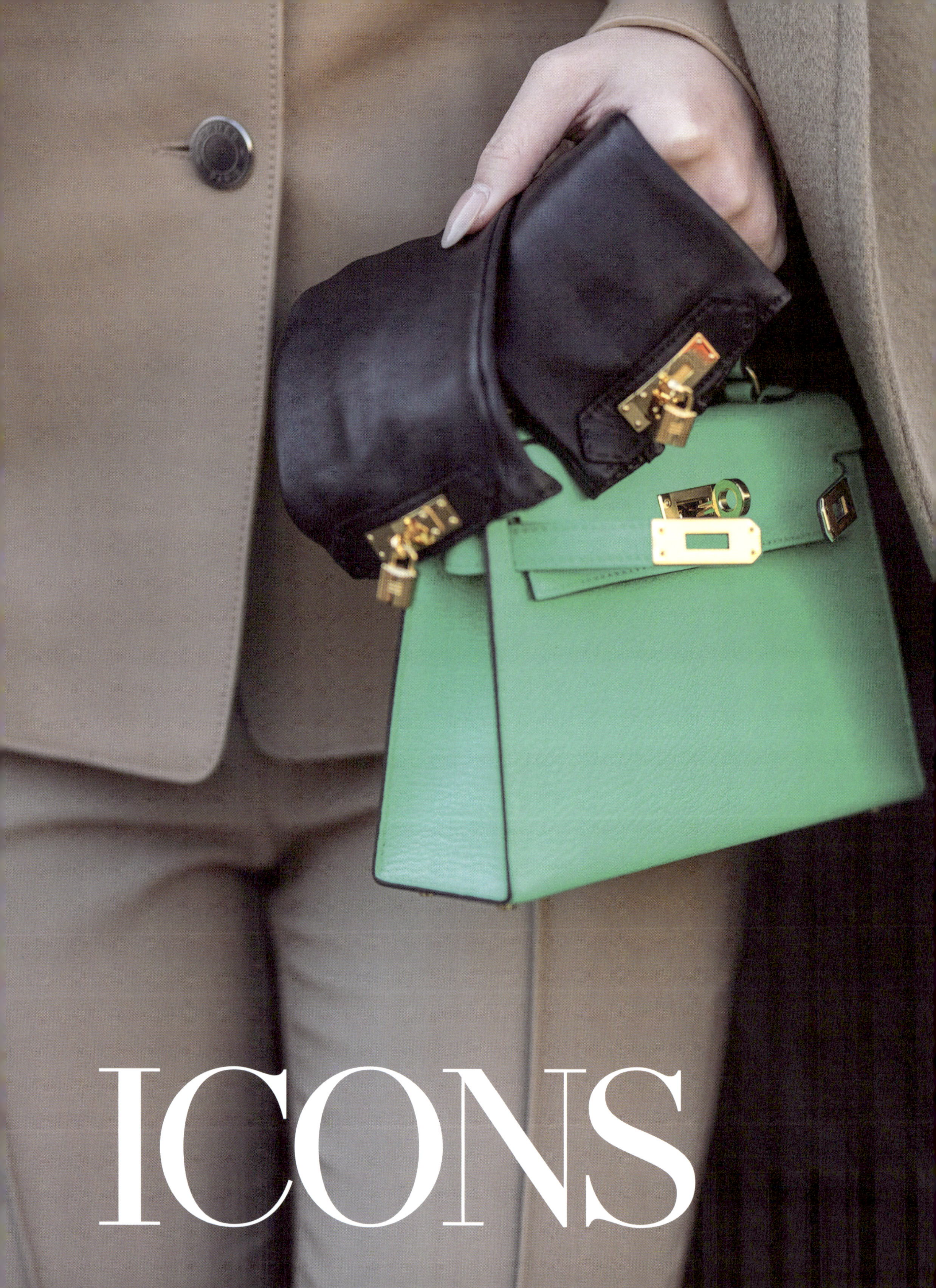

ICONS

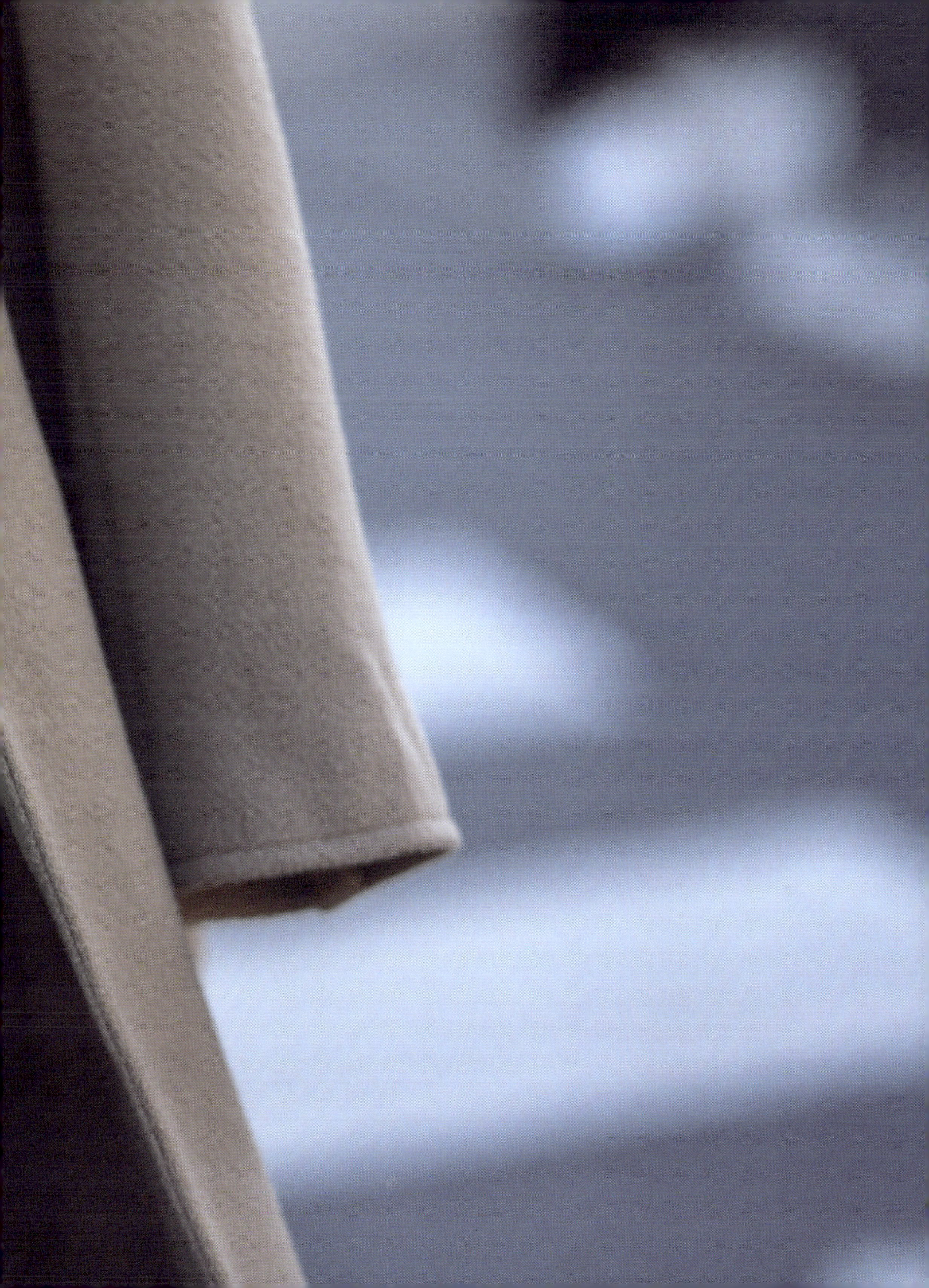

KELLY

Perhaps the world's first It bag, the Kelly's origin story is as intertwined with the 21st century's fascination with celebrity as it is the *maison's* own heritage. When Robert Dumas introduced the *sac à dépêches* in the 1930s, the elegant strap transformed the way that women could carry their bags, which were usually hand-held envelopes for upper class women, and thus wildly impractical.

It wasn't until the Alfred Hitchcock film *To Catch a Thief* (1955) that the *sac à dépêches* had its first moment in the limelight. Edith Head was the costume designer on the film and a force in the movie business at the time, winning eight Oscars over the course of her career. She inspired the cartoon character Edna Mode in *The Incredibles* (2004) *and* dressed Audrey Hepburn, Marlene Dietrich and Elizabeth Taylor. However, it was Grace Kelly who played the lead in *To Catch a Thief.* Head included the *sac à dépêches*—along with other Hermès accessories—in wealthy character Frances Steven's wardrobe. Kelly fell in love with the bag, which was a black box leather *retourné* style, and apparently refused to give it back at the end of filming. Who can blame her? While she used the bag regularly, it wasn't until after she married Prince Rainier III of Monaco and took the title of Princess Grace of Monaco that the *sac* had its second starring role. The royal couple were hounded by paparazzi, and Kelly apparently used the bag to shield a growing baby bump from photographers. A picture of Kelly and her bag made the cover of *Life* magazine in 1956, and Hermès was besieged with calls from readers desperate to get their hands on what people started calling the Kelly bag. From then on, the bag was colloquially described as the Kelly until Hermès officially renamed it in 1977.

At a retrospective of the actress's style at the Victoria & Albert museum in London in 2010, Grace Kelly's original Kelly bag was a star exhibit. Complete with scratches and scuffs, the Princess carried and loved her Kelly. At the time, Kelly's son H.S.H. Prince Albert revealed, "My mother treasured her clothes." And, clearly, her bags.

But a Kelly bag is not *just* a Kelly. There are dozens of iterations of the signature style, including the marquetry-detailed Kellywood, the sporty Kelly Lakis and the Kelly *en Désorde*, where an angled strap gives the bag a dynamic look that's a little more edgy. However, the biggest differences in Kelly bags other than their size are the variations between *sellier* and *retourné* styles, terms referring to the bag's construction. Both varieties have unique details and benefits and one top handle (in contrast to the Birkin's two-handle design).

Next page: Actress Grace Kelly and Prince Rainier III of Monaco leaving a luncheon party in Philadelphia where they announced their engagement. She hid her growing baby bump behind the *sac à dépêches* that was later renamed after her, 1956

Pages 30, 31: Twins Jyoti Babani and Snehal Babani present their impressive Hermès Kelly bag collection, including Kelly Doll Bag Charms and Mini Kelly Doll Picto bags, at Paris Fashion Week FW2024 (left) and SS2025 (right)

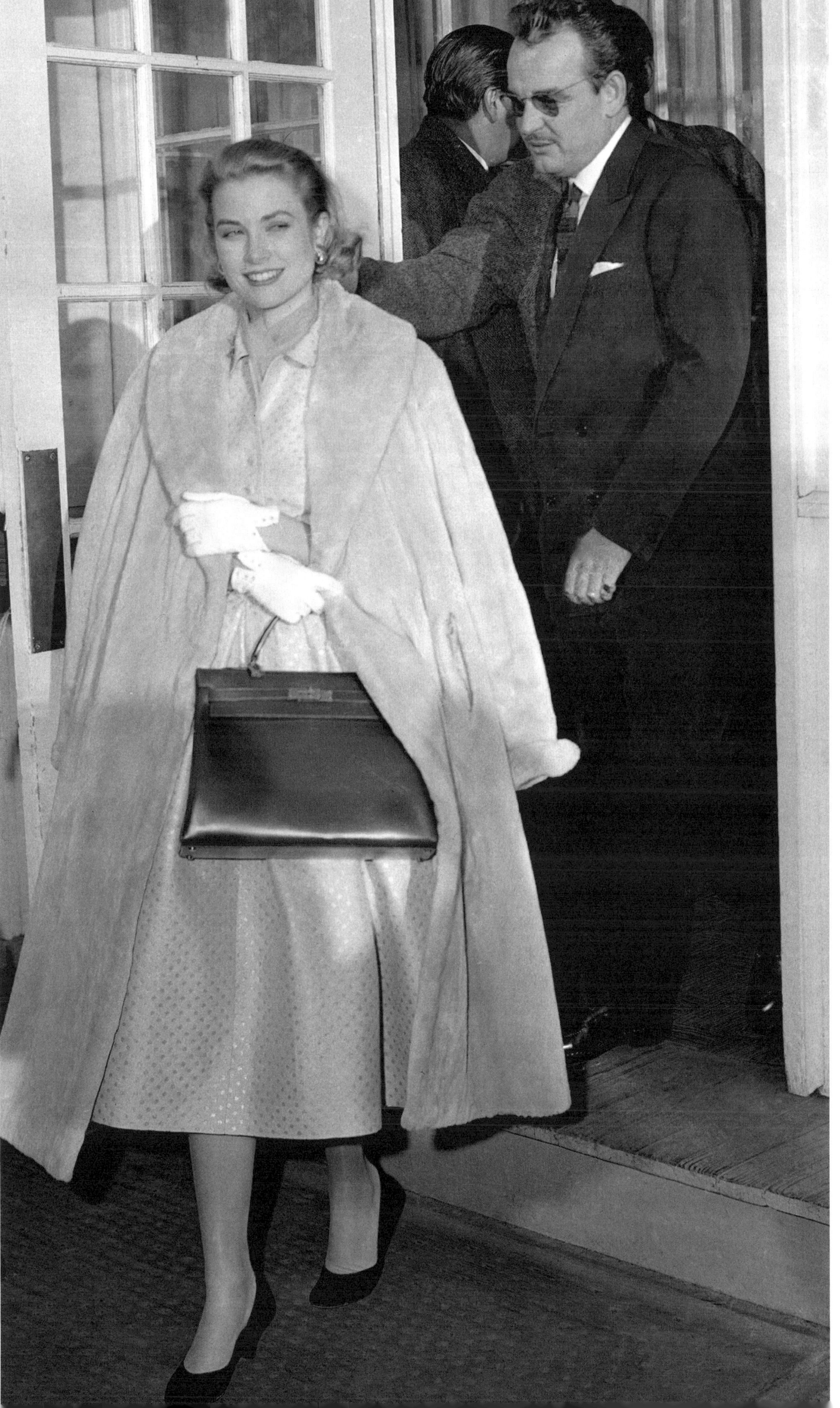

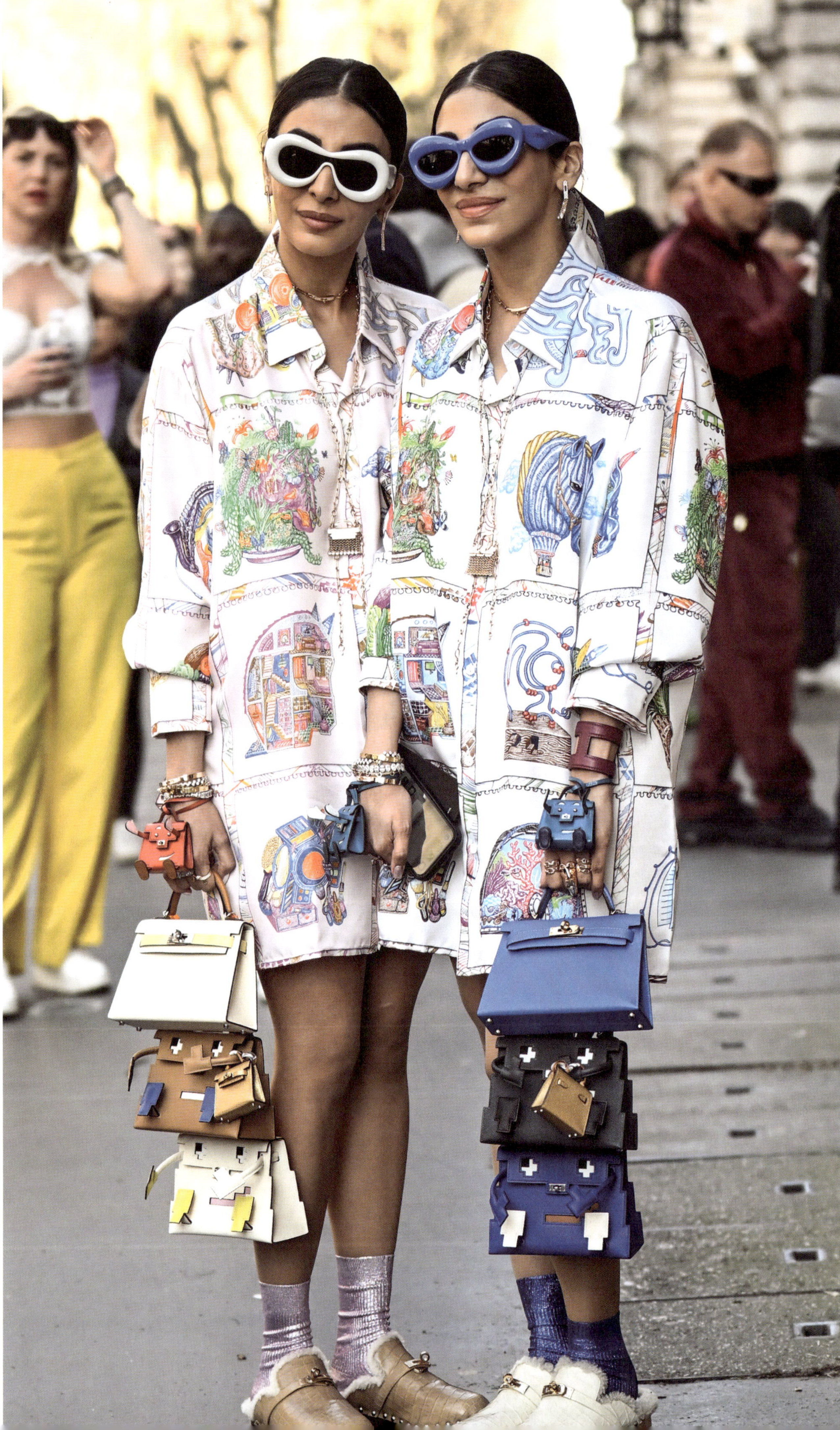

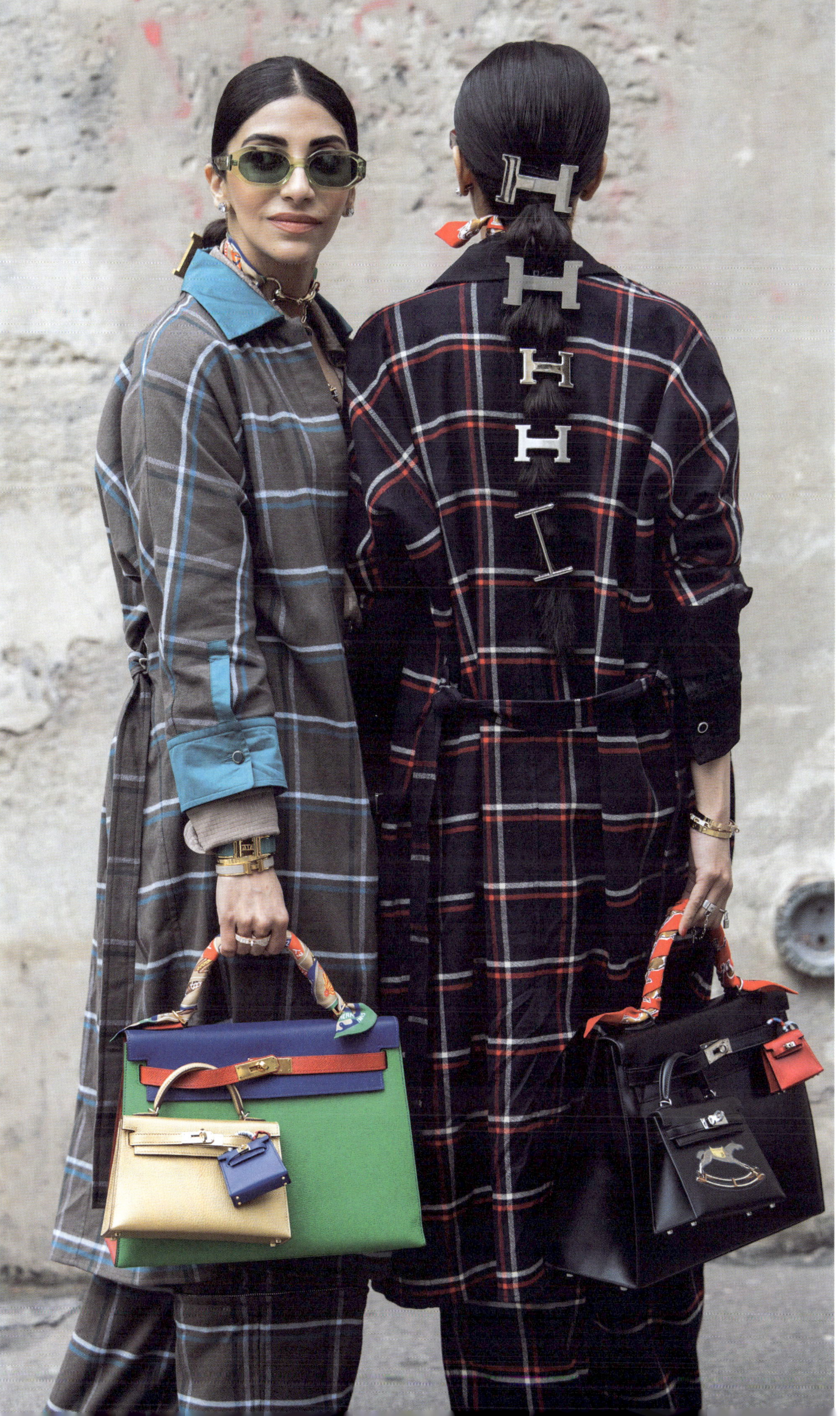

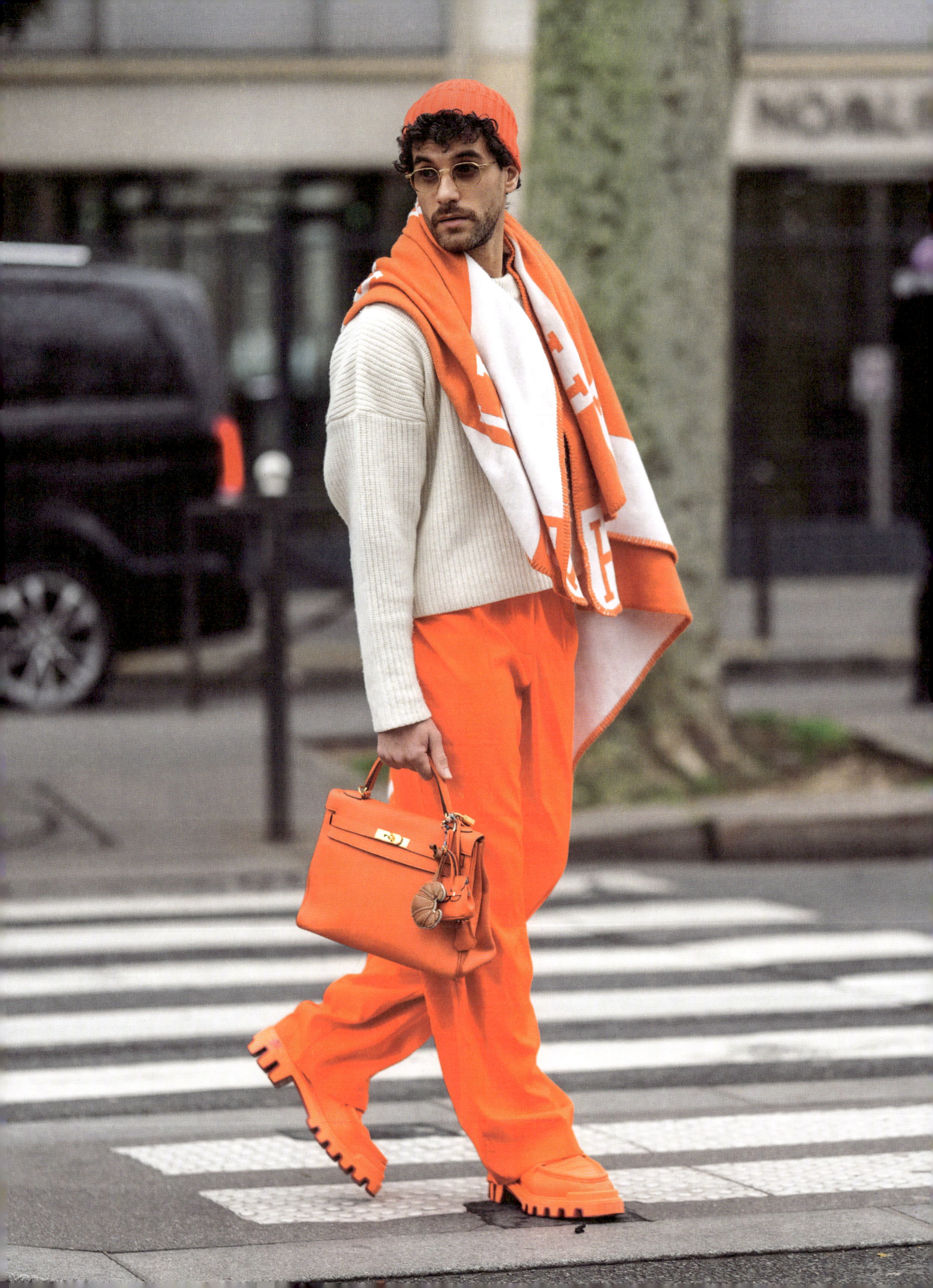

A KELLY BAG IS NOT JUST A KELLY.

Page 32: Andreas Giesen carrying a dark orange Hermès Kelly 28 *retourné* during Paris Fashion Week, January 2025

This page: Kiwi Lee with a blue leather Kelly Elan Foile bag outside the Hermès Menswear Spring/Summer 2024 show, Paris

Page 37: A Paris Fashion Week visitor wearing a red headpiece, a red leather Mini Kelly and red Mary Jane shoes, January 2025

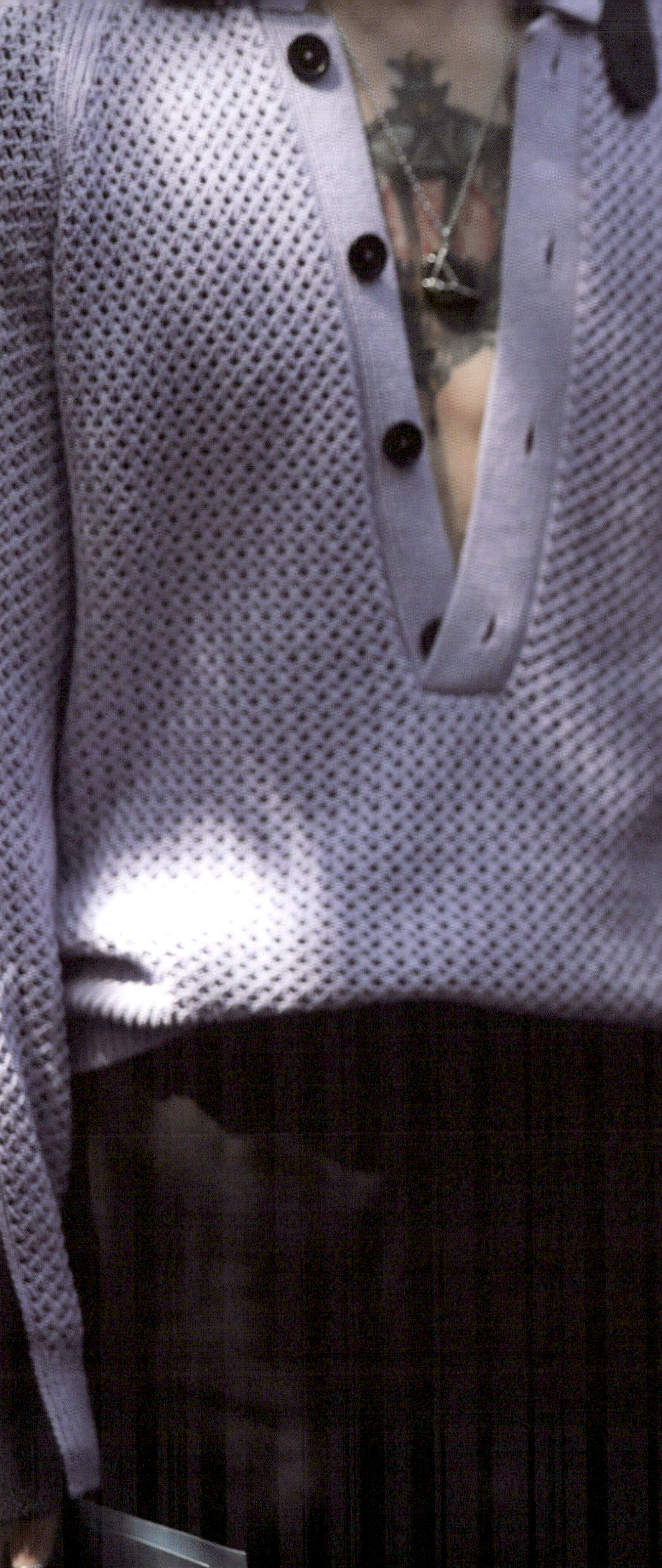

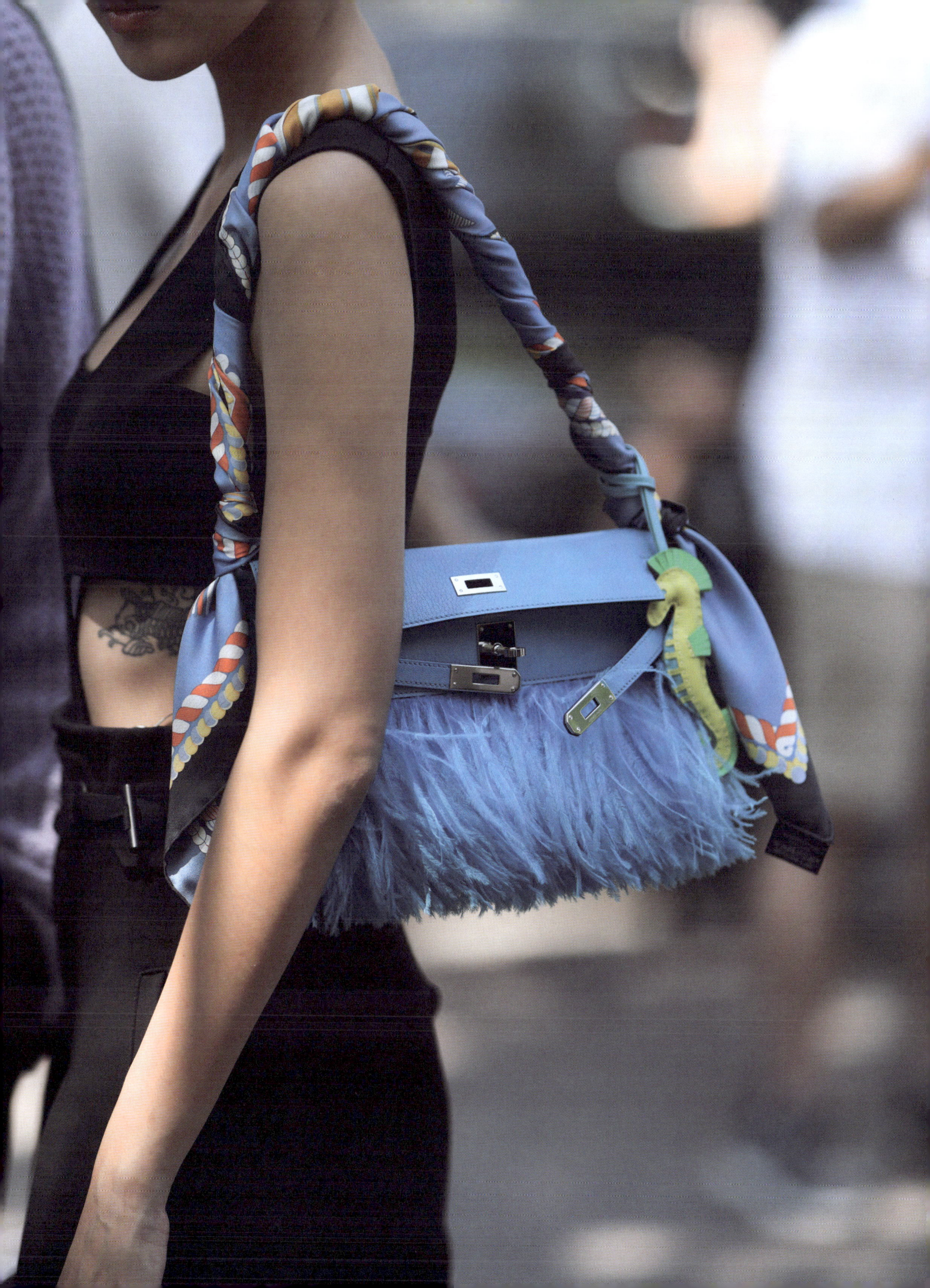

Kelly *selliers* have topstitched seams and a boxy, structured silhouette with sharp corners. They are certainly lady-like bags, perfect for formal occasions, and there is no visible piping on the bag. Often made from stiffer leathers like epsom, box, tadelakt or sombrero to keep that crisp silhouette, the Kelly *sellier* is often more expensive than a similar *retourné*. However, if you are considering a purchase, be aware that some owners complain that the *sellier*'s rigidity makes it harder to open, which increases the risk of scratching the buckle. Larger sizes are reportedly less comfortable to wear against the body. The structured shape also means that one can carry fewer belongings inside the bag.

The *retourné*, by contrast, has a look described as *souple*, meaning supple. *Retourné* means "reversed," and the bags are made by turning them inside out as they are constructed, which gives the bag a distinctive shape with relaxed, rounded edges and a flexible feel. Some say these edges can become easily scuffed although others believe they are actually more resilient to scratching. Along with visible piping, the bag looks more casual and is perfectly suited for travel or weekend wear. Often made in softer skins chosen from the ateliers, Kelly *retourné* bags can be found in togo, clemence, evercolor or swift leathers. The softer leathers also allow a more roomy interior for users' personal items.

Always eager to make their bags practical as well as impeccably constructed, a detachable shoulder strap was added to the Kelly in the 1980s. Many fans noted the lack of shoulder strap on the Birkin and believe it was introduced to differentiate between the two icons; however, there are many other variations between the bags. As an alternative to the leather strap, shoppers can add other leather or canvas straps to their Kellys, in 70, 85 or 105 cm lengths.

Models from 2000 onwards have a metal double loop holder to keep the strap neatly in place. Available hardware options include white gold, yellow gold, rose gold, permabrass (a soft champagne shade), ruthenium (a gunmetal grey), and palladium, which was introduced in 1996 and is often found on limited edition models. Most bags use 18-karat gold plating, although special orders can incorporate 24-karat gold hardware. There are also bags with PVD coated hardware, which makes the metal appear almost black, and brushed gold and brushed palladium versions where intentional microscopic scratches give a matte, satin finish to the hardware, making it less prone to accidental scratches. The newest hardware making a comeback at Hermès and appearing on the Kelly 25 is electrum, which is a scintillating mix of palladium and gold.

When describing the hardware that makes up the Kelly, Hermès uses special terms for each element. The *lock* is self-explanatory as the engraved padlock on each bag, while the *clochette* is the little leather cover that houses the keys for said lock. The *clochette* is attached to the single handle by a narrow strip of leather or *tiret*. On the front of the bag you'll find the distinctive *sangles*, or straps, which fasten onto a metal stem (the *touret)*. On the base of the bag are four *clou*: useful studs that prevent the bag from making direct contact with surfaces, which might damage the leather. Beyond these signature components, there are over 25 pieces of visible hardware and 20 invisible parts. The 36 pieces of leather require 680 stitches, and one artisan is responsible for making the entire bag, which takes 18-24 hours to construct.

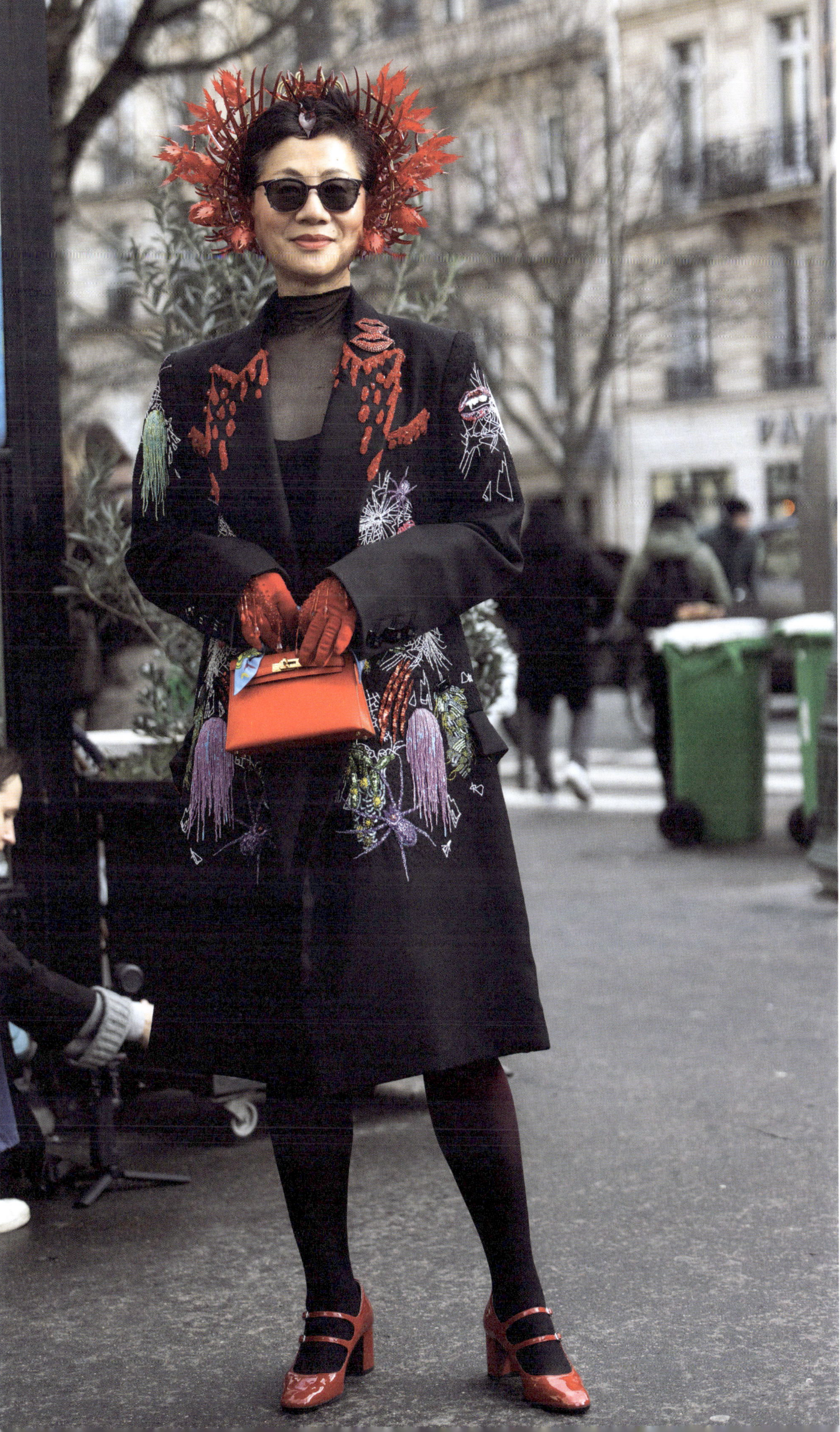

Heart Evangelista carries a dark blue Alligator Mini Kelly *sellier* during Fall/Winter 2025 Paris Fashion Week

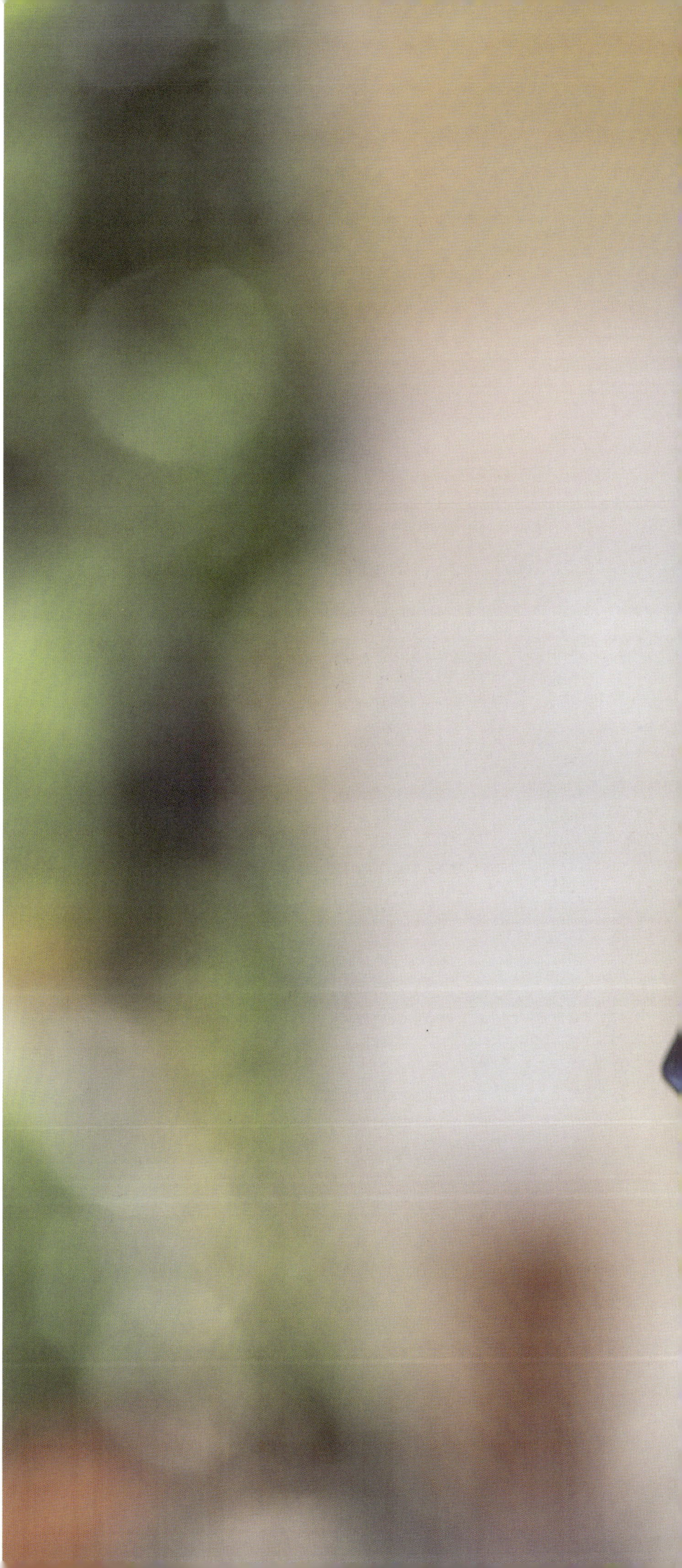

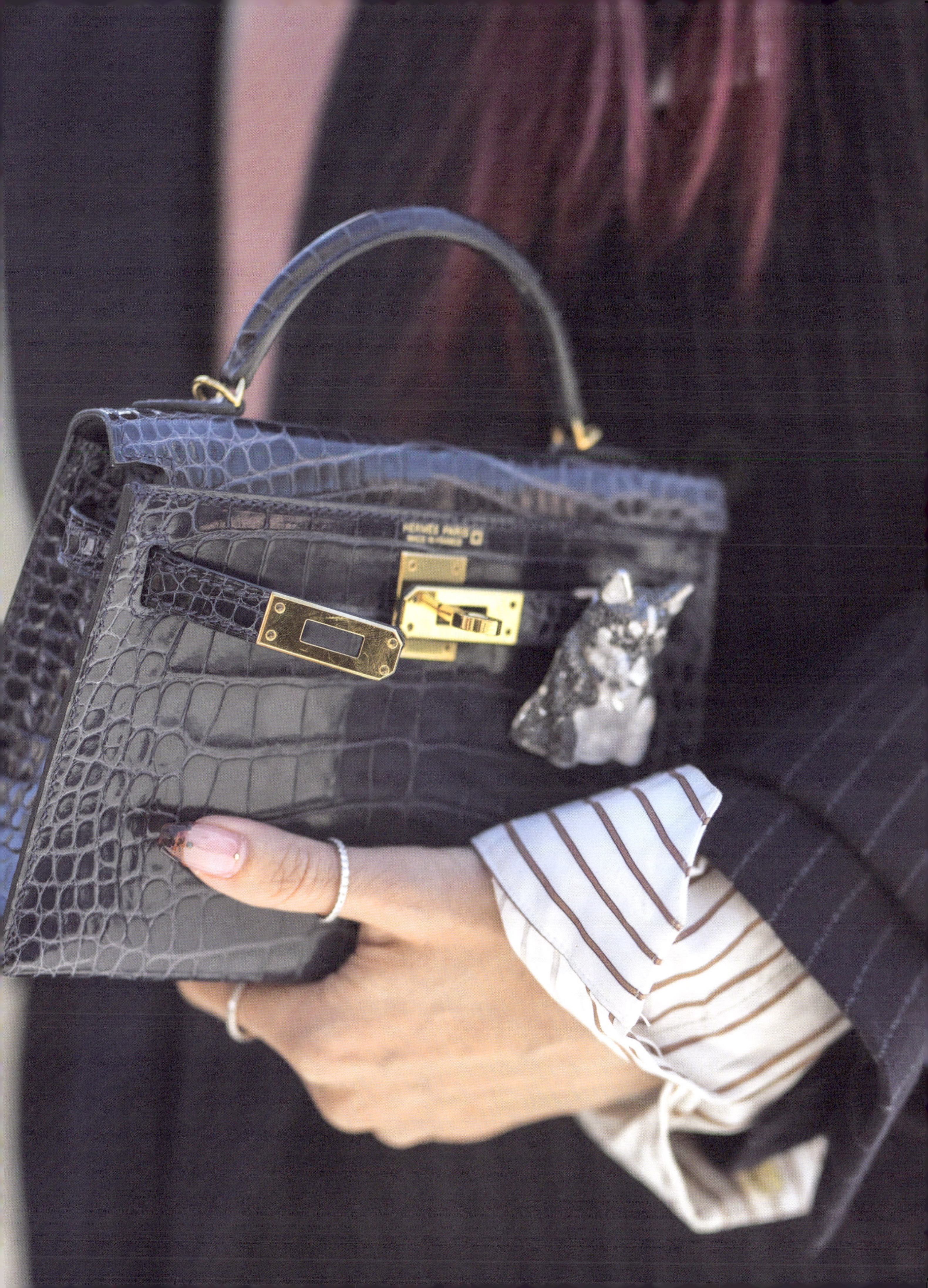

This page: A visitor to Fall/Winter 2025 Paris Fashion Week with a white Alligator Mini Kelly

Next page: Iryna Thater carrying a pink Ostrich Kelly *sellier* outside the Juana Martin Spring/Summer 2025 haute couture show, Paris

Page 42: Leonie Hanne with a green Kelly clutch during Fall/Winter 2023 Paris Fashion Week

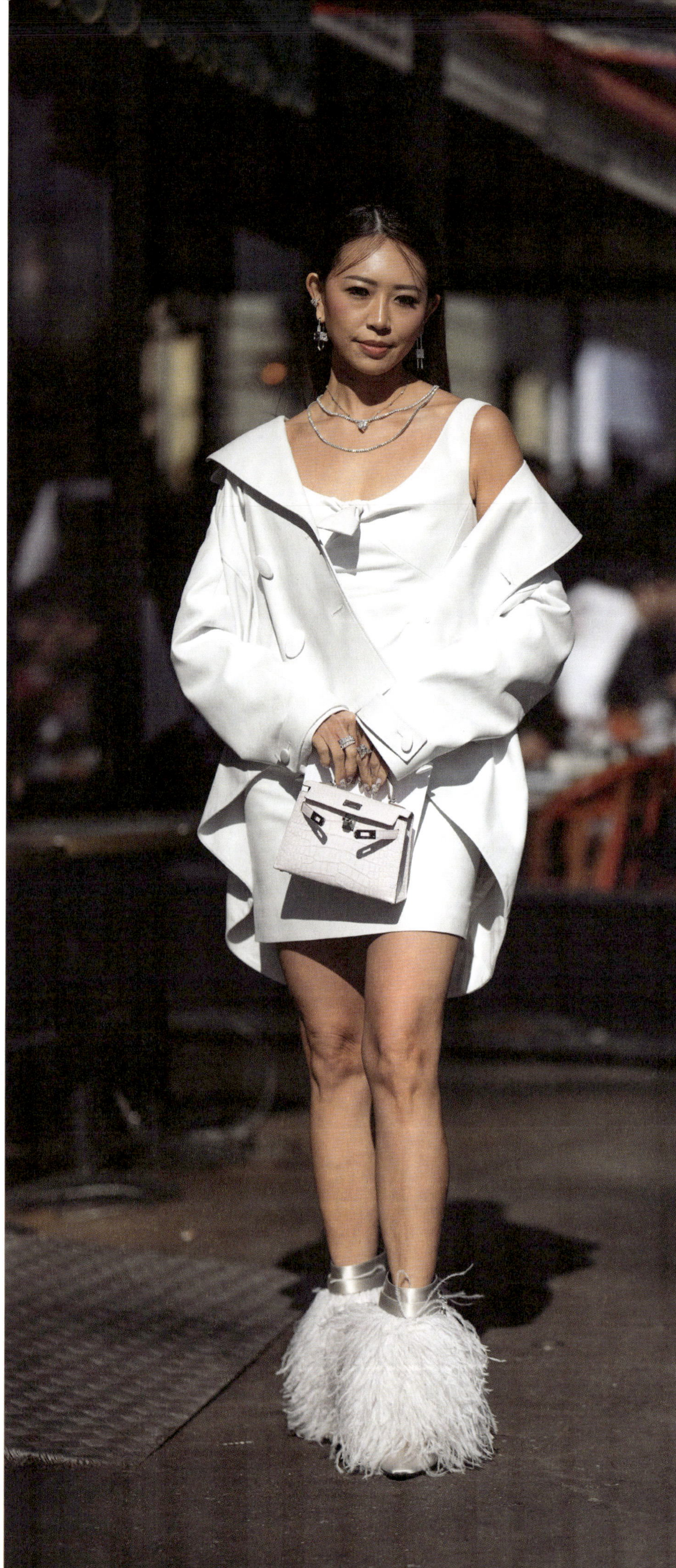

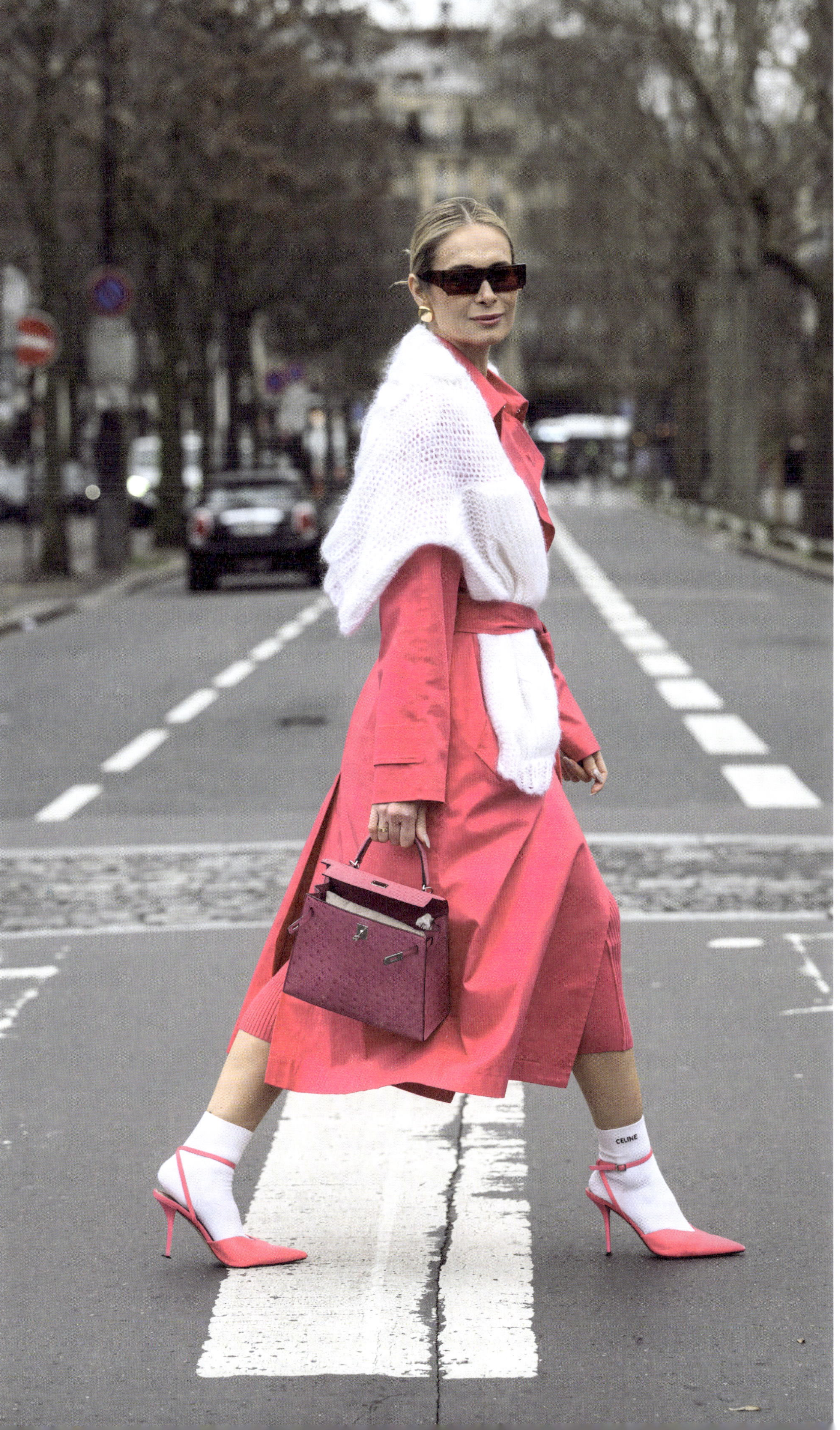
CELINE

While the Mini Kelly is apparently one of the most desired bags in Hermès boutiques, there are eight size options. Hermès often describes its bags with the initial of the style and the size in centimeters, such as K15. The bag range includes K15, K20, K25, K28, K32, K35, K40 and K50. According to Sotheby's auction house, the K25 is currently the most sought-after size for collectors.

Beyond the distinction of size, hardware and *sellier* or *retourné,* Hermès has used the DNA of the Kelly to roll out a myriad of limited edition, updated or elevated styles, so there is now a Kelly to suit every personal style. One of the oldest variations on the classic is the Kelly Sport, noted for its open top design and casual feel. Preserving the classic trapezoid shape, this bag was launched in 1987 and has a taller, narrower footprint which can be worn crossbody as well as shoulder-style. Unfortunately, it was discontinued in 2001.

In 1996 Jean-Louis Dumas' wife Rena designed the Kelly Ado. In line with the Nineties' minimal-yet-sporty mood, the Kelly Ado was created as a backpack and was available in two sizes. The larger size incorporated a top handle while the smaller came without. Discontinued after just a few years, Hermès brought the style back and relaunched the Kelly Ado II in 2018. Inside the new style, you'll find a handy phone pocket.

Another casual Kelly style is the Kelly Danse, which Jean Paul Gaultier added to the line in 2008. It was discontinued in 2013 before being revamped as the Kelly Danse II for the Fall/Winter 2019 collection. With an adjustable strap that transforms the bag into six different styles, this is one of the most versatile iterations of the Kelly, offering clutch, wristlet, shoulder bag, waist bag, crossbody or backpack wear options.

Small yet mighty and in high demand on the vintage market, the Micro Kelly was made in limited runs between 1984-1985 and 1991-1992. Everything about this sweet style is miniaturized, from the thinner shoulder strap to the shrunken hardware. They often came in lizard or crocodile with box or courchevel leather options and are a particular favorite with vintage collectors.

If you prefer something more whimsical, the Kelly Doll first became available in 2000. The hardware of the bag was turned into a face (the *touret* became a nose) and arms were added, which owners could style into different poses. It was adorable but was discontinued in 2005. Relaunched in 2008, new styles are often unveiled as special editions attached to the opening of new Hermès stores across the globe. Following the Kelly Doll, the Kelly Doll Picto was brought to market as part of the Spring/Summer 2002 collection. The cute face remains, but is now pixelated, and the bag wears its own mini backpack. Both the Kelly Doll and Kelly Doll Picto are highly collectable. At launch, the Kelly Doll Picto retailed for approximately $15,600, but sales at auction see the bag reach prices in excess of $80,000.

The newest member of the Kelly family is the Mini Kelly Pampilles, launched in 2025. With swishing swathes of fringe across the front, the style nods to the prevailing bohemian mood of fashion. For many Hermès aficionados, the Kelly is the ultimate Hermès bag, treasured by collectors, and is apparently the hardest to secure. The Mini Kelly Pampilles is set to become a collectible of the future, just like every Kelly ever made.

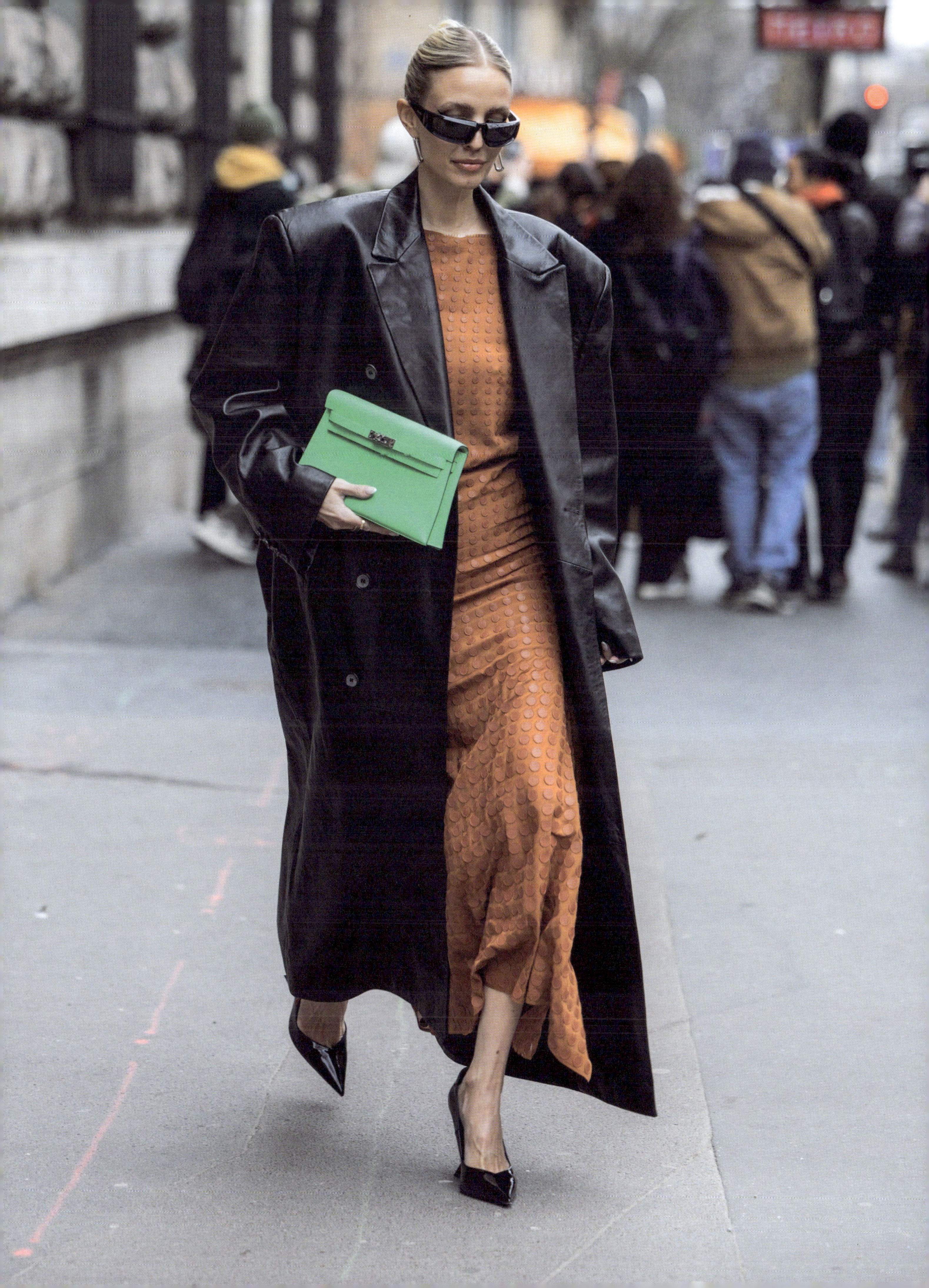

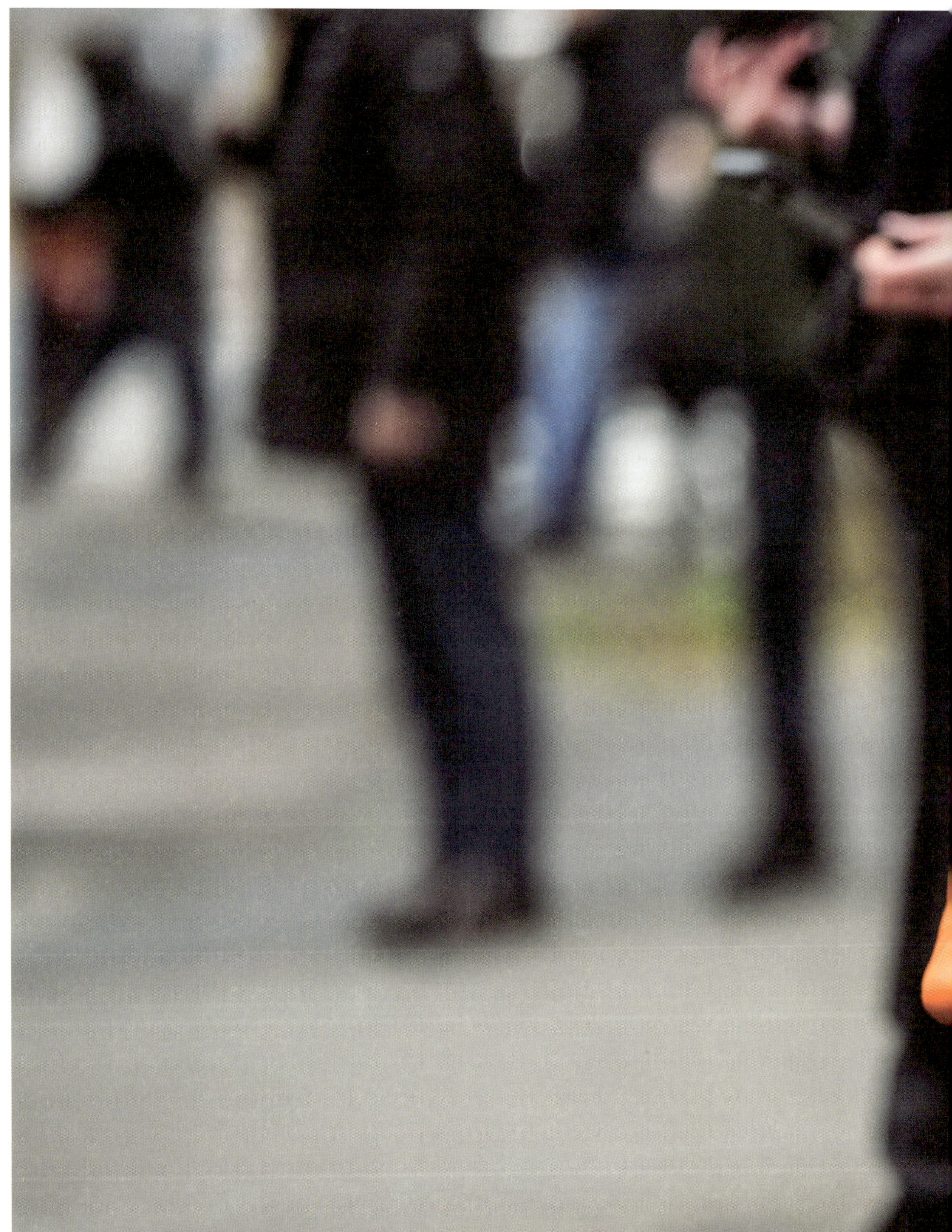

A visitor to the Menswear Fall/Winter 2025 show carries a shiny orange leather Kelly 40 retourné bag, Paris

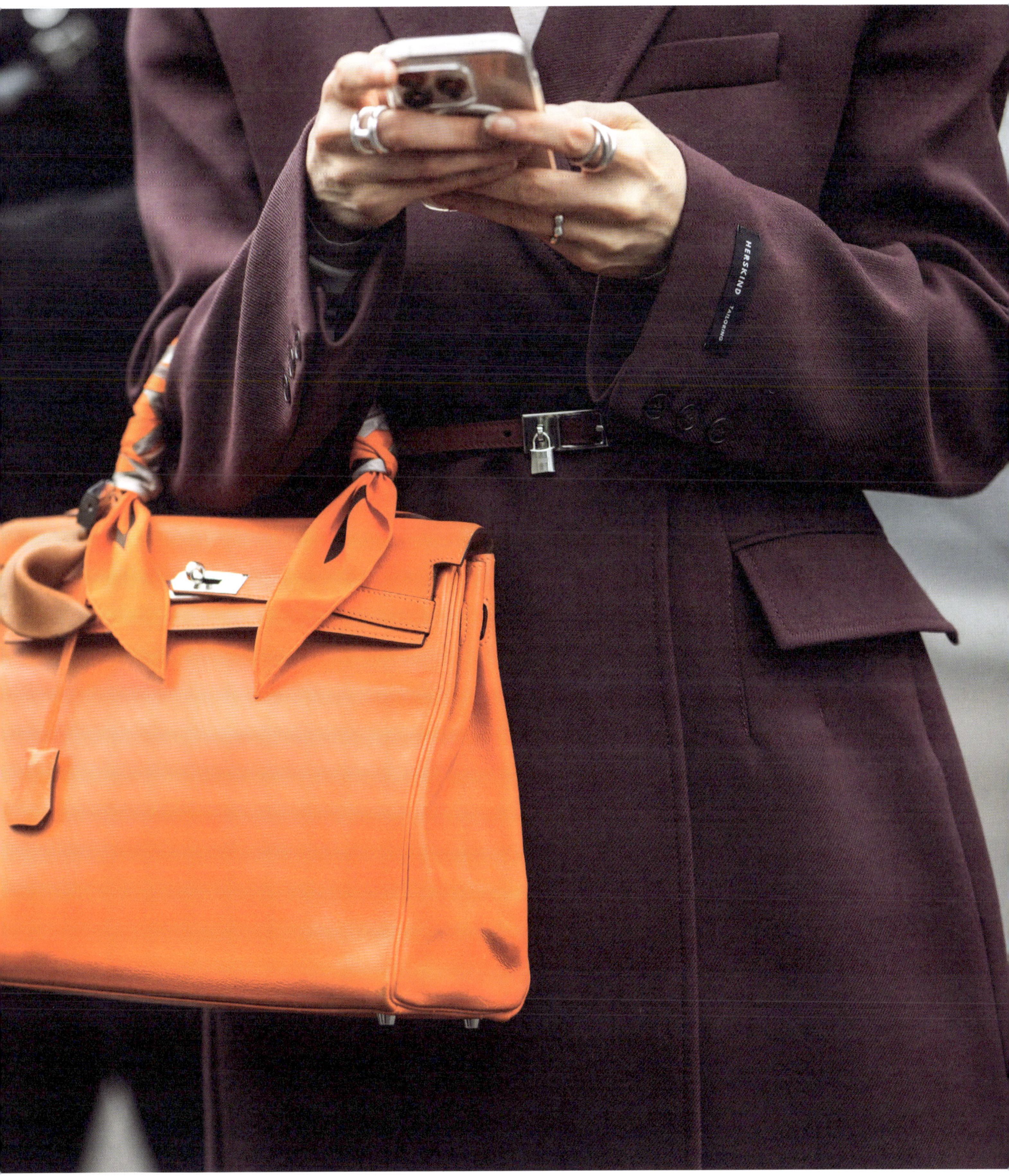
HERSKIND
TAILORING

BIRKIN

Staking a claim as the most famous bag in the world, and certainly the most expensive, the Birkin's origin story is a legendary tale mixing celebrity, practicality and serendipity. When actress and singer Jane Birkin was seated next to Jean-Louis Dumas (Hermès CEO at the time) on an Air France flight between Paris and London in 1983, fashion history was made. As luck would have it, Jane was upgraded, but her belongings (including a Hermès diary) spilled from her bag as she tried to fit it into the overhead compartment. As Birkin retold the story to fashion writer Luke Leitch, "The man next to me said, 'You should have one with pockets.' I said, 'The day Hermès makes one with pockets I will have that.' And he said: "'But I am Hermès, and I will put pockets in for you.'" Dumas got to work and, so the story goes, sketched the first Birkin on an air-sickness bag on the flight, incorporating Birkin's suggestions and requests. Twelve months later, the Birkin bag was born.

Hermès asked Birkin's permission to name the bag after her and she received annual royalties amounting to £30,000 in 2011. Birkin donated the sum to charity each year. The original bag was completely unique, as it was a one-off prototype, with several elements that made the bag special which weren't replicated in the commercially created Birkin. One of the differences between the Kelly and Birkin is that Birkin bags do not have a shoulder strap (other than a 1990s limited edition that included straps in the design); however, Jane's bag *did* come with a strap. It was an unusual hybrid, with the width and height of the Birkin 35 paired with the depth of the Birkin 40, while the B40 was the first bag available to the public. Birkin's own Birkin hardware was gilded brass, but the bag at launch had gold-plated hardware, with other options such as palladium, rose gold and ruthenium added later. The four metal feet on the base were smaller than the commercial ones would be. Jane made her Birkin unmistakably hers, stamping JB on the flap and hanging nail clippers from the inside. With remnants of stickers on the outside, it was as much a diary of her life as any written document could be. In later years, Jane was given four other Birkin bags, but none were like the original, which was donated to a charity auction in October 1994. Sold to benefit the Association Solidarité Soda, an AIDS foundation, that bag was sold again in May 2000 and now is in private hands. Birkin donated another of her bags, this one in black calfskin, to auction in 2009 to benefit the International Federation of Human Rights. It went under the hammer for €74,352.

Next page: Singer Jane Birkin attends the "Jane Birkin sings Serge Gainsbourg 'VIA JAPAN'" press conference at L'Institut Franco-Japonais de Tokyo, March 26, 2013

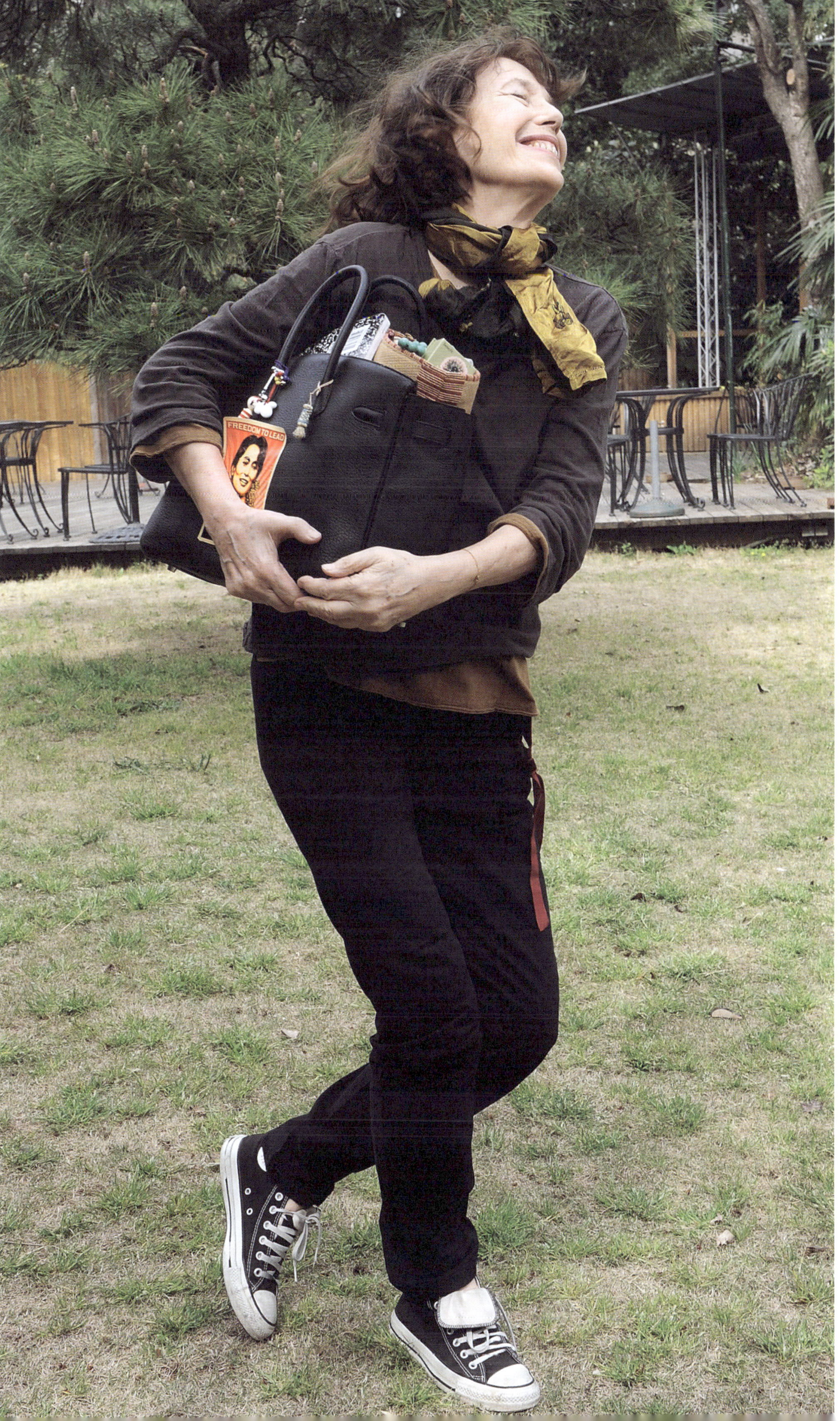
FREEDOM TO LEAD

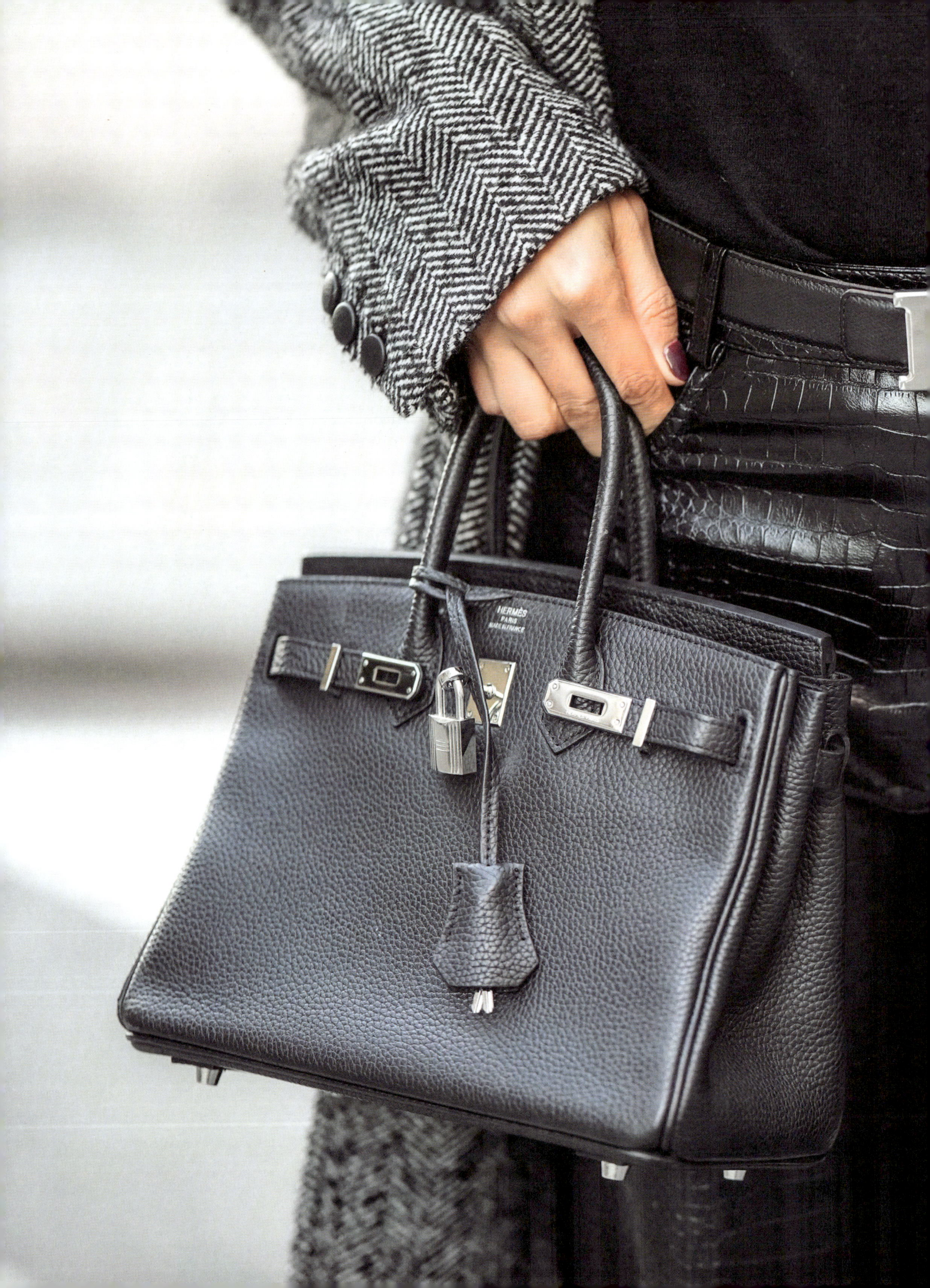
HERMÈS
PARIS

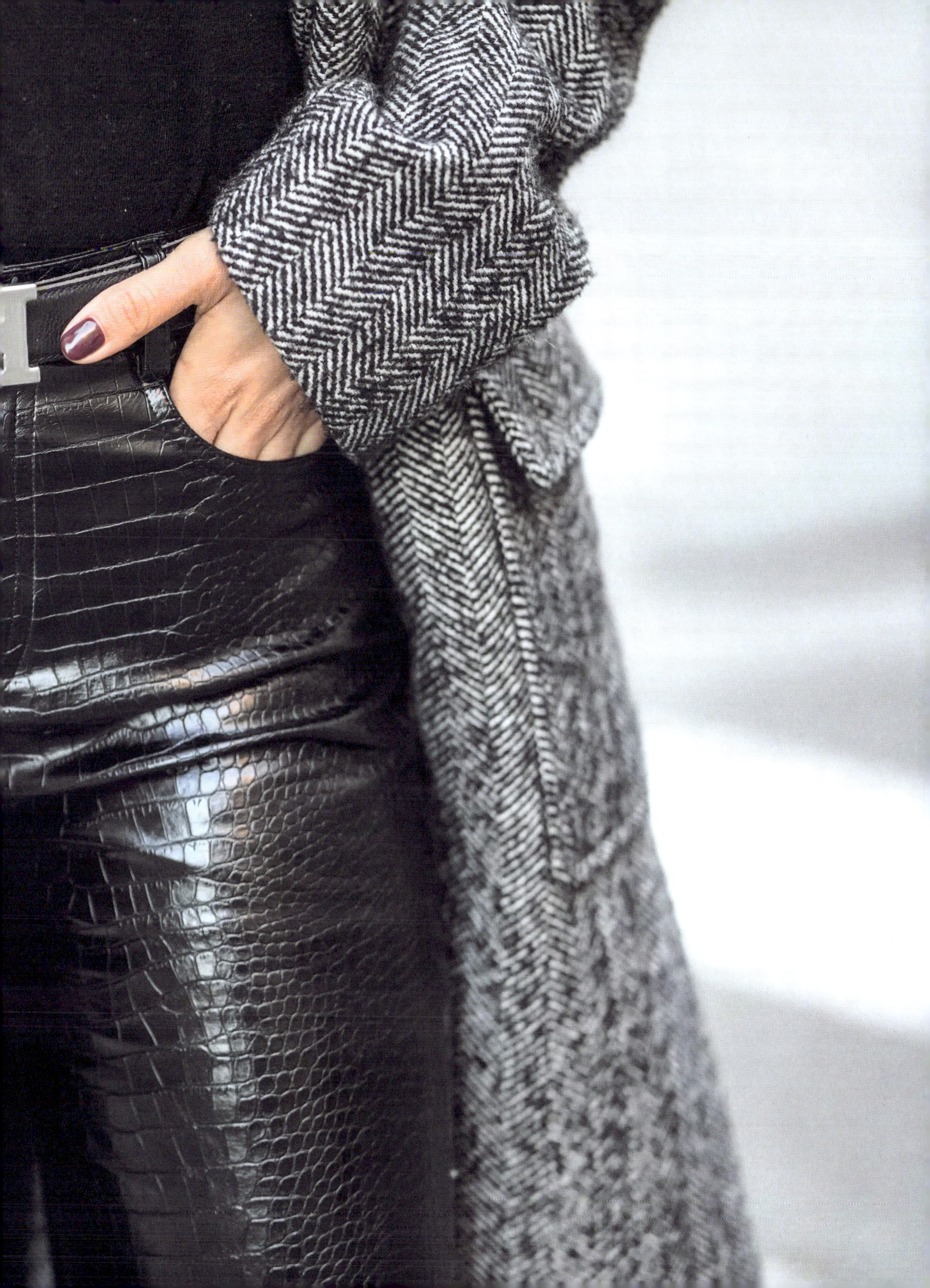

Page 48: Patricia Gloria Contreras wears a black leather Birkin bag during a street style fashion photo session, Paris, January 2025

This page: Mary Leest carrying an étoupe Birkin 25, Spring/Summer 2025 Paris Fashion Week

Next page: Visitors to the Spring/Summer 2025 Yanina Couture show with a black Birkin 35, Paris Fashion Week

Page 52: Close-up of a limited edition Hermès *Birkin 20 Faubourg sellier Sous La Neige*, Paris, September 30, 2023

Page 54: Rapper Travis Scott carrying a Birkin Cargo bag, New York City, December 19, 2023

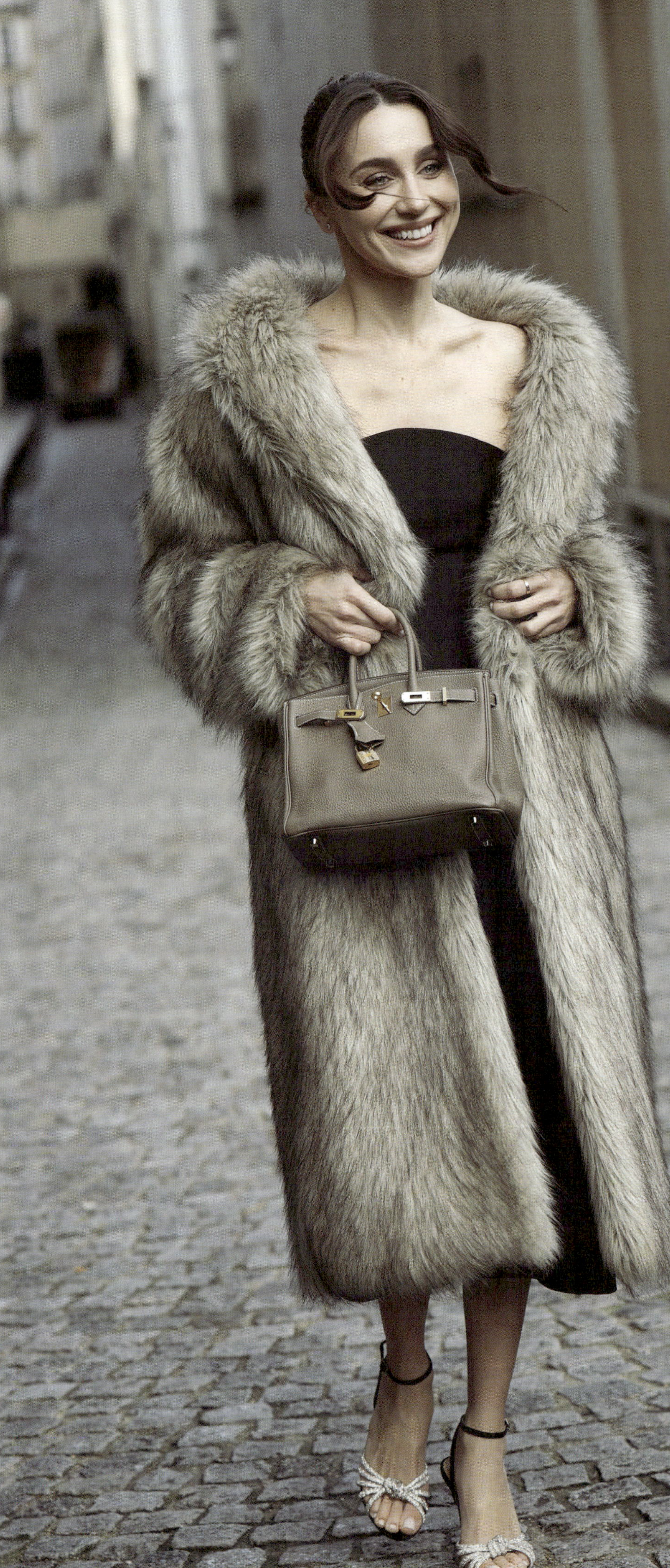

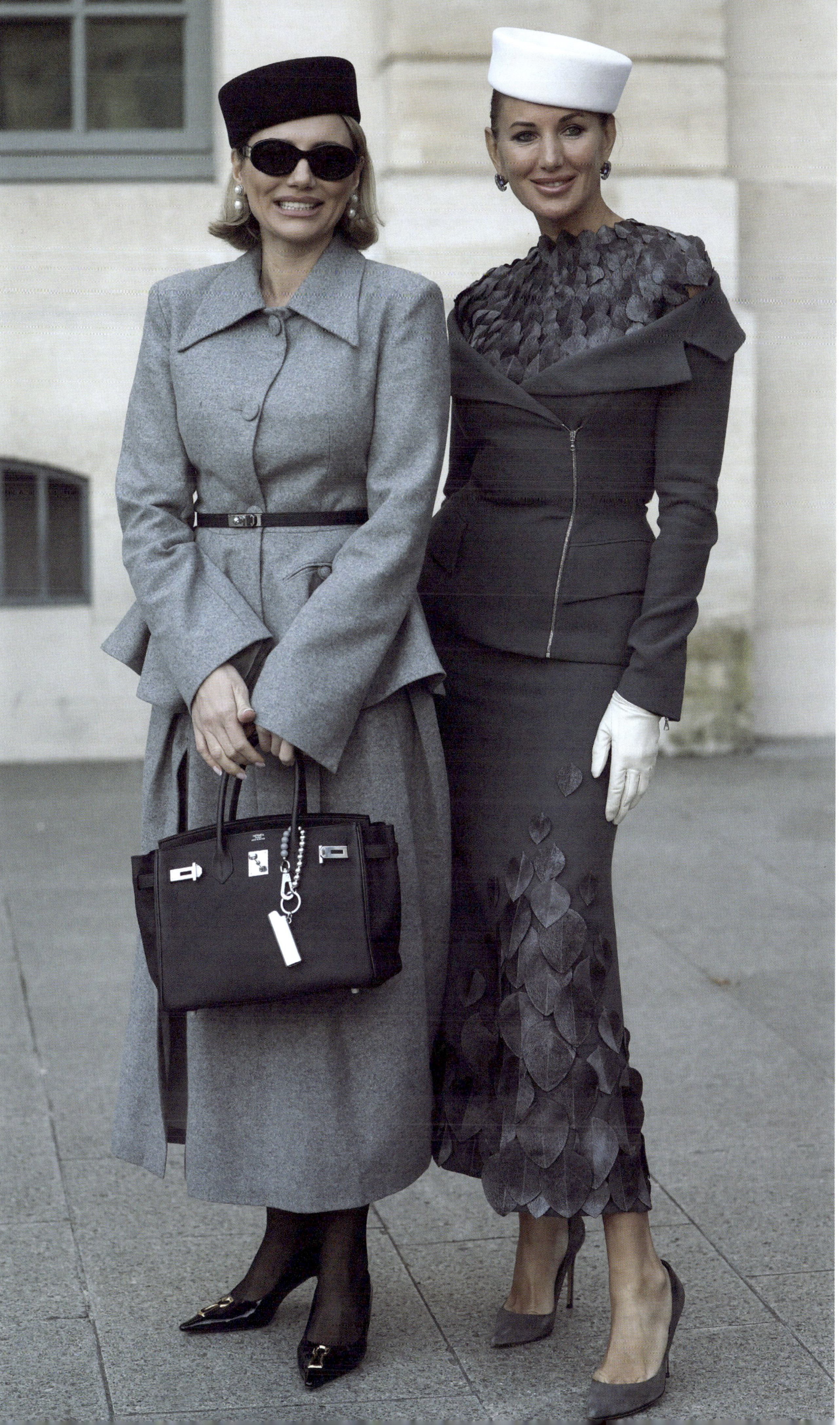

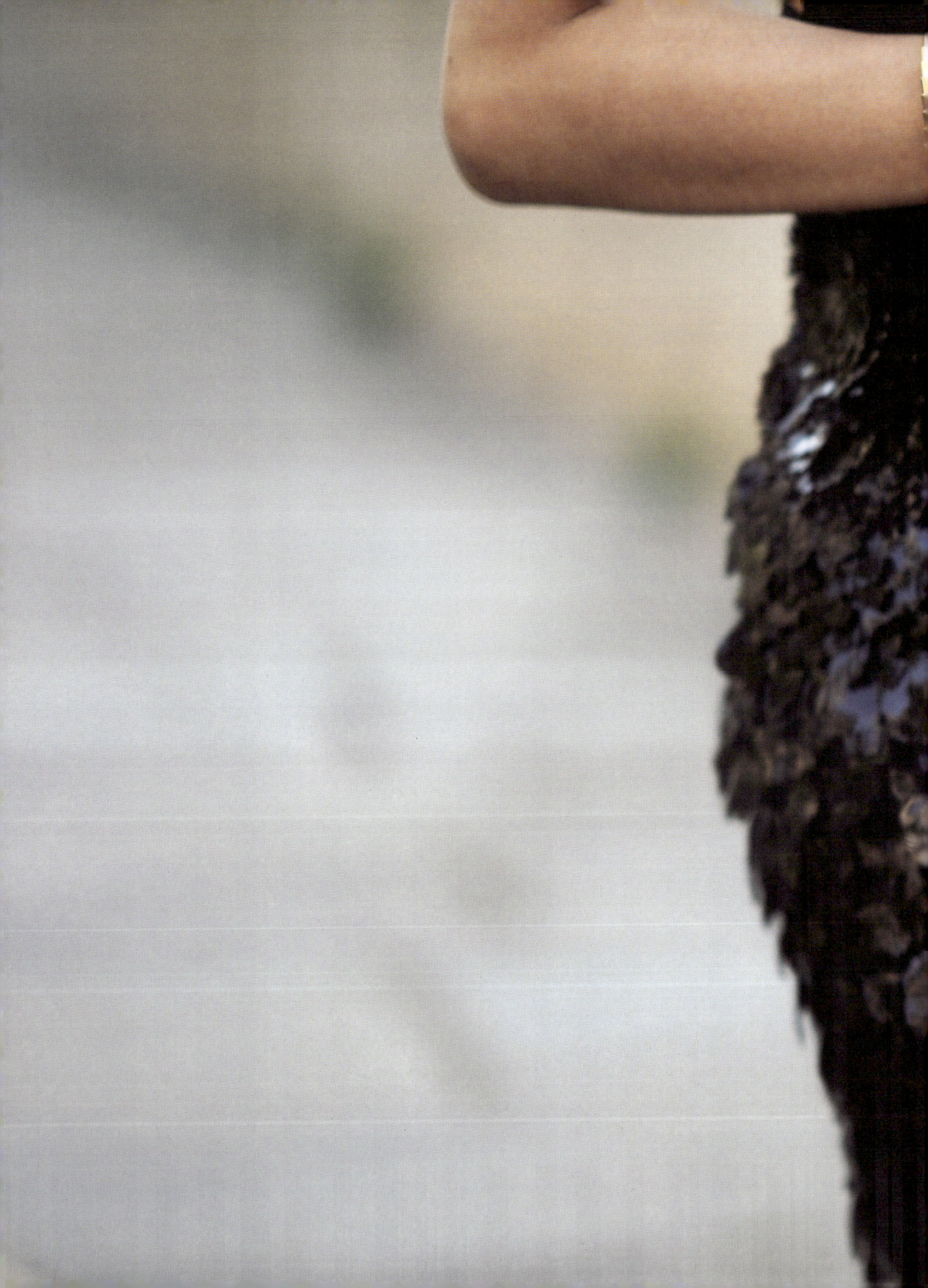

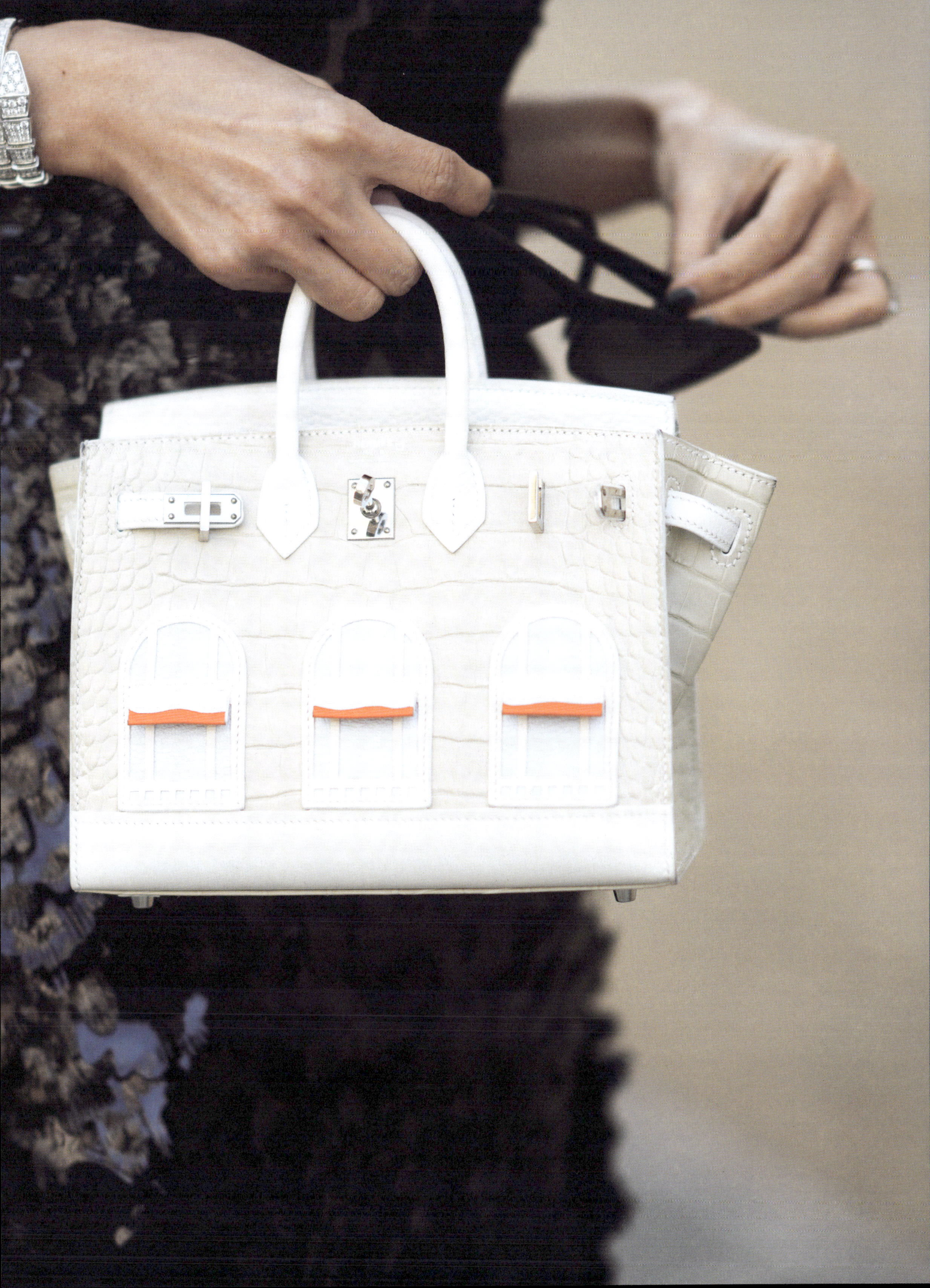

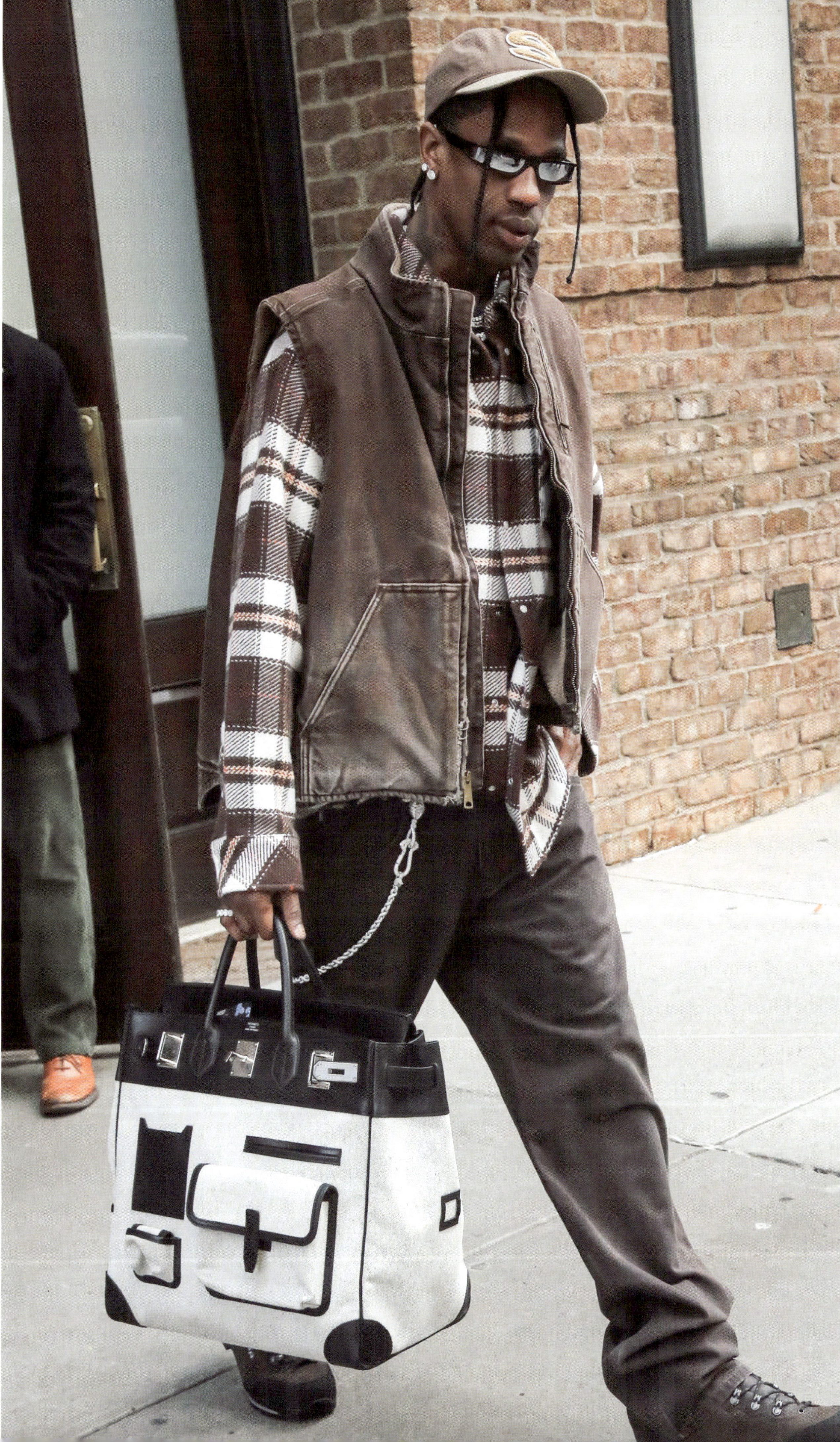

Jane Birkin had a seemingly complicated relationship with her eponymous bag and Hermès. Although she used the bags heavily before moving on to a fresh one, often donating the old bag to charity, Birkin described the bags as impractical, telling the BBC in 2017 that overfilling the bag with "junk" as she was wont to do, made it "a very, very heavy bag."

Hermès still uses exotic skins to make many of their bags, and although these products are covered by the Convention on International Trade in Endangered Species of Wild Fauna and Flora to ensure that any item using a protected species is produced in accordance with the Convention's rules, Birkin publicly disagreed with the practice of using exotic skins.

In 2015, animal rights group PETA released footage showing horrific methods of killing crocodiles by alleged employees on a Texas farm, supposedly supplying Hermès at the time. Birkin released a statement asking Hermès to 'debaptize' the exotic-skin version of the bag bearing her name. In an open letter, Birkin wrote, "Having been alerted to the cruel practices reserved for crocodiles during their slaughter to make Hermès handbags carrying my name, I have asked Hermès to debaptize the Birkin Croco until better practices in line with international norms can be put in place." In response, Hermès spokespersons swiftly announced that they "respect and share her emotions and (were) also shocked." The *maison* shared that crocodile skins from the implicated farm are not used for Birkin bags, nor do they own the farm in question, but that they were investigating the allegation. Birkin was satisfied with that response, although PETA US continues to lobby Hermès because they hold shares in the house.

Creating Birkin bags, or any bag, from an exotic animal skin ensures that the final piece is rarer, more expensive and therefore more desired in some circles. Each Birkin bag reportedly requires three crocodile skins to create. Hermès currently uses a variety of skins in their production. The most prized leather is from the saltwater crocodile (*Crocodylus porosus*) farmed in Australia. These crocodiles are highly territorial, so they must be kept separately to ensure they don't fight and potentially scar the expensive skins. Hermès rejects a significant number of hides that fail to meet their exacting standards. The saltwater crocodile hide has a small, neat square pattern and tiny pores across the skin. Available in matte and *lisse* versions, *lisse* is shiny and buffed with agate stones to achieve a glossy finish. Each exotic skin has a symbol next to the Hermès stamp; saltwater crocodile is marked with a ^.

Hermès also uses Mississippi alligator, Nile monitor, Asian water monitor and ostrich skins, while some vintage bags feature caiman hide. The Nile crocodile (*Crocodylus niloticus*) is marked with a ·· next to the Hermès stamp and has a larger and more random scale pattern. Usually Nile crocodile skins are cheaper than saltwater crocodile skins, but matte Nile crocodile, which is dyed in ombré shades to create the Hermès Himalaya Birkin and Kelly, is an exception. Reminiscent of the Himalayan mountains, the hides take on a rocky and snow-capped appearance (and are often adorned with sparkling diamond hardware). In 2022, Sotheby's sold a Himalaya Birkin 30 for $450,000—the most expensive Hermès bag in the world. Compared to the humbler $2,000 price tag that buyers were faced with on the bag's release in 1984, even the most plain Birkins now start at around $10,000. Yet they still remain a wise investment. A 2016 report showed that a Birkin bag purchase has returns of approximately 14%. That is, if

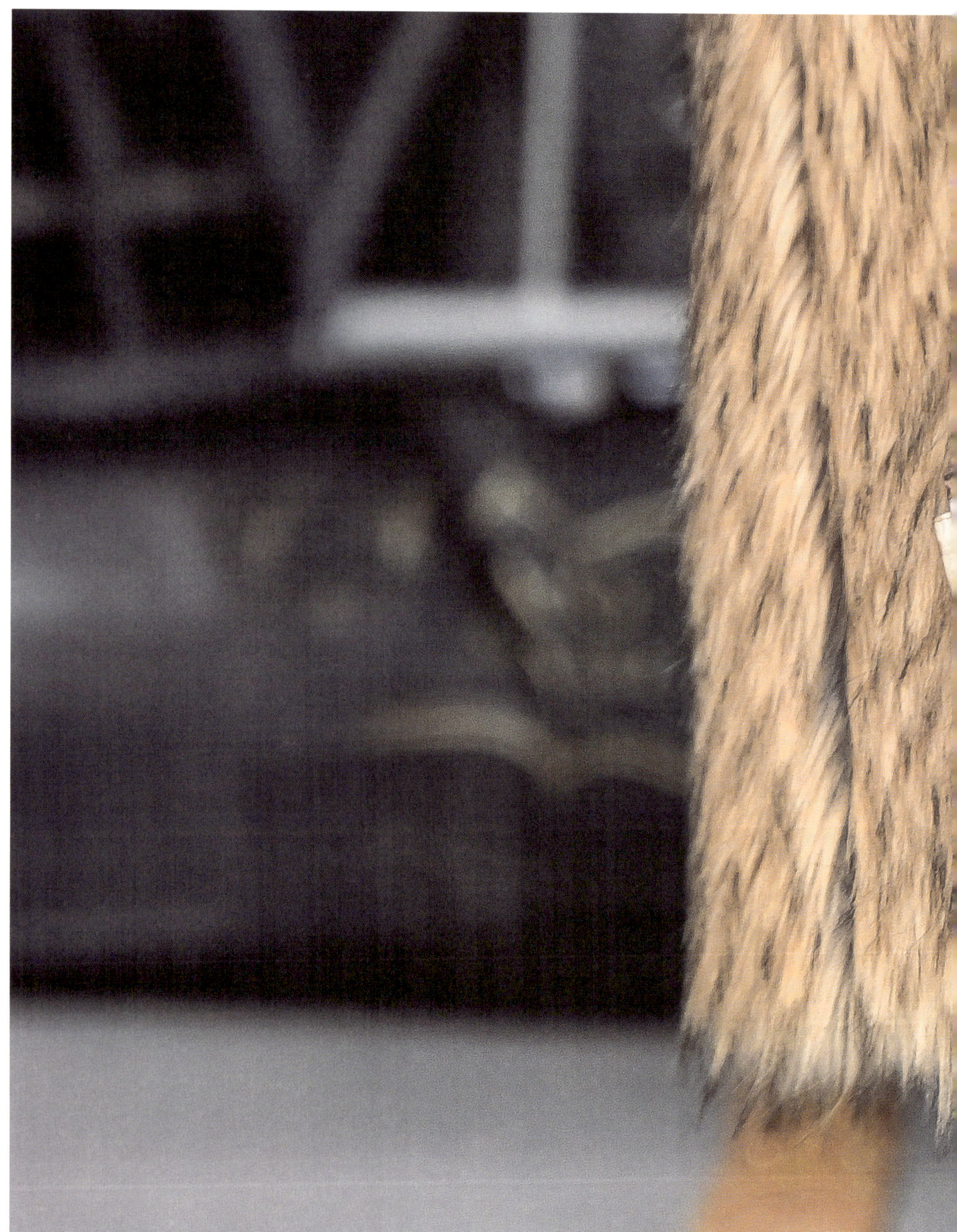

Close-up of Jennifer Lopez's Himalaya Birkin 25, New York City, February 15, 2024

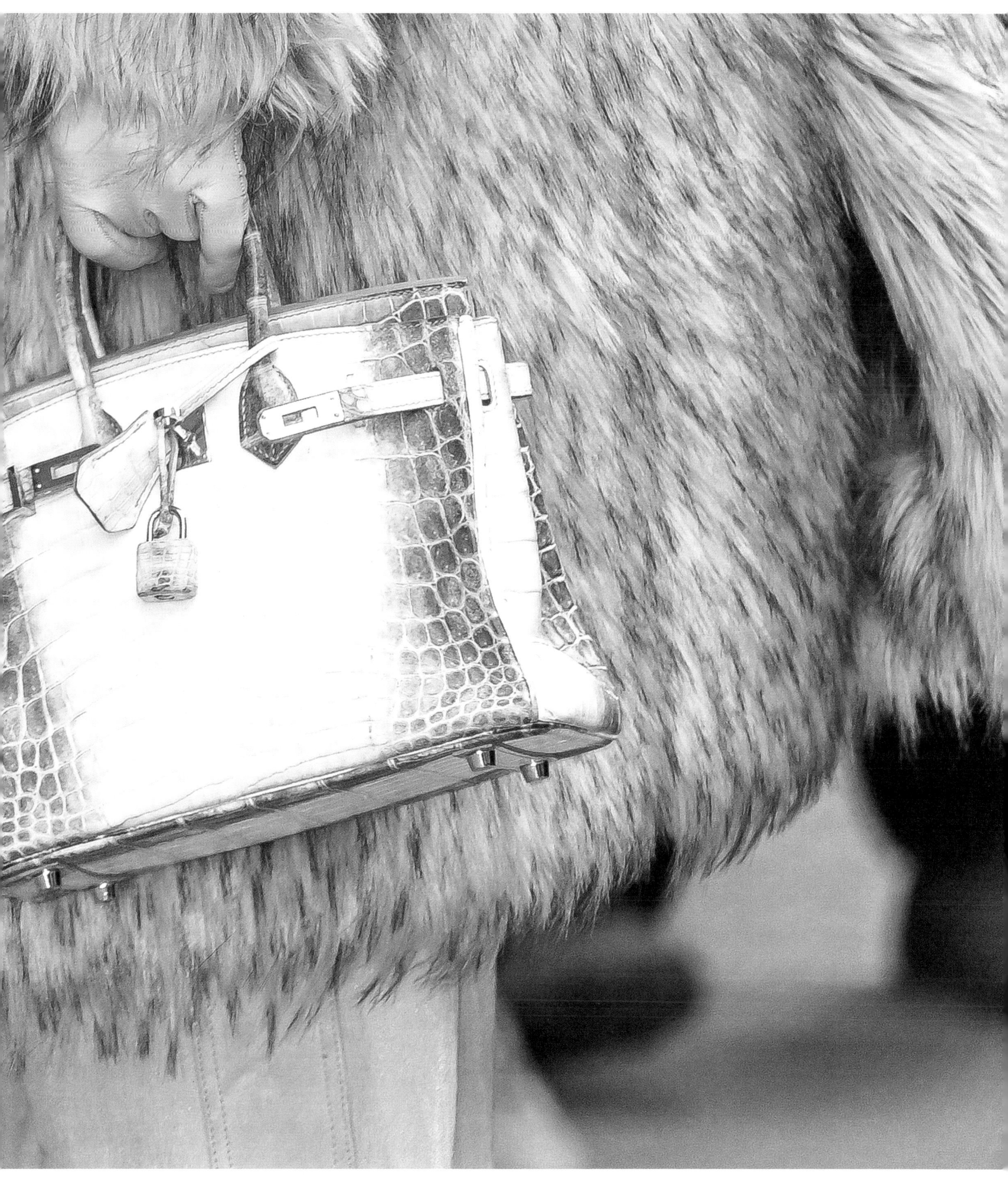

This page: A visitor to London Fashion Week Fall/Winter 2025 with a green Birkin

Next page: Caro Daur carrying a black Birkin outside the Hermès Womenswear Fall/Winter 2025 show, Paris

Pages 60/61: Snehal Babani and Jyoti Babani with their limited edition Sunset and Sunrise Birkins, Paris Fashion Week, March 02, 2024

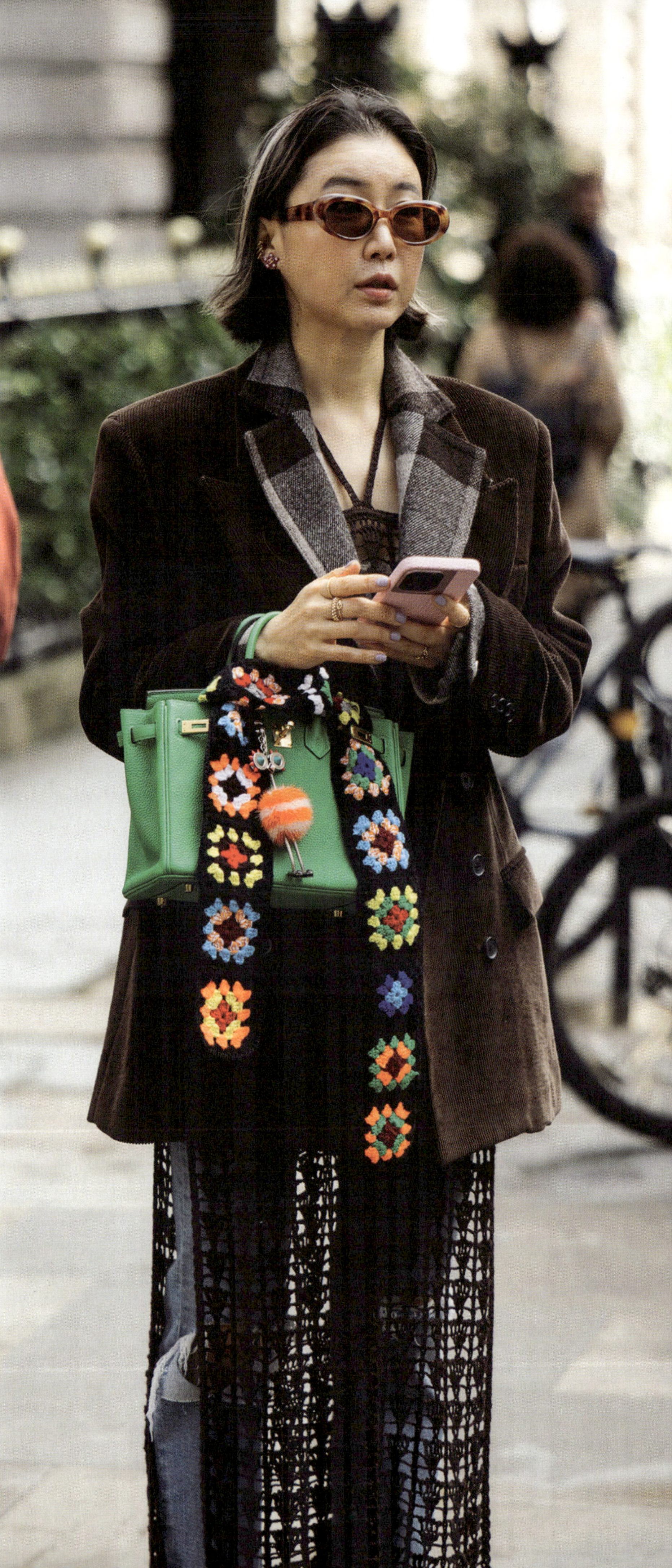

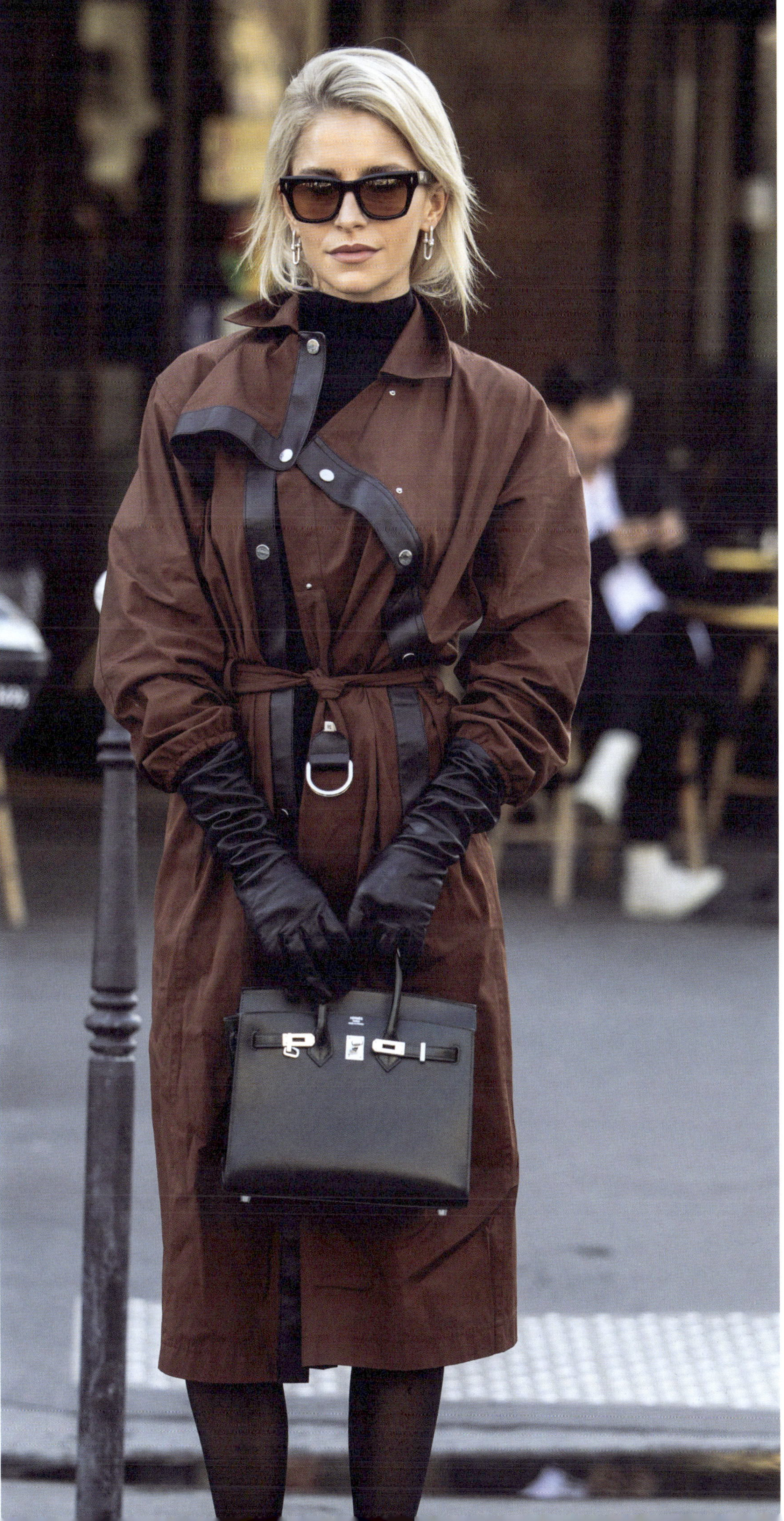

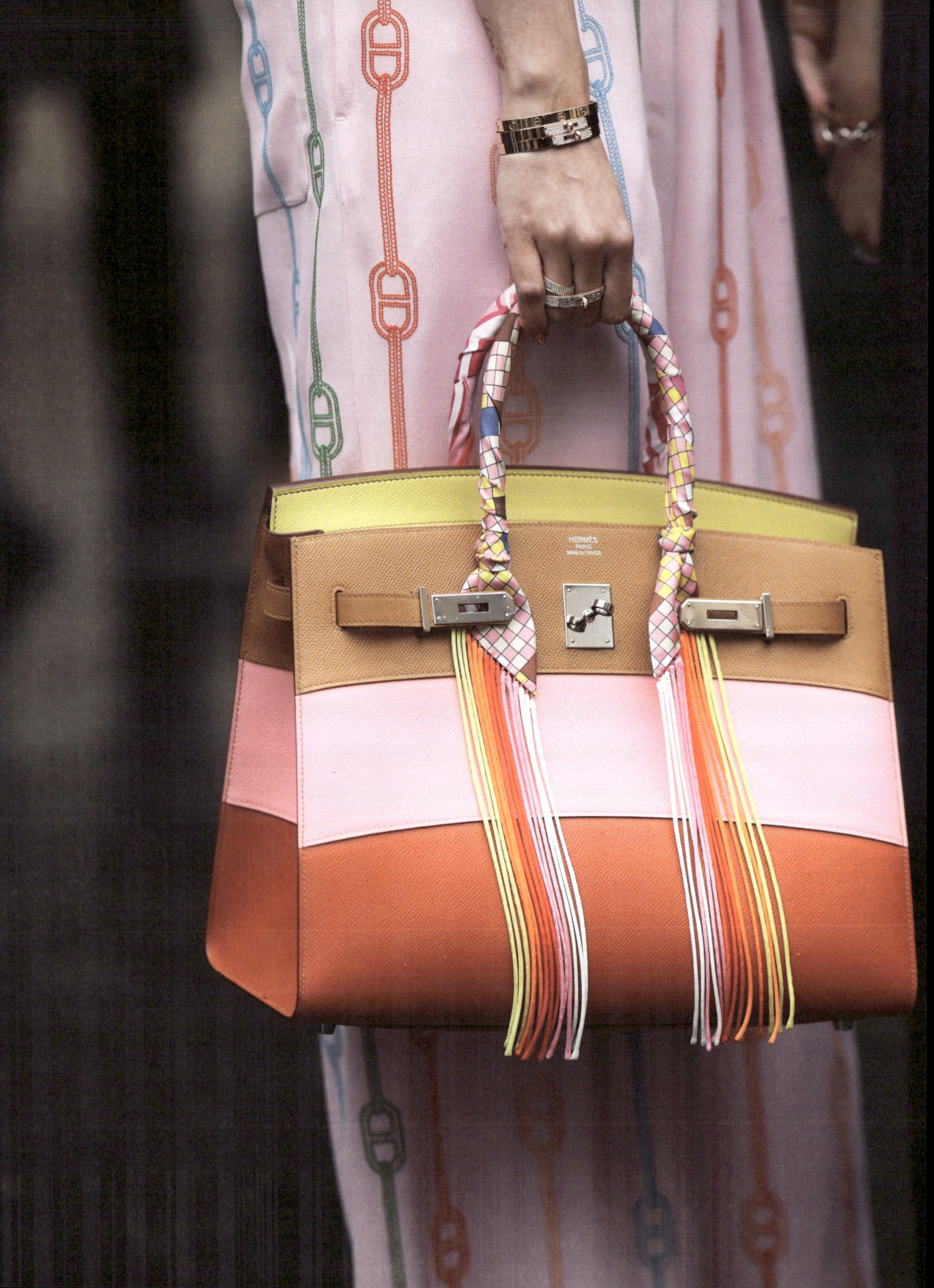
HERMÈS
PARIS

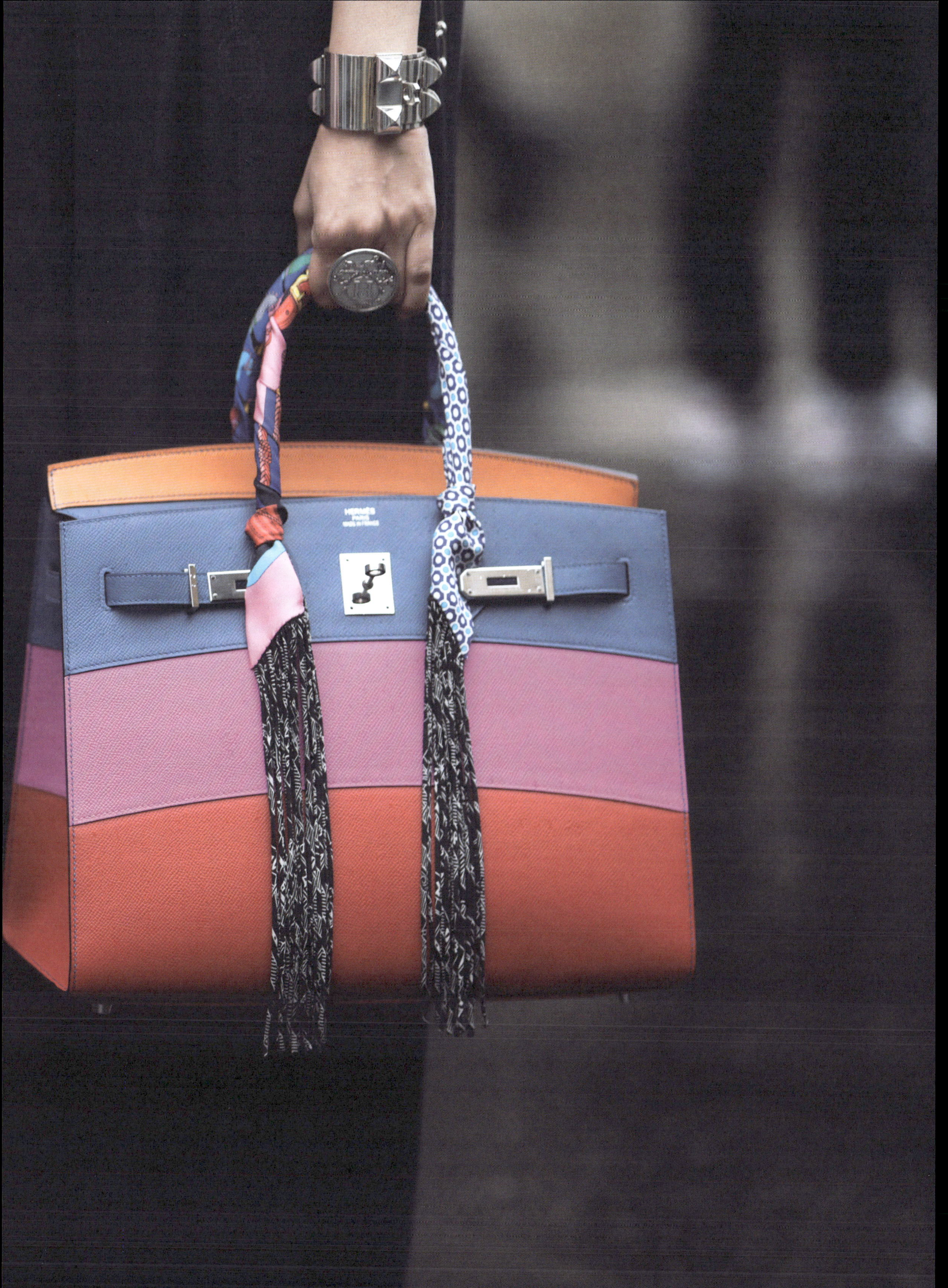

you can bear to keep your Birkin box-fresh. Wearing your bag, even once, can knock around £5,000 off the resale value. Of course, that assumes you have the means to be able to buy one in the first place...

While there are urban legends of people strolling into an Hermès store and walking out with a Birkin bag, the desirability of the style is in direct correlation to its availability. Birkins are so-called 'quota' bags, along with the Kelly (and Constance bags, in some countries), which mean customers are limited to two purchases a year. However, before a sale can occur, potential customers need to make a 'wish' and be offered a bag. Most Birkin buyers cultivate relationships with a specific sales associate and allegedly spend six-figure sums on other Hermès products before making a wish and then receiving an offer. Being as specific as possible with your wish will help with your order, apparently, but in the London stores a wish will expire after 8 months. Those who re-wish are more likely to get their dream bag, and while it's not explicitly described as a waiting list, customers can wait up to five years for their Birkin. It's that long wait that drives some impatient customers to shop resale options. They want a bag *immediately*, despite resale prices of brand new bags often being higher than in Hermès stores. Hermès doesn't reveal how many bags they make per year, but it takes one artisan up to 48 hours to make a bag from start to finish. Around five bags leave the workshops each week to supply global demand, so it explains both the market scarcity *and* the waiting time to purchase.

Other than the Himalaya bags, the most expensive Birkin is actually a piece of jewelry. Known as the Sac Bijou Birkin and part of the Hermès Haute Bijouterie Collection from 2012, the bag is a miniature Birkin designed to be worn as a bracelet. Encrusted with over 2000 diamonds set in rose gold, only three pieces were ever made. The price tag? $2 million.

If you're looking to add a Birkin bag to your collection or invest in your first handbag, once you've chosen the leather and color, available sizes are 25, 30, 35 and 40 cm. For 2025, the Birkin à *l'envers* is an exciting twist on the classic style, taking the interior pocket and placing it on the outside and switching the *touret* fastening to inside the bag. Available in a combined canvas and leather style, it's set to become a modern classic alongside the Shadow Birkin. Designed by Jean Paul Gaultier and launched in 2009, the Shadow Birkin's exterior signature details are removed, but instead appear as embossed details to create a sleek minimalistic look. The JPG Shoulder Birkin is also a Gaultier creation undergoing a resurgence. With a deep and practical shoulder strap, the 2004 original was re-released in 2024 to adoration from influencers. Despite its legion of celebrity fans and infinite appearances on social media, the Birkin bag still manages to be the most elusive handbag of our time.

Next page: Fashion blogger Bryanboy carrying a green crocodile Birkin at Milan Fashion Week, September 23, 2022

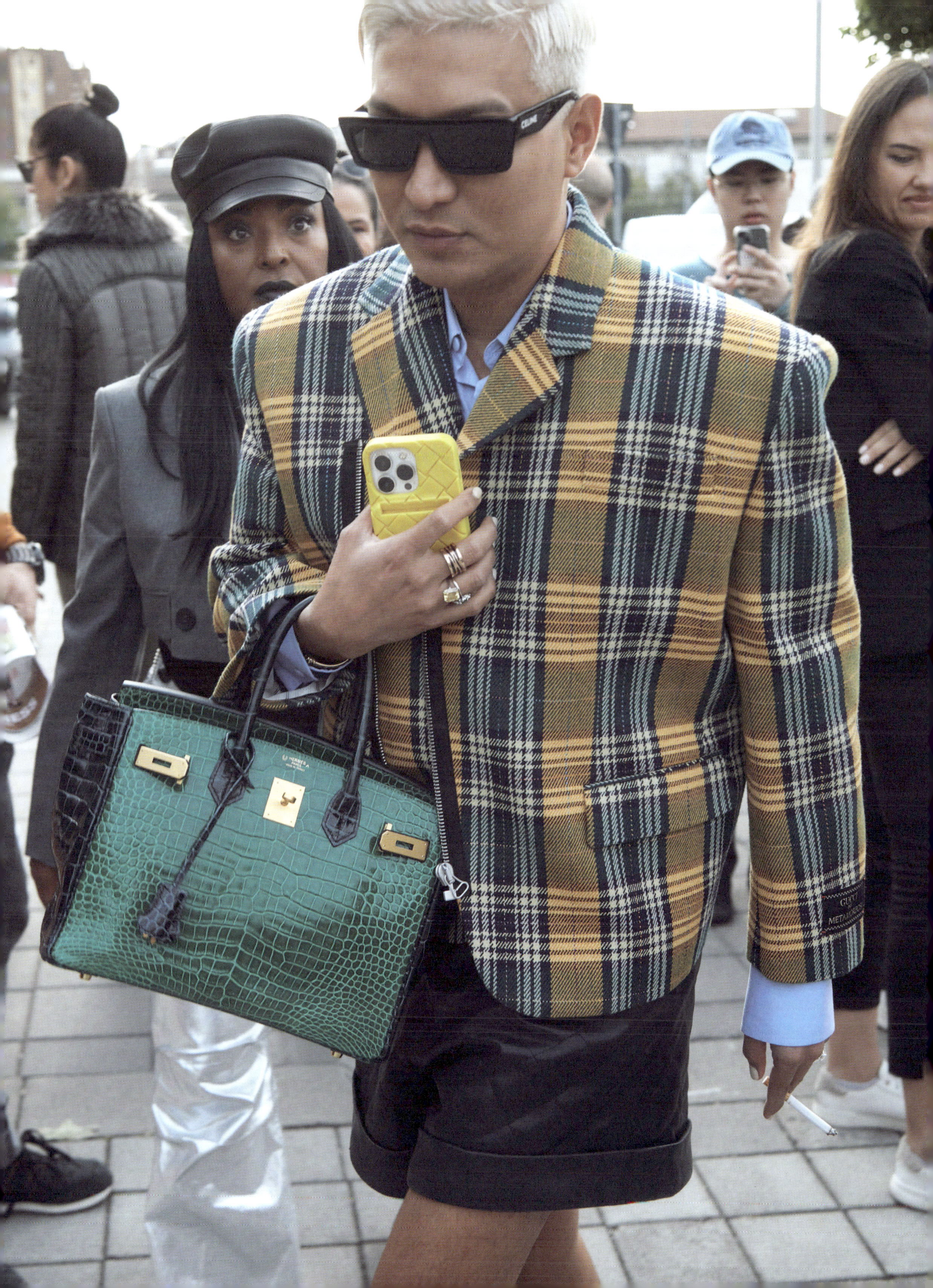

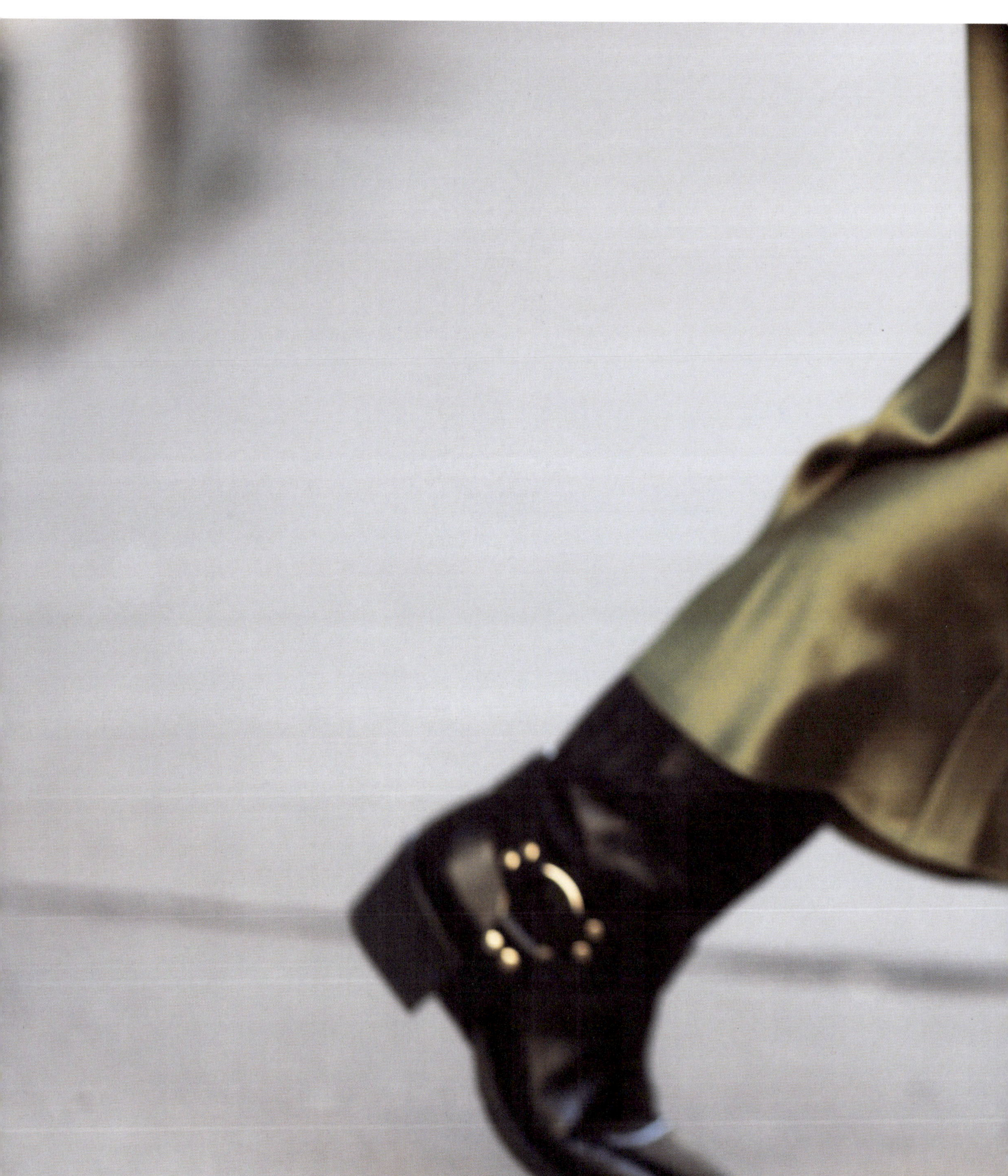

Karin Teigl adorns her black leather Birkin bag with colorful bag charms, Vienna, 2025

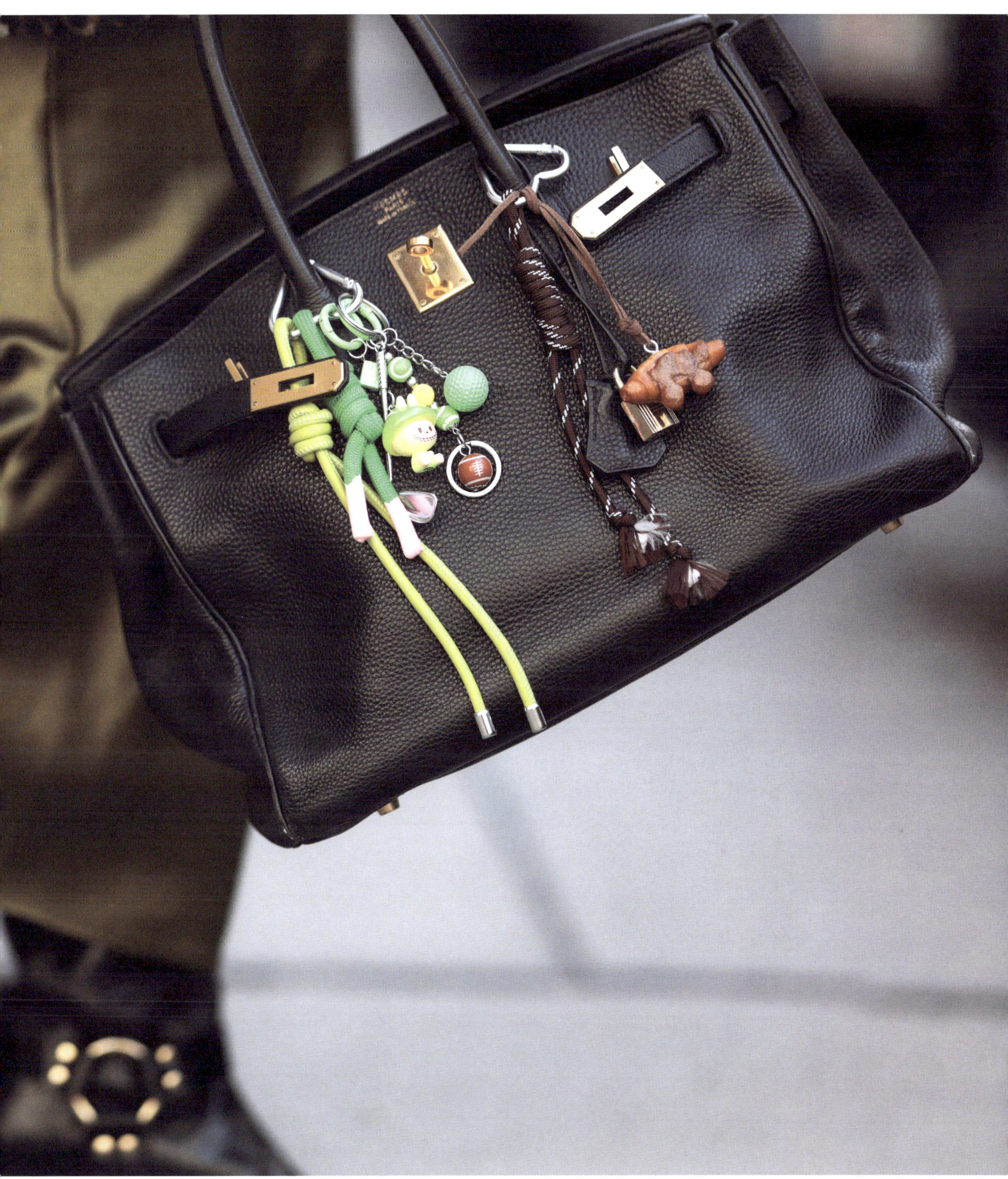

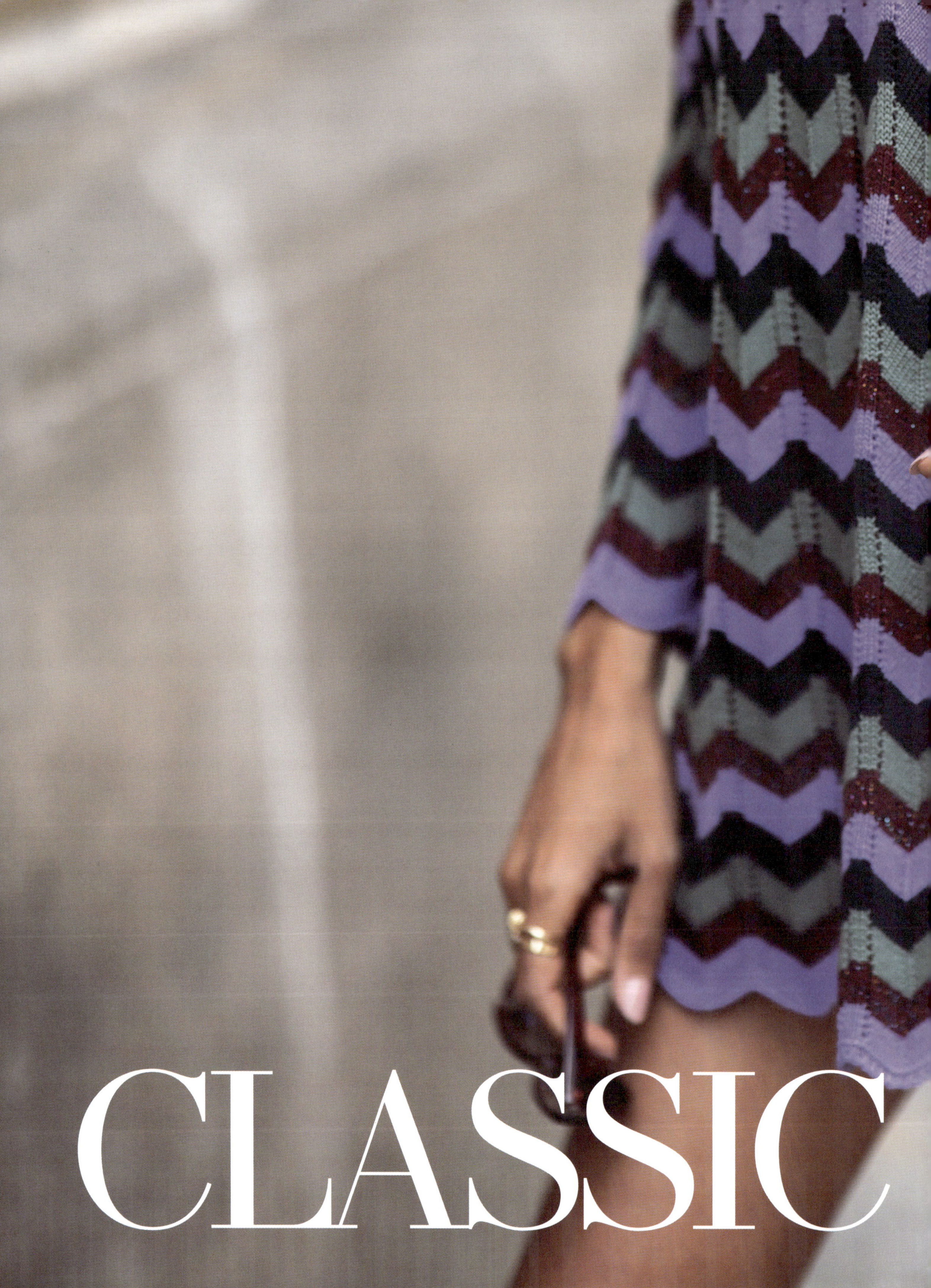
CLASSIC

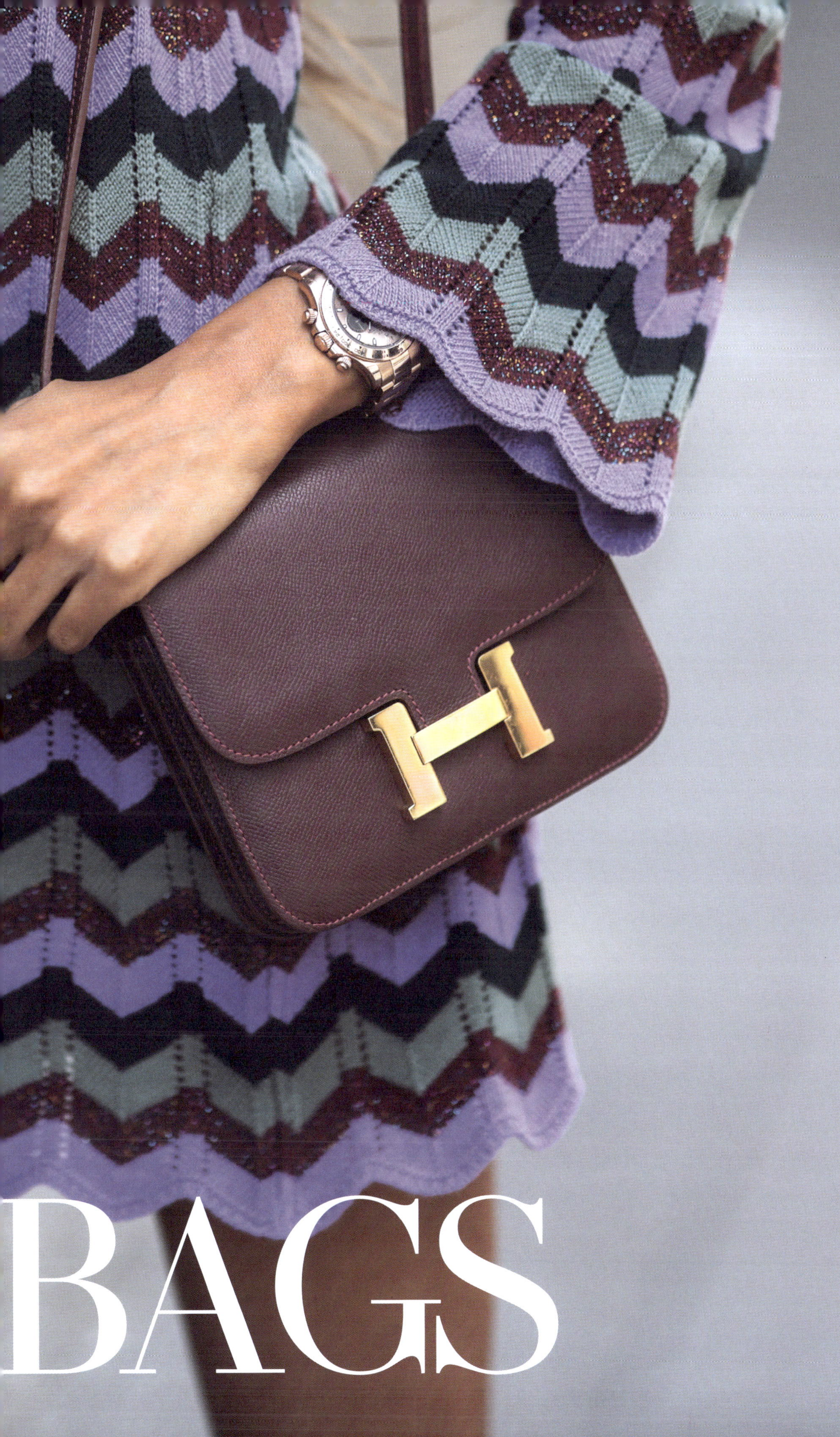

BAGS

CONSTANCE

Beyond the Birkin and Kelly, Hermès is home to a cavalcade of chic bags that are just as legendary, even without a serendipitous celebrity origin story. Perhaps the third most well-known bag from Hermès' stable is the Constance bag. The bag dates back to 1967, when Jean-Louis Dumas asked in-house designer Catherine Chaillet to create a new bag. Chaillet was pregnant with her fifth child and named the bag after her new baby daughter with the style going on sale the day Constance was born.

Jackie Kennedy Onassis became an early fan of the bag, with Diane Kruger, Emily Ratajkowski and Rachel Bilson all more recent converts to the Constance's easygoing appeal. Where the Birkin is the go-to everyday tote, and the Kelly is the formal evening option, Constance is the bag that transcends every occasion with flair.

In most locations, Constance doesn't count as a quota bag, so customers can buy several each year if their pockets are deep and supplies are plentiful, although that never seems to be the case. In China, Japan, Singapore, Australia, France and Canada, the Constance counts towards a customer's annual quota. And, anecdotally, in some locations customers are less likely to be offered a Constance than a Birkin or Kelly due to finite stock coupled with insatiable desire. The Constance is undergoing a resurgence in popularity, leaving many potential customers turning to the resale market to secure their dream bag.

One Hermès artisan takes 14-18 hours to bring each bag to life, but the Constance bag is certainly worth the wait, being hailed as the ultimate day-to-night bag. Infinitely versatile due to the long sliding strap, which can be worn crossbody, shoulder style or on the hip, and noted for its bold H buckle, the Constance's concealed spring mechanism fastening is clever yet simple. Offered with an array of hardware, some styles are enameled in tonal or contrasting shades, and there is also a version in *marqueterie de paille*.

Available in a variety of finishes including simpler and more affordable leathers like epsom, swift and box, the Constance also dons exotic skins and can be purchased in a kaleidoscopic marbled silk version. Sizewise, the Constance comes in a mini size (18cm), the 1-24 (which comes with a tiny compact mirror tucked into a pocket) and the Elan, an elongated rectangular shape which was launched in 2010, discontinued, and then brought back for spring 2024. The new Elan was first presented in box leather, which recalls the 'old money' aesthetic, but can also be found in a wide range of finishes. Prices for a box leather Constance Elan start at almost £12,000 in Hermès boutiques, while the mini size is currently the most popular, retailing at around $9,000 for epsom leather and $10,000 for *chèvre*.

Pages 66/67: Jill Asemota is seen wearing a brown Hermès Constance bag, Berlin, 2022

Next page: Emili Sindlev carries a green Constance with palladium hardware during Paris Fashion Week, 2022

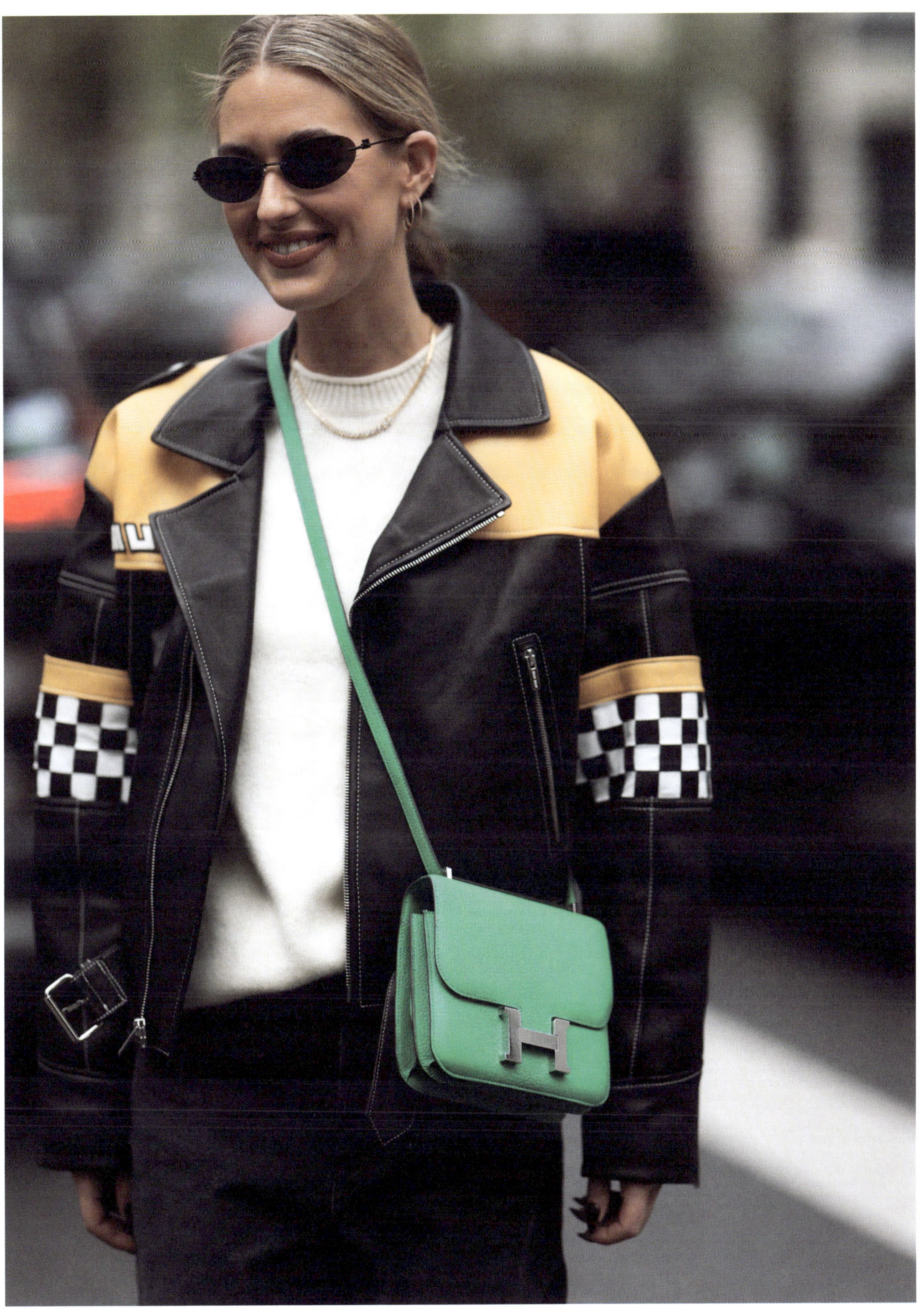

If you find a vintage Constance from the 1980s or 1990s, you might be surprised to find a slip pocket on the back of the bag. This was removed from later models, while the original large middle compartment was divided into two smaller, expandable pockets. The silhouette changed to a wider shape with the introduction of gussets, but the newly reimagined Constance Elan has returned to the sleeker vintage shape.

While less expensive than Birkin bags or Kellys in comparable materials, the Constance bag can still shatter price expectations. A Constance 24 Himalaya Crocodile from 2023 sold at auction with Sotheby's for nearly $100,000, while resale site Xupes is listing an unworn Constance 24 Blanc Himalaya Matte Crocodile bag, with palladium hardware, also with a 2023 stamp, for $160,000.

For people who don't want to wait and who insist on getting their bag in a boutique, choosing a non-quota bag is the best way to secure an Hermès bag, *fast.*

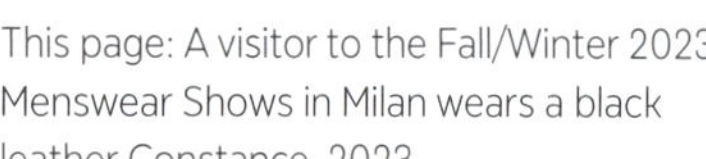

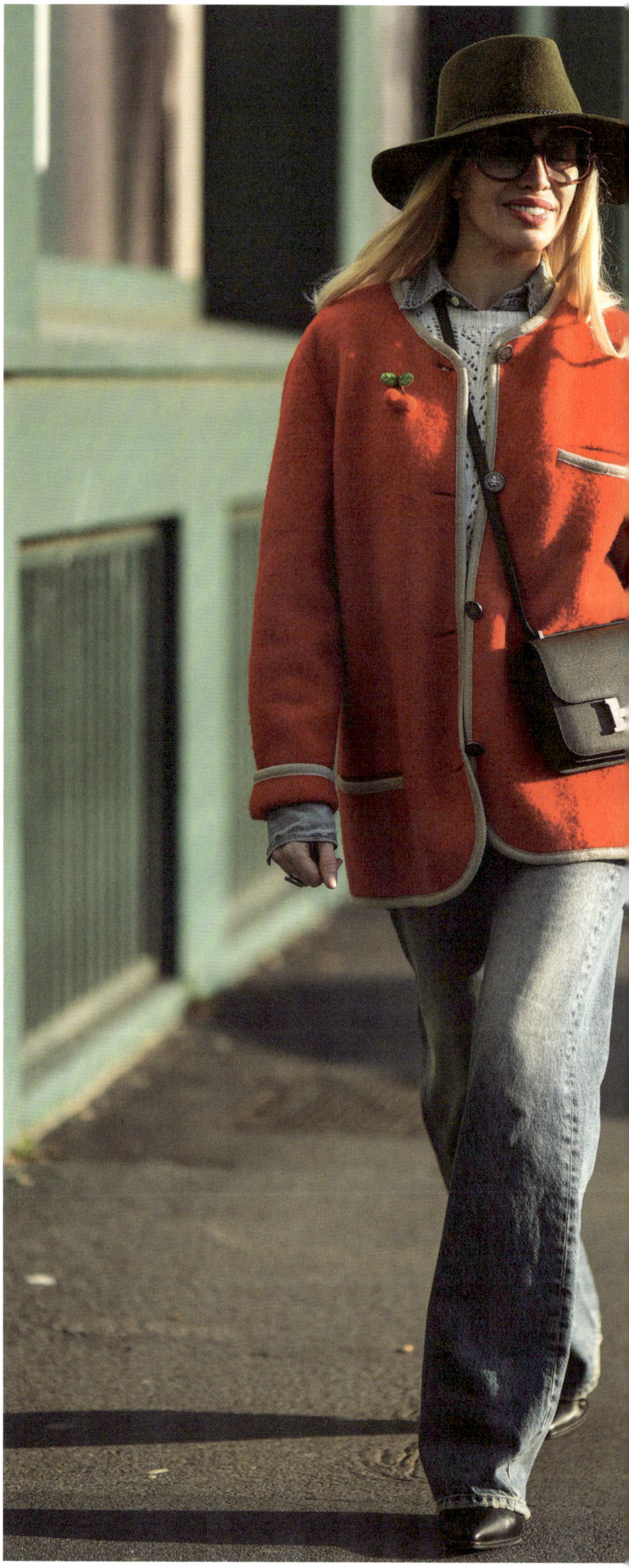

This page: A visitor to the Fall/Winter 2023 Menswear Shows in Milan wears a black leather Constance, 2023

Next page: At the Spring/Summer 2023 haute couture shows in Paris, a visitor carries a purple Alligator Constance

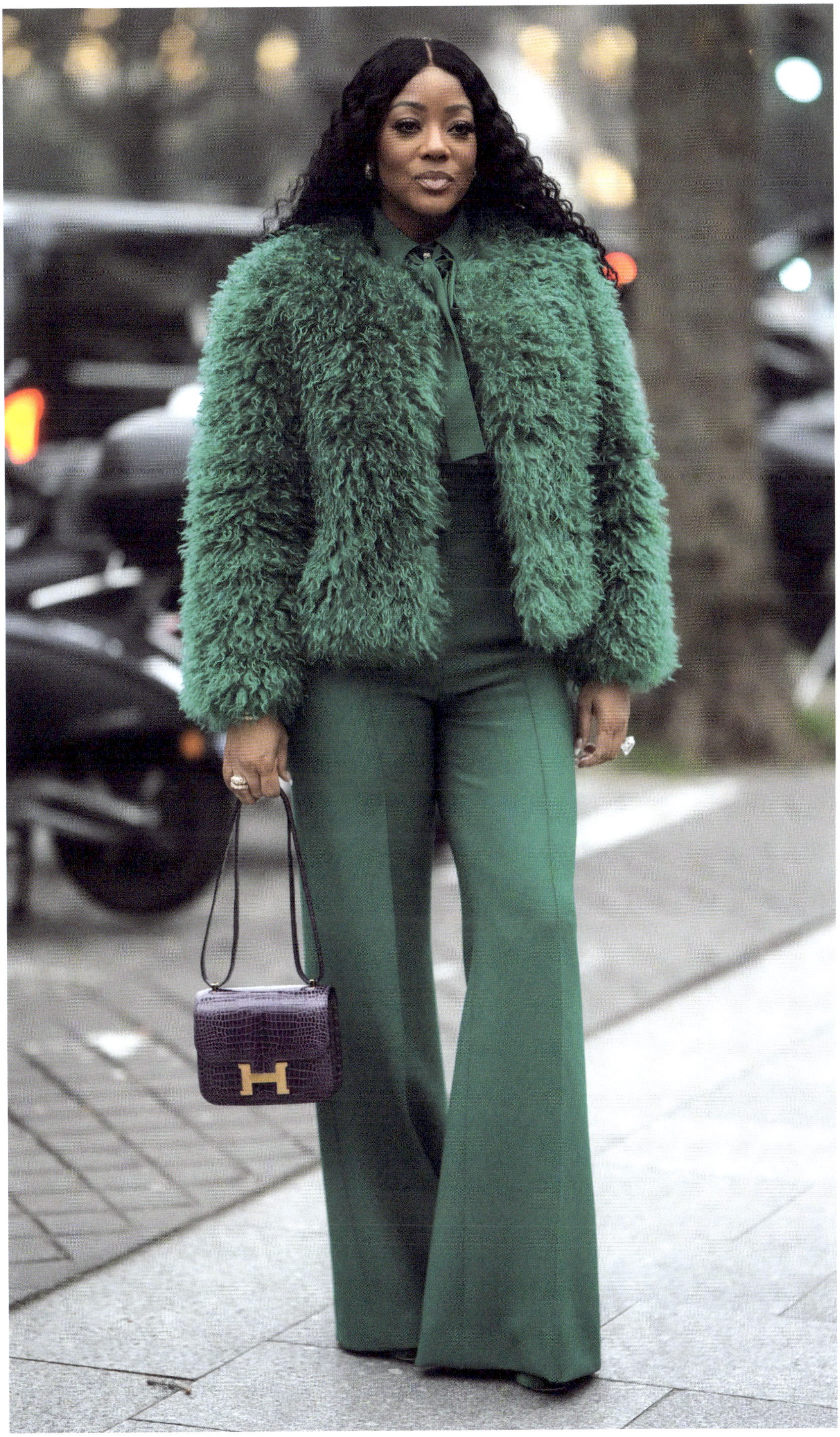

EVELYNE

Harking back to Hermès' horsey past, this bag was originally designed for grooms to carry equestrian equipment. Unlined and easy to wear, the perforated H logo helped air circulate around the bag and dry wet gear. That logo was meant to be worn facing the body, but as the bag became popular as a fashion accessory, wearers eager to showcase their designer credentials turned it face out. The bag was named for Evelyne Bertrand, Hermès Riding Department Head, and launched in 1978. Currently available for around £1400 in Hermès European boutiques, the bags sell for between £2900-£3600 at resale outlets, depending on color, age and wear.

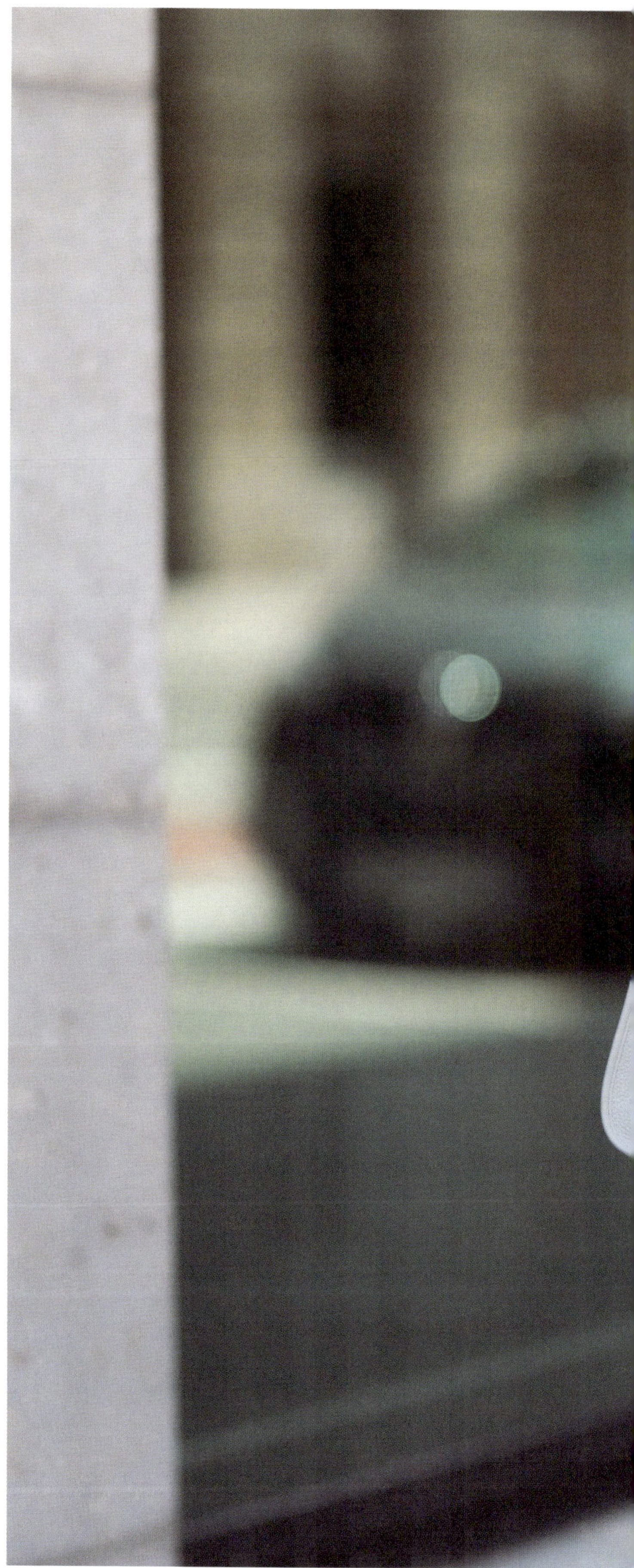

Kathrin Bommann is seen wearing a gray-blue Evelyne 33 bag, Düsseldorf, May 28, 2023

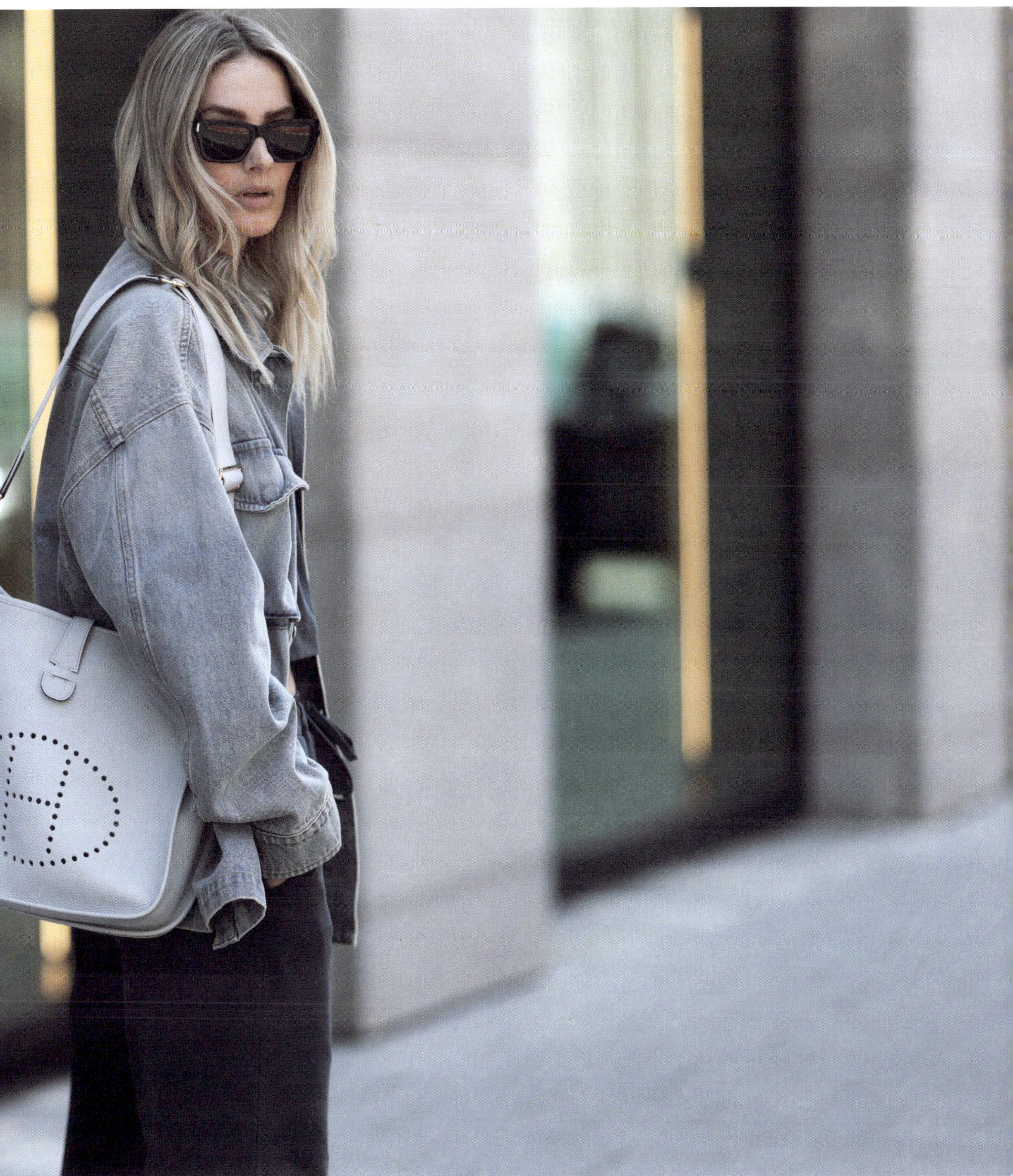

This page: A guest carries an orange patent leather Evelyne outside the Fall/Winter 2022 Bluemarble show in Paris

Next page: Emili Sindlev carries a blue leather Evelyne during Fall/Winter 2022 Paris Fashion Week, 2022

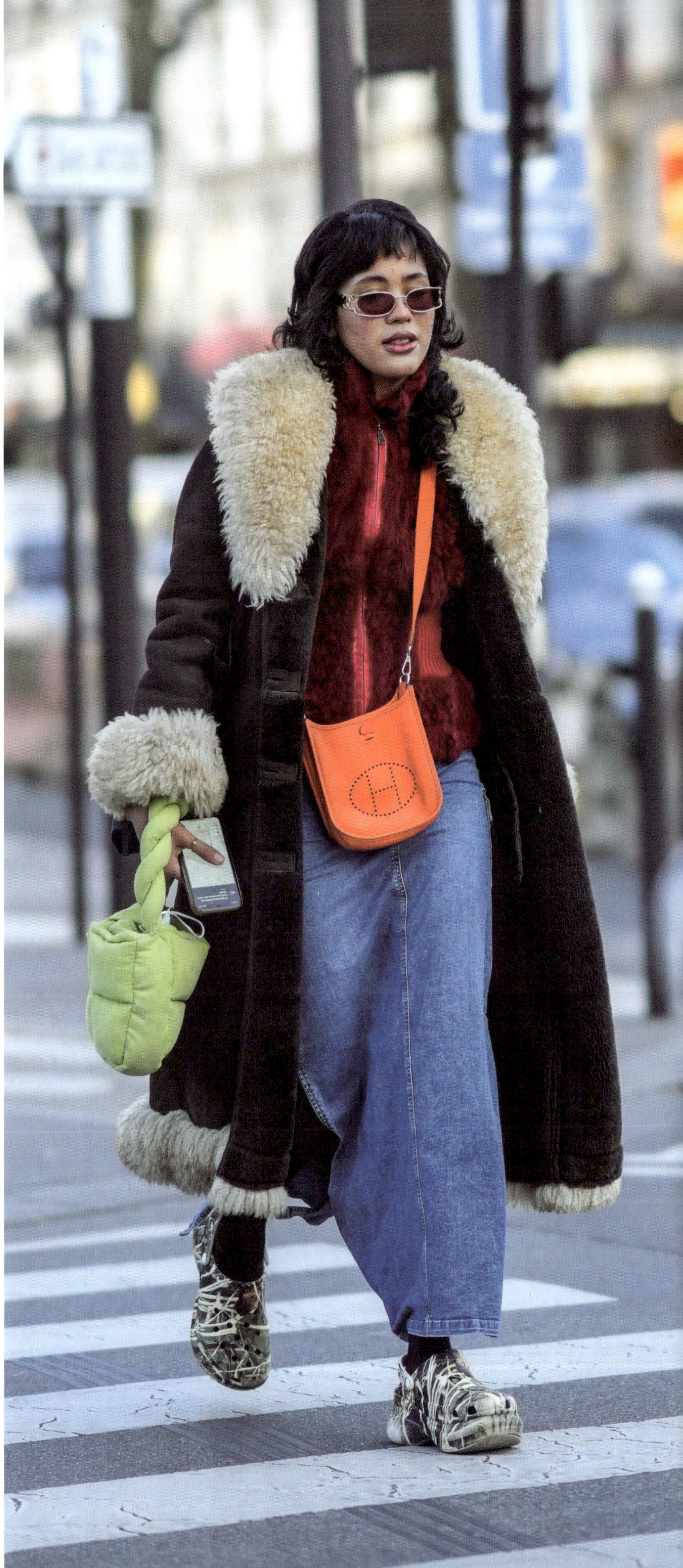

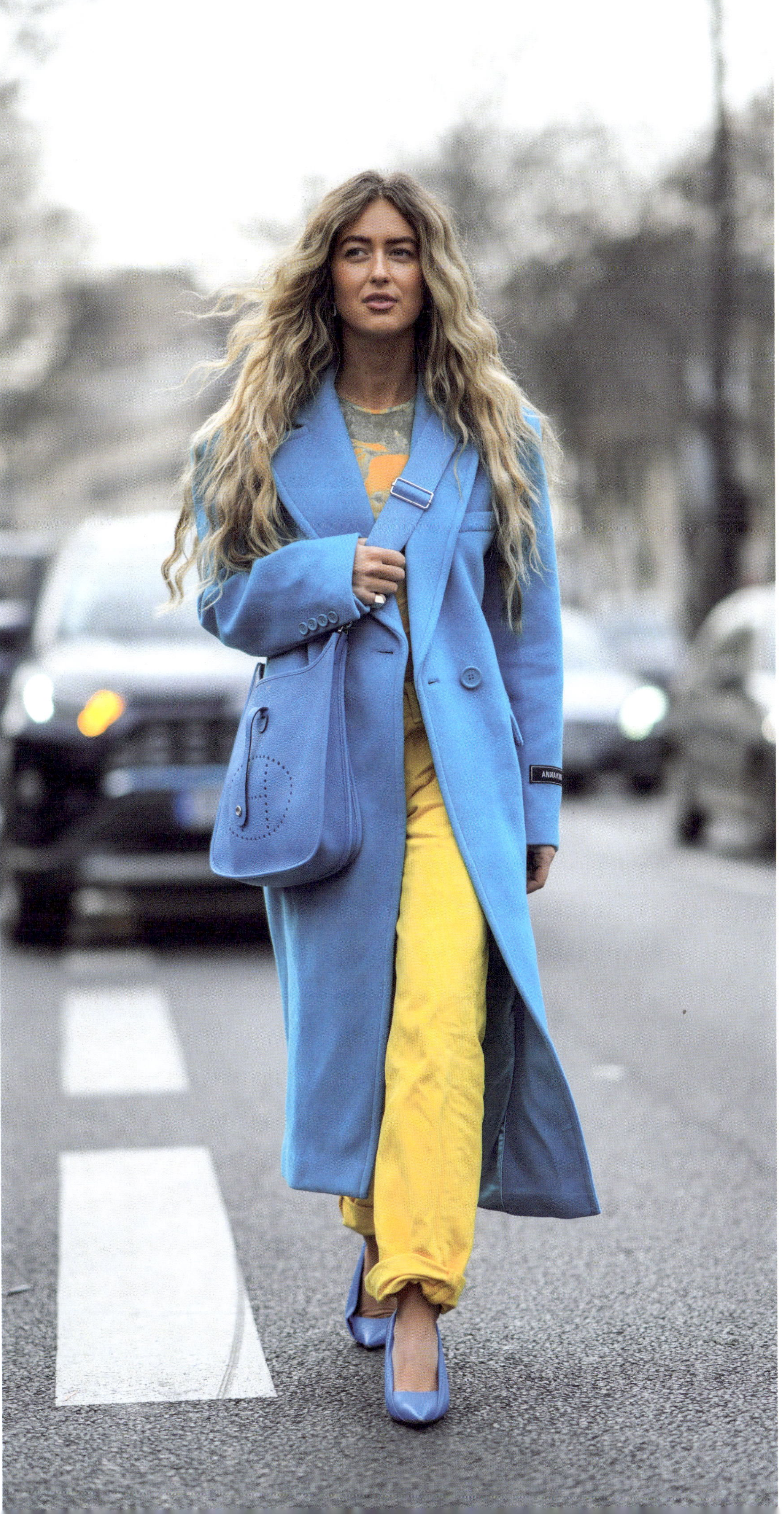

PICOTIN

Launched in 2002, the Picotin's popularity shows no signs of waning. Inspired by a feed bucket, the P18 is the smallest and most popular size, although there are also micro P14, P22 and P26 sizes available. The style is supple and casual and is made from unlined leather, although it can also be found in canvas finishes. Closed with a strap and padlock, the most popular versions come in clemence or epsom leathers, which are both matte, grainy and scratch-resistant. However, for 2025 a new P26 was presented in Barenia™ leather, a heritage hide made from calf leather. Renowned for its smooth, glossy finish, Barenia™ was originally used for saddles.

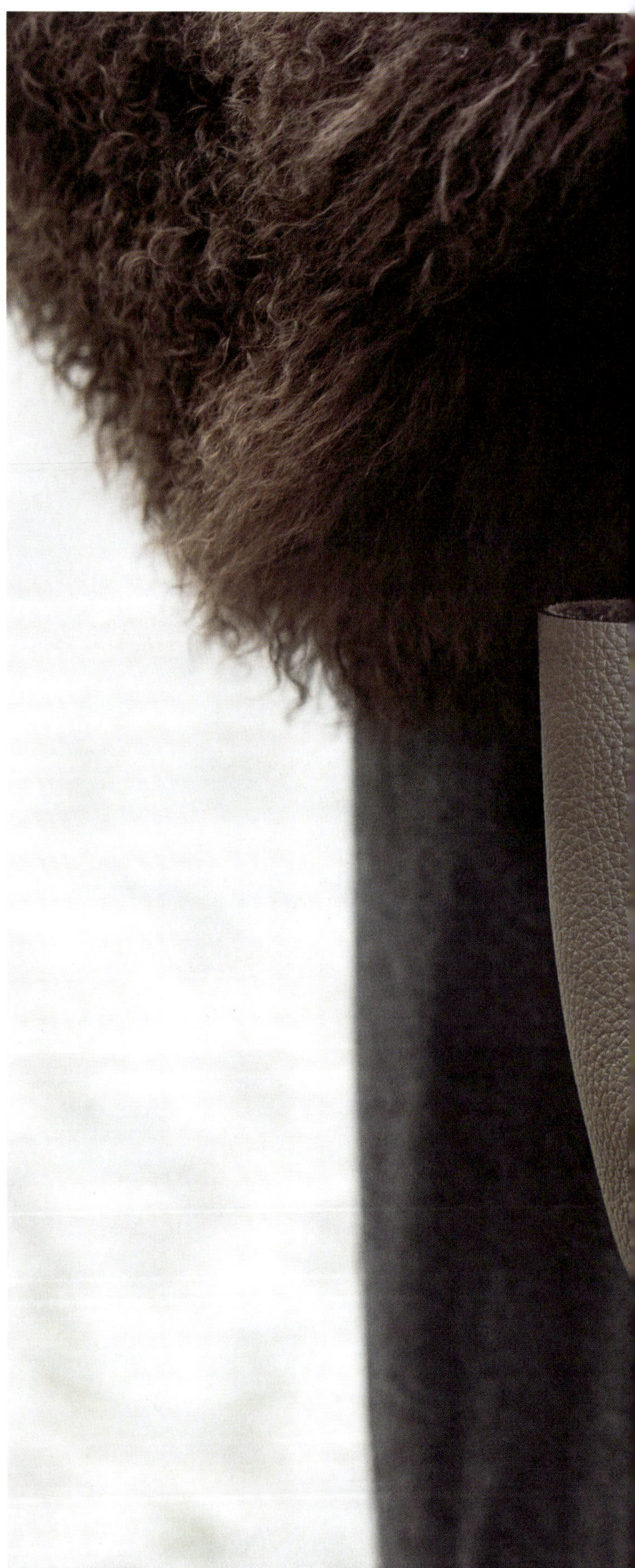

Sonia Lyson with a Picotin, Berlin, 2024

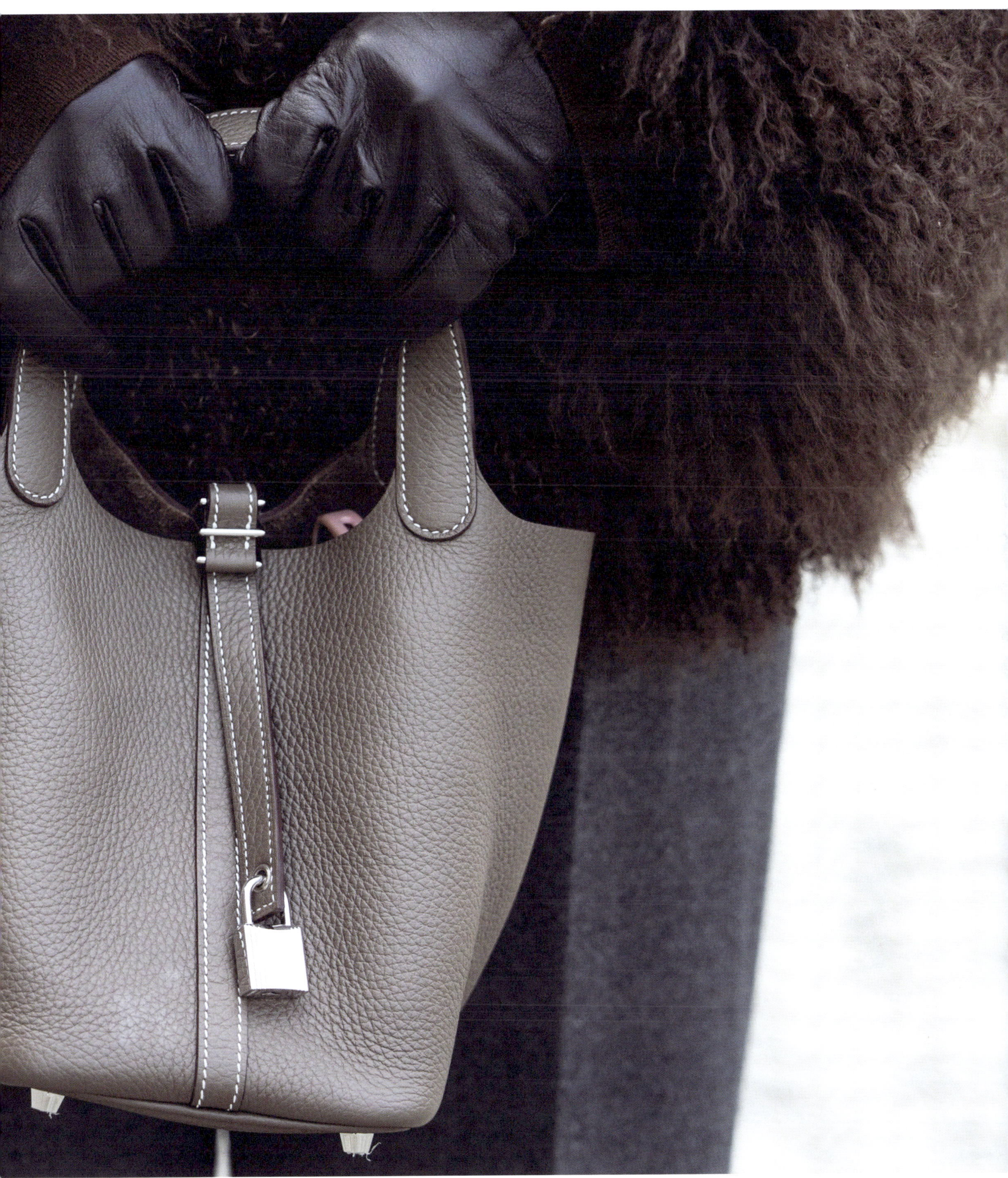

HERBAG

A sporty canvas bag that could be described as ludicrously capacious, the Herbag takes inspiration from the Kelly: clean lines paired with a trapezoid silhouette. The lightweight construction makes it an ideal tote for travel and weekend wear, and fresh colors and finishes are released every season.

A staple of Hermès' collections in the 1980s, the Herbag was discontinued in the mid-2000s before returning to stores in 2009 as the Herbag Zip. The bag now features an external pocket, useful interior pouch and zipped pocket, but what is its most versatile feature? The *vache* hunter leather top can be detached from the *officier* cotton canvas bottom and switched, earning the Herbag the name the "two-in-one bag." Maybe you'd like to wear a print for summer and a dark shade for winter? You get to choose! Available in Zip 31, Zip 39, Zip Cabine 50 and Zip 52 sizes, the Herbag usually sells for $1000 more than the boutique price in resale stores.

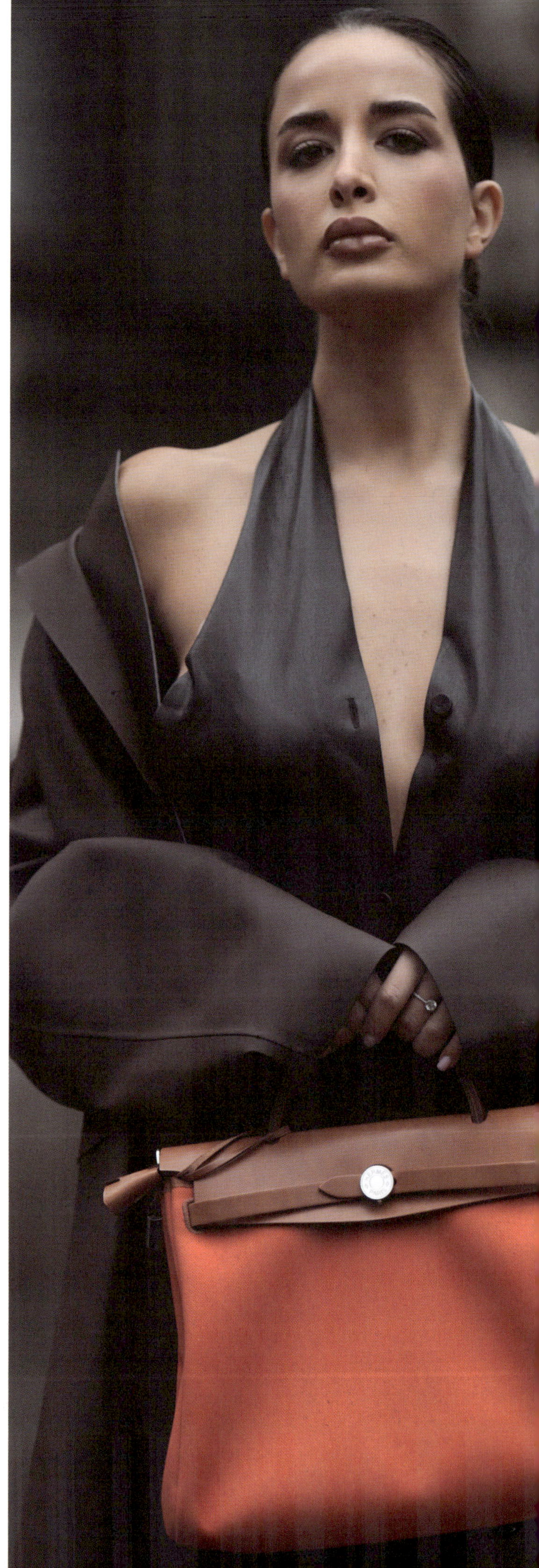

This page: A show-goer carries a red Herbag Zip 31, Paris Fashion Week, March 02, 2024

Next page: A visitor to Hermès Fall/Winter 2025 show, with a beige canvas Herbag Zip 39

Pages 80/81: Close-up of a Bolide on Wheels, Paris Fashion Week, 2024

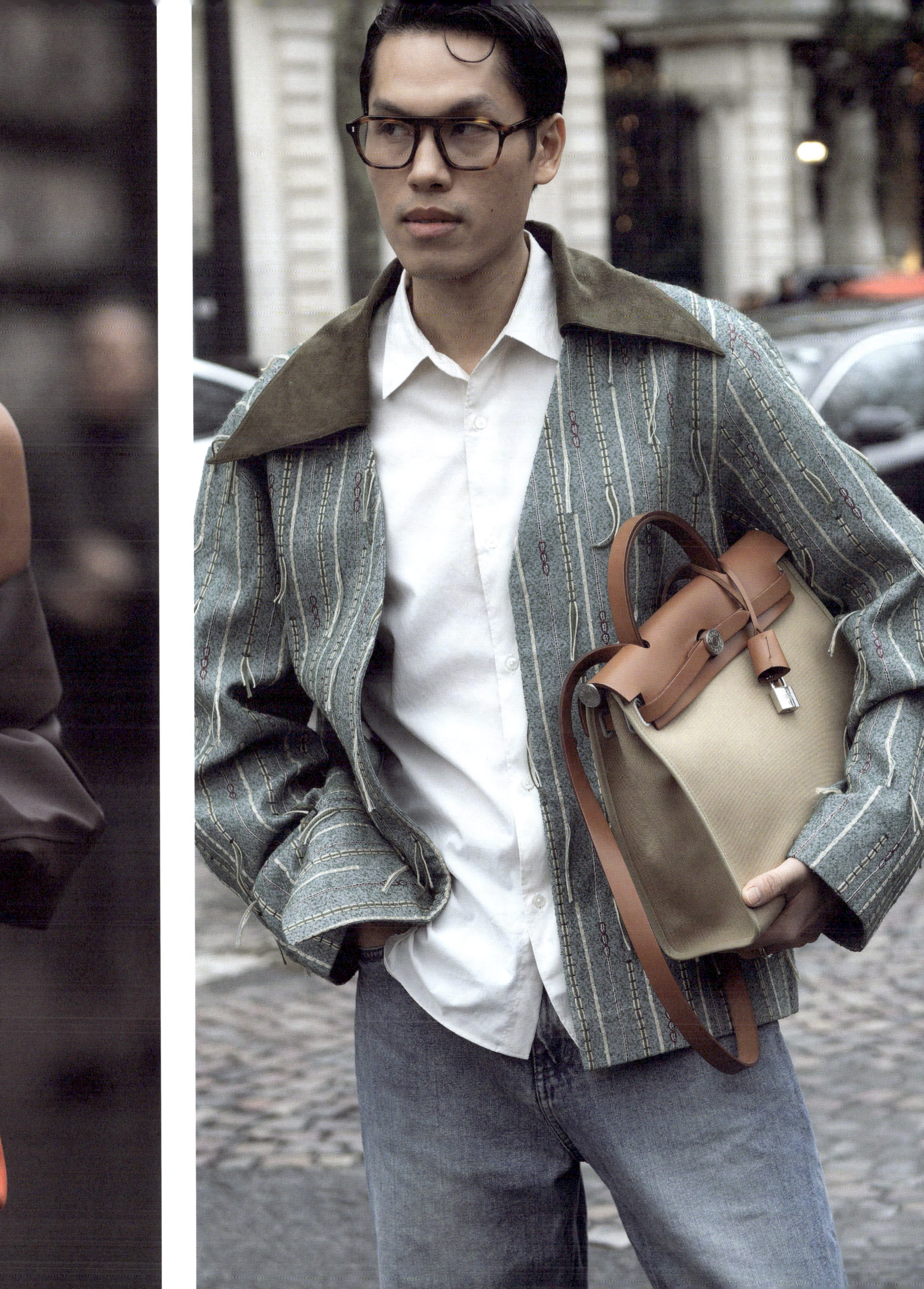

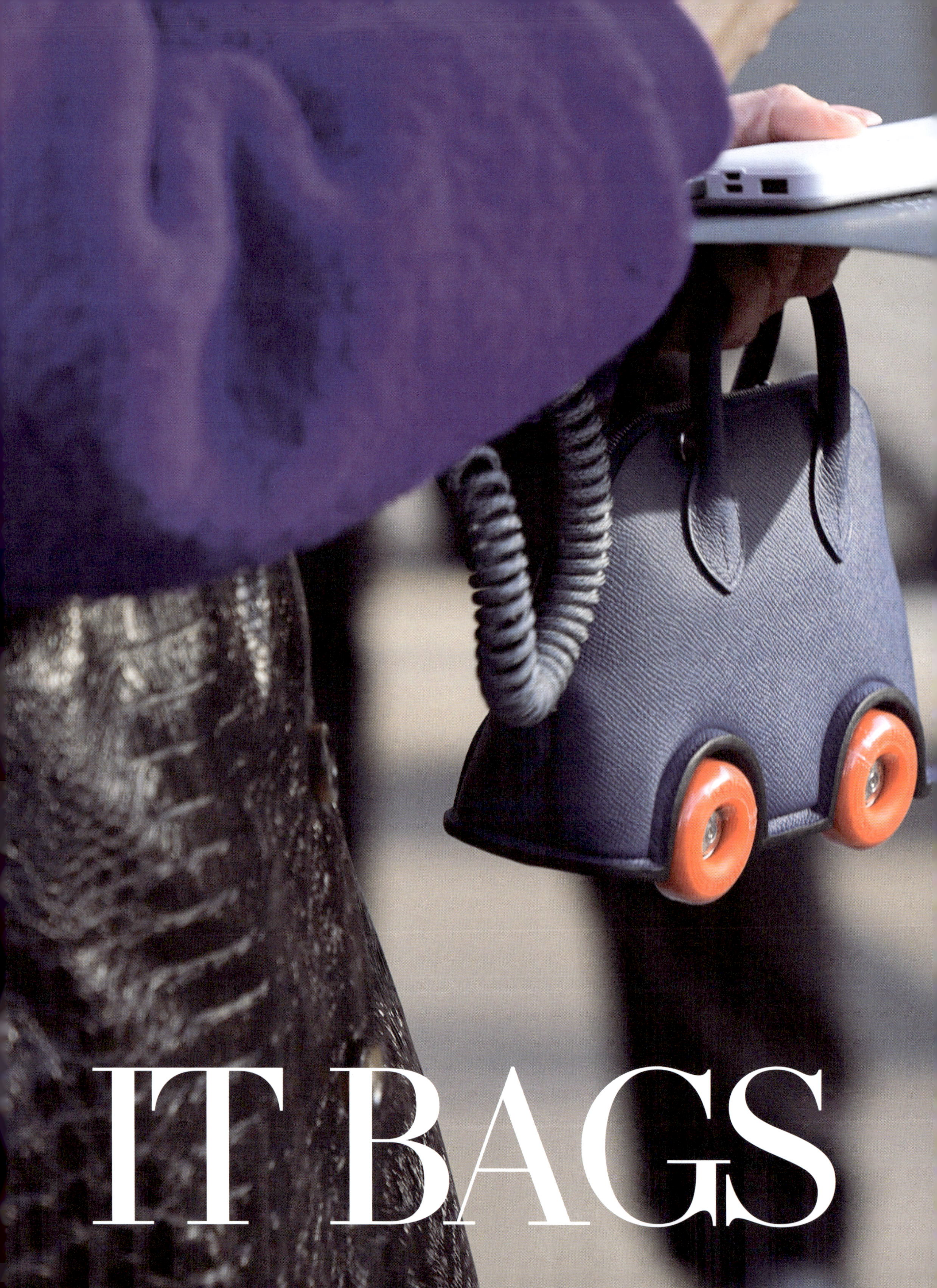

IT BAGS

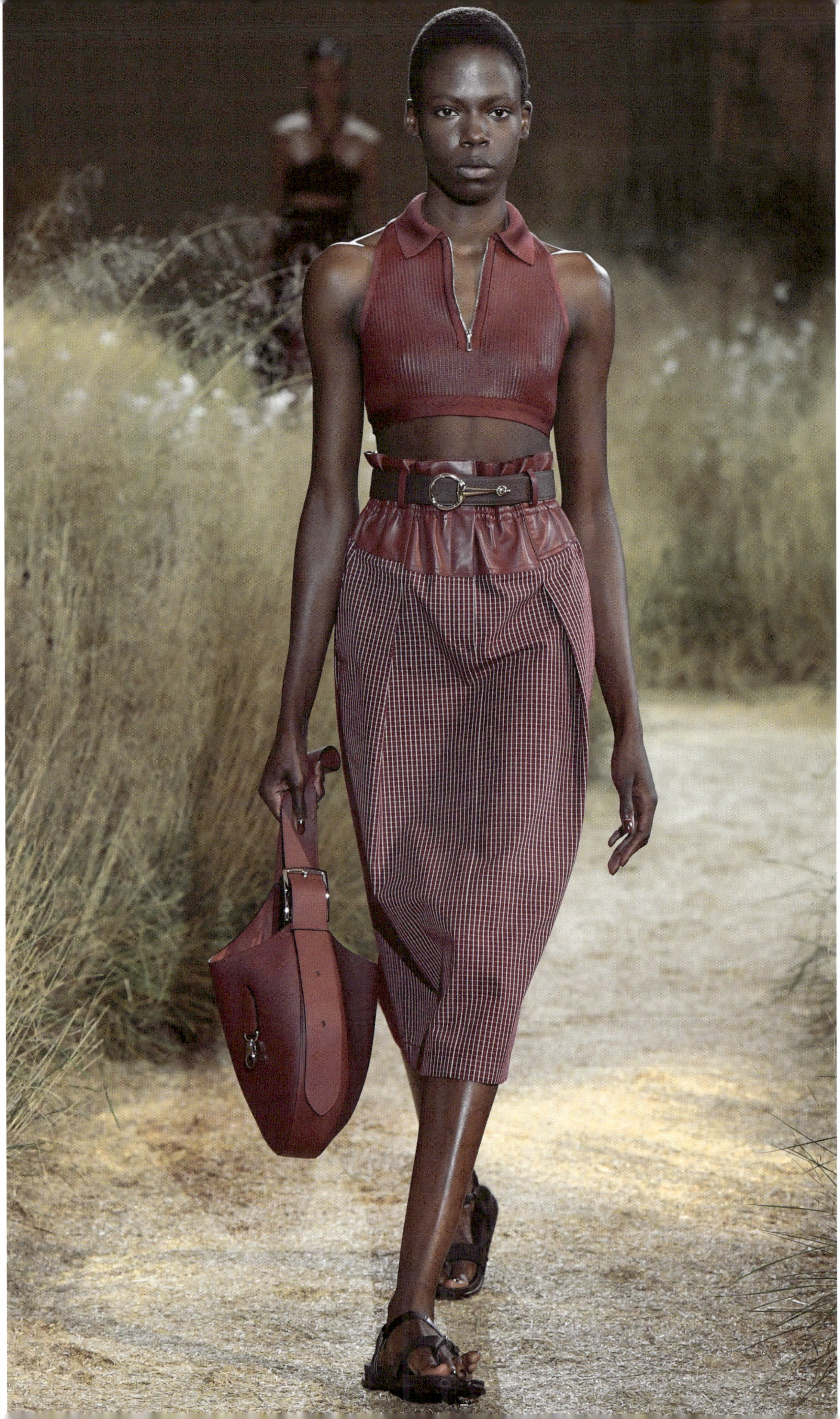

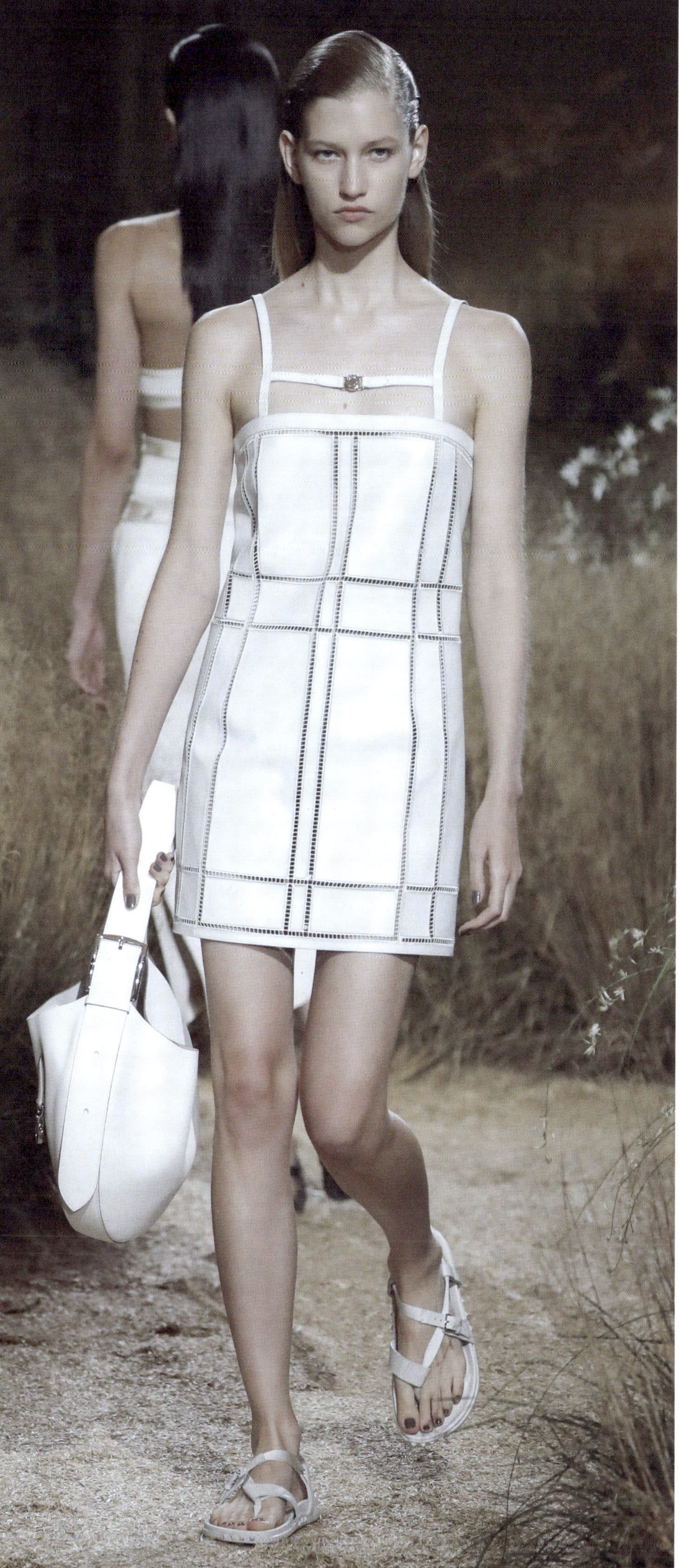

ARÇON

Pages 82/83: Models on the runway at Hermès Spring/Summer 2024 show in Paris carrying Arçon bags, which was first presented in Spring/Summer 2023. It's round shape mimics a saddle flap. It is available in two sizes and all-leather or canvas and leather versions.

BOLIDE

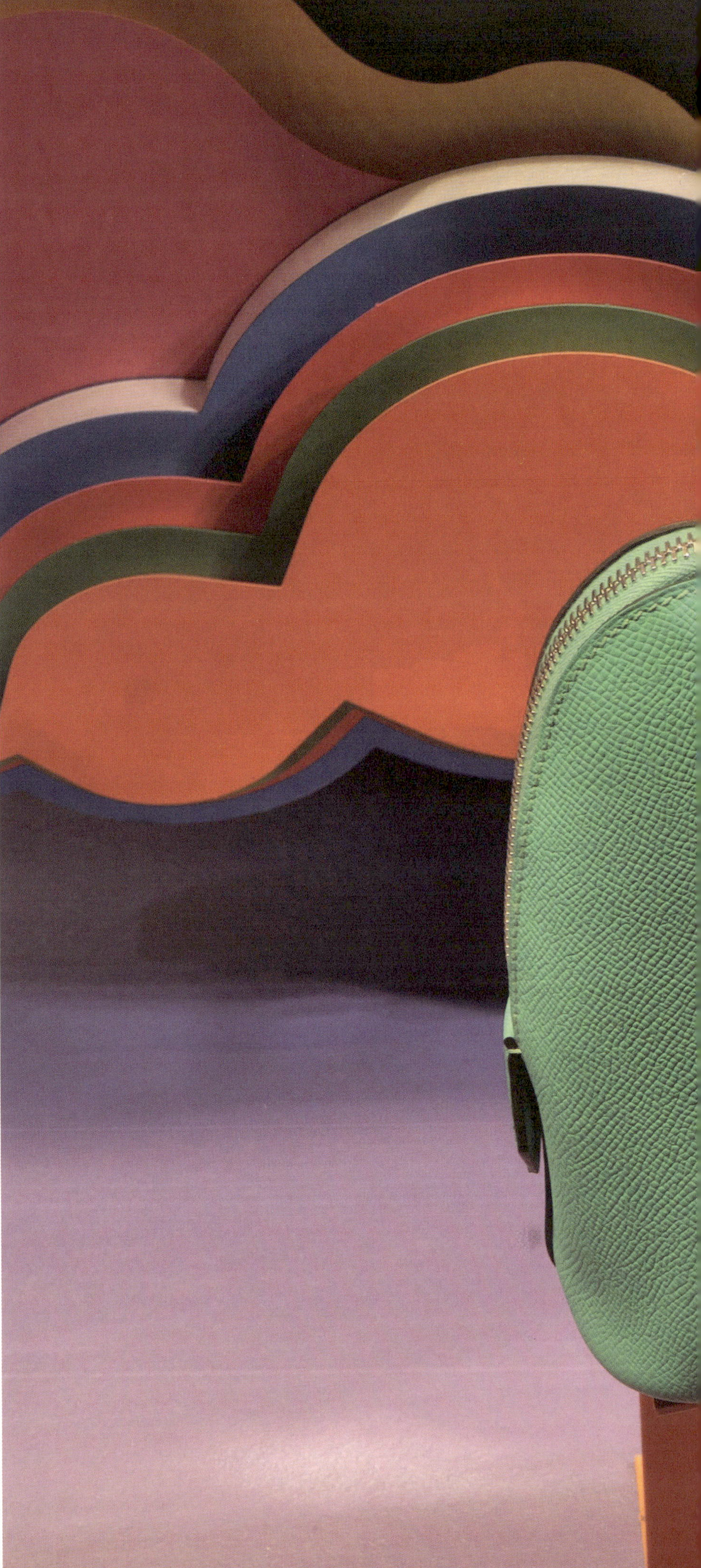

Bolide bag on display in a Hermès boutique.
The first Bolide was created in 1923.

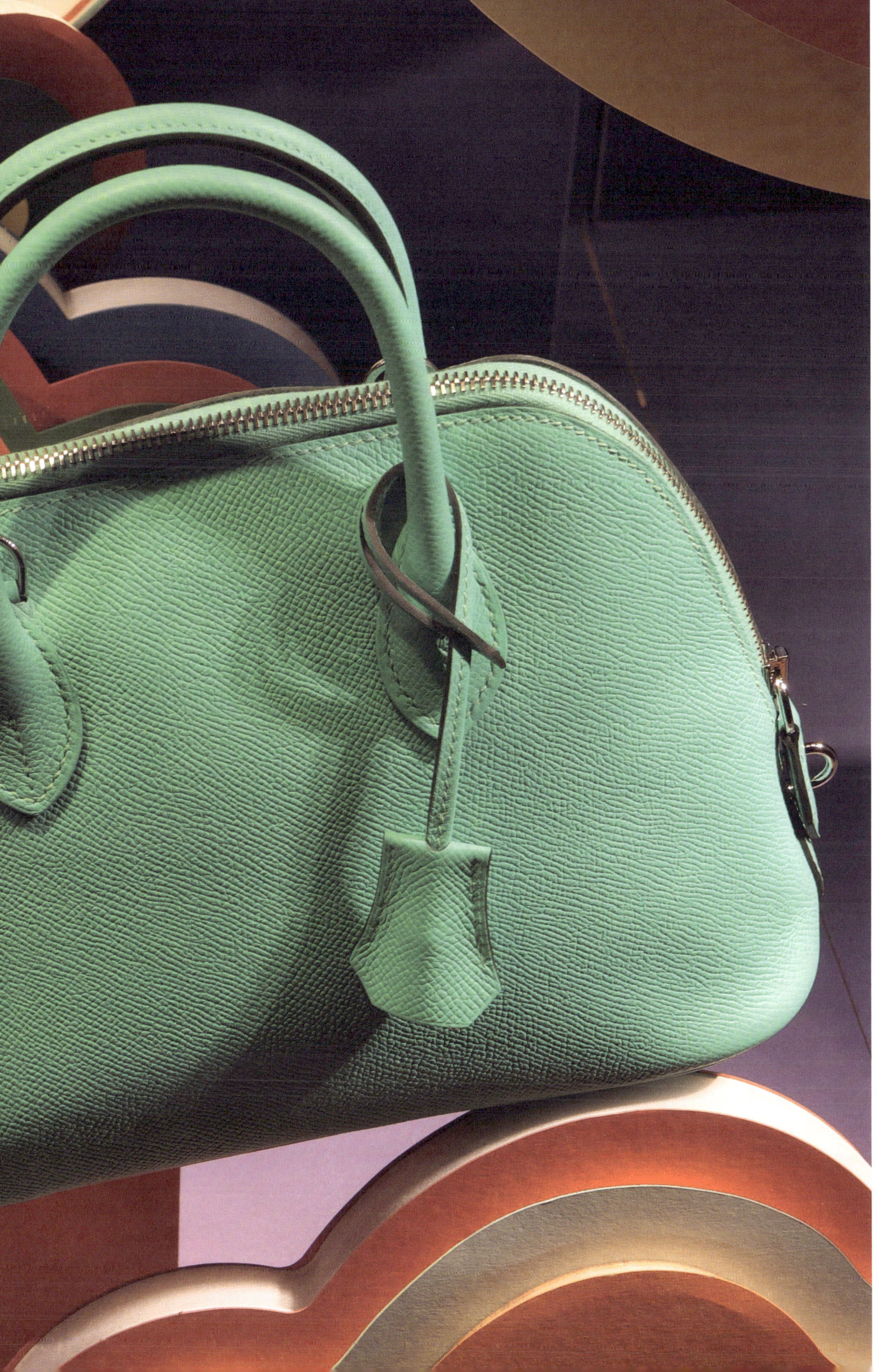

85

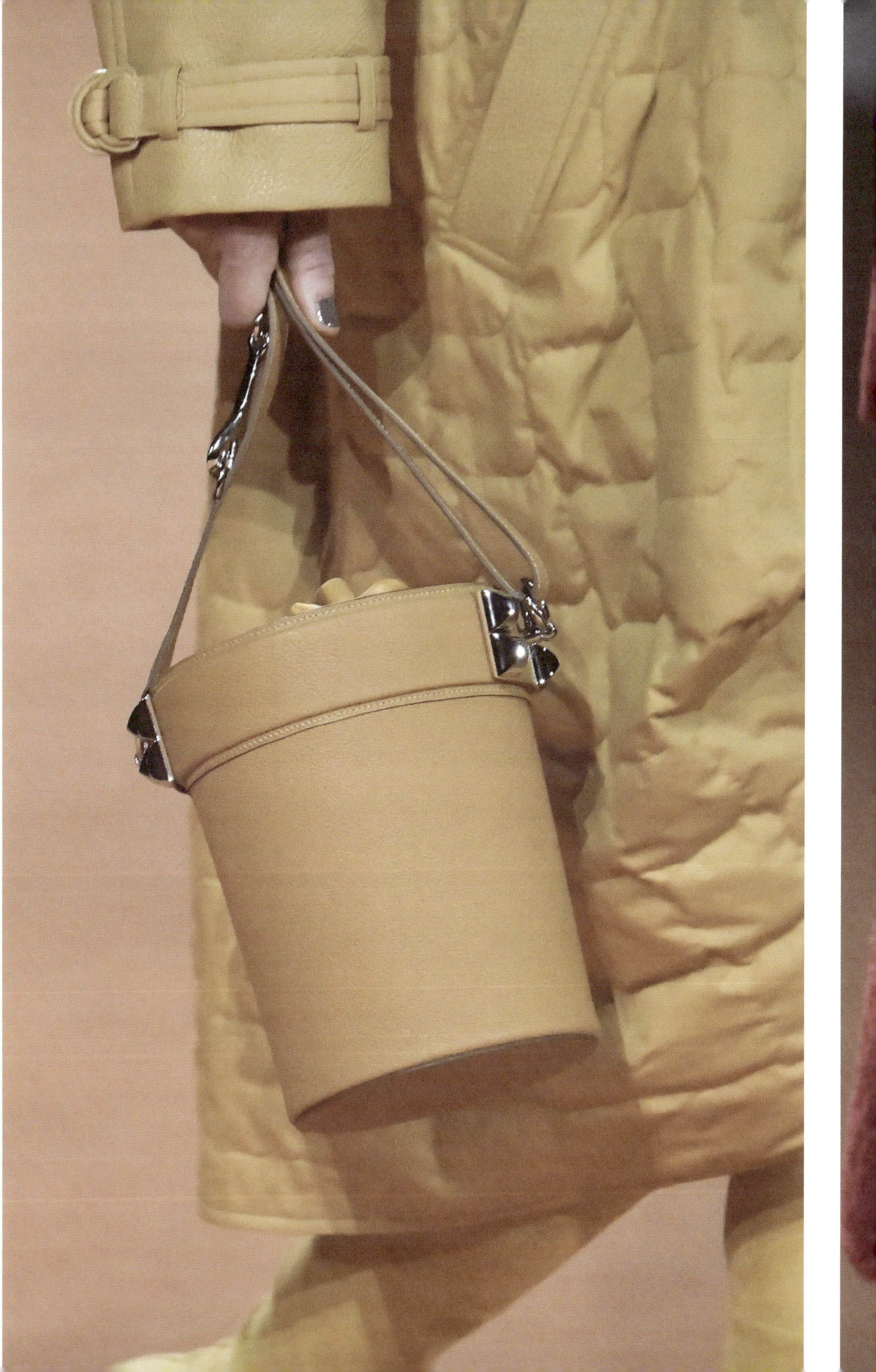

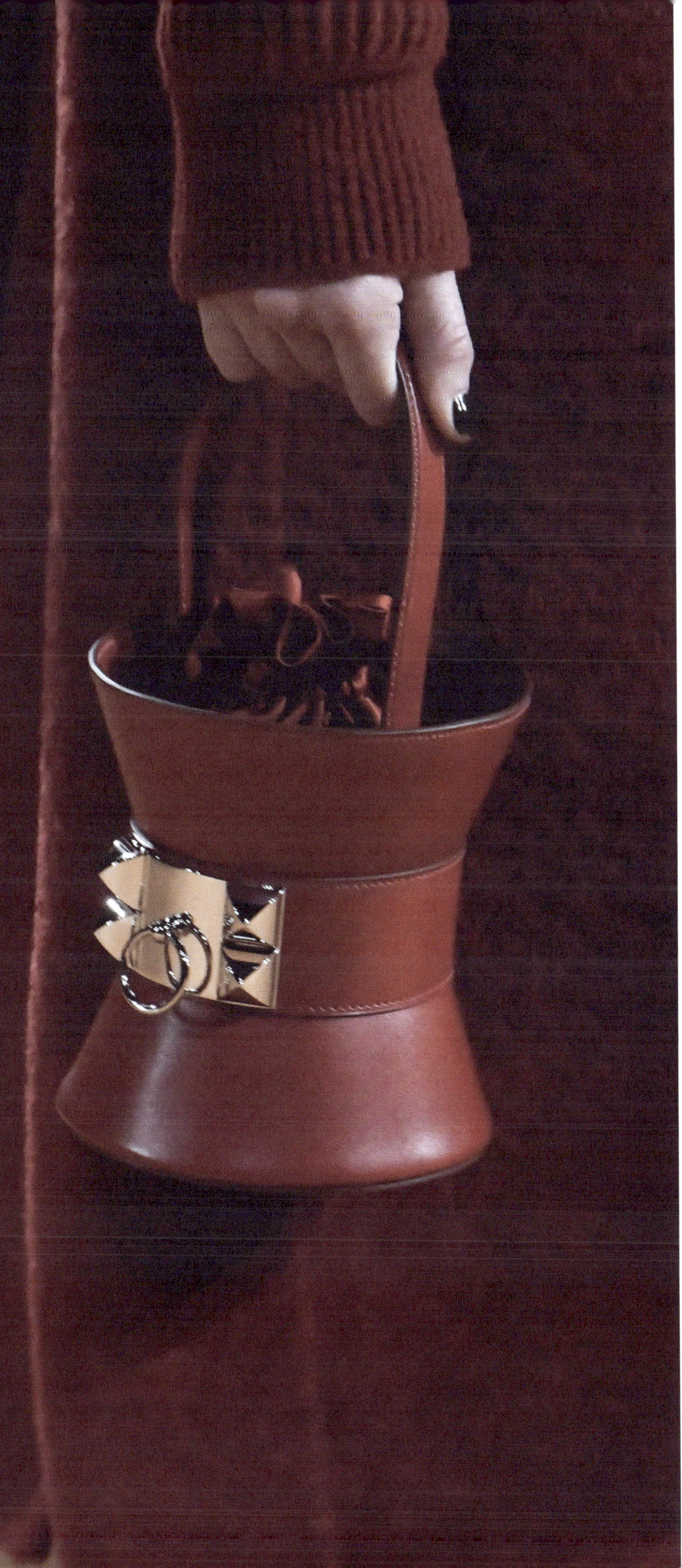

BUCKET BAGS

Pages 86/87: During the Fall/Winter 2023 ready-to-wear collection in Paris, the togo calfskin leather Sac So Médor (left) and the box calfskin Sac Mini Médor (right) were presented. March 4, 2023

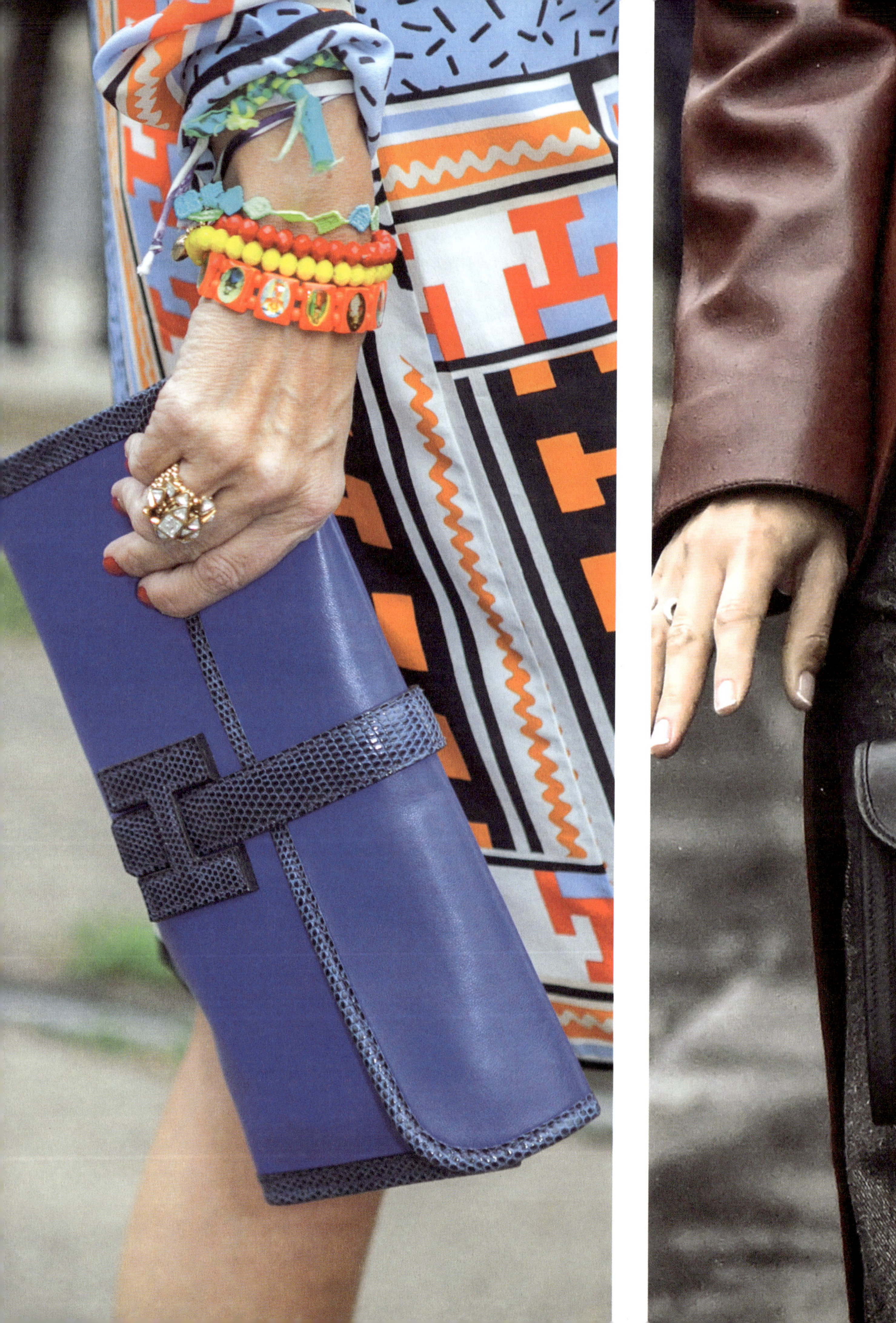

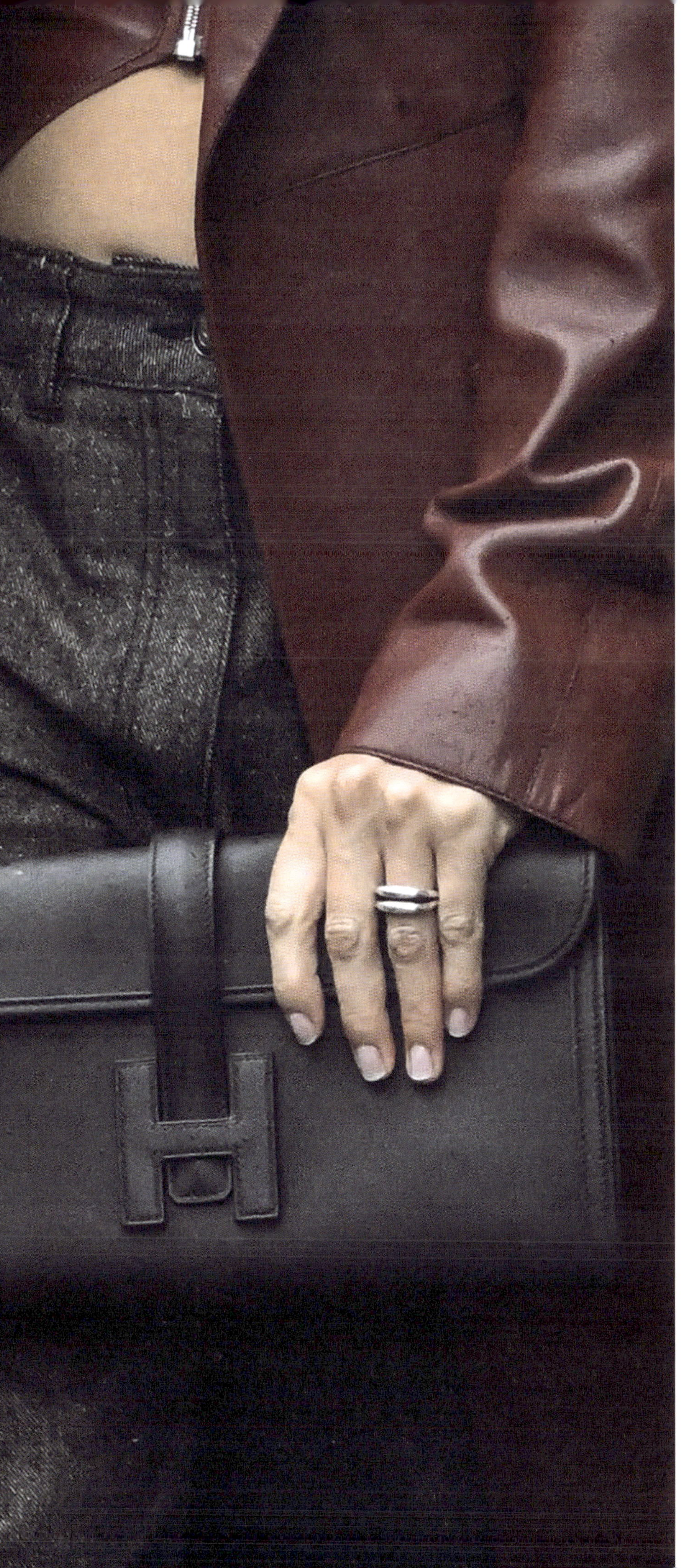

JIGE

Previous page: Close-up of a blue leather Jige clutch with Lizard trim, Milan, 2013. The first Jige was created in 1975 by Jean René Guerrand. He gave it to his future daughter-in-law as a wedding gift.

This page: Diana Louise Bartlett is seen carrying a black Jige clutch during the Fall/Winter 2024 Paris Fashion Week shows

JYPSIERE

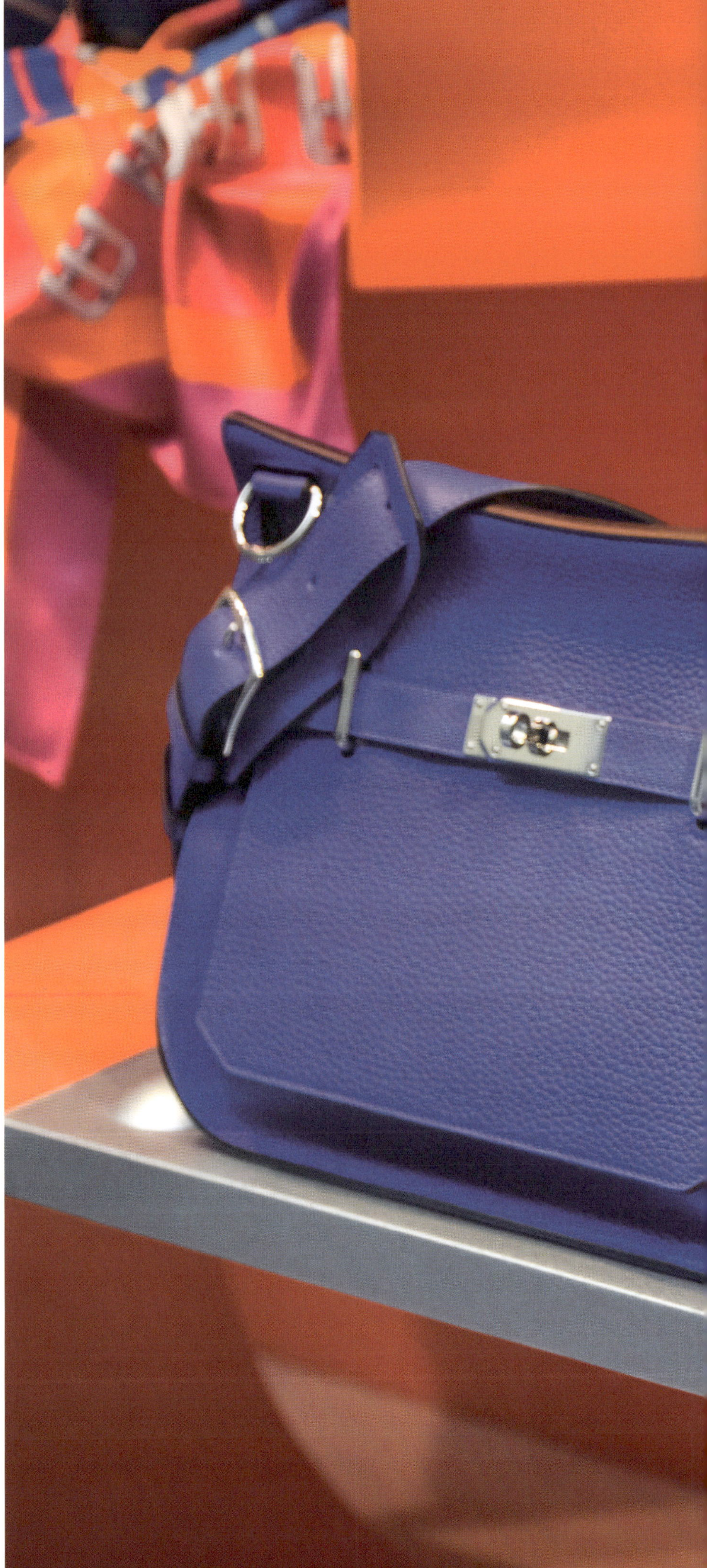

Jypsiere bag on display in a Hermès store in Milan, 2017. This model was designed by Jean Paul Gaultier for the Fall/Winter 2008 collection and is available in four different sizes (28, 31, 34, and 37 centimeters in length).

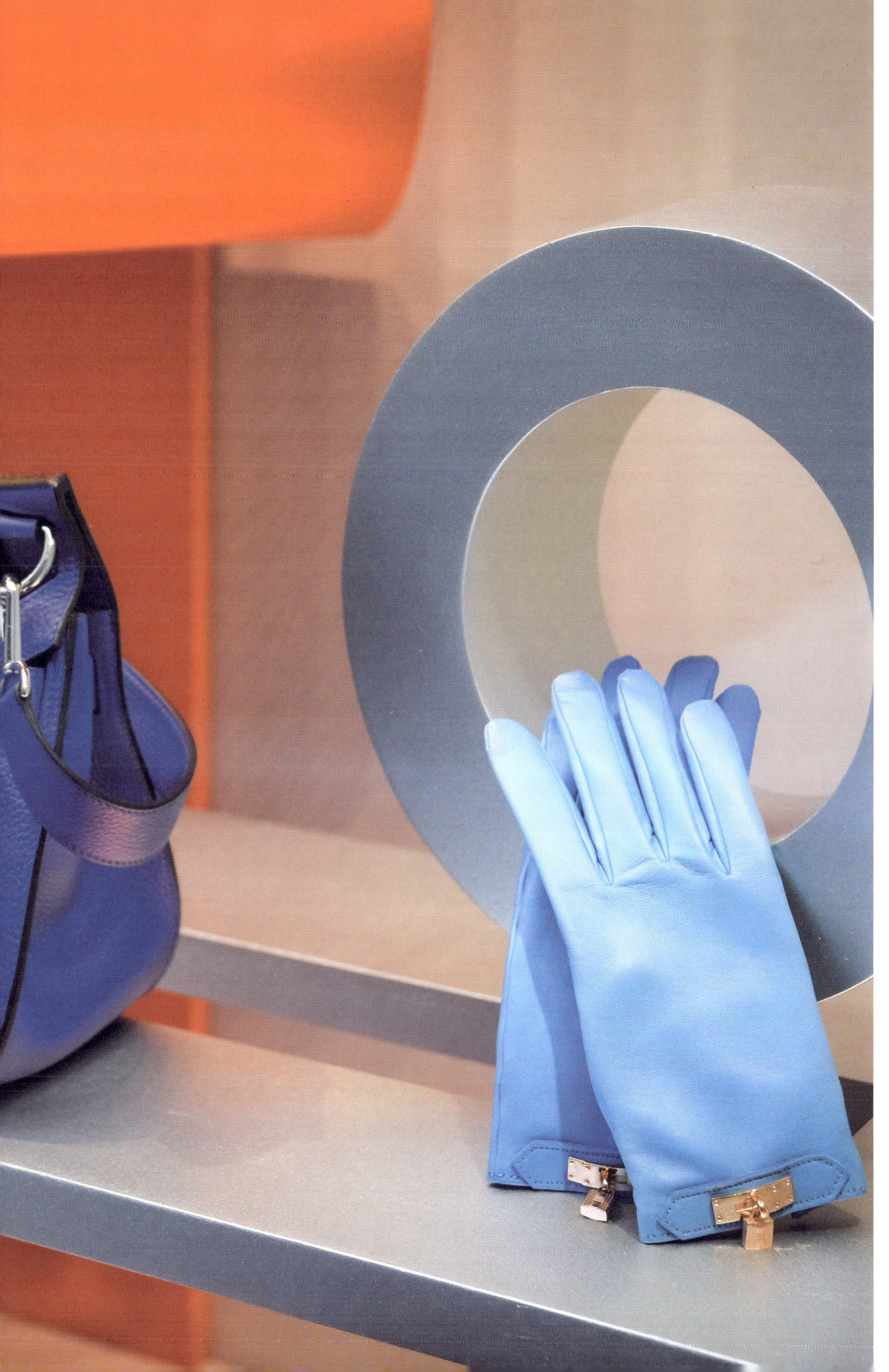

GETA

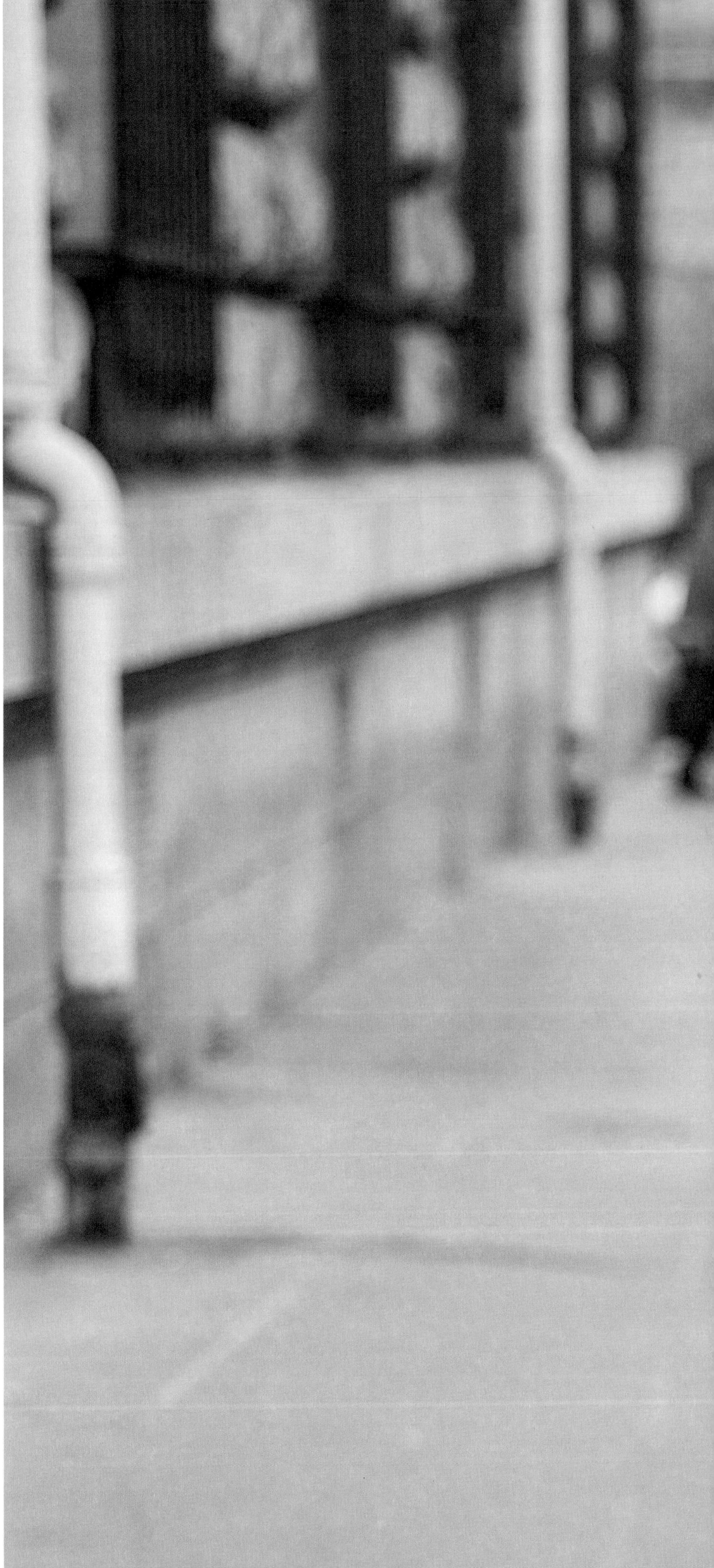

A visitor to Fall/Winter 2023 Paris Fashion Week wears a red Geta bag. The Geta was first introduced in 2022.

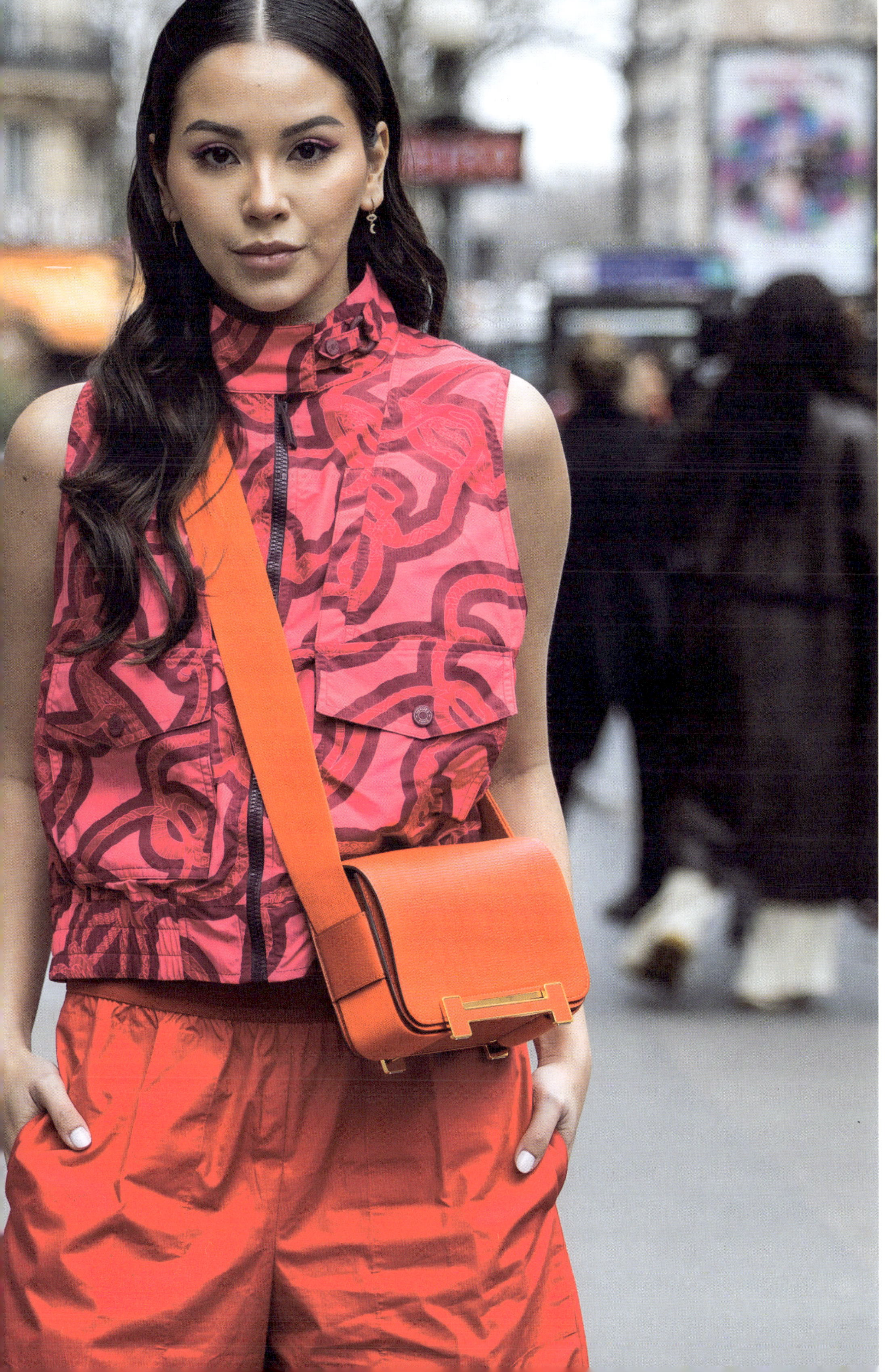

24/24

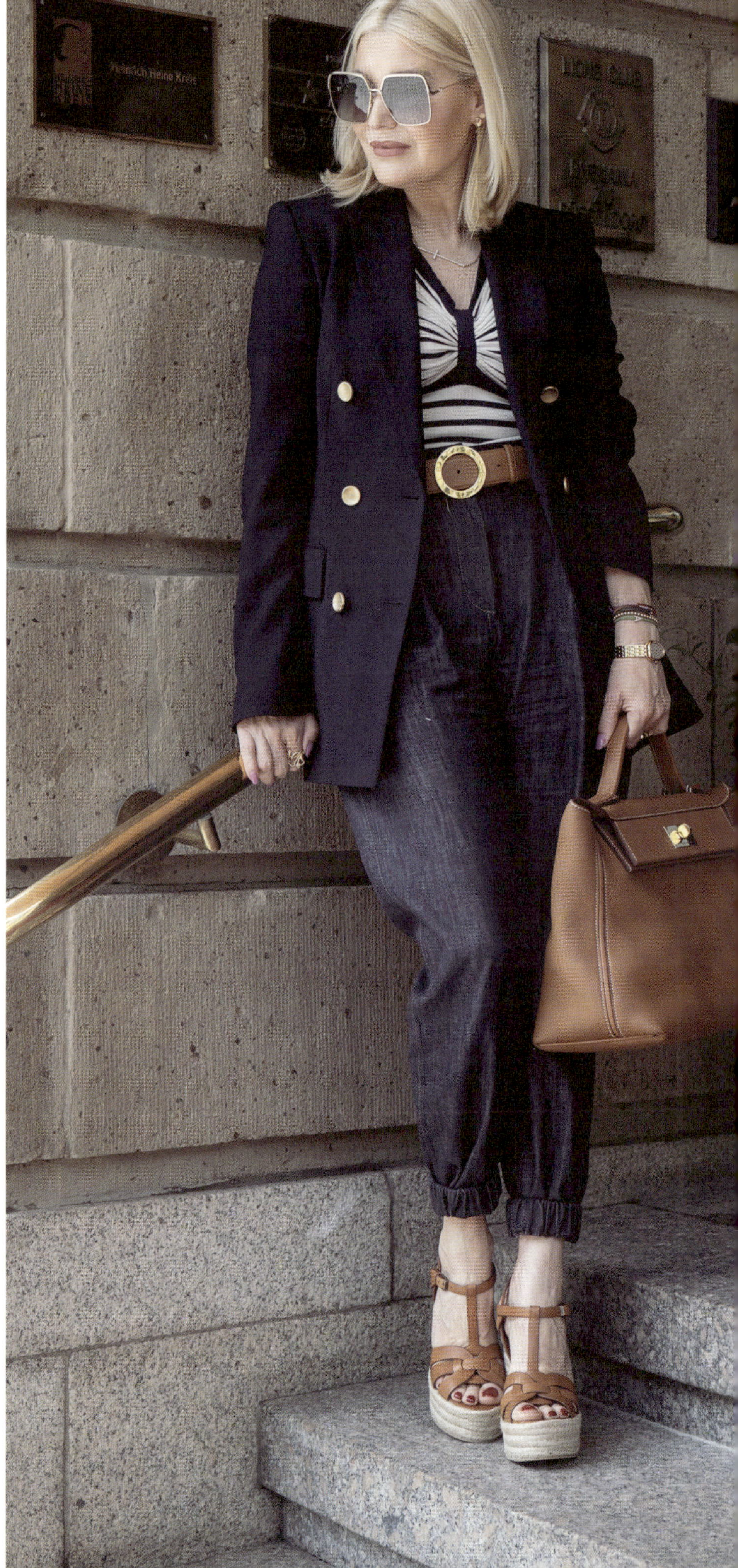

This page: Fashion influencer Petra Dieners carrying a 24/24 bag, Düsseldorf, 2022. The 24/24 debuted in the pre-Fall 2018 collection.

Next page: Kathrin Bommann with a black Togo leather 24/24 bag with a flap made from alligator, Düsseldorf, 2023

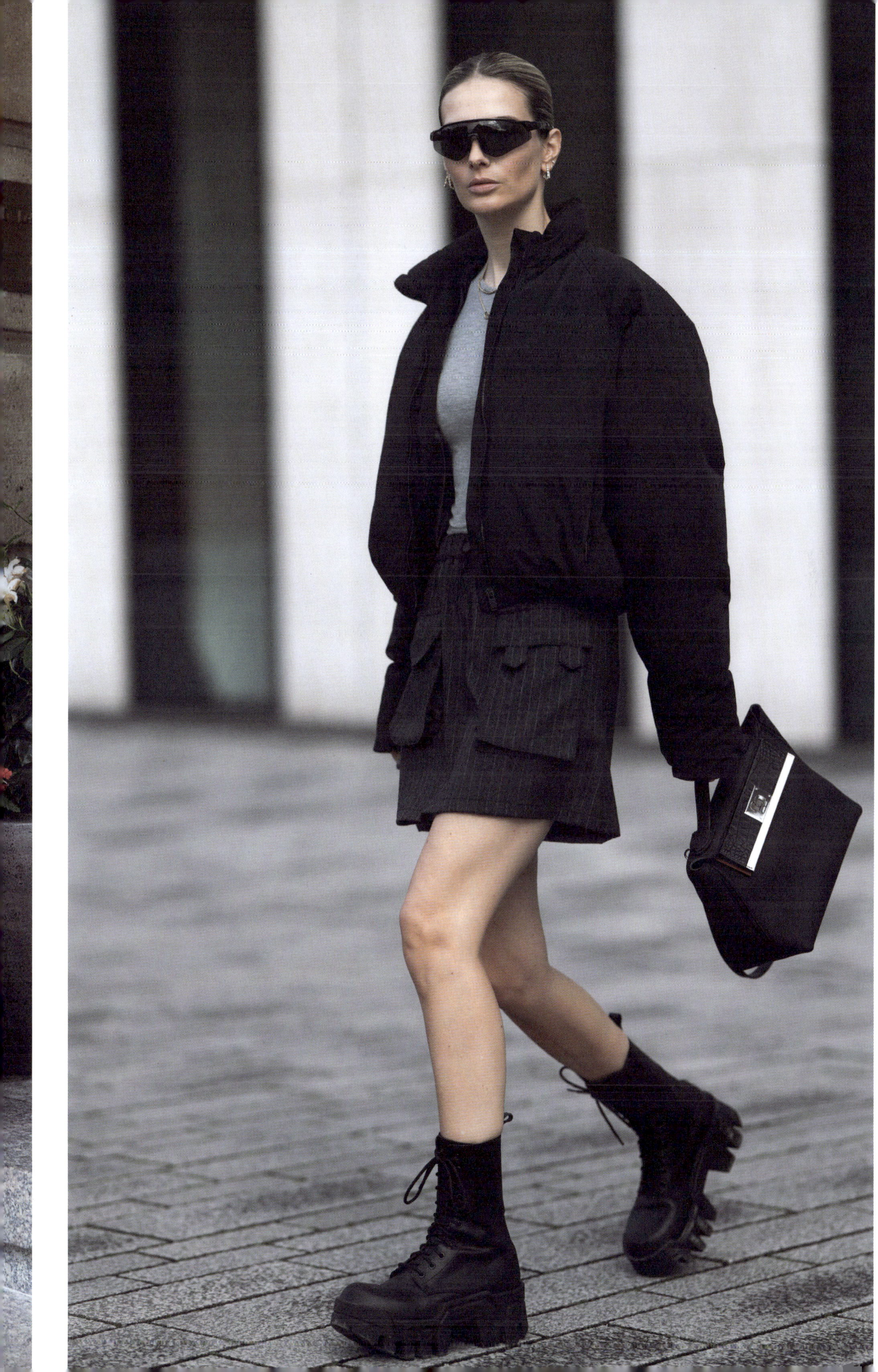

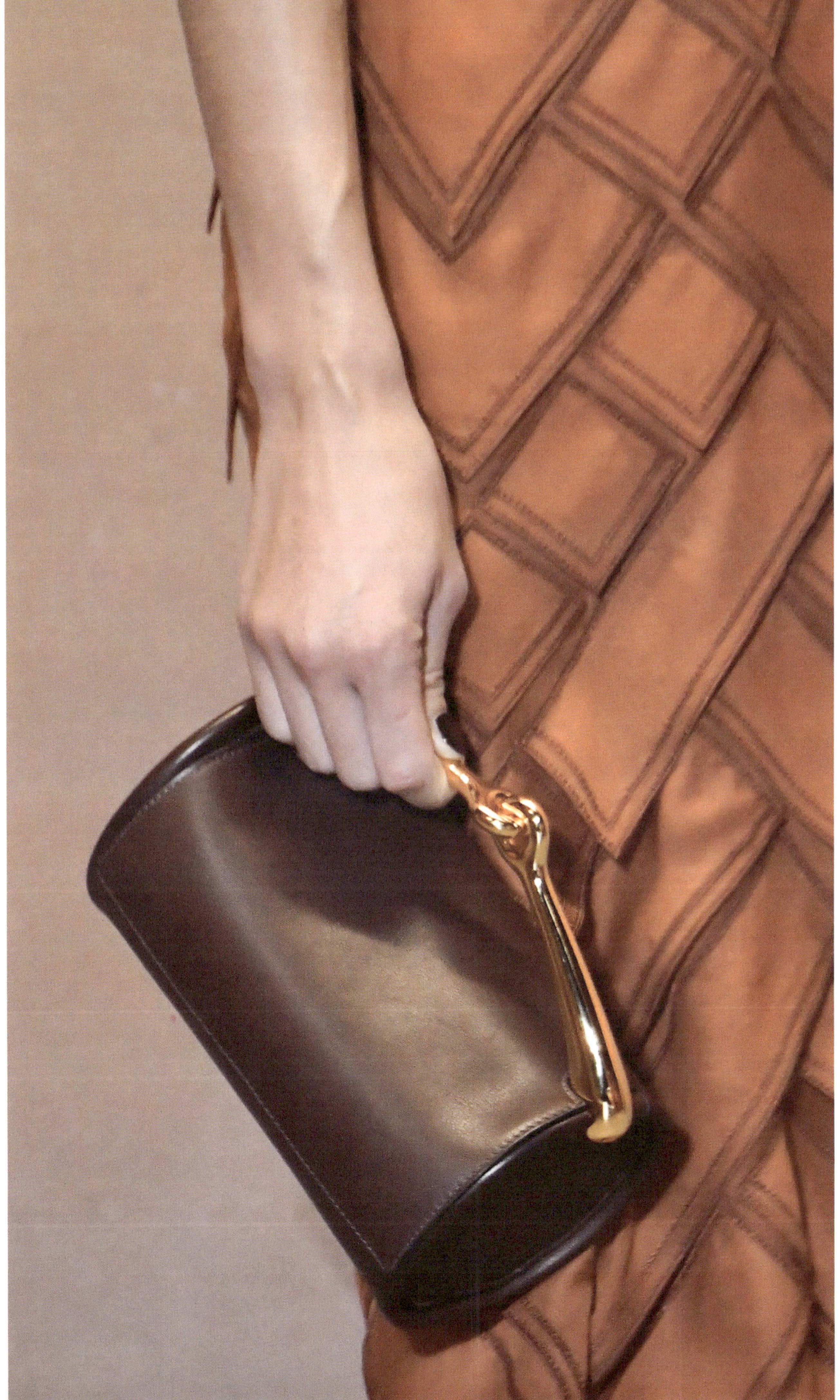

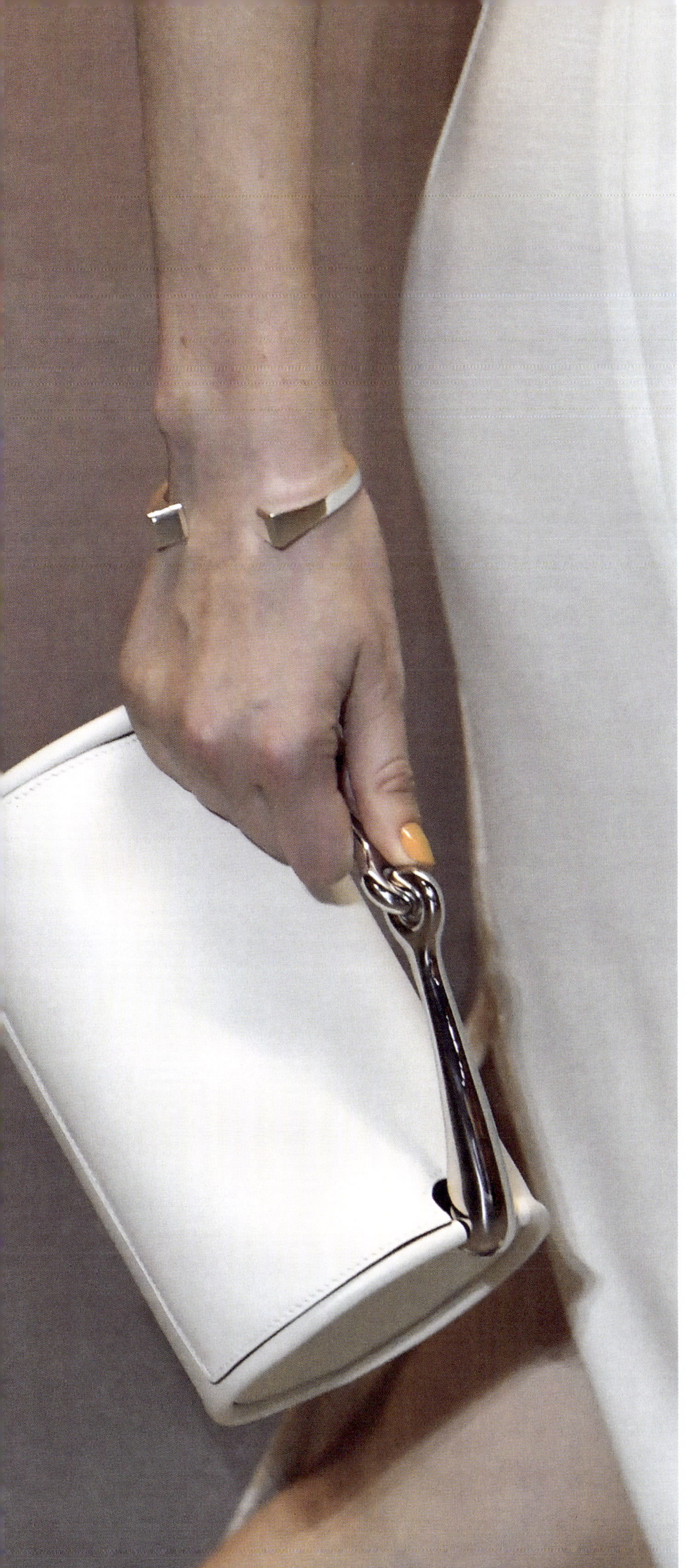

MAXIMORS

Pages 96/97: Close-ups of Maximors bags from the ready-to-wear Spring/Summer 2022 collection presented at Paris Fashion Week, October 2021. The precious handle is inspired by horse bits and Hermès' equestrian heritage.

VERROU

A visitor to Paris Fashion Week's Menswear Fall/Winter 2022 show carries a pink Verrou bag. First introduced in 2010 as a strap-free clutch, the chain-strap Verrou with the characteristic lock was added to the *maison* in 2017.

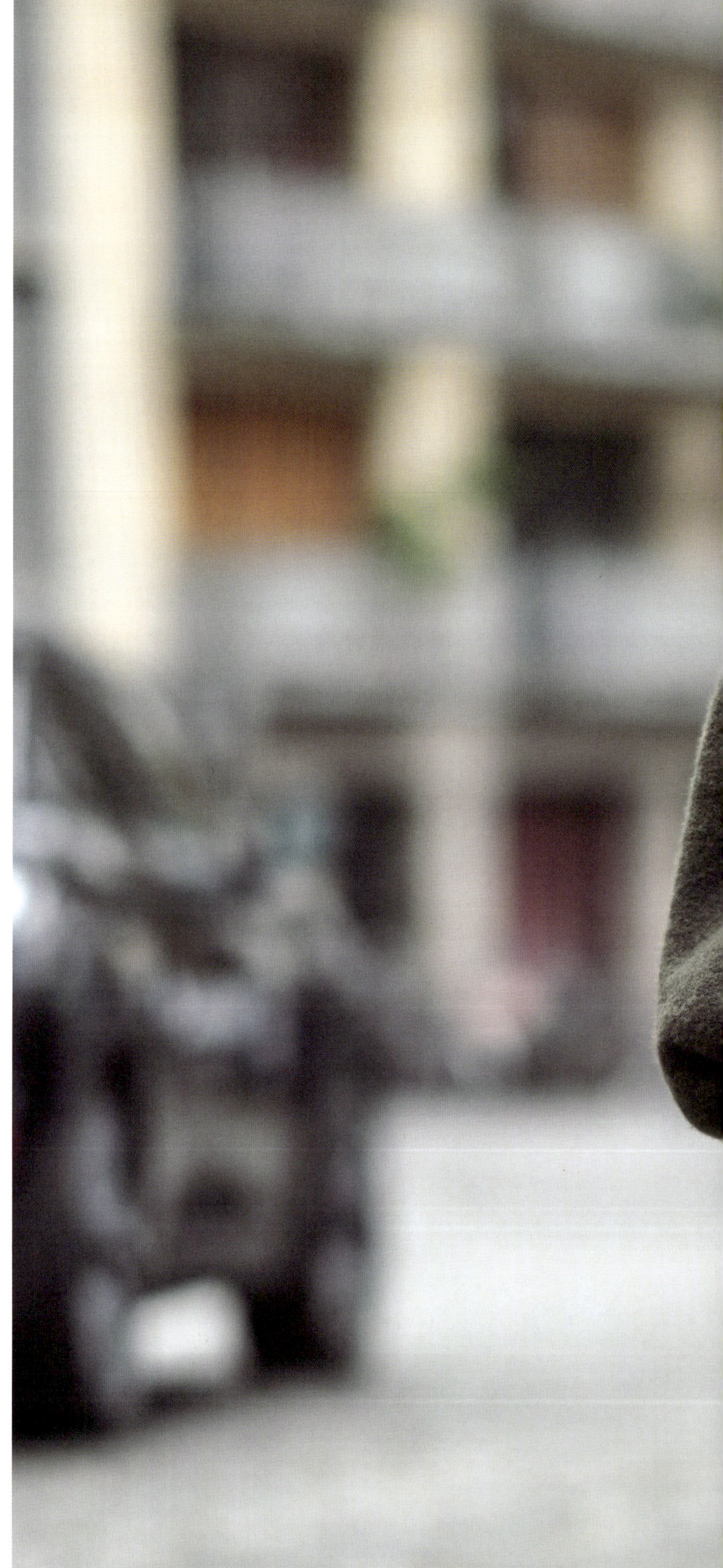

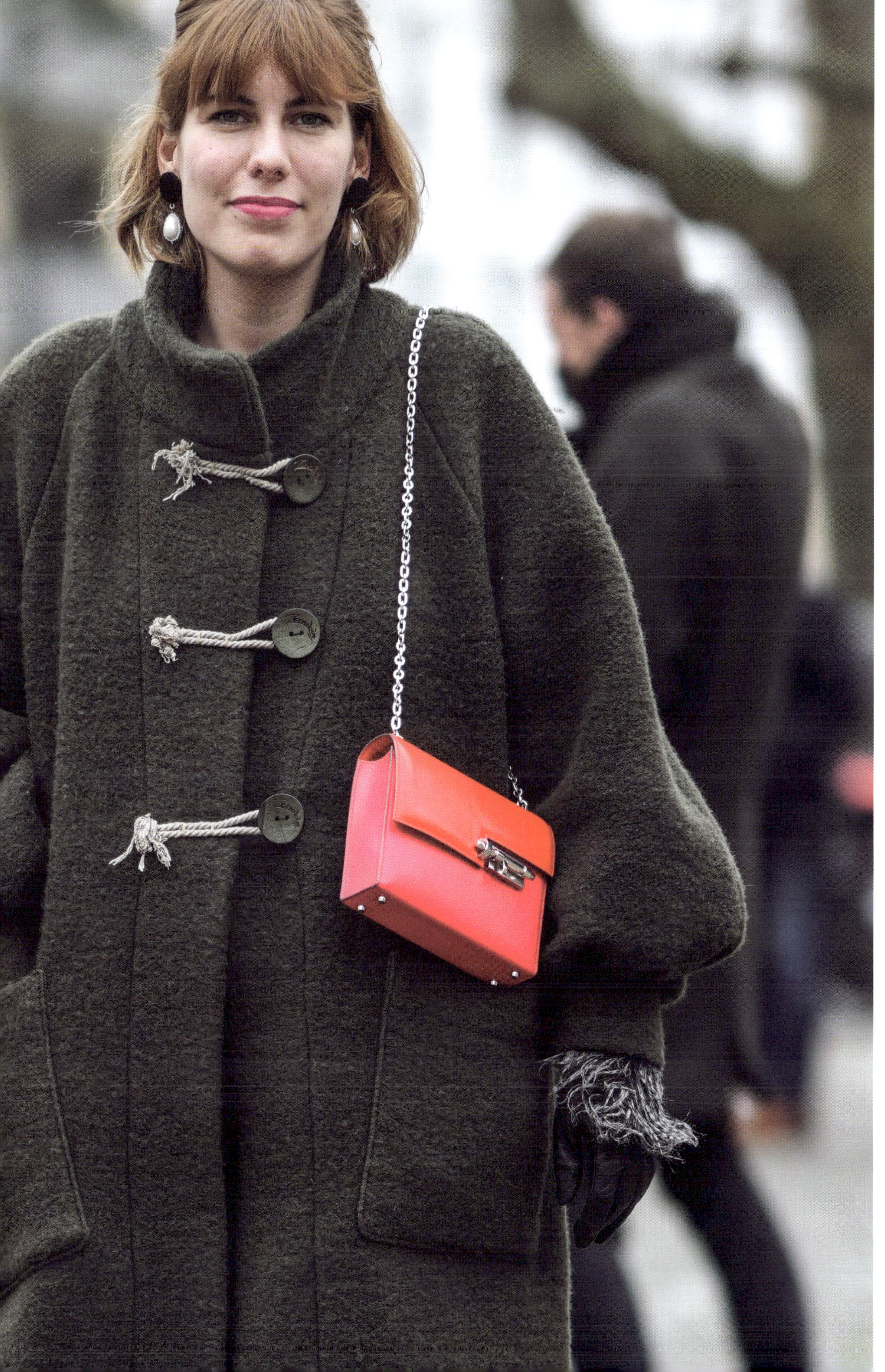

IN-THE-LOOP

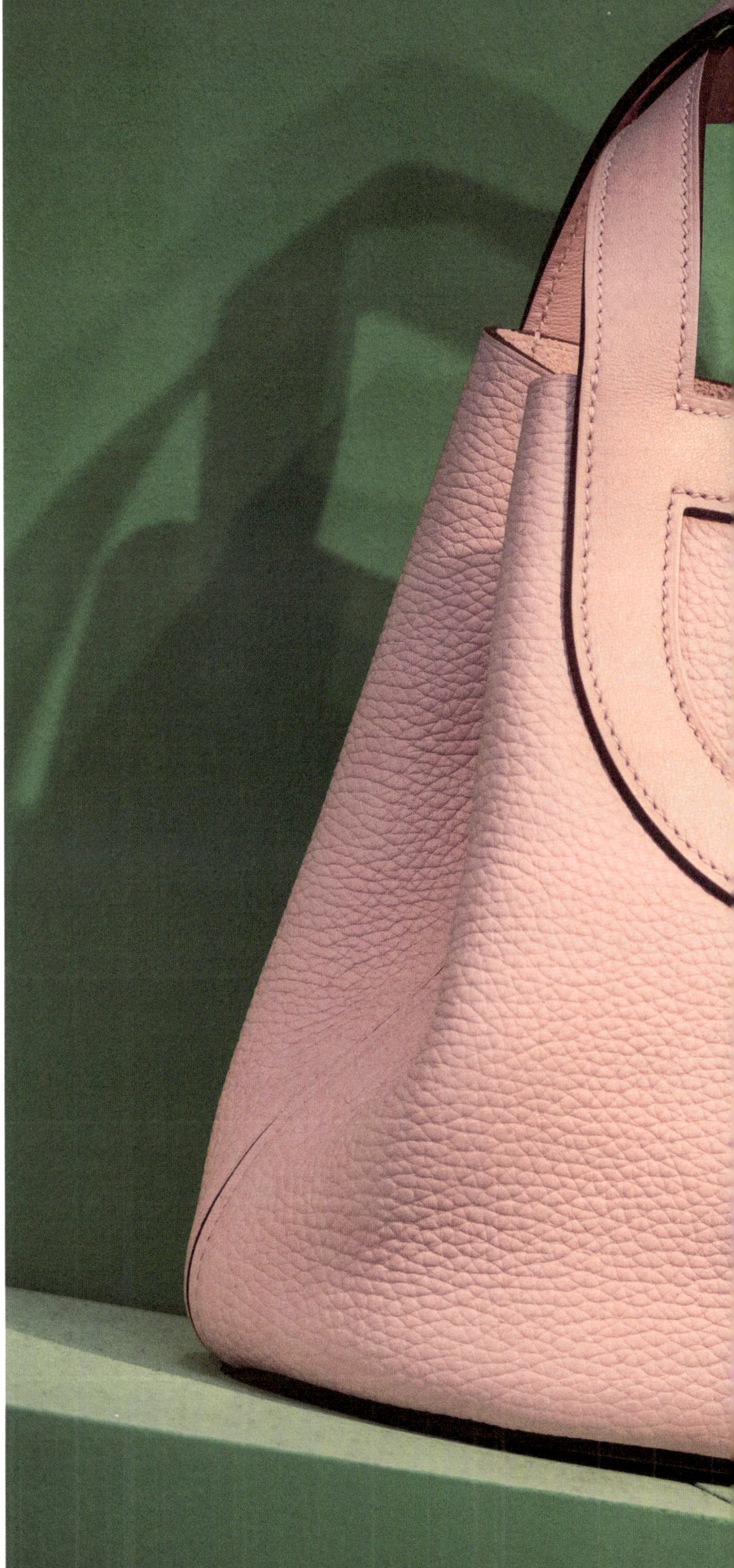

Pink In-the-loop leather handbag as seen in a Hermès store in Milan, 2024. The bucket style In-the-Loop bag was launched in 2022 and is available in two sizes. It combines smooth (for the handles) and grained leather.

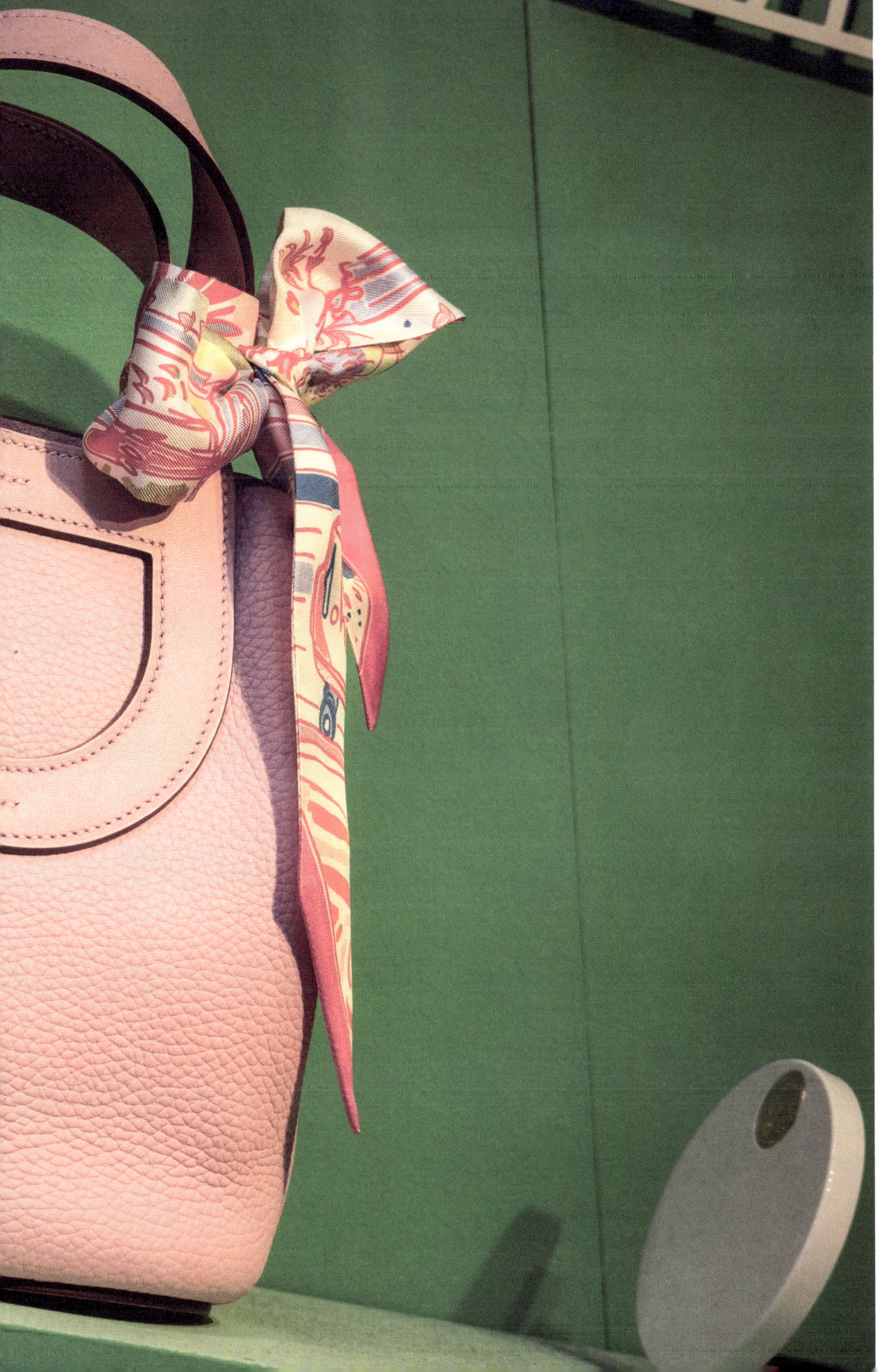

LINDY

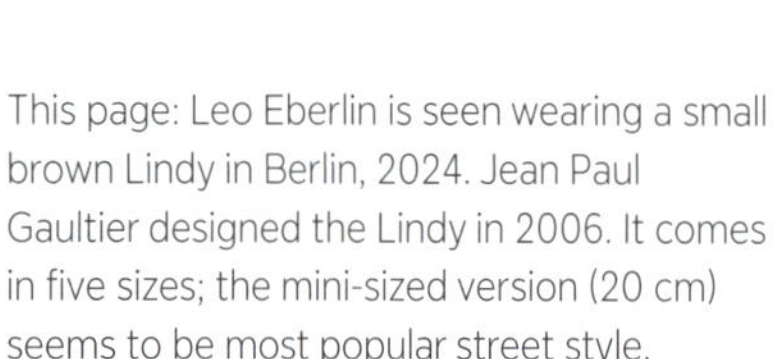

This page: Leo Eberlin is seen wearing a small brown Lindy in Berlin, 2024. Jean Paul Gaultier designed the Lindy in 2006. It comes in five sizes; the mini-sized version (20 cm) seems to be most popular street style.

Next page: A black clemence leather mini Lindy. Paris, 2022

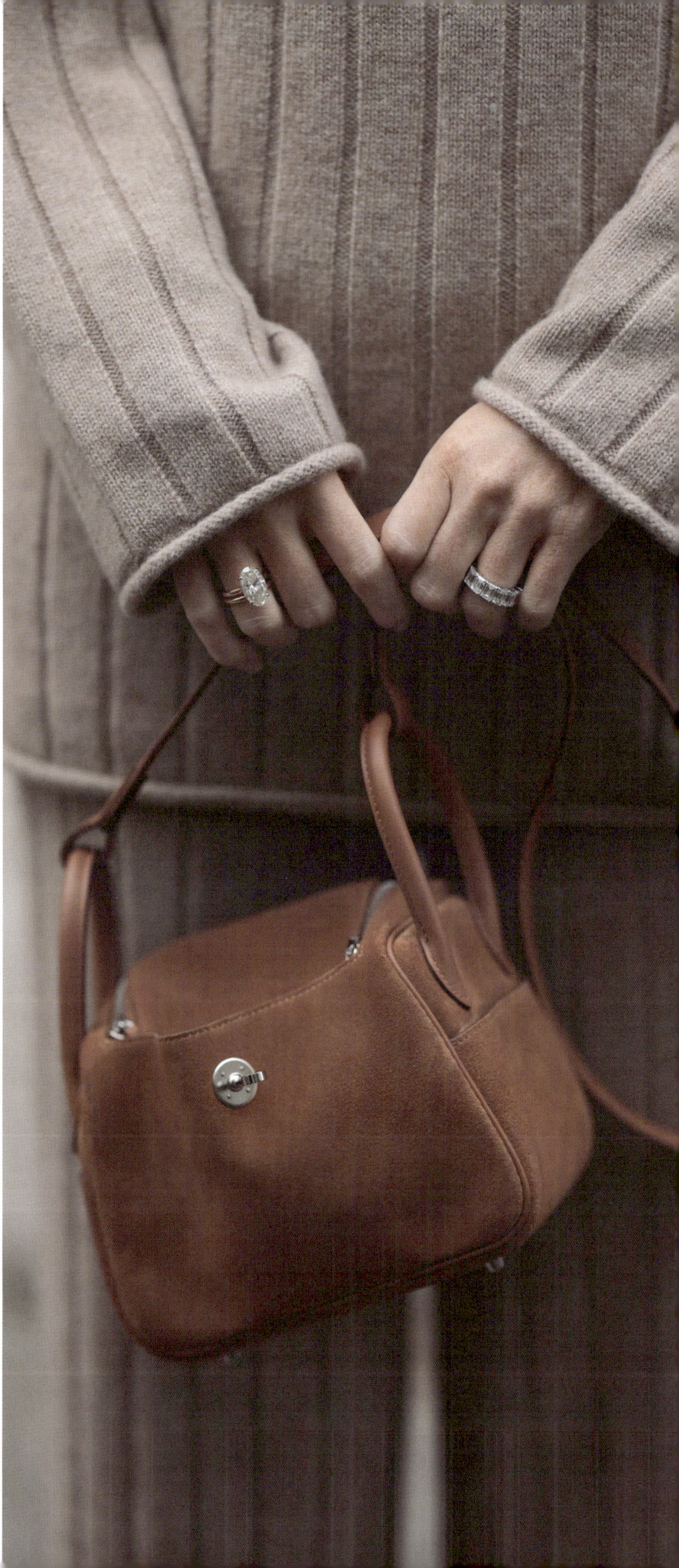

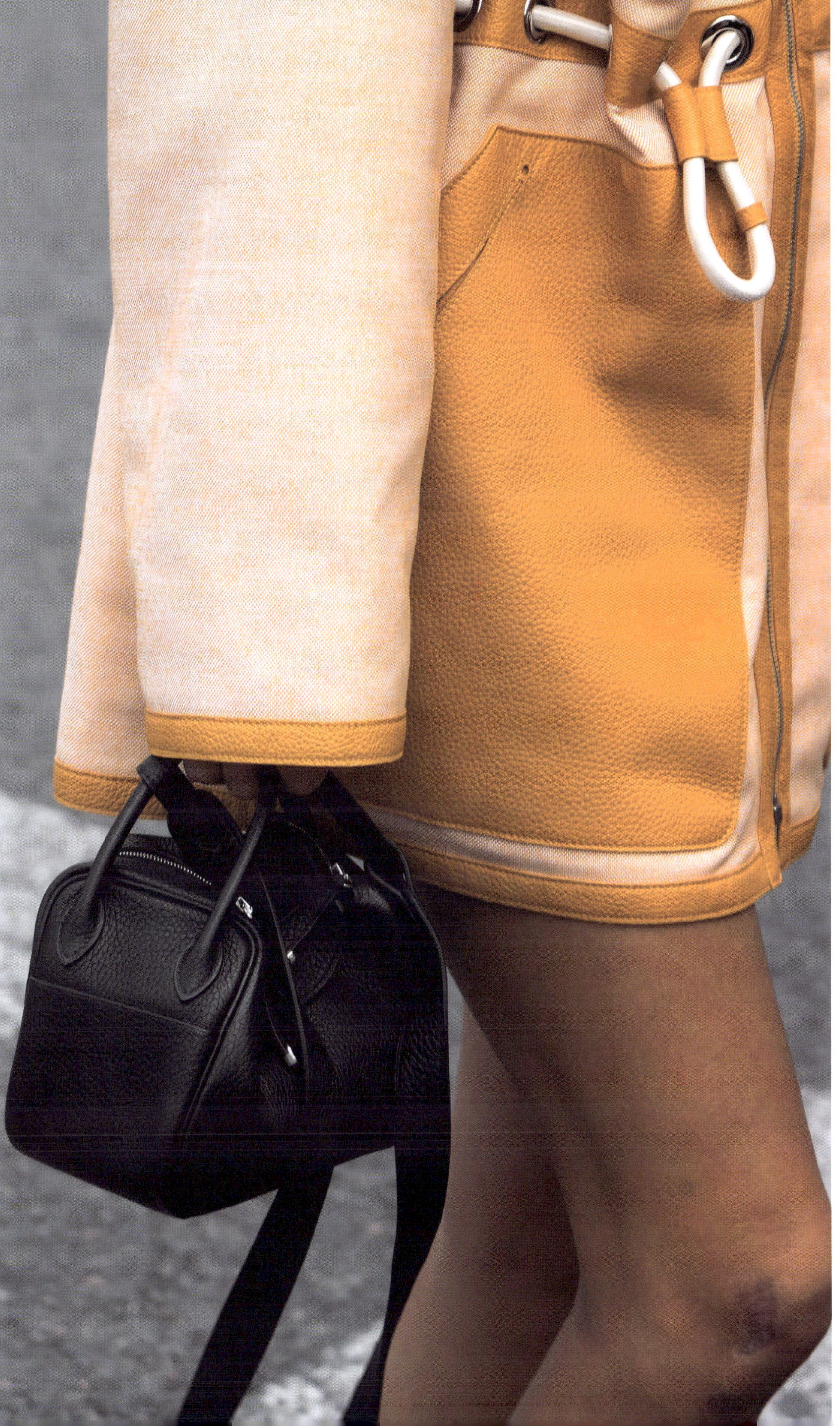

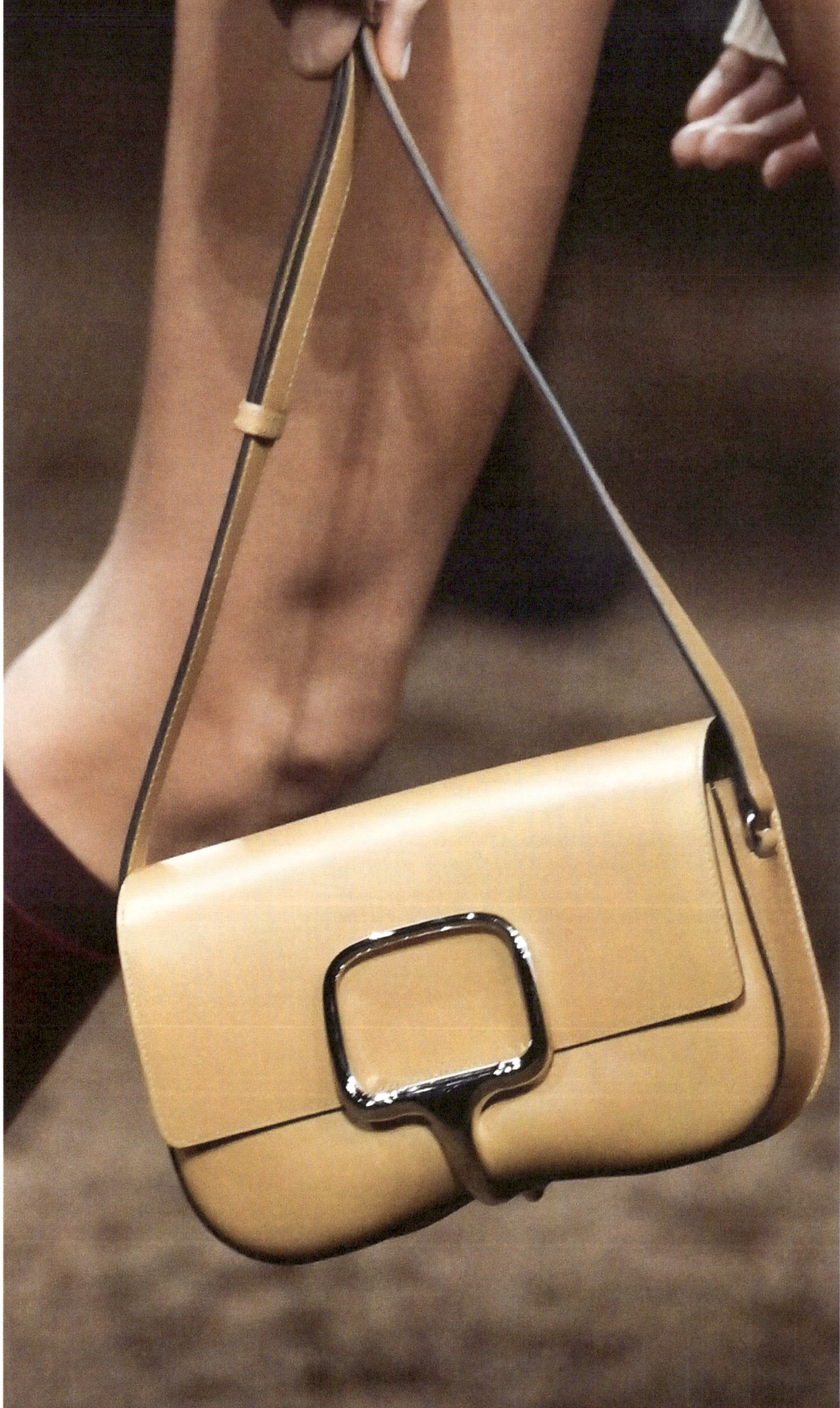

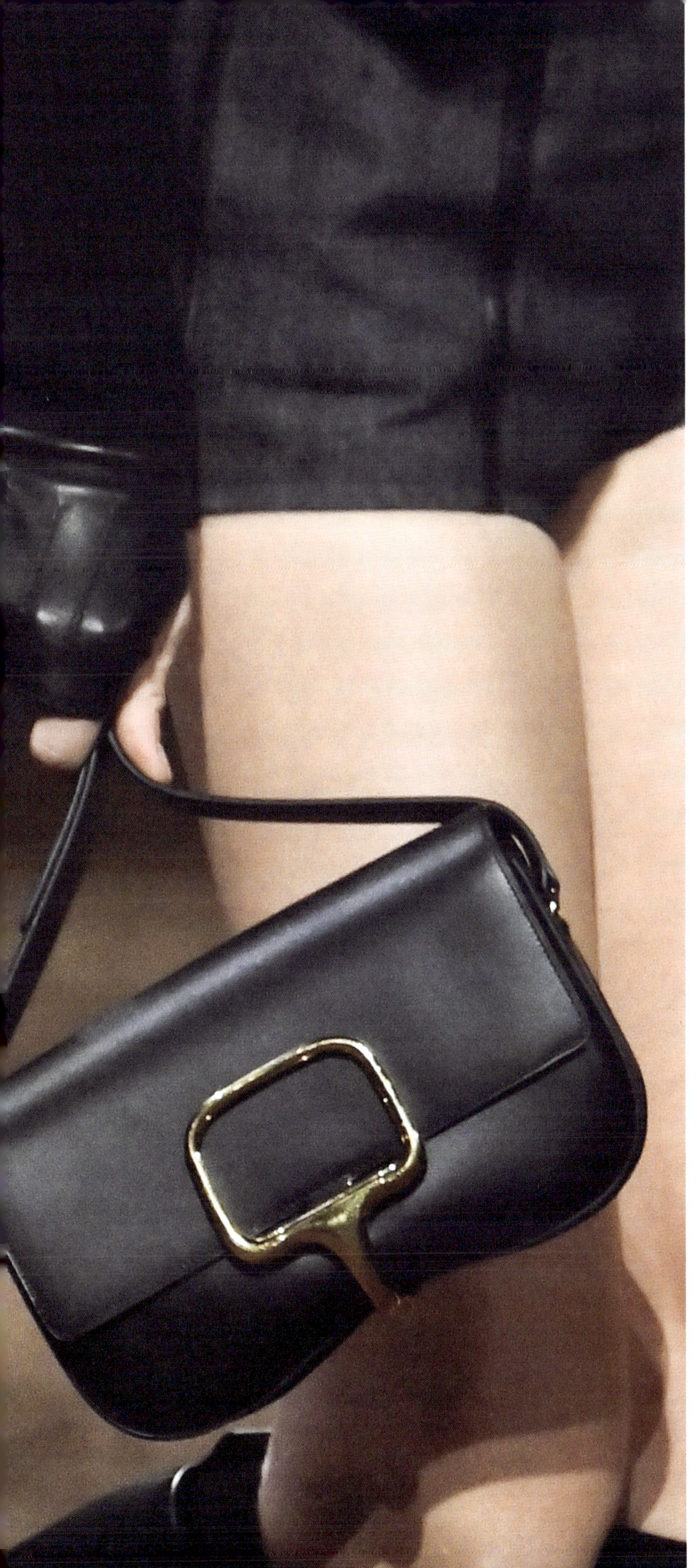

DELLA CAVALLERIA

Pages 104/105: Models presenting the Della Cavalleria Elan at the Hermès ready-to-wear Fall/Winter 2025/2026 fashion show, Paris, March 2025. The Della Cavalleria was first introduced in 2020 and received a refreshed silhouette (from almost square to rectangular) in 2023.

ROULIS

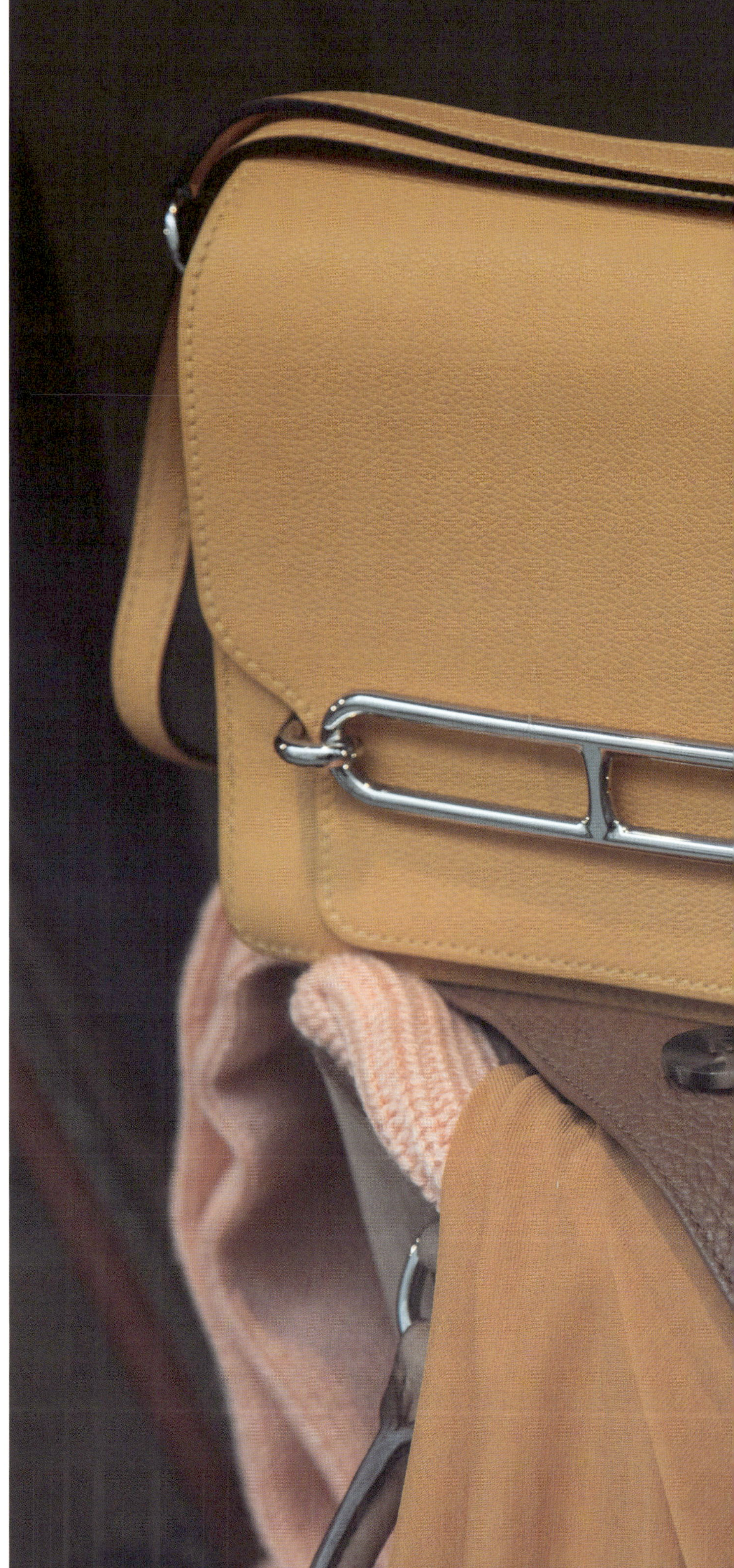

Roulis handbags in the window of the Hermès boutique on Rue du Faubourg Saint-Honoré, Paris, 2023. The Roulis made its first appearance in 2011 and features a *chaîne d'ancre* buckle.

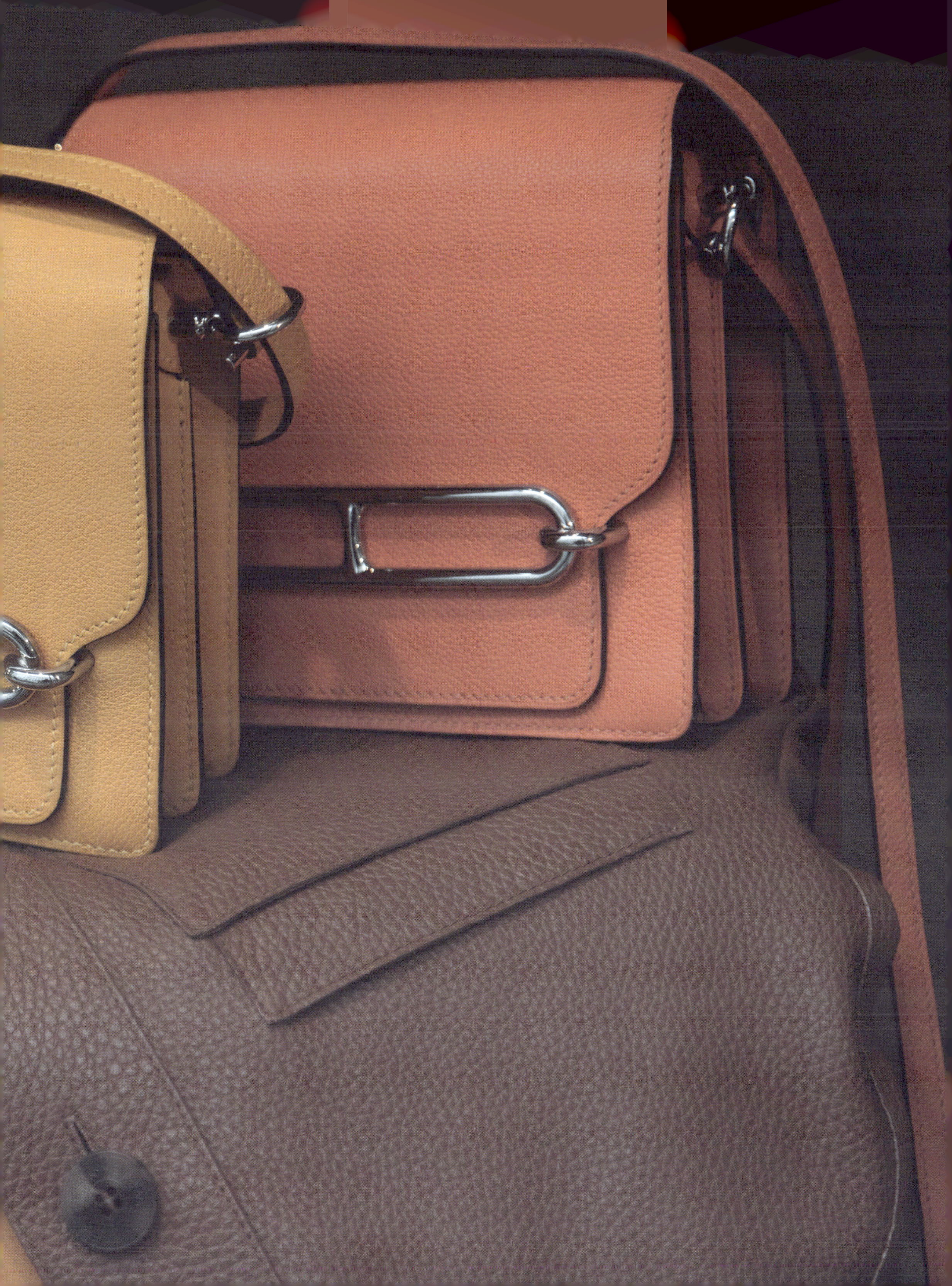

STEEPLE

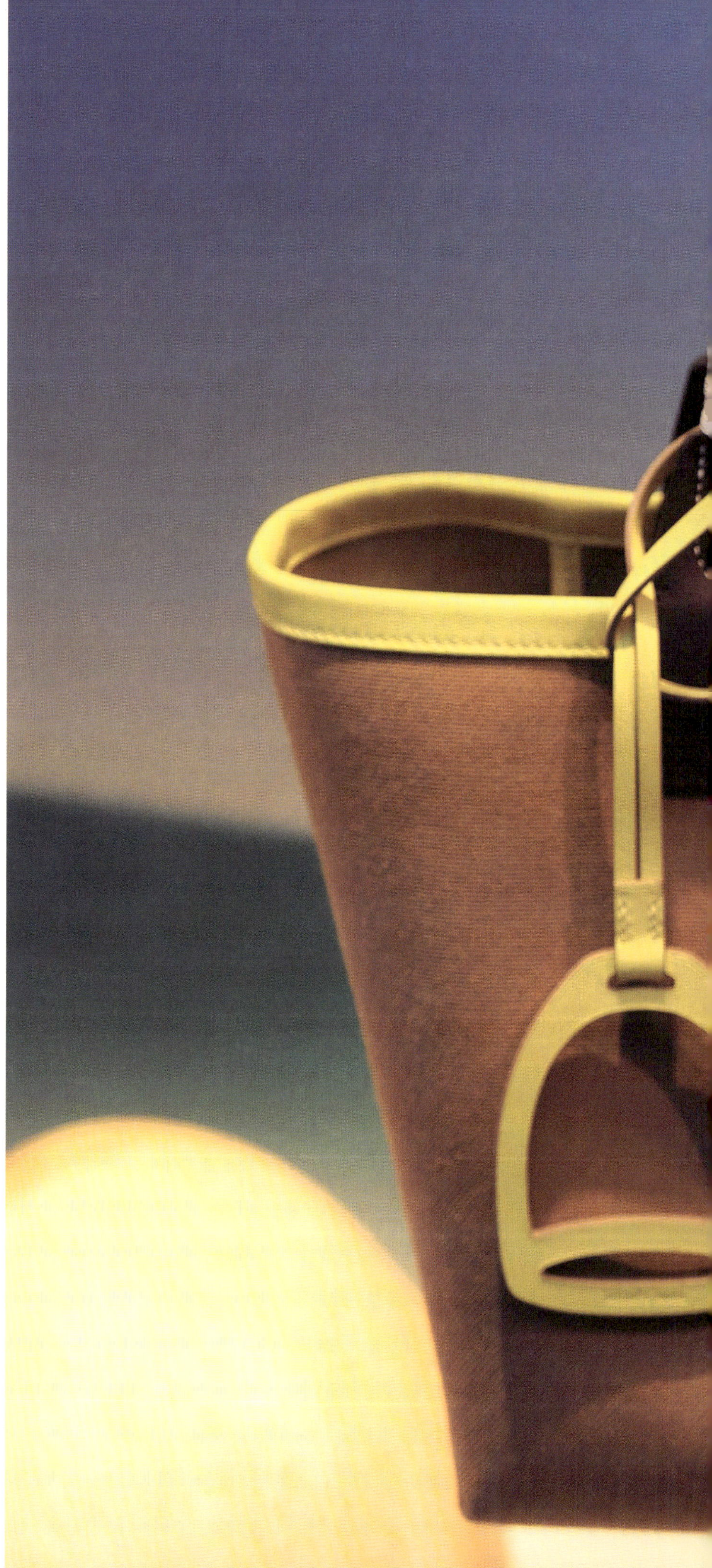

The Steeple presented in an Hermès store window. This bag is a two-tone cabas bag mixing canvas and leather.

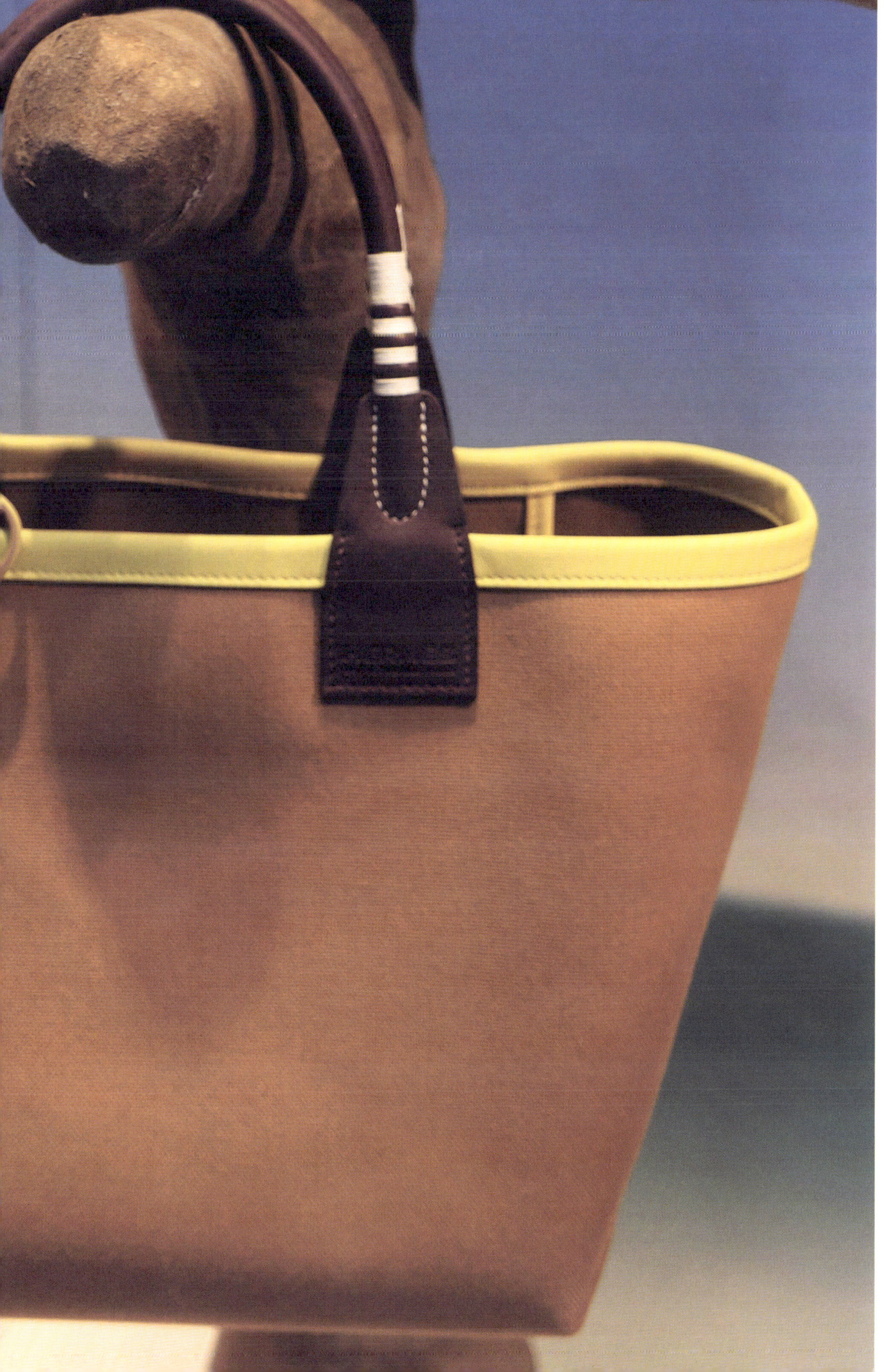

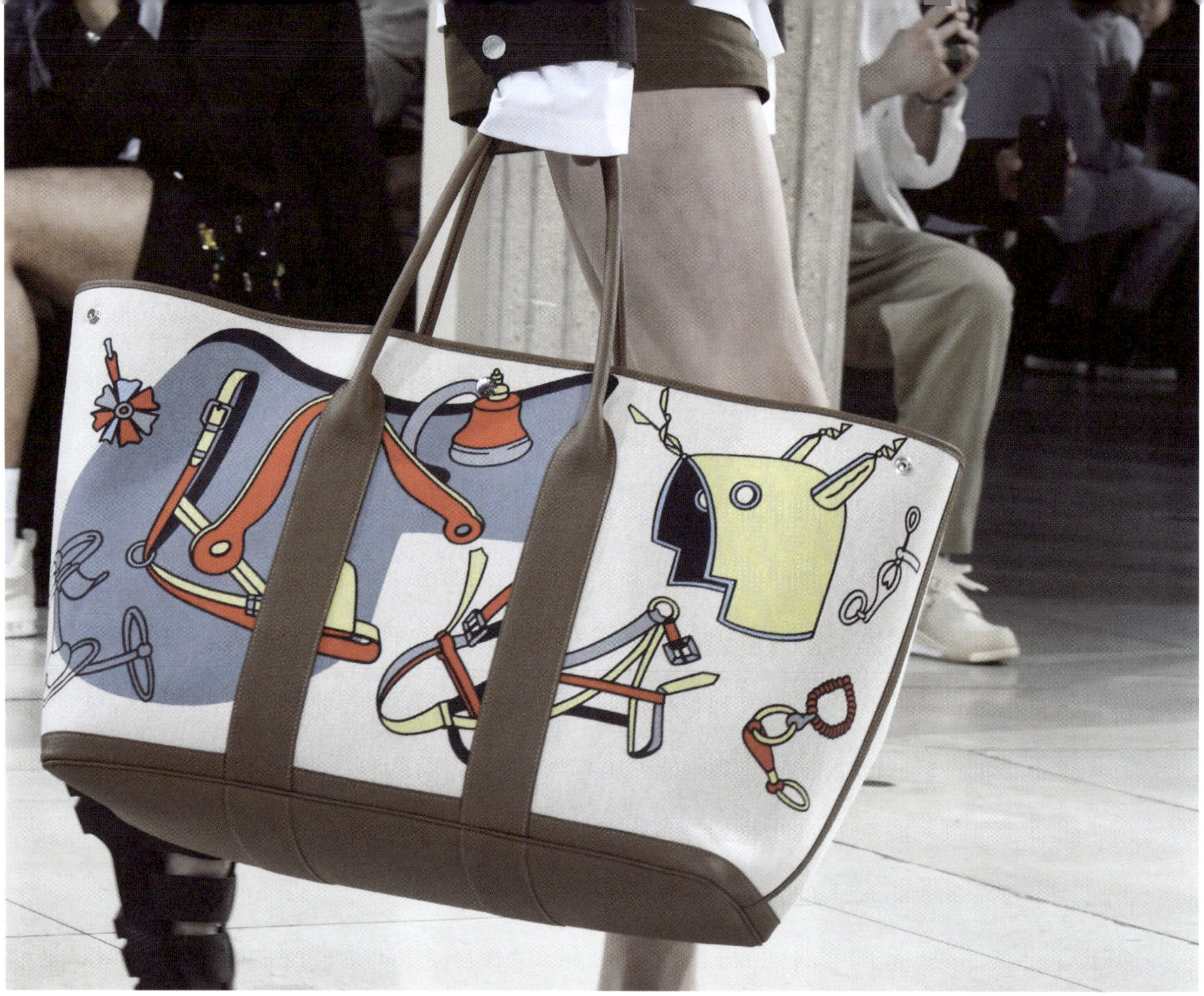

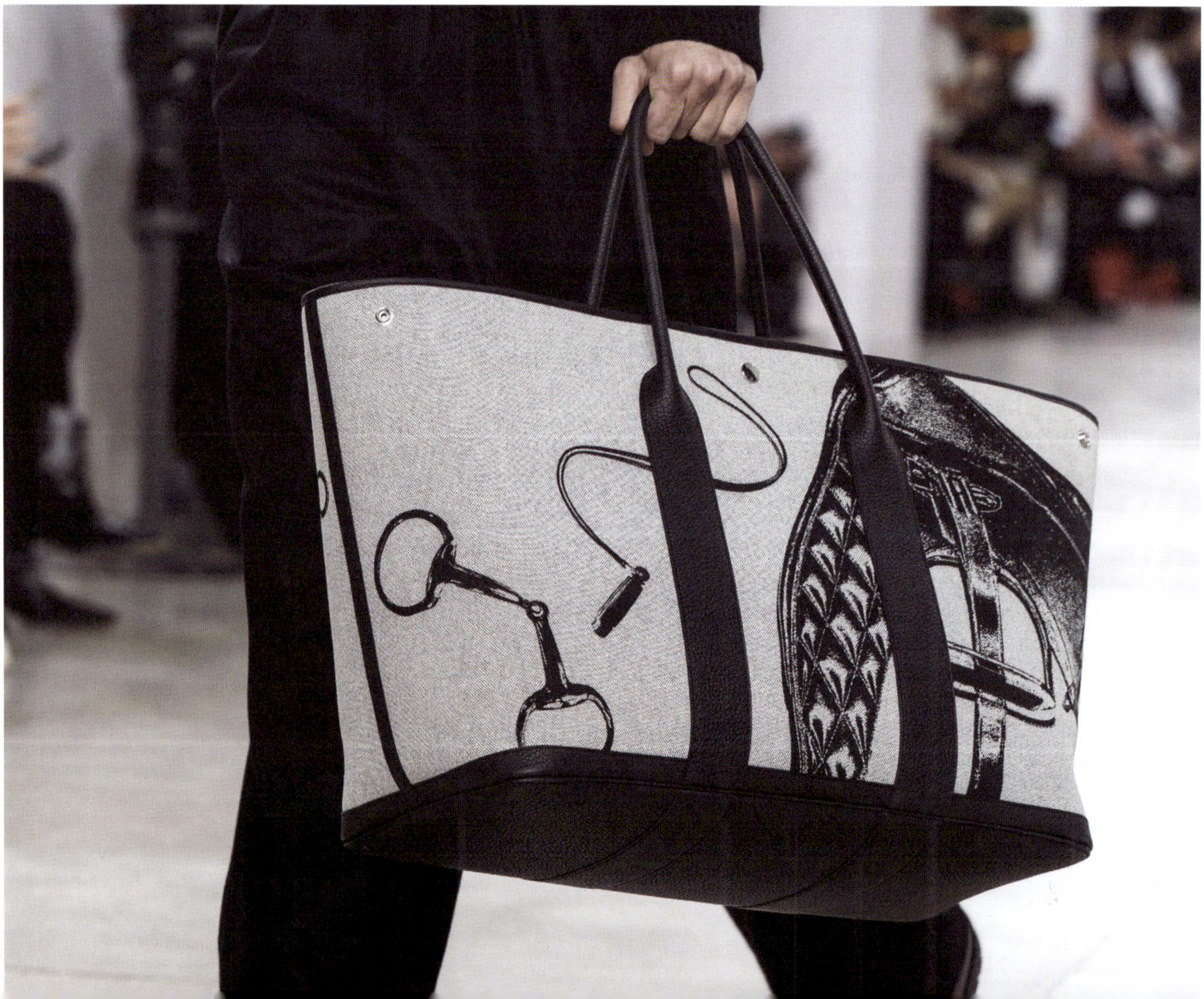

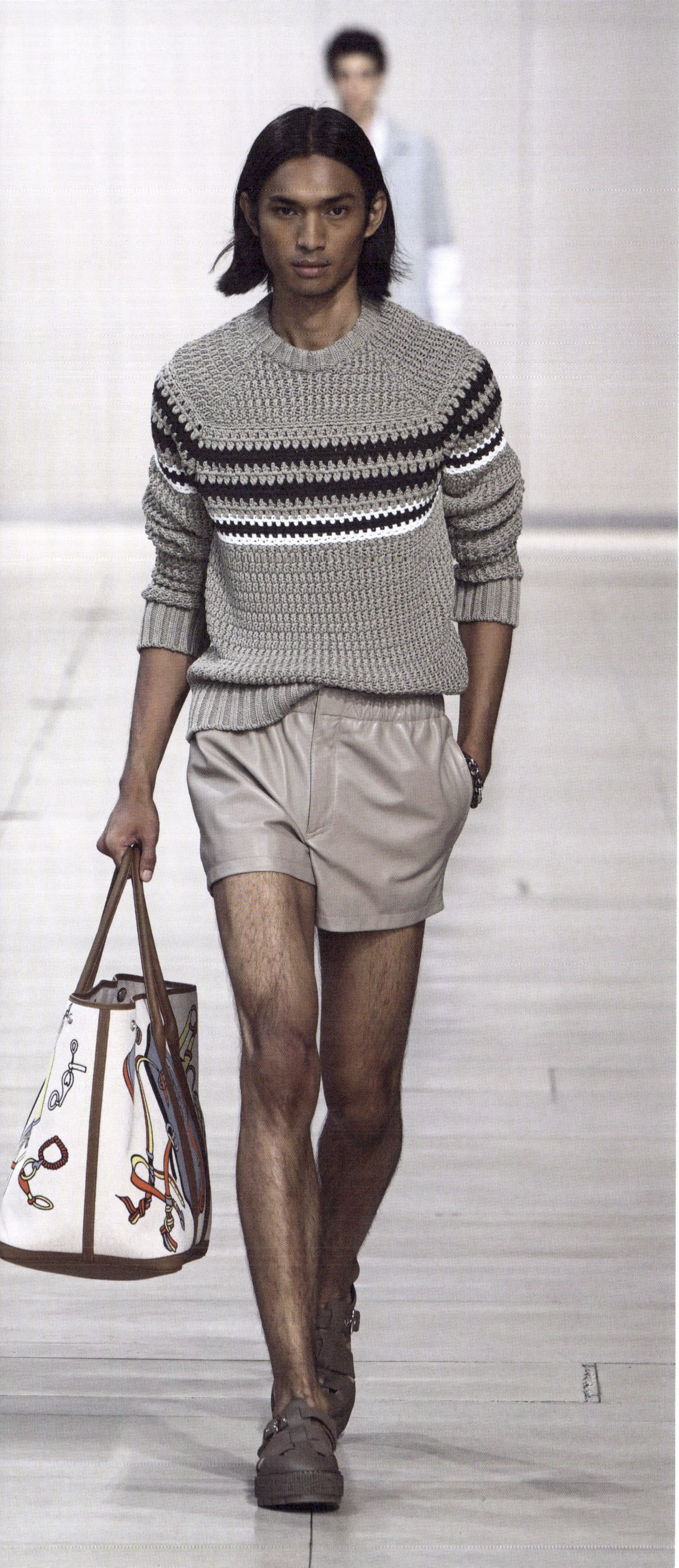

GARDEN PARTY

Pages 110/111: Models present large Garden Party bags on the runway at Hermès Fall/Winter 2024 and Spring/Summer 2024 fashion shows, Paris. The tote bag is available in three sizes and in either all leather (smaller sizes only) or canvas with leather trim options. It is a celebrity favorite.

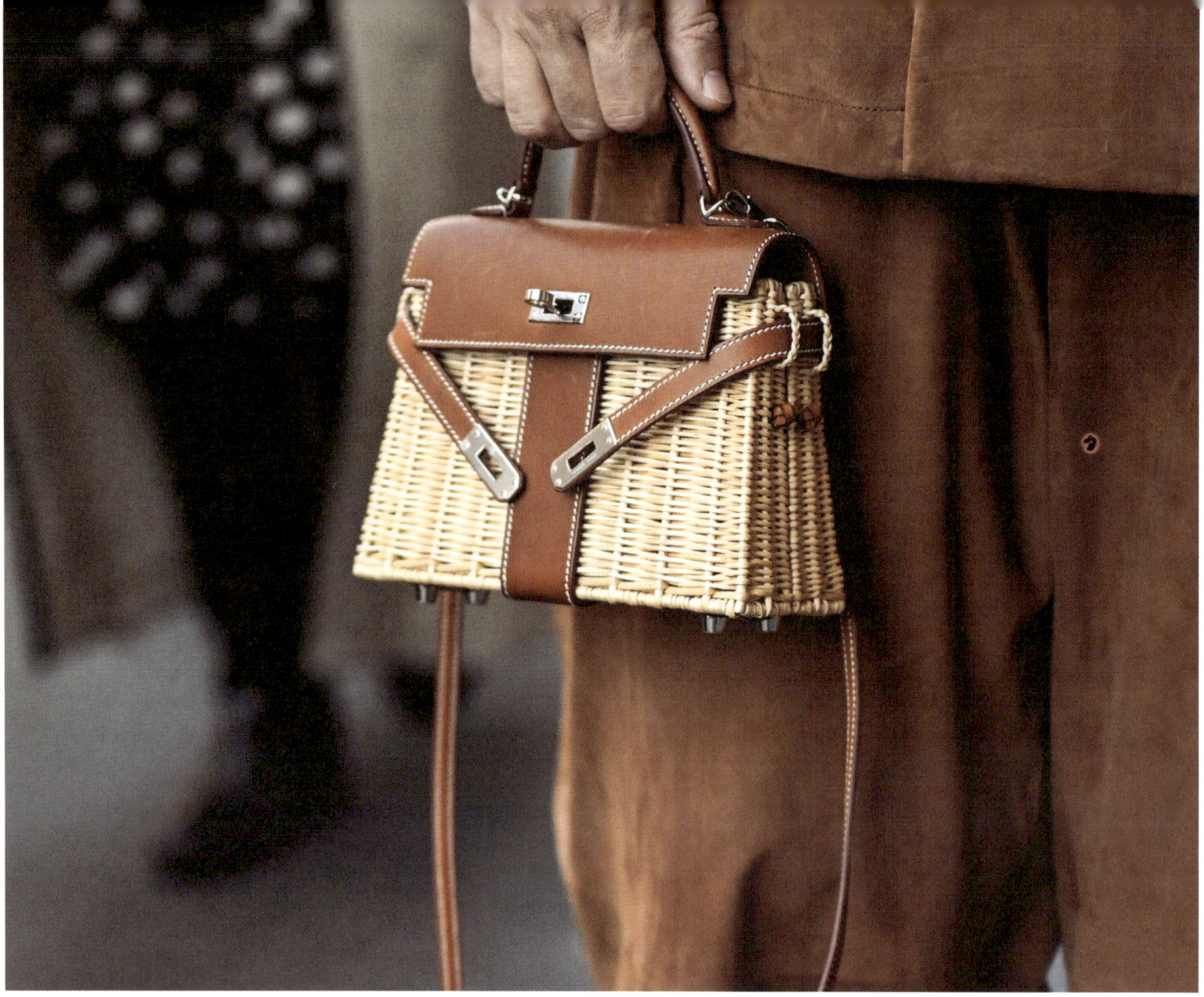

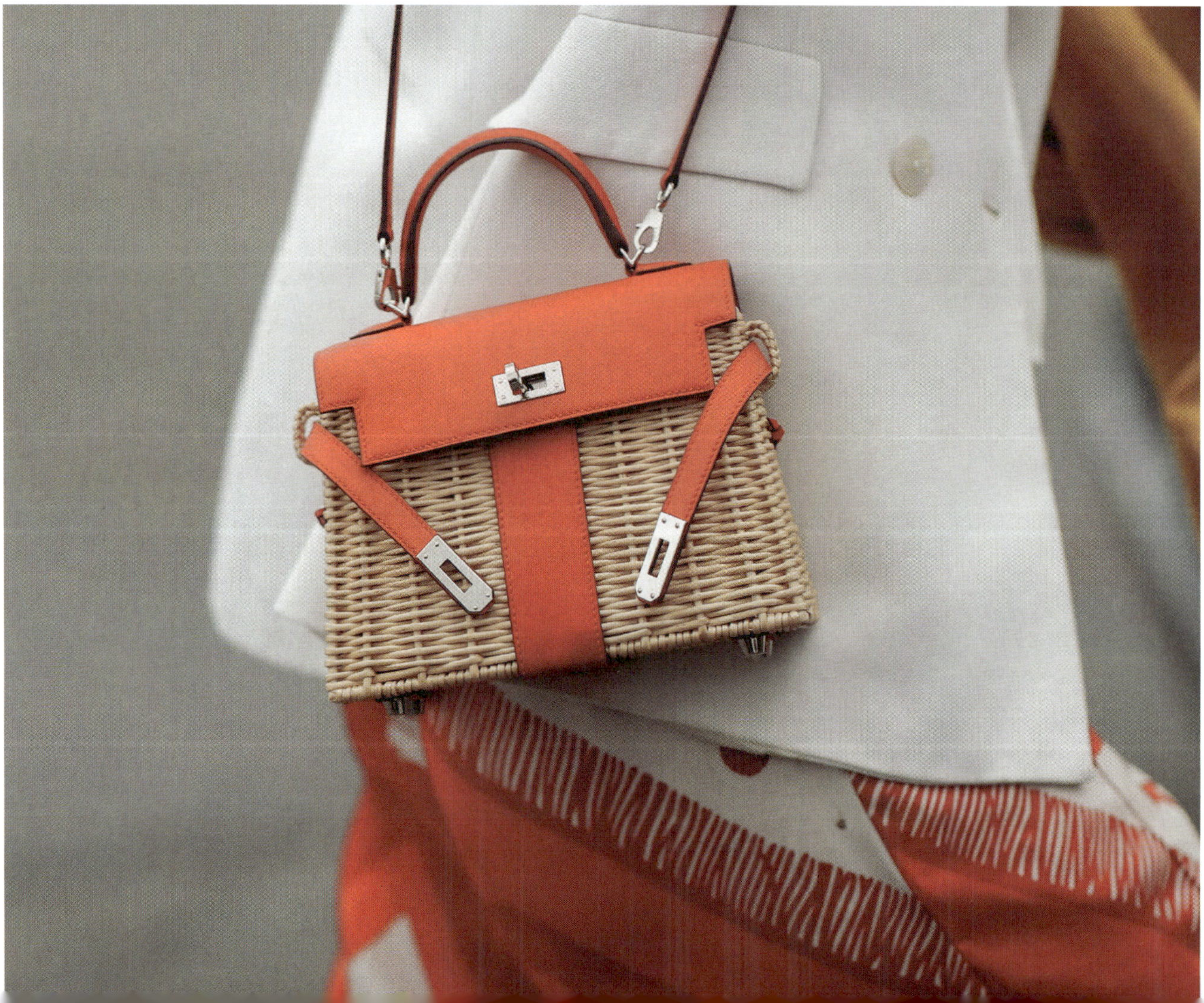

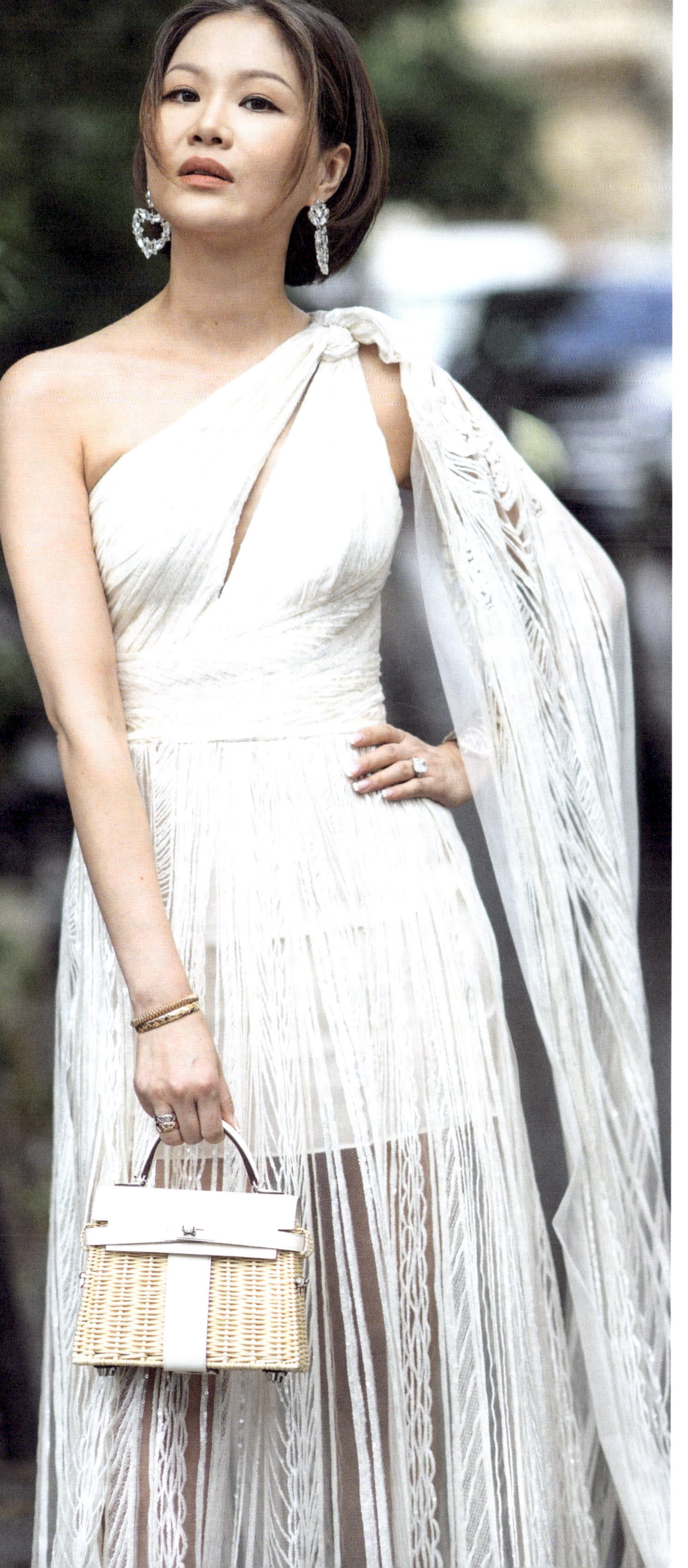

PICNIC BASKET

Previous page: Close-ups of Hermès' Picnic Kelly bags outside the Hermès shows in Paris, 2025 and Le Bourget airport, 2021

This page: A visitor carries a Picnic Kelly outside Elie Saab's Fall/Winter 2022 show during Paris Fashion Week

Next page: Cate Blanchett carries a gold Birkin in Woody Allen's 2013 movie *Blue Jasmine*

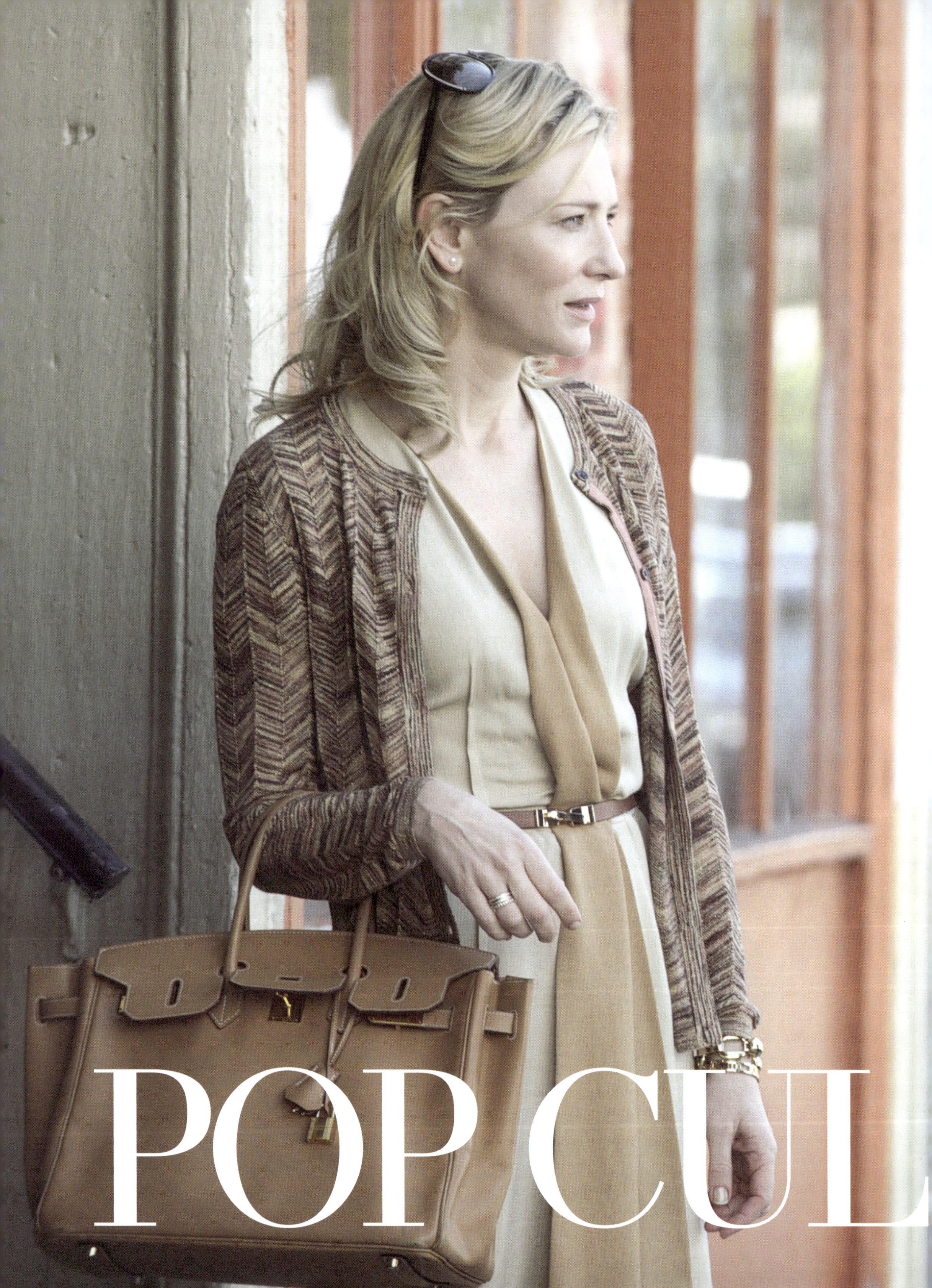

POP CUL

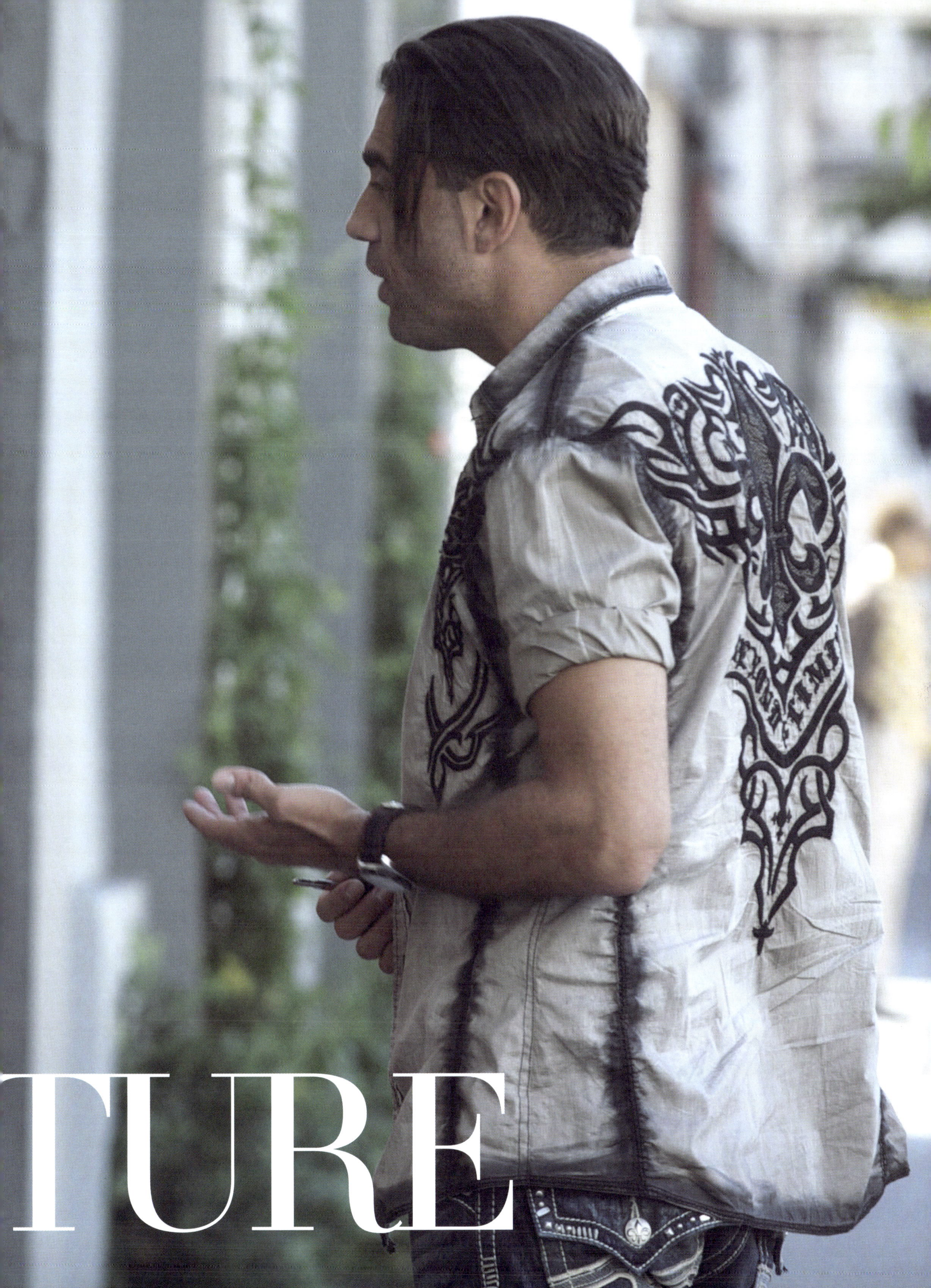
TURE

ON STAGE AND SCREEN

The elegant and refined brand values of Hermès mean that courting celebrity fans with freebies is not part of their PR strategy. However, the story of Hermès' success is still inextricably linked with star power over the past centuries, whether via the influence of Empress Eugenie on her court, the appearance of Princess Grace of Monaco with the soon-to-be Kelly bag, or Jane Birkin's involvement in the creation of her eponymous tote. Capitalizing on the brand's elite and glamorous associations, managing supply by using slow and intricate handcrafting, and charging jaw-droppingly high prices, Hermès has assumed a unique position in popular culture.

Along with the legions of celebrity fans spotted in paparazzi shots and on fashion shoots that have helped Hermès become a household name, the house can be seen in high-profile roles in TV and film, too. Perhaps the most notorious appearance is the Birkin bag vs. the character of Samantha Jones in Season 4 of *Sex and The City* (2001). Desperate to get a red Birkin 35, Jones is told her potential bag will cost $4000, to which she replies, "For a bag?" The sales associate responds with the iconic line, "It's not a bag, it's a Birkin." And proceeds to inform Samantha that along with the cost, the bag would require a five year wait. Today, one would be hard pressed to find any authentic Birkin for under five figures.

Samantha *did* get a Birkin in the end, sort of. In the movie spinoff *Sex and The City 2* (2010), the characters travel to Abu Dhabi and visit a fake goods store. The shop owner follows Samantha, played by actor Kim Cattrall, into the street and mistakes her orange ostrich Birkin for one of his counterfeits, thinking she has shoplifted. There's an angry tussle for the bag and the personal contents of Samantha's bag—condoms and all—spill out onto the street. Samantha cries, "You broke my Birkin!" The real tragedy is that the bag used in the scene was actually a fake: the handles are too long for that specific style to be an authentic Hermès.

Featuring niche luxury goods on popular TV has gone a long way towards increasing brand awareness and creating demand.

In the US comedy-drama series *Gilmore Girls* (2005), the character Rory is gifted a Birkin 25 Rose Tyrien in ostrich with palladium hardware—worth over $40,000 at the time—but doesn't appreciate its significance, leaving viewers gnashing their teeth and fantasising over how *they* would cherish such a present.

Next page: Cardi B arrives at E11EVEN Miami carrying a Birkin on December 13, 2024

Page 119: Sarah Jessica Parker carrying a blue Birkin as her character Carrie Bradshaw on the set of HBO's *Sex and the City*, 2002

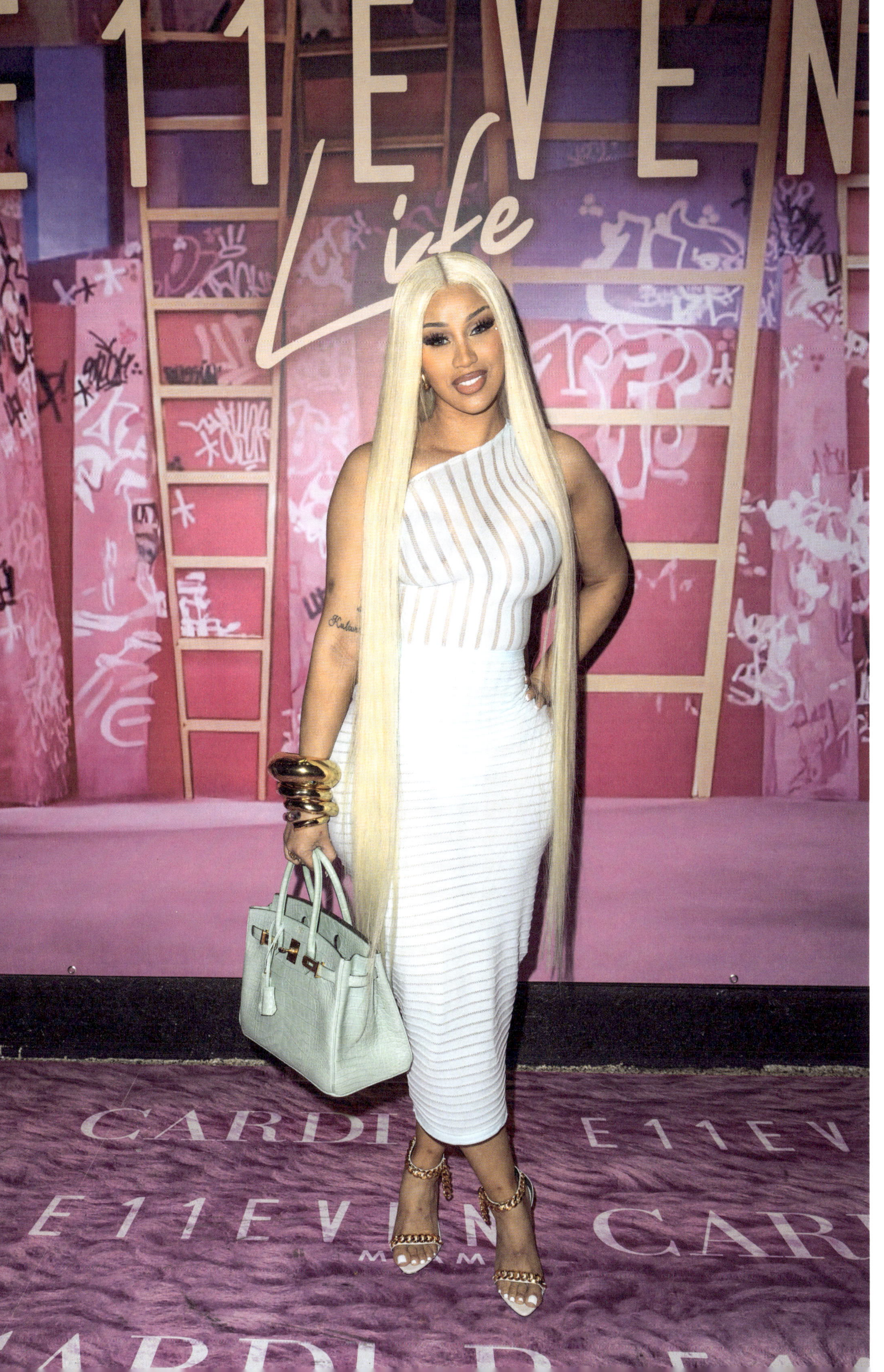
Life

FEATURING LUXURY GOODS ON POPULAR TV HAS GONE A HUGE WAY TO INTRODUCE MANY BRANDS TO THE WIDER PUBLIC

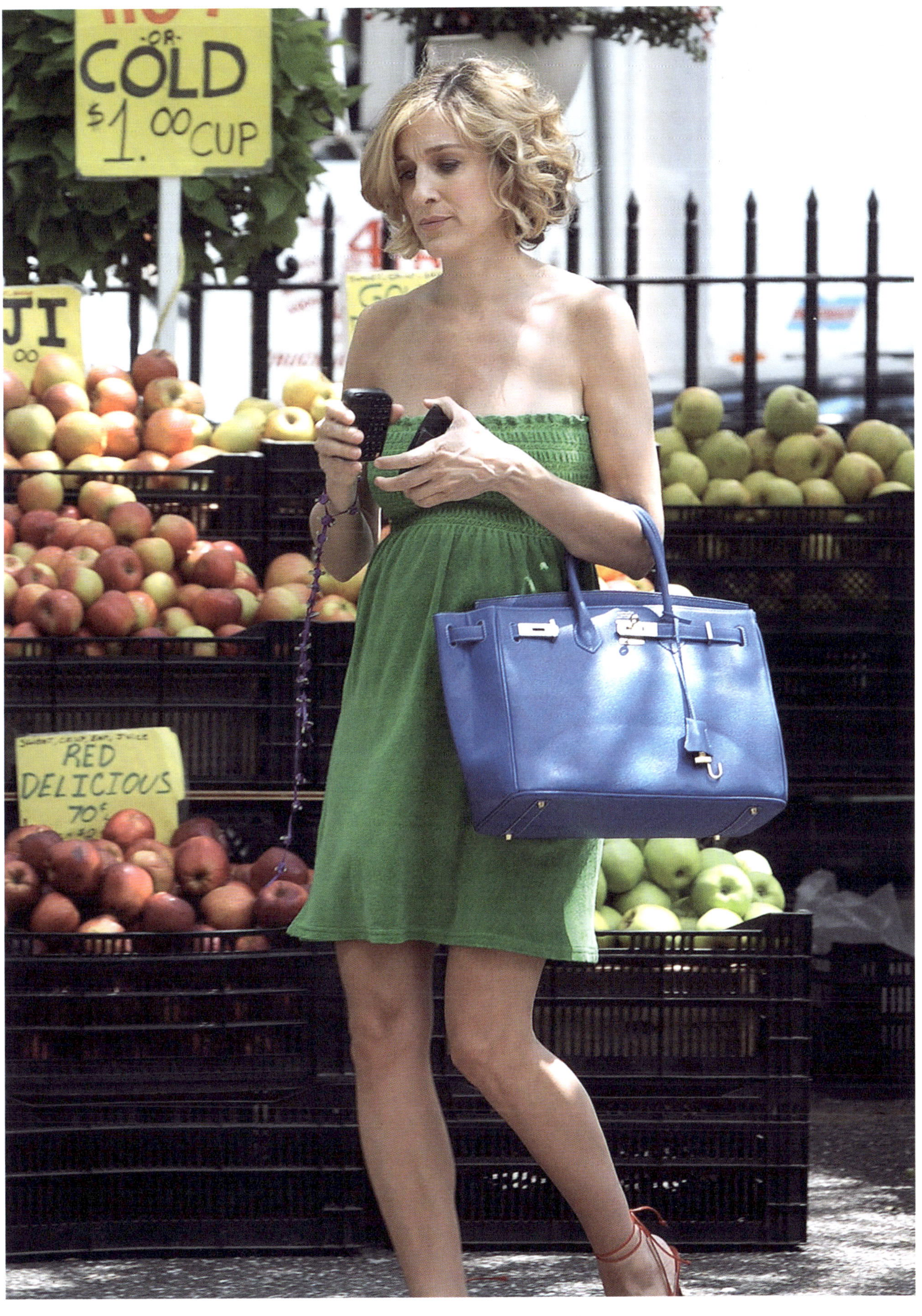
-OR-
COLD
$1.00 CUP
RED
DELICIOUS
70¢

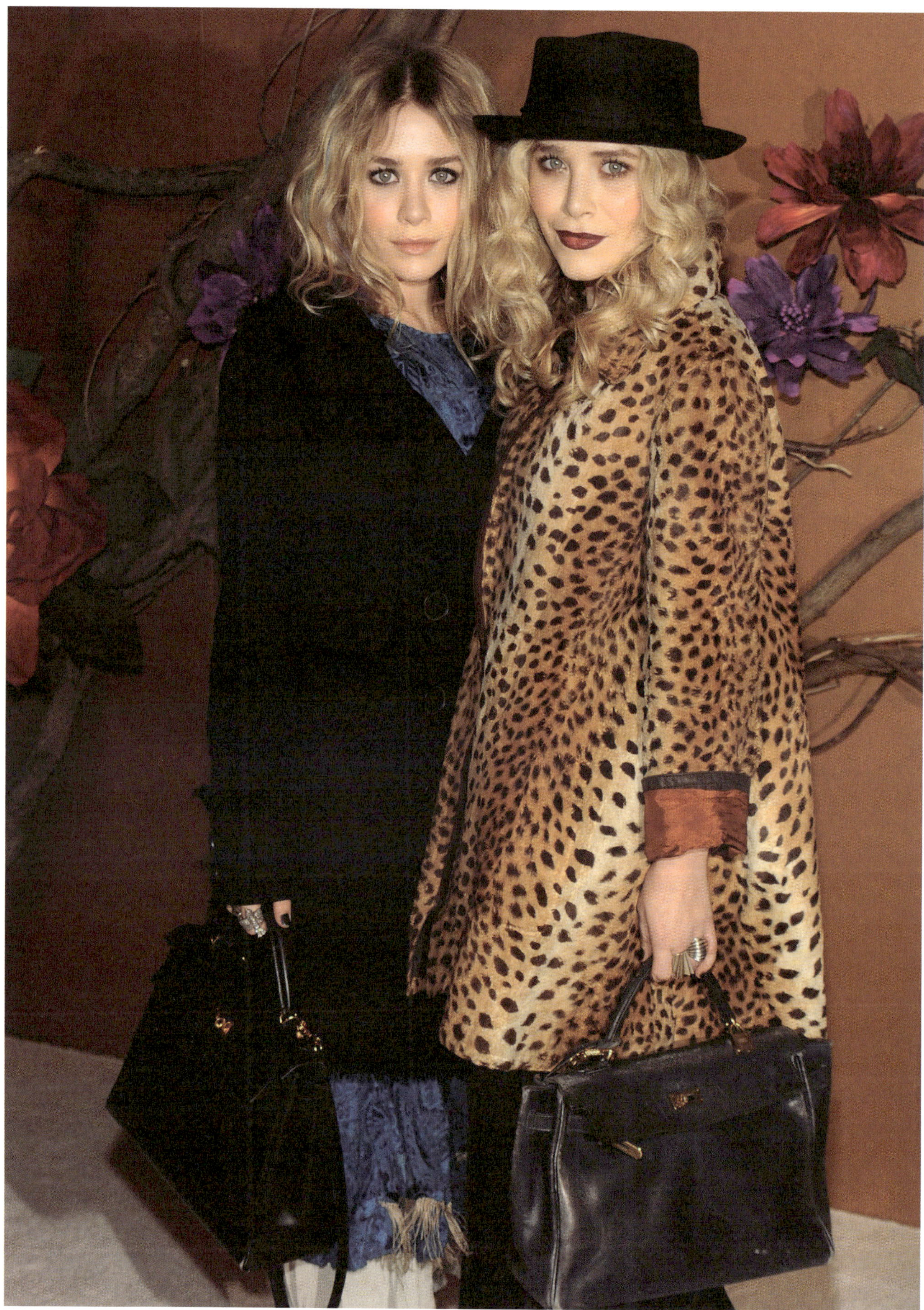

Ashley and Mary-Kate Olsen carry Kelly bags while attending "The Museum of Modern Art Film Benefit: A Tribute To Tim Burton", New York City, 2009

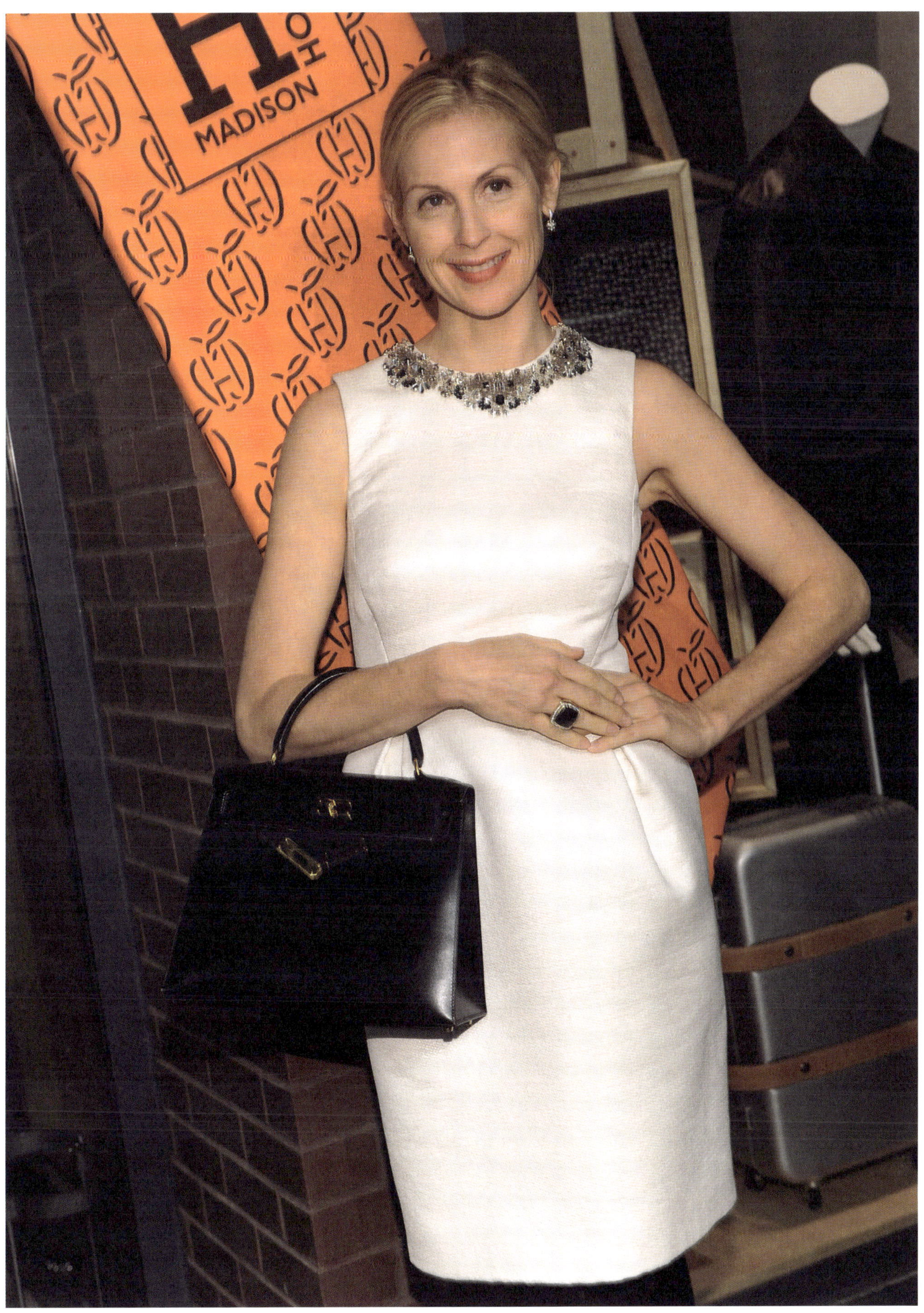

Actress Kelly Rutherford with a Kelly bag at the opening of the first Hermès Men's Store on Madison Avenue, New York City, 2010

In *Gossip Girl* (2007-2012), which followed the lives of rich kids in Upper Manhattan, the lead characters often carried the latest designer bags. However, it was an adult character, Lily van der Woodsen, whose elite collection of Hermès bags elicited the wildest lust in fans watching the show for its style credentials. With an array of Birkins (and Kellys) at her disposal, van der Woodsen's character was played by Kelly Rutherford, who often used bags that were part of the actor's *own* collection. Rutherford often bought herself a Hermès bag after wrapping a season of filming, and her portrayal of van der Woodsen is the epitome of the "Birkin Mom." The phrase is used to describe slick, well-groomed mothers who are confident and extremely affluent (and always have a Birkin nestled in the crook of their arm). This type has definitely found its leader in Rutherford. She even named her son Hermés—but the accent in his name is acute, not grave as it appears on Hermès.

However, the fame of Hermès has spread far beyond the confines of American TV. *Zindagi Na Milegi* (2011) is a Bollywood film detailing the road-tripping adventures of three friends—Arjun, Kabir and Imran. They are also joined by the character Bagwati, an orange ostrich Kelly bag. Bagwati is looked after like a person, given sunglasses and a hat, and has inspired the nickname that many Indians use to describe Hermès bags today.

Wondering what movies you should add to your Hermès bag research project? Try *The Royal Tenenbaums* (2001)—featuring a gold Birkin; *Le Divorce* (2003)—spot the red crocodile Kelly; *The Proposal* (2009)—note the incongruity of the orange Birkin; and *Blue Jasmine* (2013)—a gold Birkin is carried by Cate Blanchett's character.

Today you're more likely to spot an influencer or celebrity carrying Hermès in a reality TV show or on their own YouTube channel than at the cinema. As one of the most famous families in the world, the Kardashian-Jenners have substantial collections of Hermès pieces, which they are more than happy to show off to viewers. By rough calculations, it looks like Kim has the largest selection, followed by little sister Kylie. Both own bags in Himalaya Niloticus Crocodile—Kim's is a Birkin and Kylie's a Kelly *retourné*. Kylie has said, "This one... is really special. If my house is on fire, I could take this one out of all of them if I could only choose one." Clan matriarch Kris Jenner also owns a Himalaya Kelly, among many, *many* others. Estimates suggest Kim owns over 30 Birkin bags, while Kylie's collection comprises approximately 13 Birkin bags and 10 Kellys, according to the calculations of the Australian edition of *ELLE* magazine.

As social media shows no sign of losing its chokehold over the general public, sneaking a peek at the carefully dehumidified and air-conditioned wardrobes of the rich and famous is an ever more accessible hobby. Usurping the Kardashians, Jamie Chua is the woman credited with owning the largest collection of Hermès bags in the world (over 200); her collection focuses on rare and limited edition versions. The Singaporean socialite shares her lifestyle—and the bags she owns—on her Instagram page (1.5 million followers) and unboxes new purchases for her 587,000 subscribers on YouTube. Chua's collection has been valued at over $2 million. While she was divorcing her millionaire ex-husband, Chua revealed to listeners of the *Pass the Power with Paige Parker* podcast that she had to sell some of her bags "to feed her children" in the process.

THE WEEKND, YOUNG THUG AND LIL WAYNE HAVE ALL INCLUDED HERMÈS MENTIONS IN THEIR LYRICS

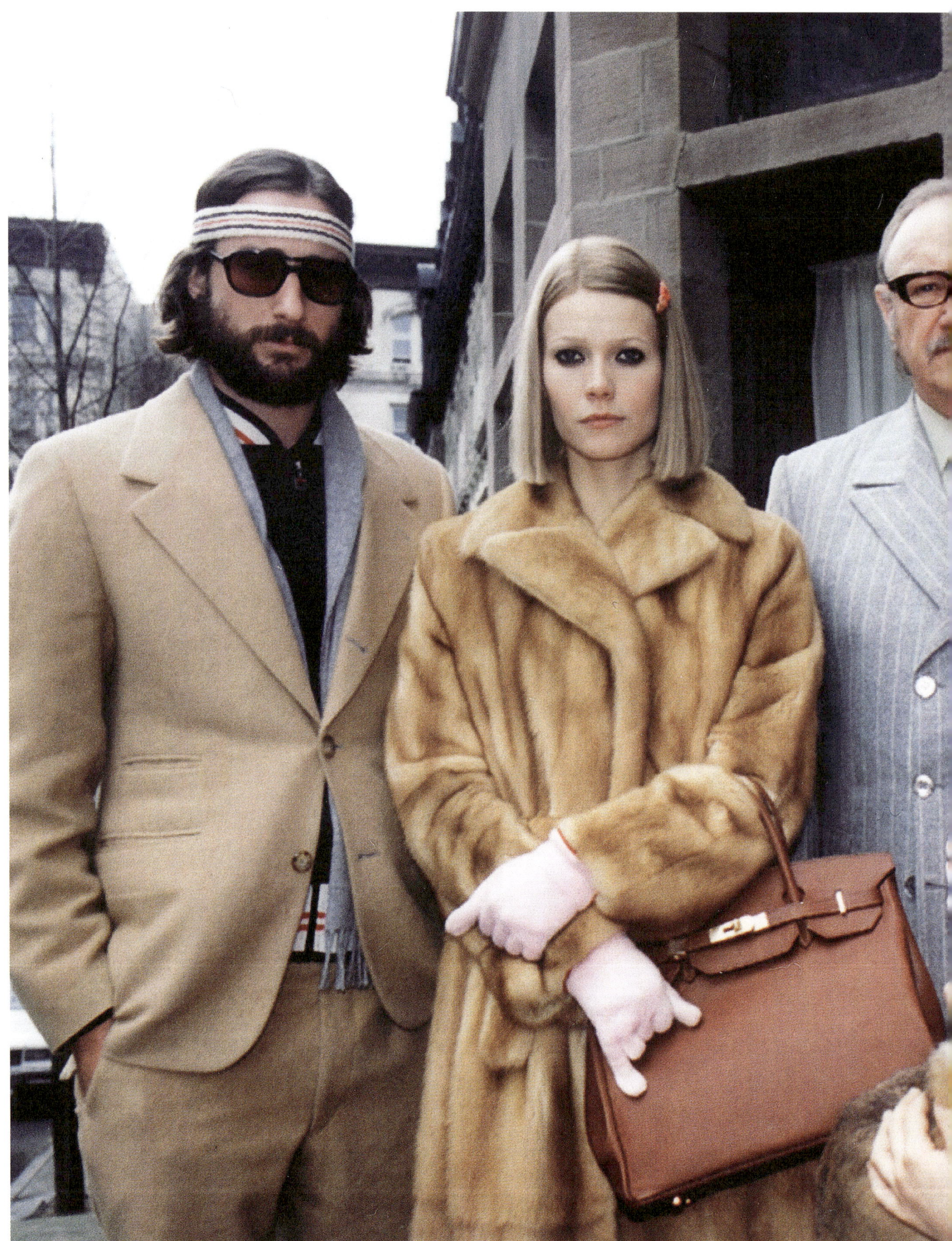

Gwyneth Paltrow carries a Birkin in Wes Anderson's movie *The Royal Tenenbaums*

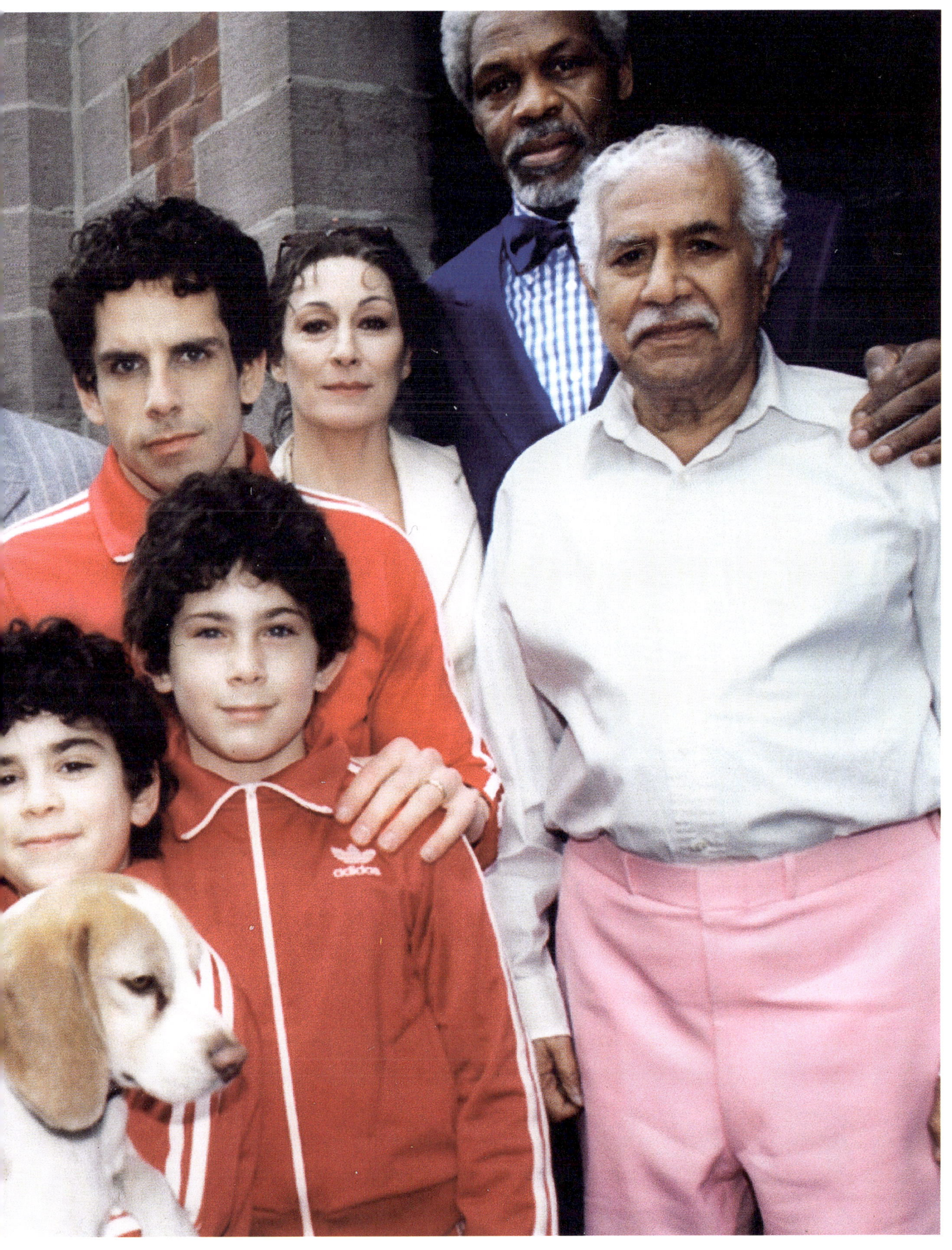
adidas

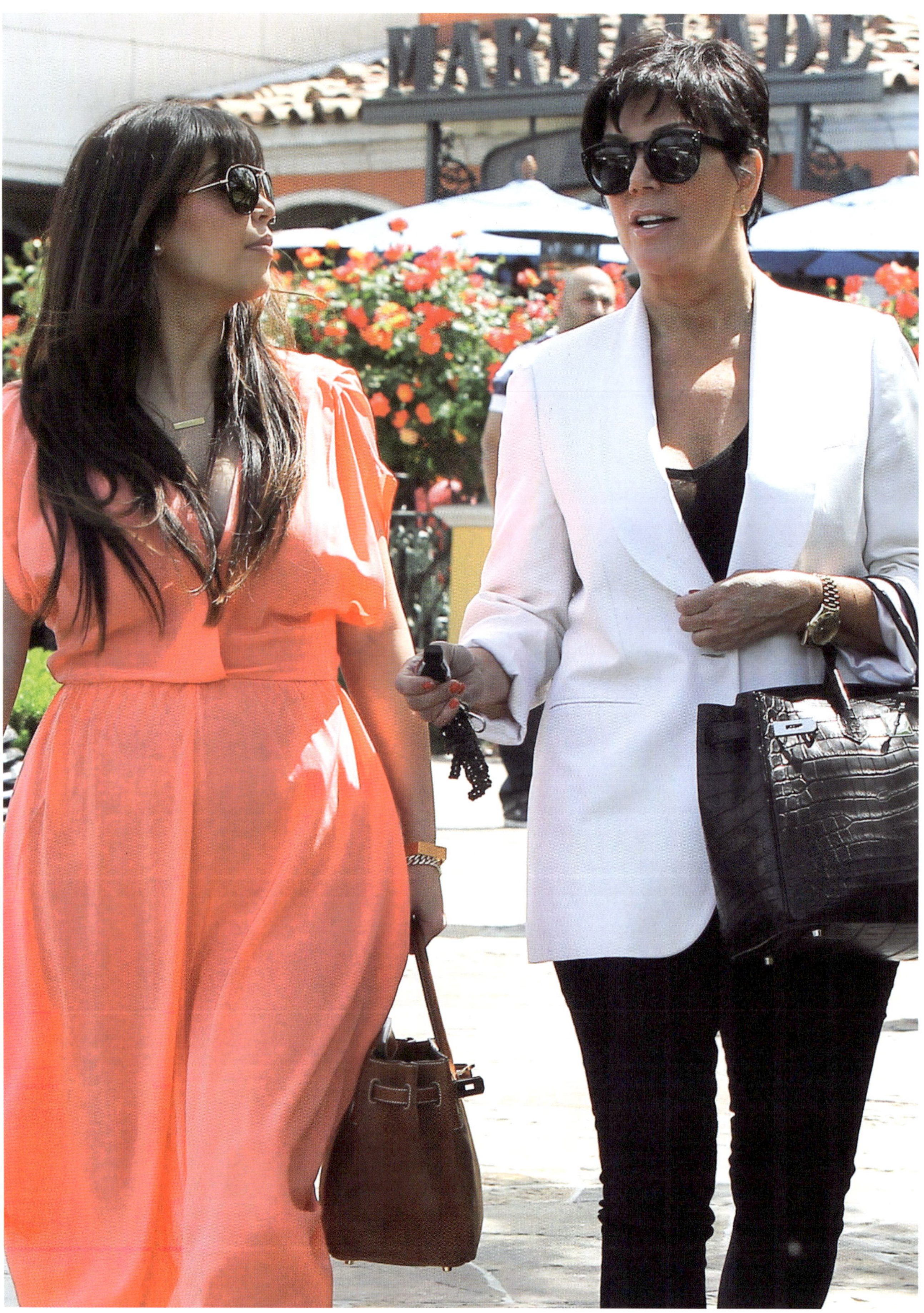

Kim Kardashian and Kris Jenner carry Birkin bags, Calabasas, 2013

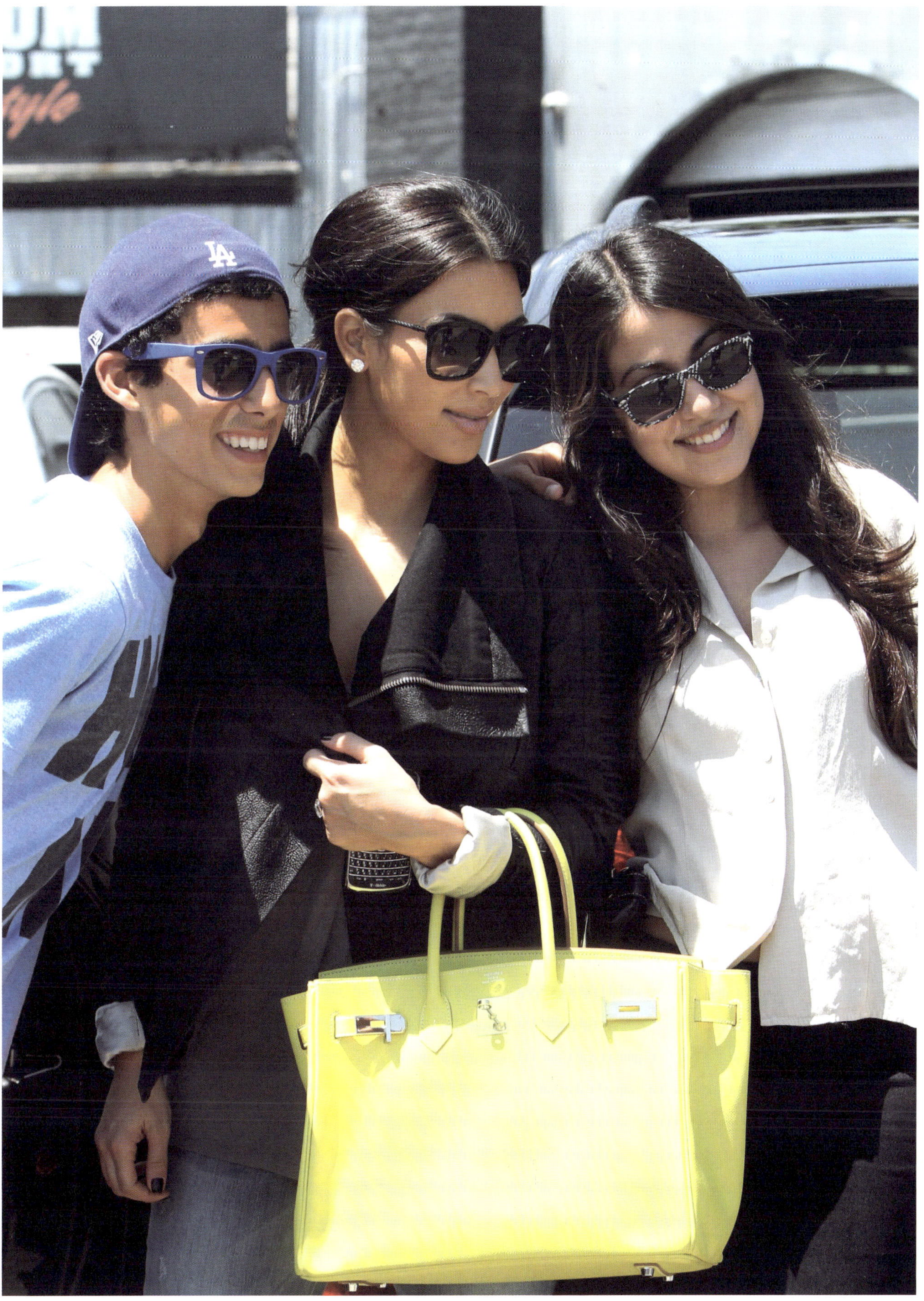

Kim Kardashian poses with fans in Beverly Hills while carrying a yellow Birkin from her impressive collection, 2011

This page: Sarita Choudhury is seen carrying a Birkin on the set of the TV series *And Just Like That...*, New York City, 2022

Next page: Julianne Moore (carrying a Birkin) and Justice Smith are seen on the film set of *Sharper* on October 1, 2021 in New York City

Page 130: Kelly Rutherford and Caroline Lagerfelt on the set of *Gossip Girl*, New York City on March 26, 2009

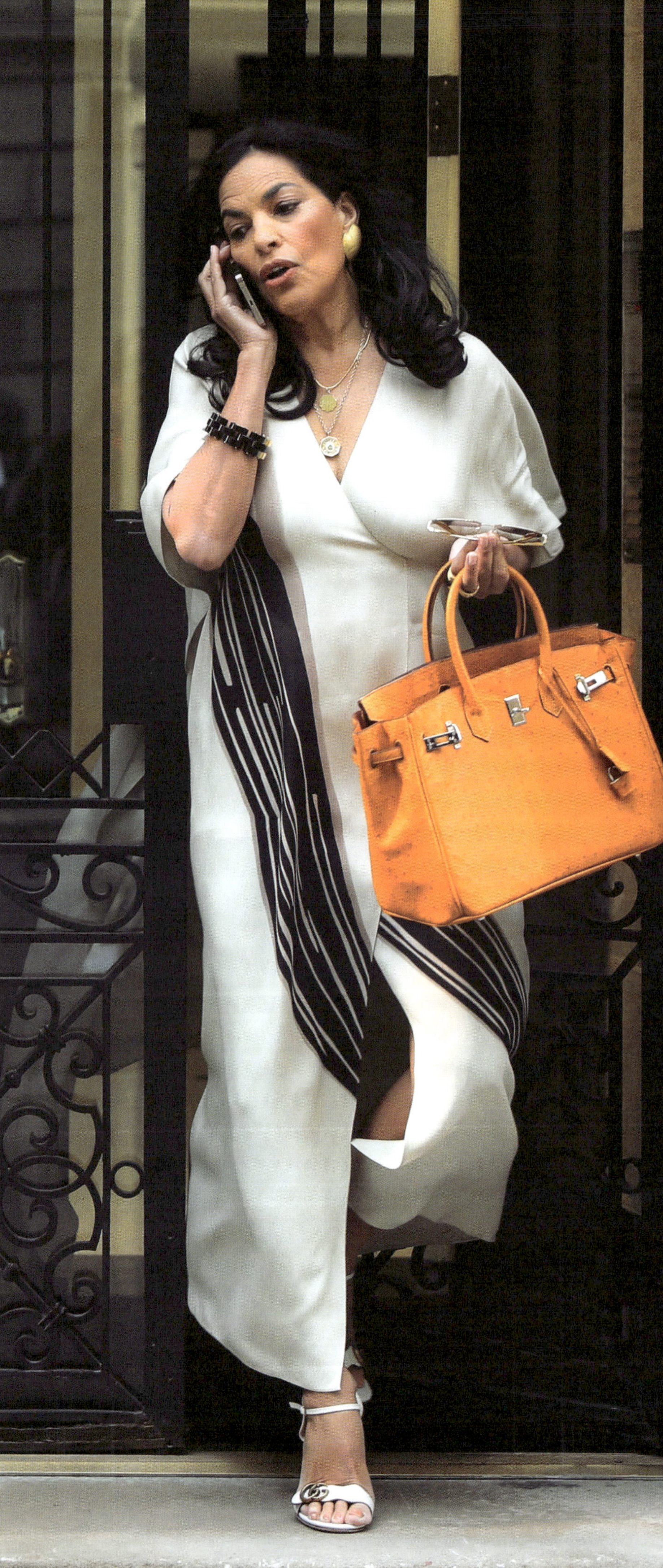

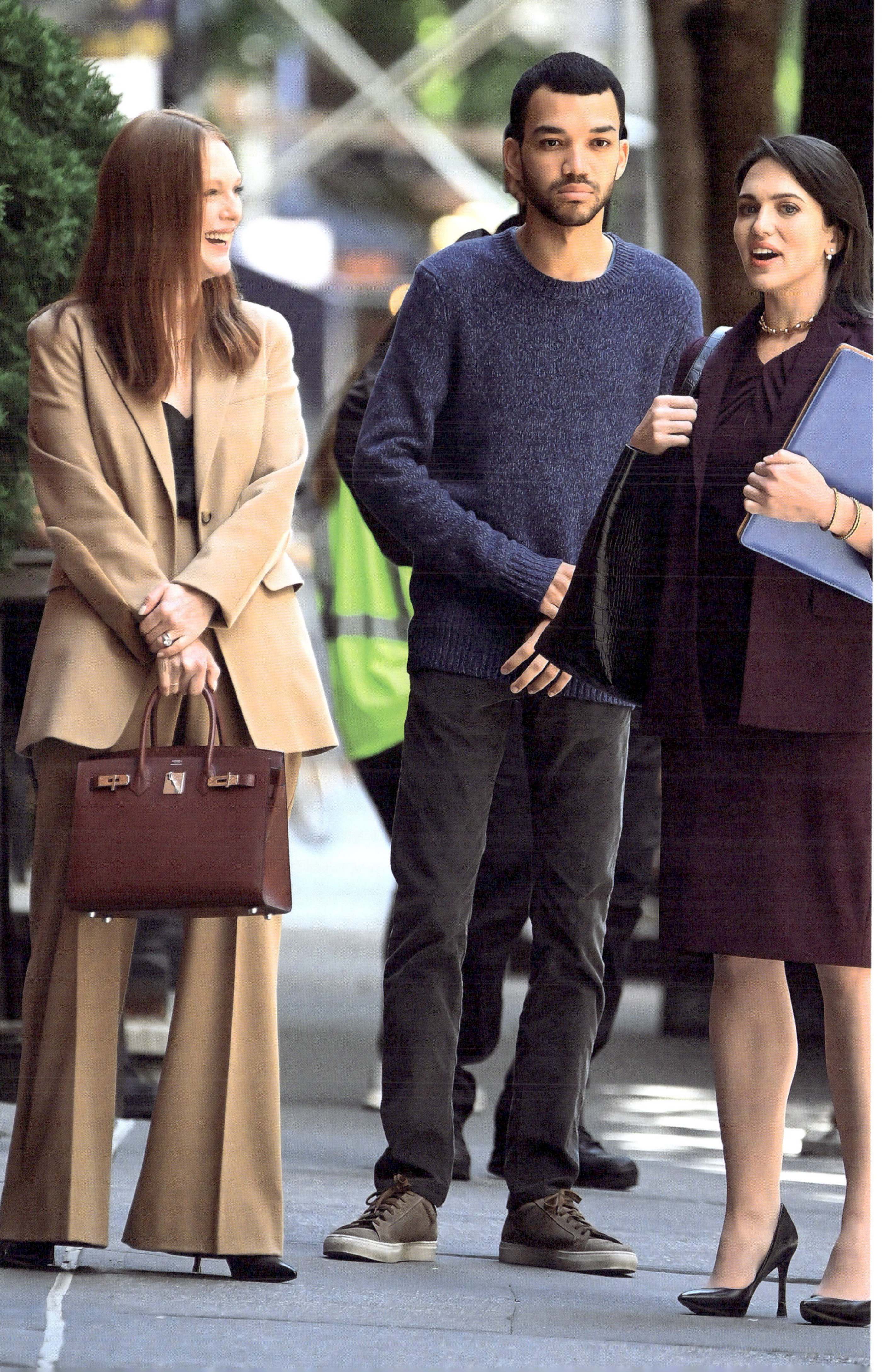

If potential clients must make a wish and wait for a bag to be offered to them in stores, online shops allow the elusive world of Hermès to become more accessible. Charles Gross is a TikTok content creator who shares his knowledge of Hermès bags with his 1.3 million followers. In an interview with *Vogue* in 2022, Gross said that his goal is "to share my understanding of luxury fashion in the most diplomatic and conversation-starting way. Inclusivity is at the heart of everything I do." Gross opens each video with his catchphrase, "Let's talk about it." By doing so, he hopes to "open up the discussion to the world—even if someone isn't buying these pieces, why can't they be part of the conversation?" Absorbing the knowledge Gross shares is a surefire way to inspire future fans of the brand.

In the world of music, hip-hop often boosts luxury brand awareness with well-placed name checks. The Weeknd, Young Thug and Lil Wayne have all included Hermès mentions in their lyrics, while Cardi B is a vocal fan of the *maison*. The rapper also owns a significant Hermès collection of her own. The centerpiece is a Birkin 30 in Himalaya crocodile (naturally!), but her 26 bags also include a Faubourg Birkin—sometimes called the 'House' Birkin—which pictures Hermès' 24 Rue du Faubourg Saint-Honoré HQ in Paris. The Faubourg Birkin has an estimated value of just under $400,000.

Despite being a fashion designer herself, Victoria Beckham is also the curator of a growing collection of Birkins that began with her first purchase of a tan bag in 2004. Now numbering over 100, it's clear that aside from her own designs, the Birkin is likely her favorite bag. Perhaps the Birkin could be called the fashion insider's ultimate handbag? Ashley and Mary-Kate Olsen, former child actors turned fashion designers of quiet luxury brand The Row, are also Hermès Birkin afi-

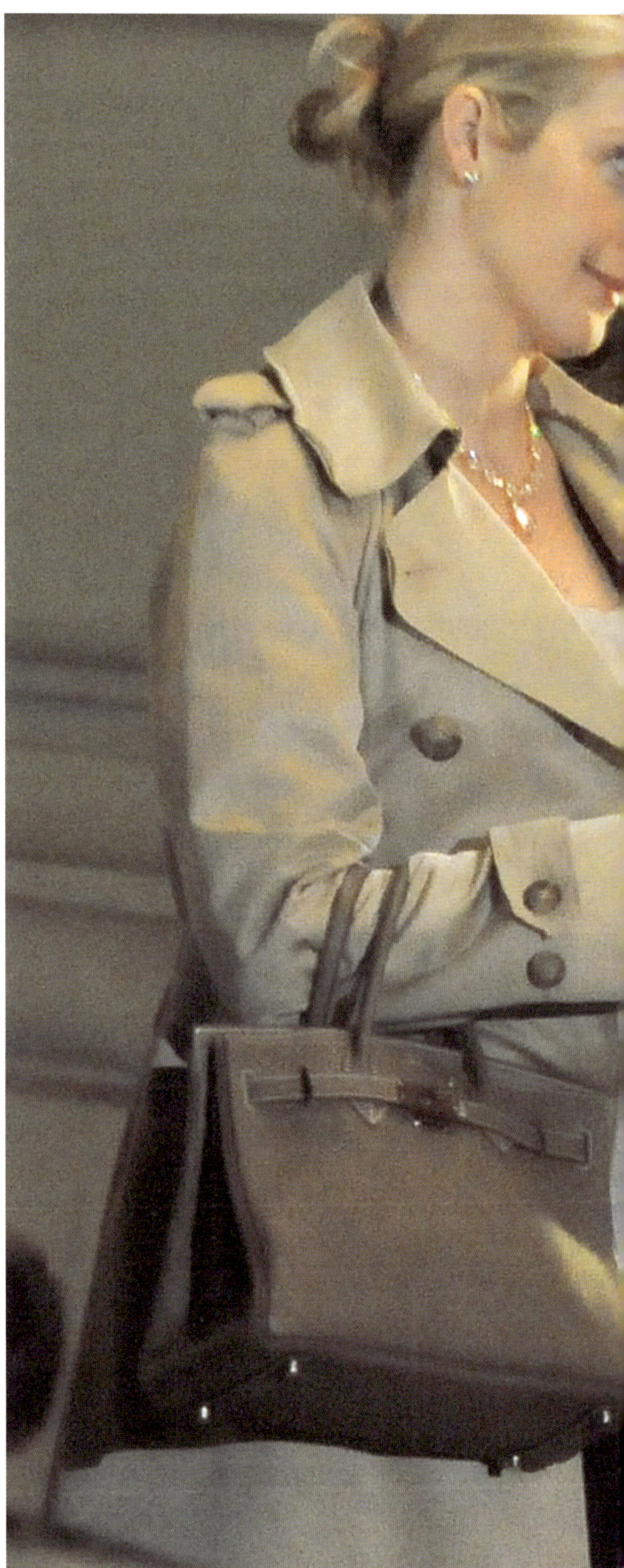

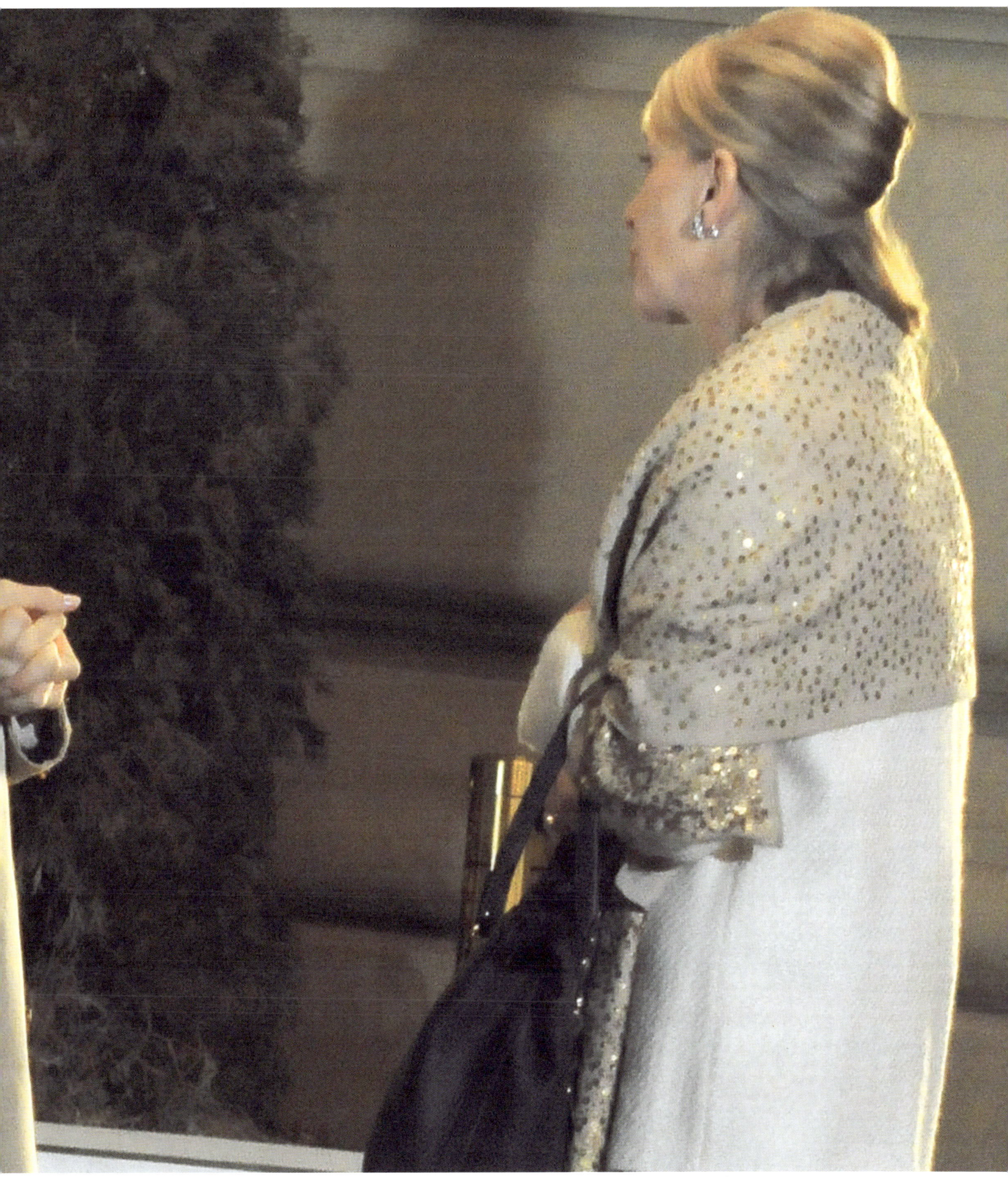

This page: Kim Kardashian with a Birkin that features a painting by artist George Condo, Paris, 2020

Next page: Kelly Rutherford carrying an ostrich Birkin on location for *Gossip Girl*, New York City, 2009

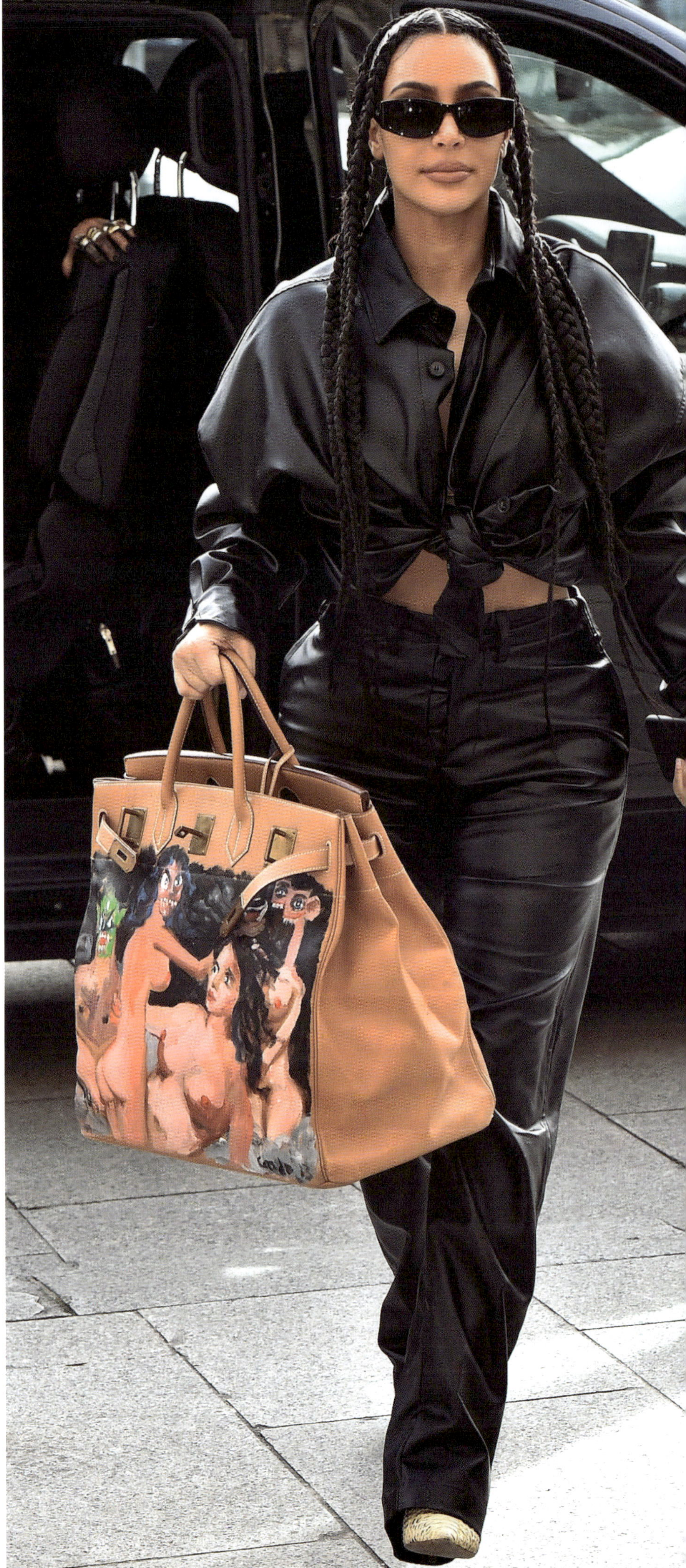

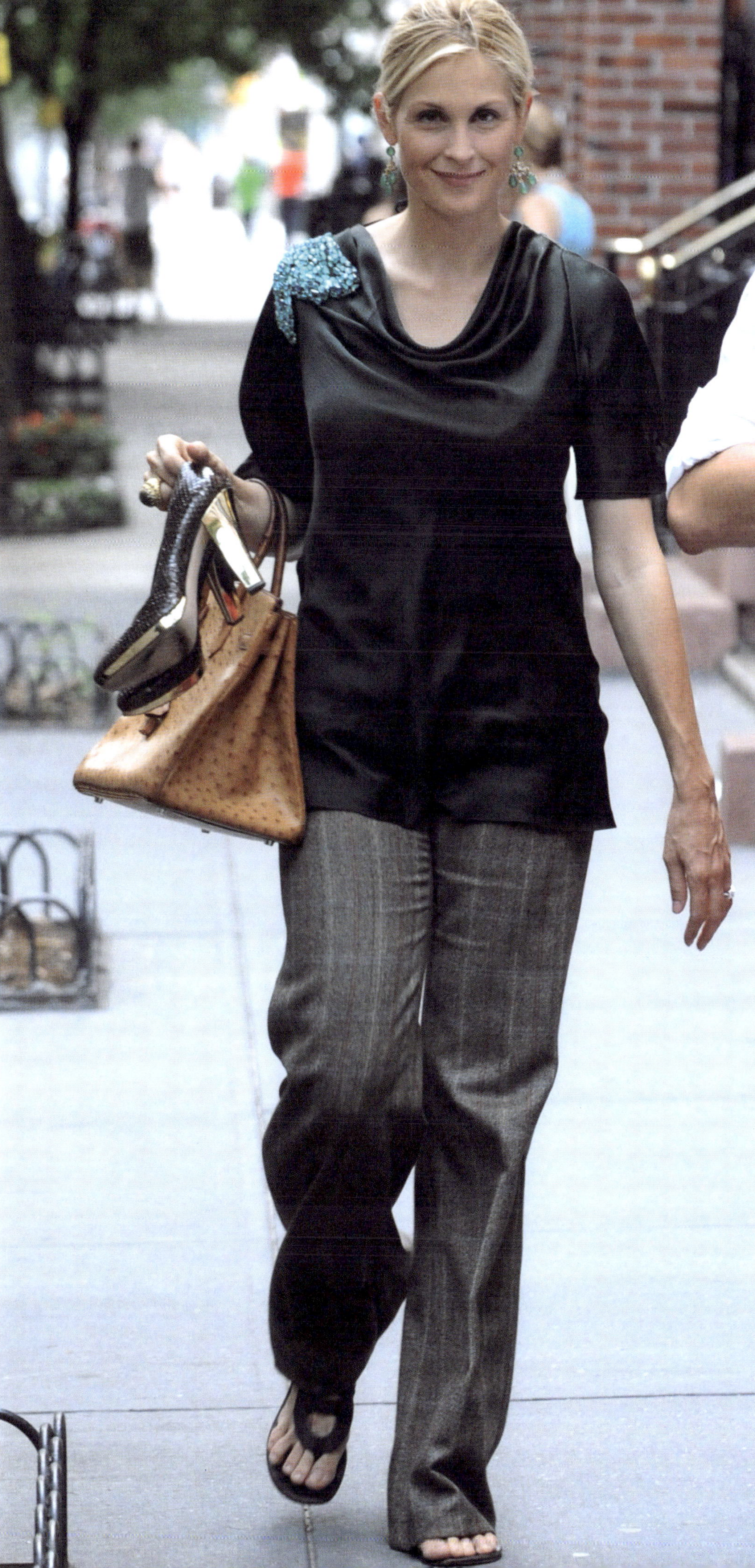

cionados. But unlike the box-fresh investments of other stars, who keep their bags pristine and barely used or displayed in their own rooms, the Olsens have been seen stuffing their bags full, carting them around, scratches and all, and generally *using* them.

These Birkins are the fabled "beater bag," the workhorse of a woman's wardrobe, and therefore subject to having coffee spilled on them, being left on the floor, and generally being put through a lot. Jane Birkin used to wear her own bags until they were worn out, even putting stickers directly onto the leather. This casual disregard for such an expensive, coveted investment piece is hailed by many as the most authentic way to use such a pricey bag.

Beyond bags that are worn every day, loved and filled with life, the rarest bags spend their days locked in vaults and safes. Due to their incredibly high value and their status as an investment rather than an accessory, owners will protect them from use at all costs.

If you are hoping to add years to the life of your own Hermès bag, consider a ribbon scarf wrapped around the handles. The narrow silk scarves look adorable, offer a sweet way to further personalize your bag and serve a practical purpose as well. The silk scarves offer protection from grease and oils that could potentially damage your bag and stain the handles, lowering its value, particularly for lighter-colored styles.

Whether it's likes for a celebrity's special-order bag presented in a coveted blue-lined box; an incredible vintage piece handed down through generations and displayed in a museum; or paparazzi pictures pasted onto a moodboard and dreamed into existence, the power of Hermès has been magnified by the *maison's* incorporation into popular culture and the collective consciousness.

Next page: Jennifer Lopez is seen carrying a Himalaya Birkin 25, New York City, 2024

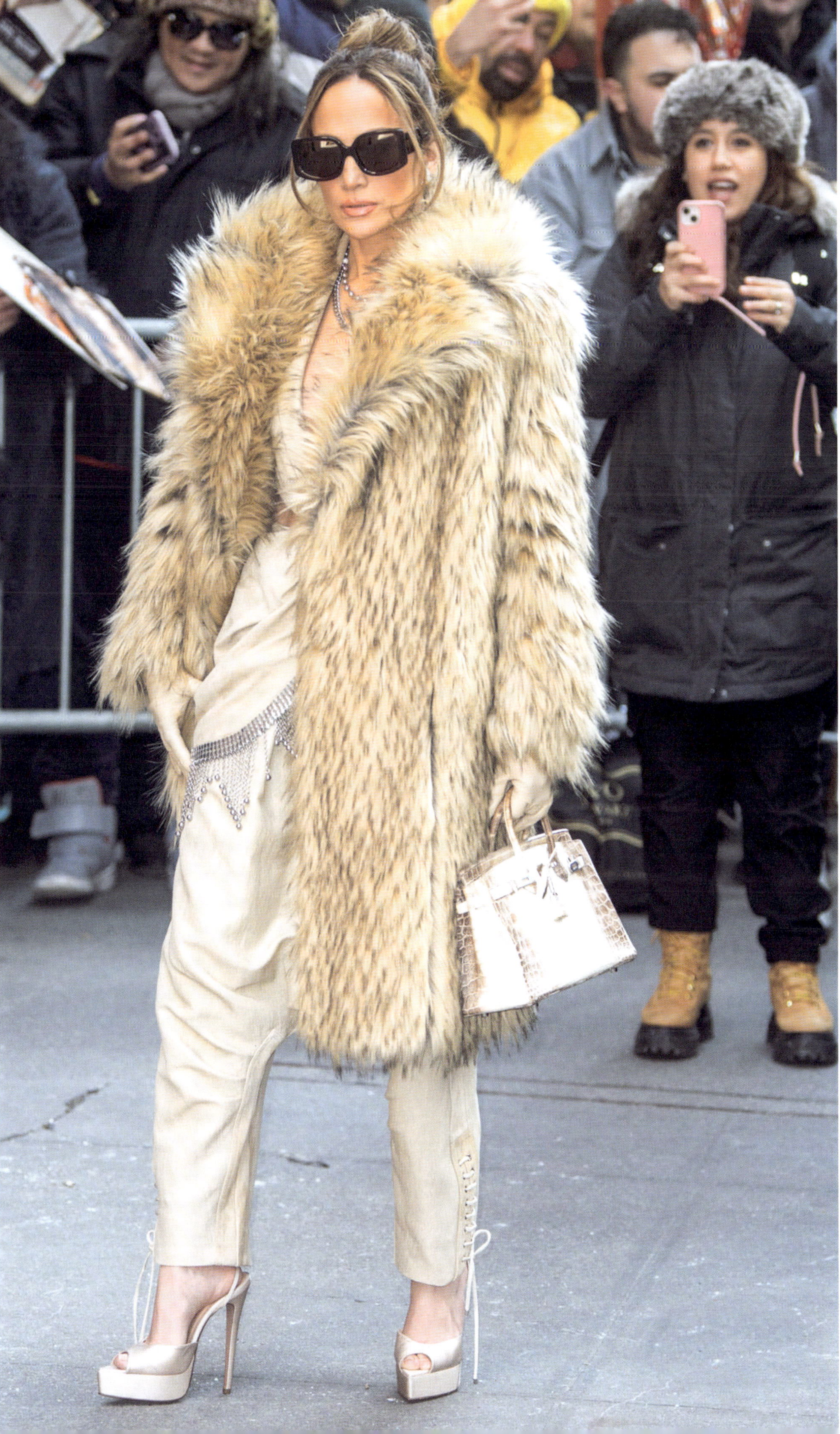

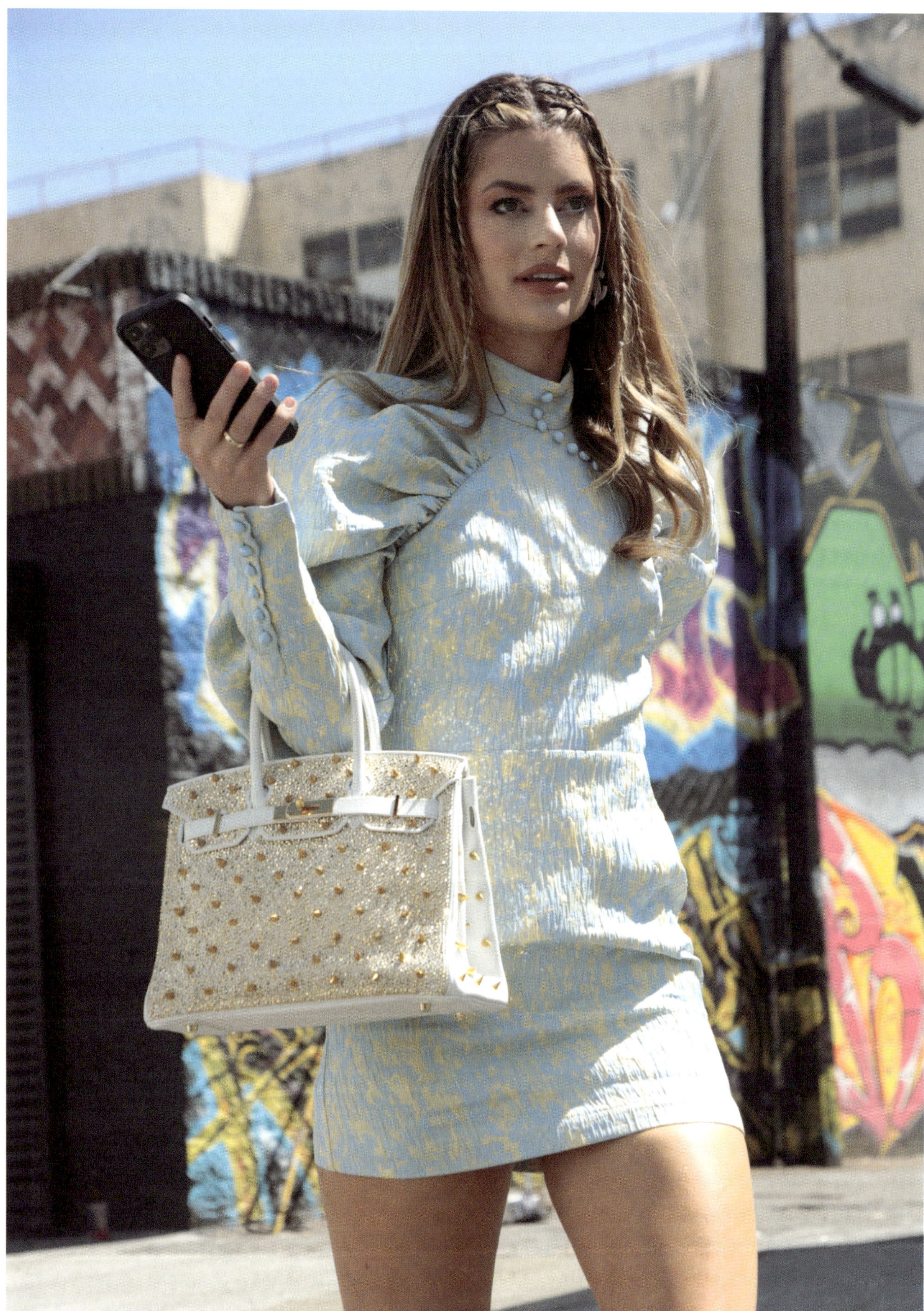

Content creator Hannah Stocking presents a Birkin that has been customized by Privé Porter for their MoneyBags x MB range. Los Angeles, 2021

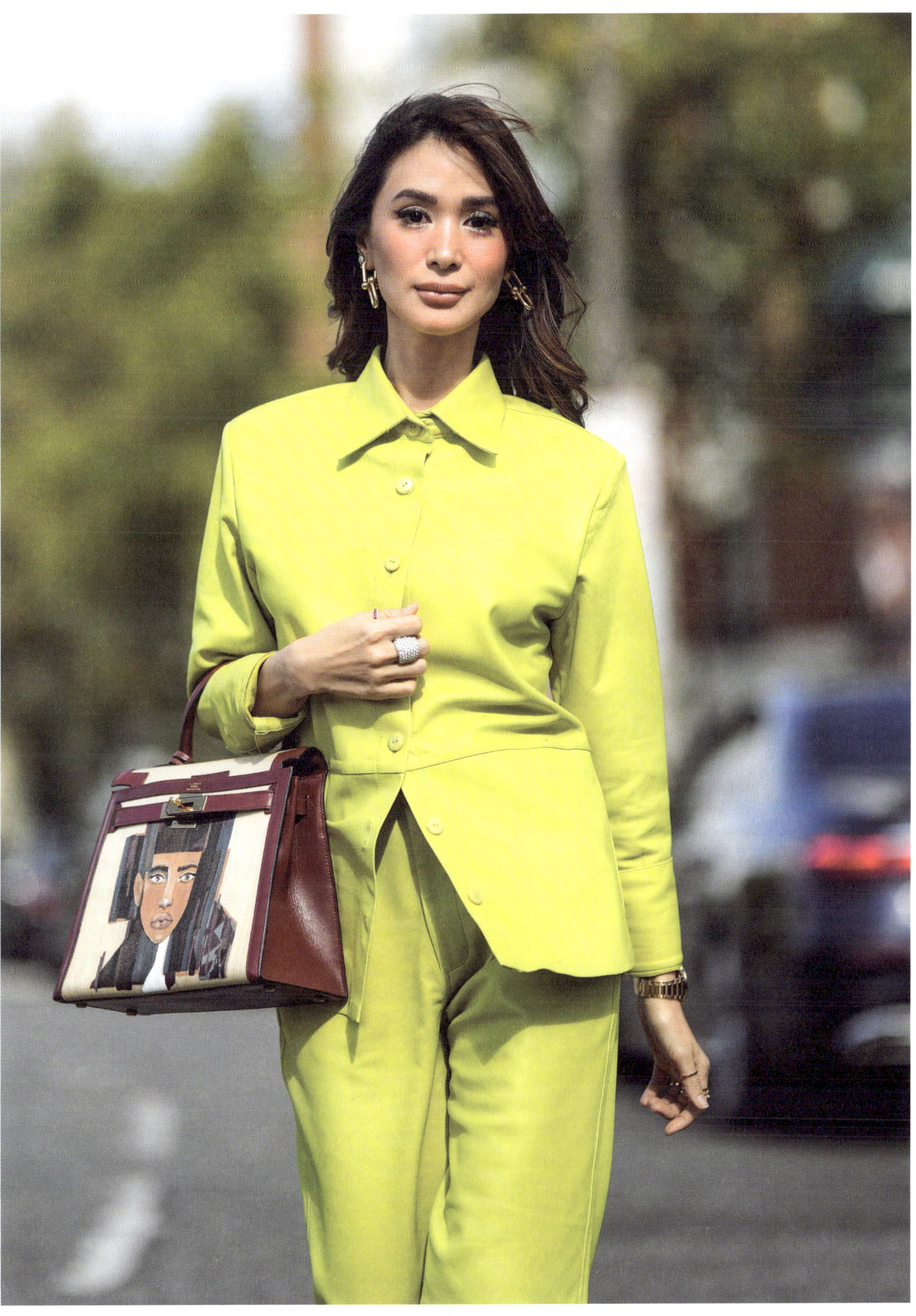

Heart Evangelista carrying a Kelly bag with print, Paris Fashion Week, October 2022

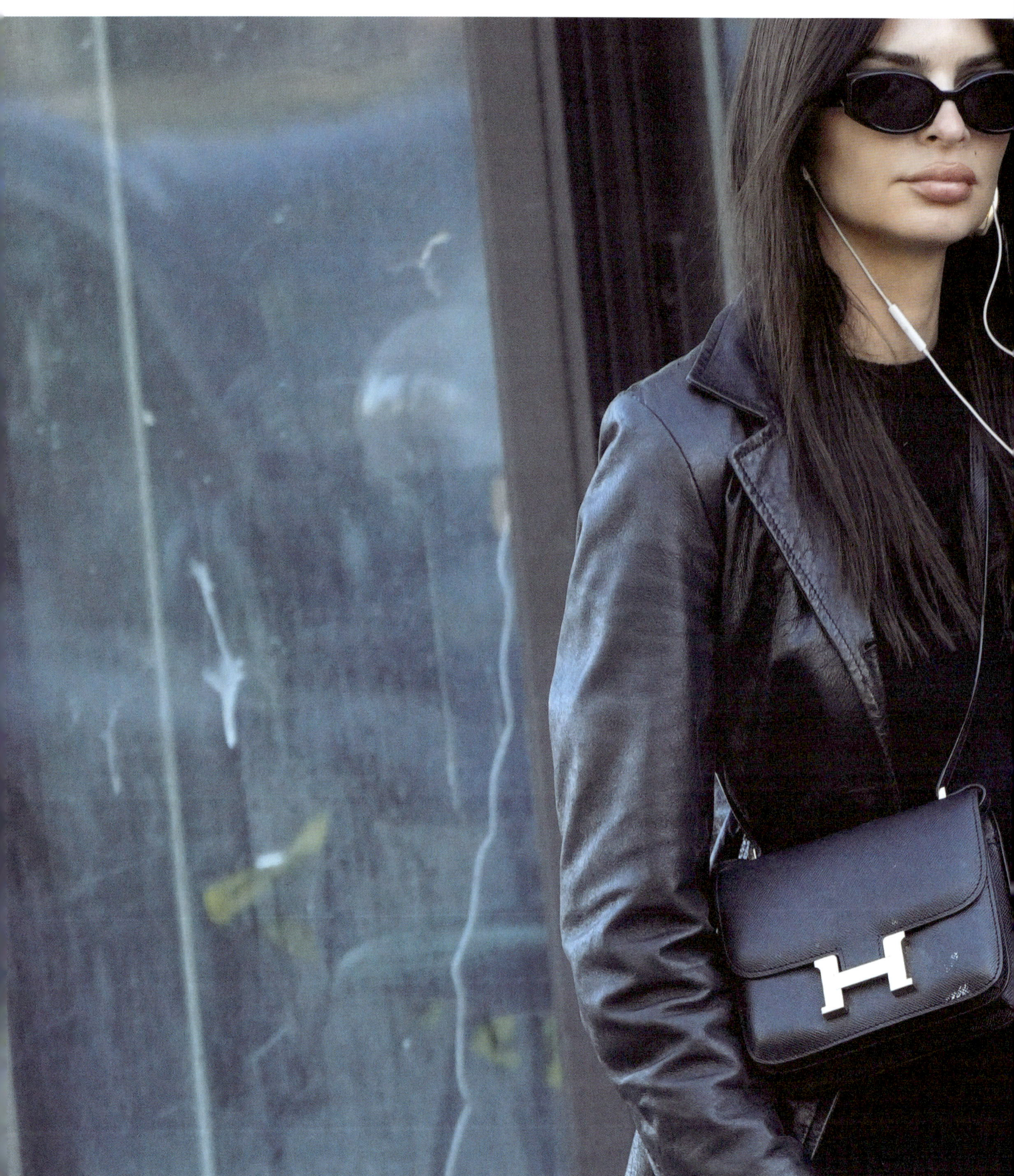

Emily Ratajkowski with her black Constance, New York City, 2023

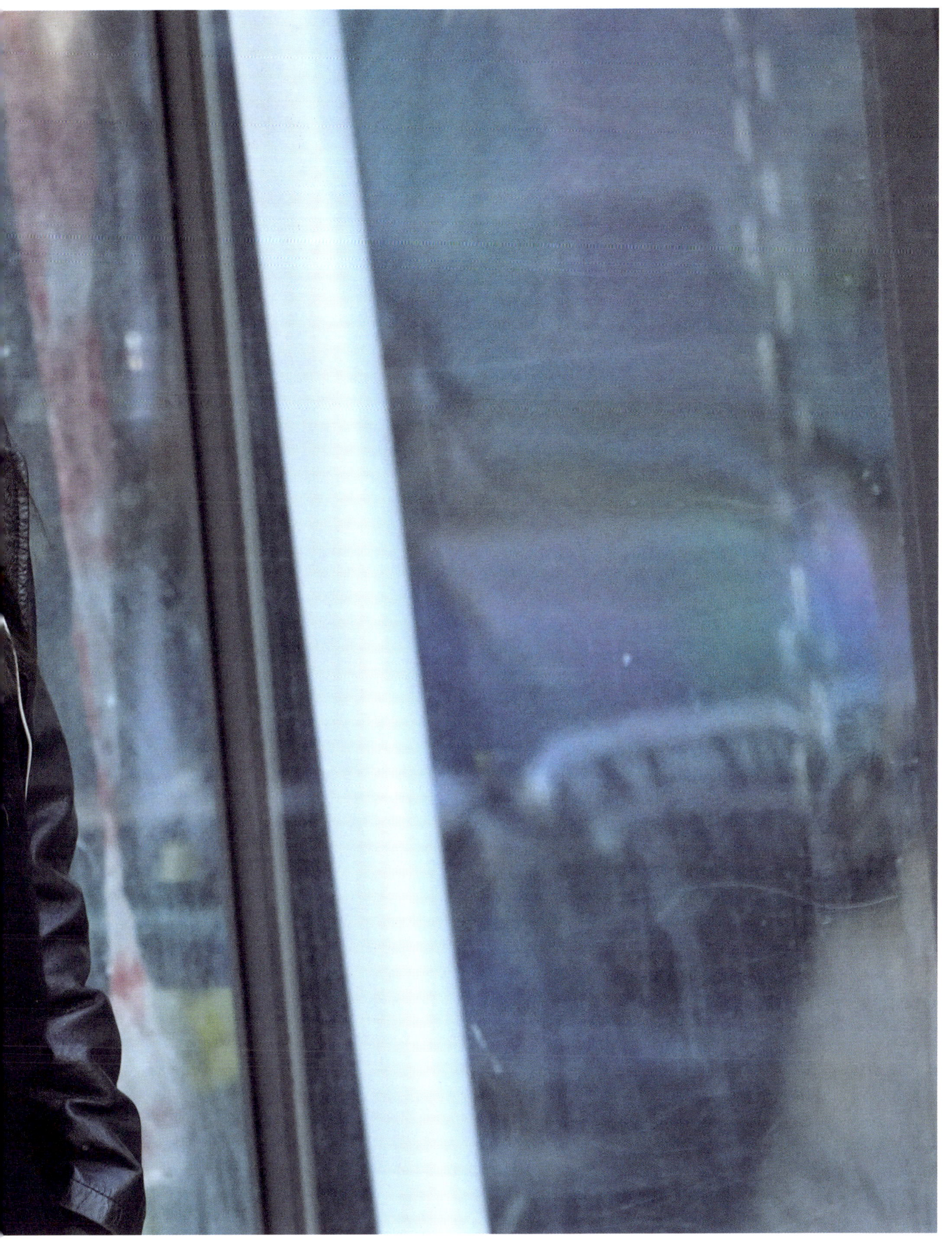

Cardi B carries Birkins at Red Martini Nightclub in Atlanta, 2020 (left) and at HOT 107.9's Birthday Bash in Atlanta, 2023 (right)

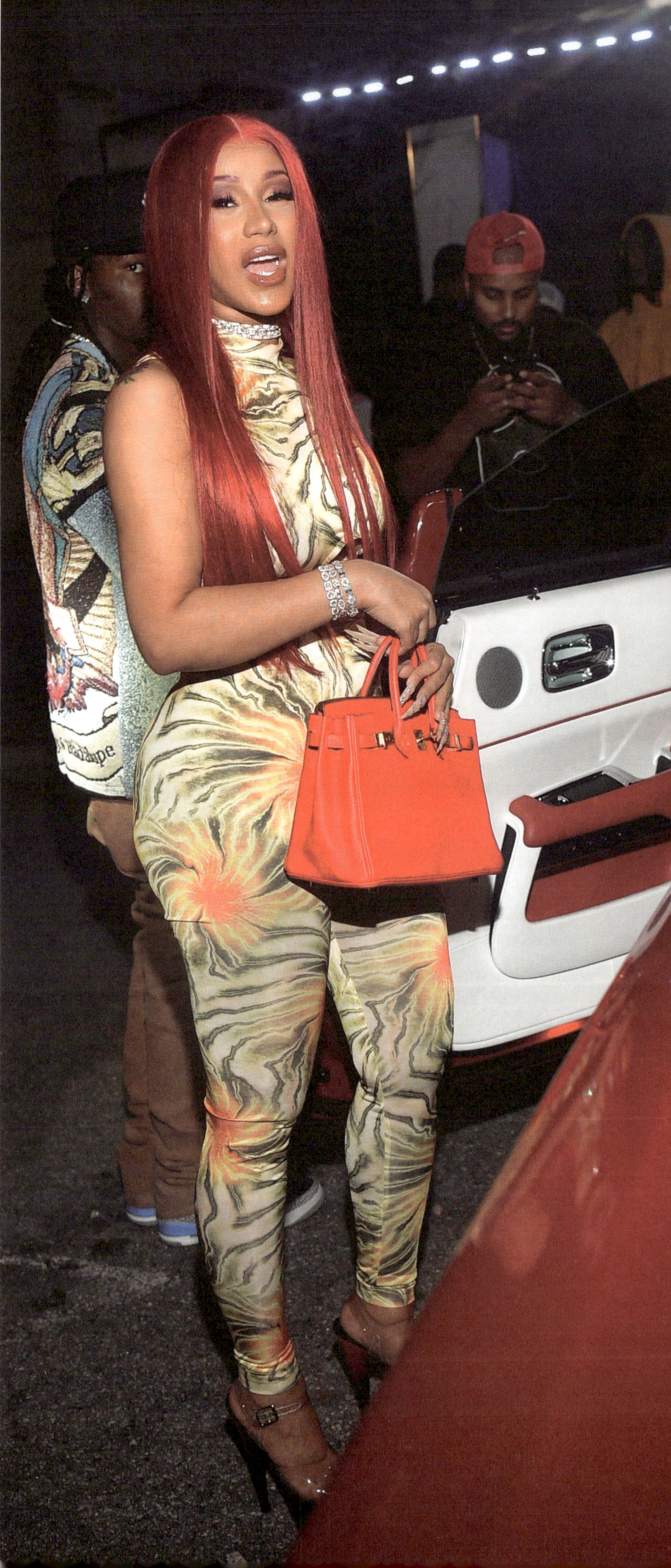

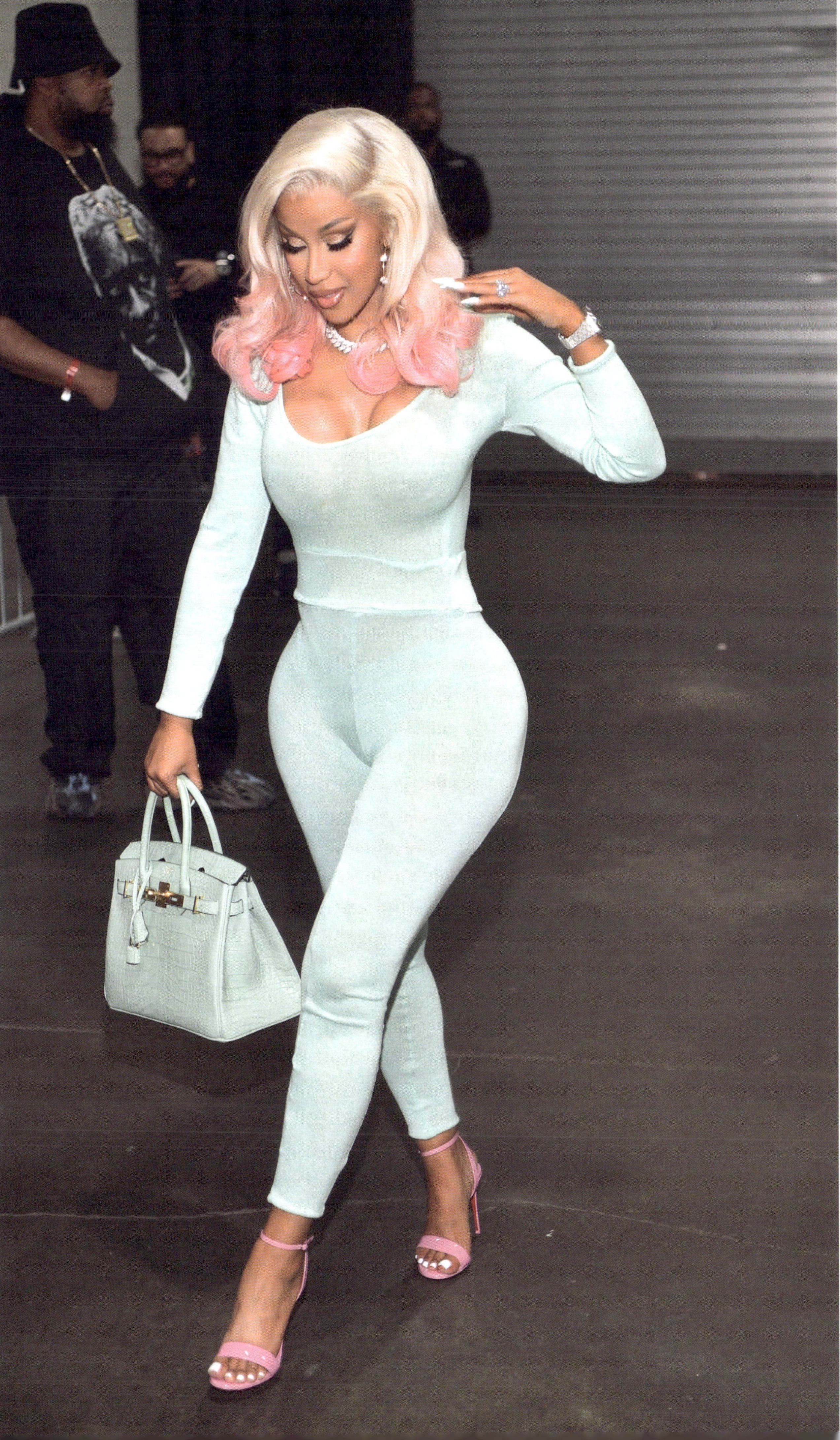

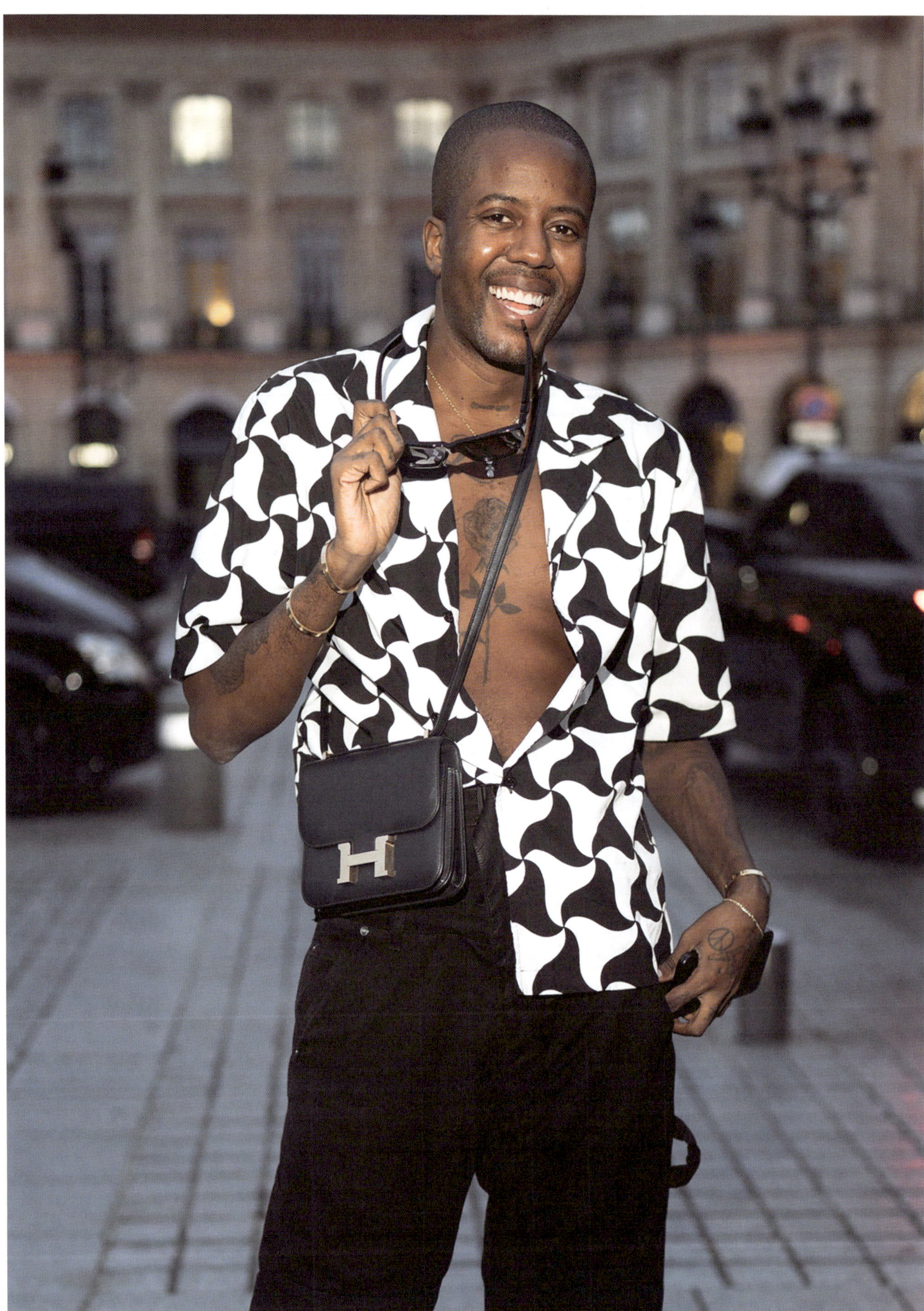

Vas Morgan wearing a Constance during Paris Fashion Week, September 2024

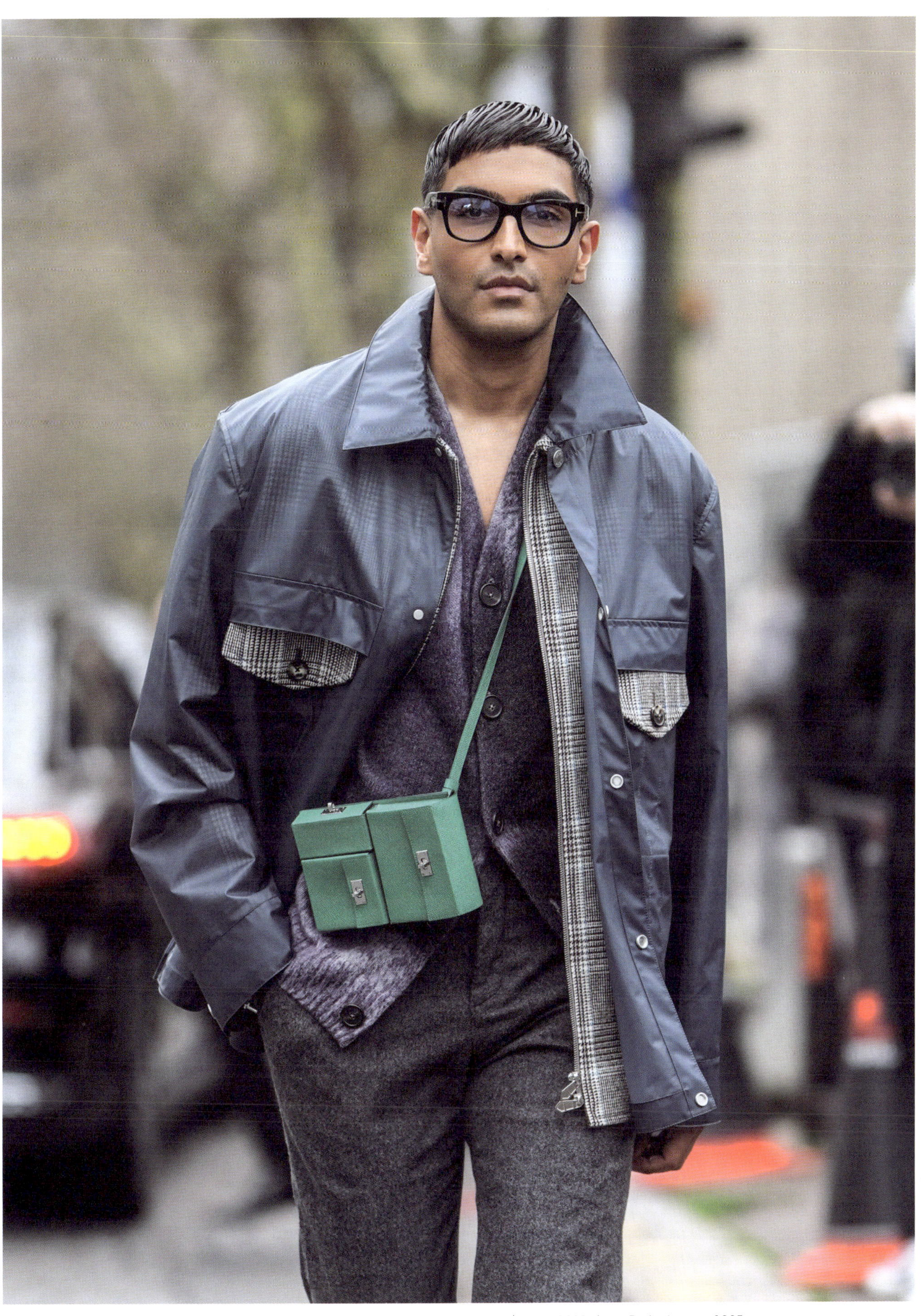

Rahi Chadda carries a Kelly Multipocket pouch outside Hermès during the Men's Fall/Winter 2025 show, Paris, January 2025

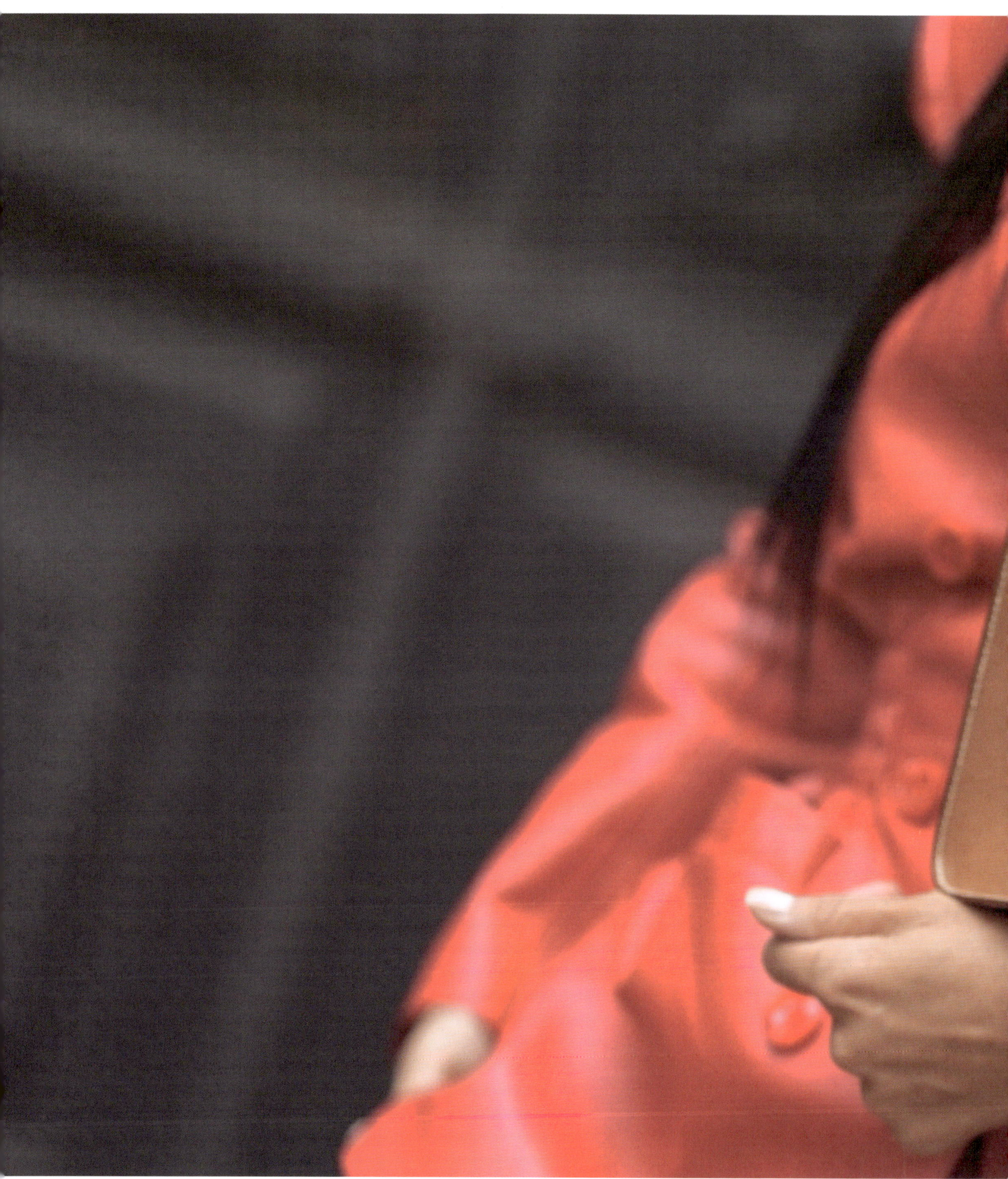

A gold on gold Birkin carried by a visitor to the Spring/Summer 2025 show, Paris, September 2024

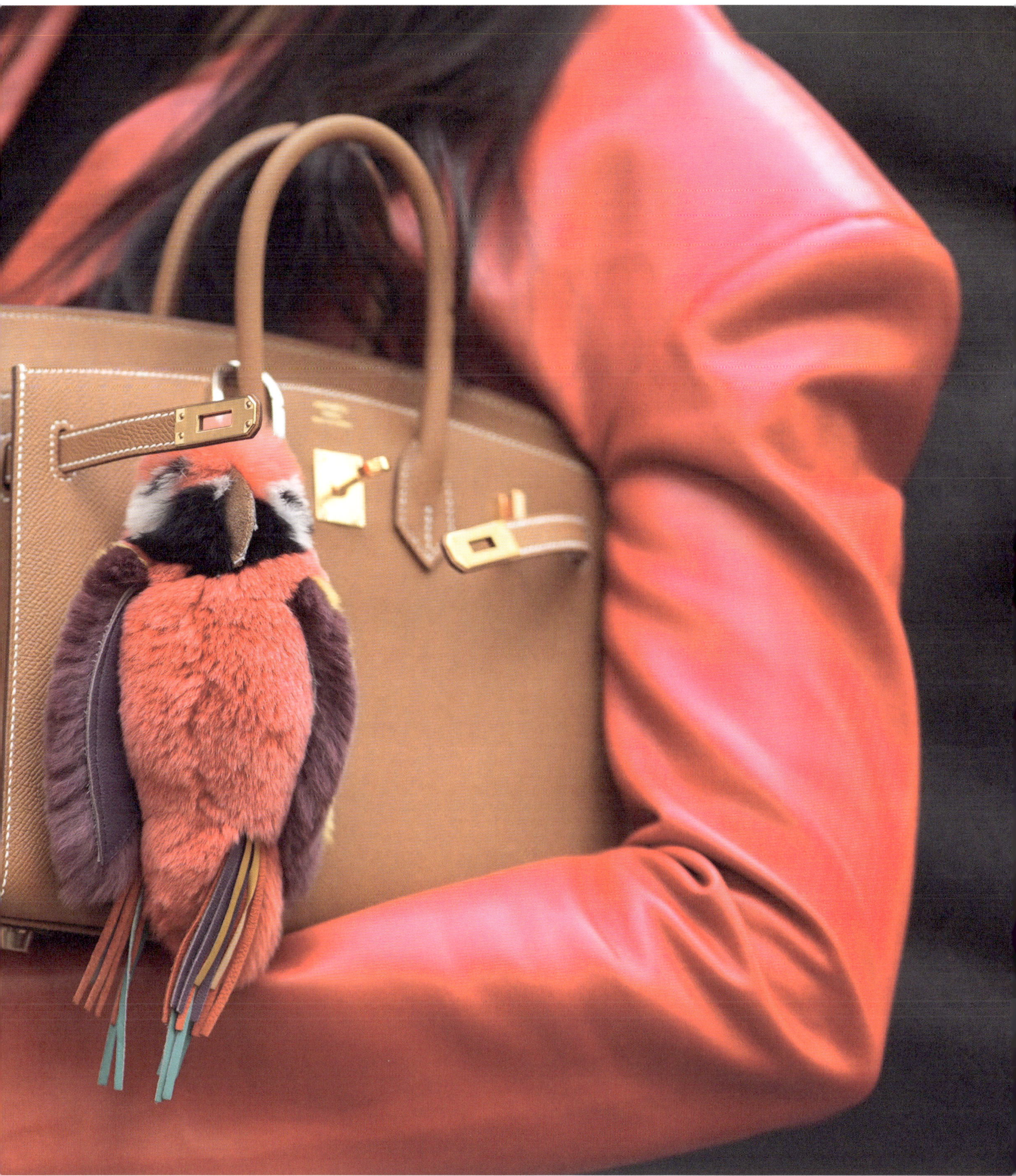

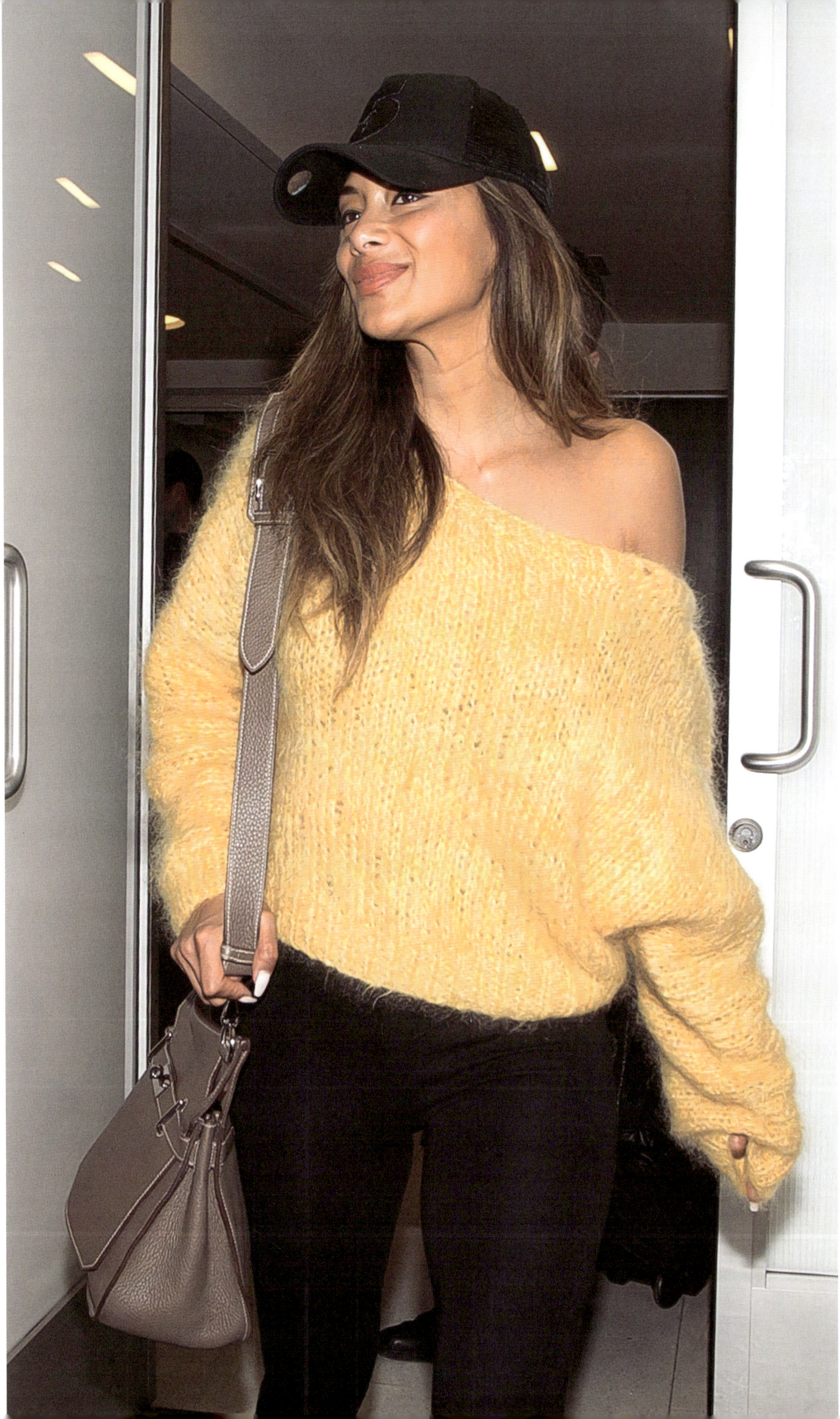

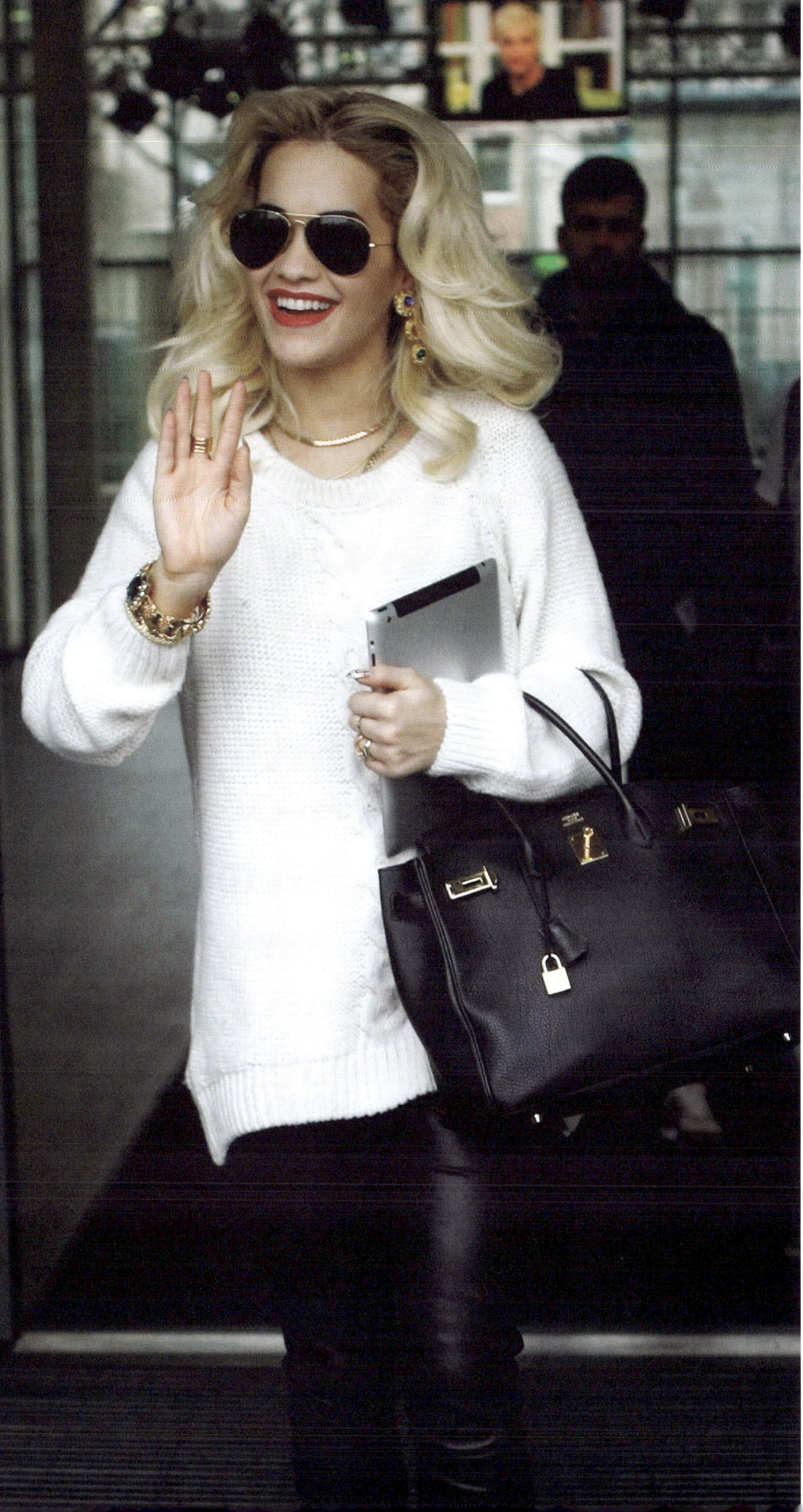

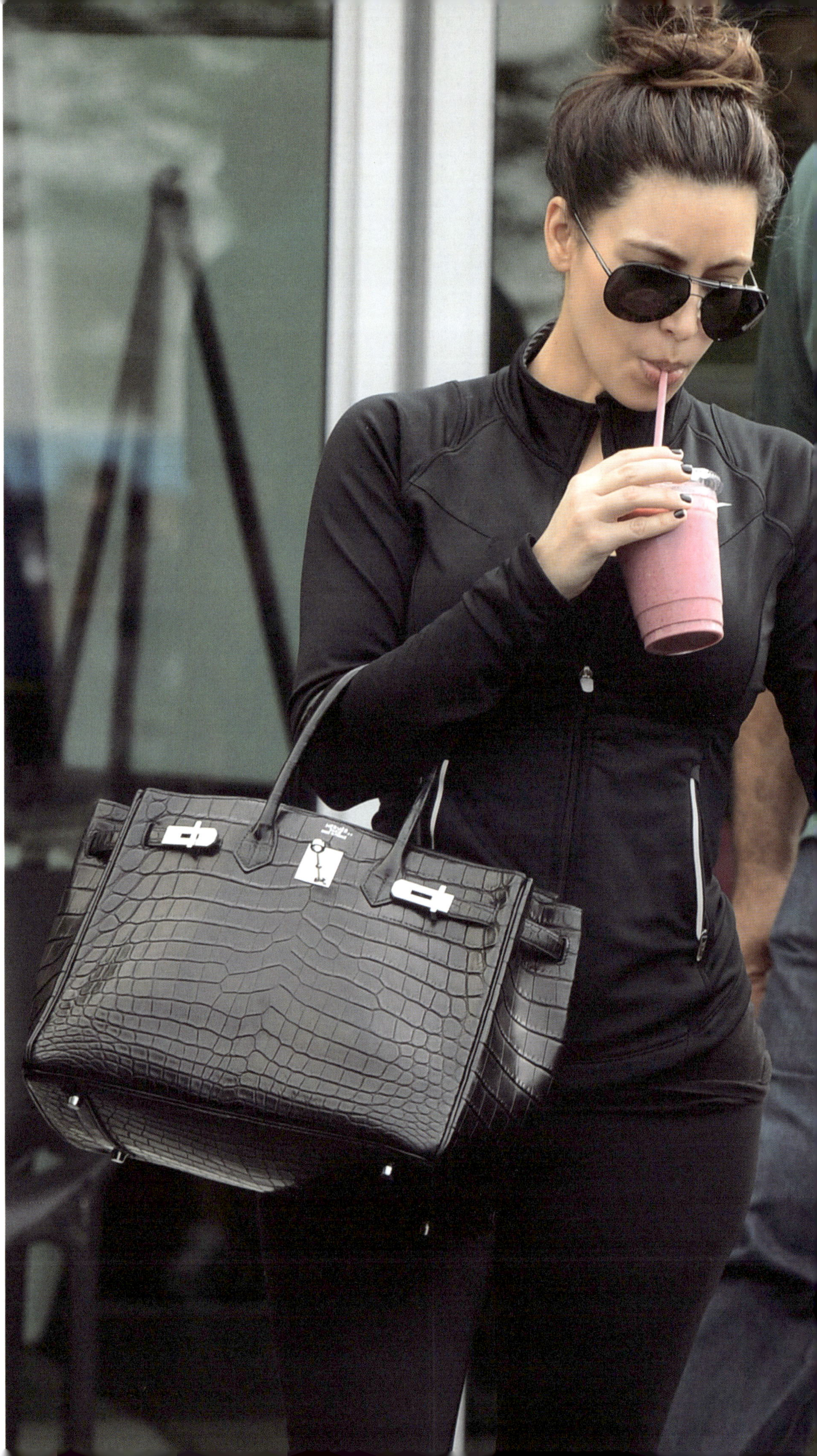

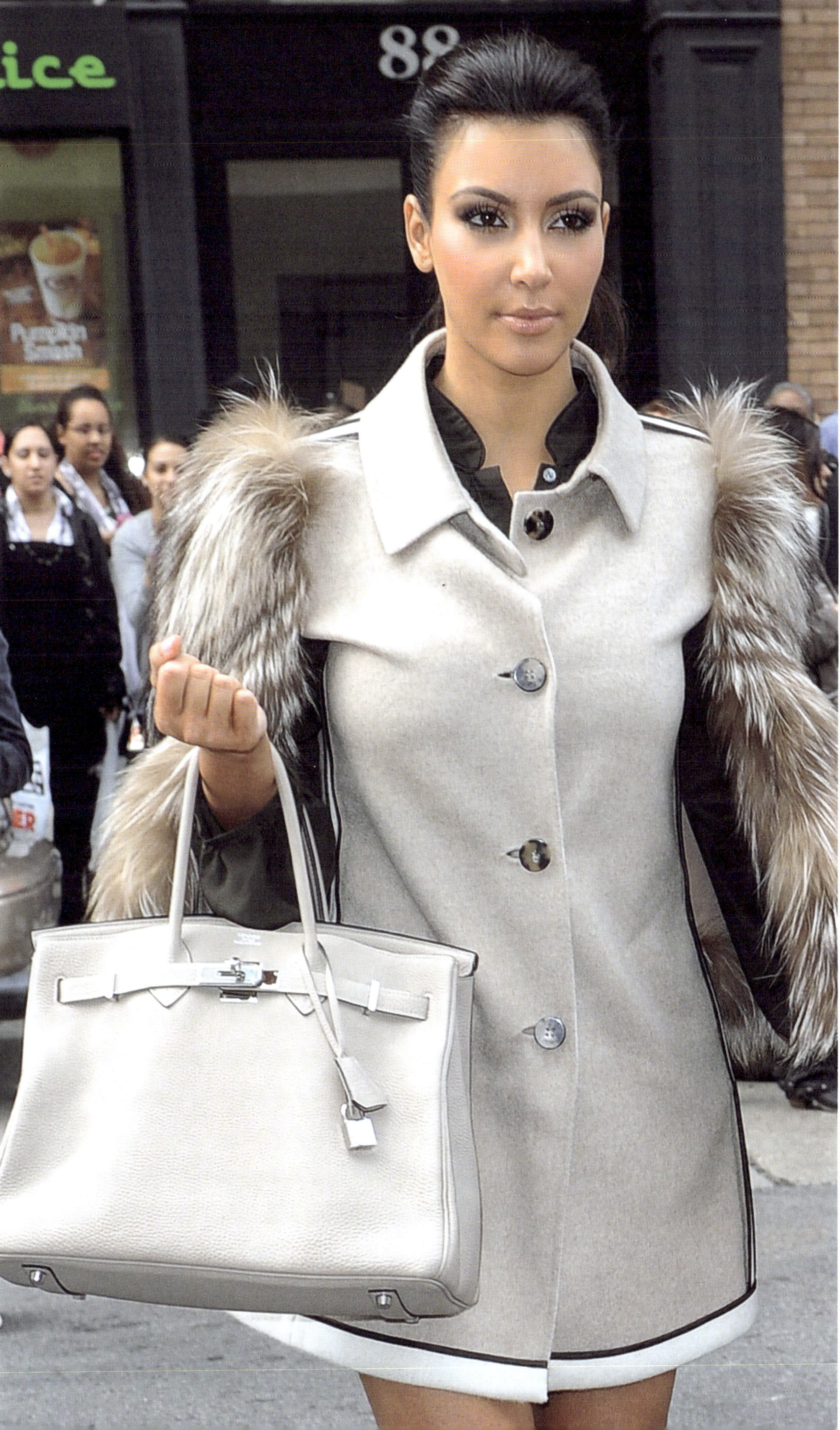
88

Page 146: Nicole Scherzinger carrying a Jypsiere bag at Los Angeles International airport on February 01, 2014

Page 147: Rita Ora leaves a TV studio carrying a Birkin, Berlin, November 2012

Pages 148–151: Kim Kardashian with Birkin bags from her seemingly infinite selection.

Page 152: Stylist Law Roach attends the launch of Tiffany Titan by Pharrell Williams at the Tiffany & Co. Landmark store on May 02, 2024 in New York City. He is carrying a Birkin in "Tiffany Blue"

Page 153: Jennifer Lopez with a Birkin bag in Paris, 2024

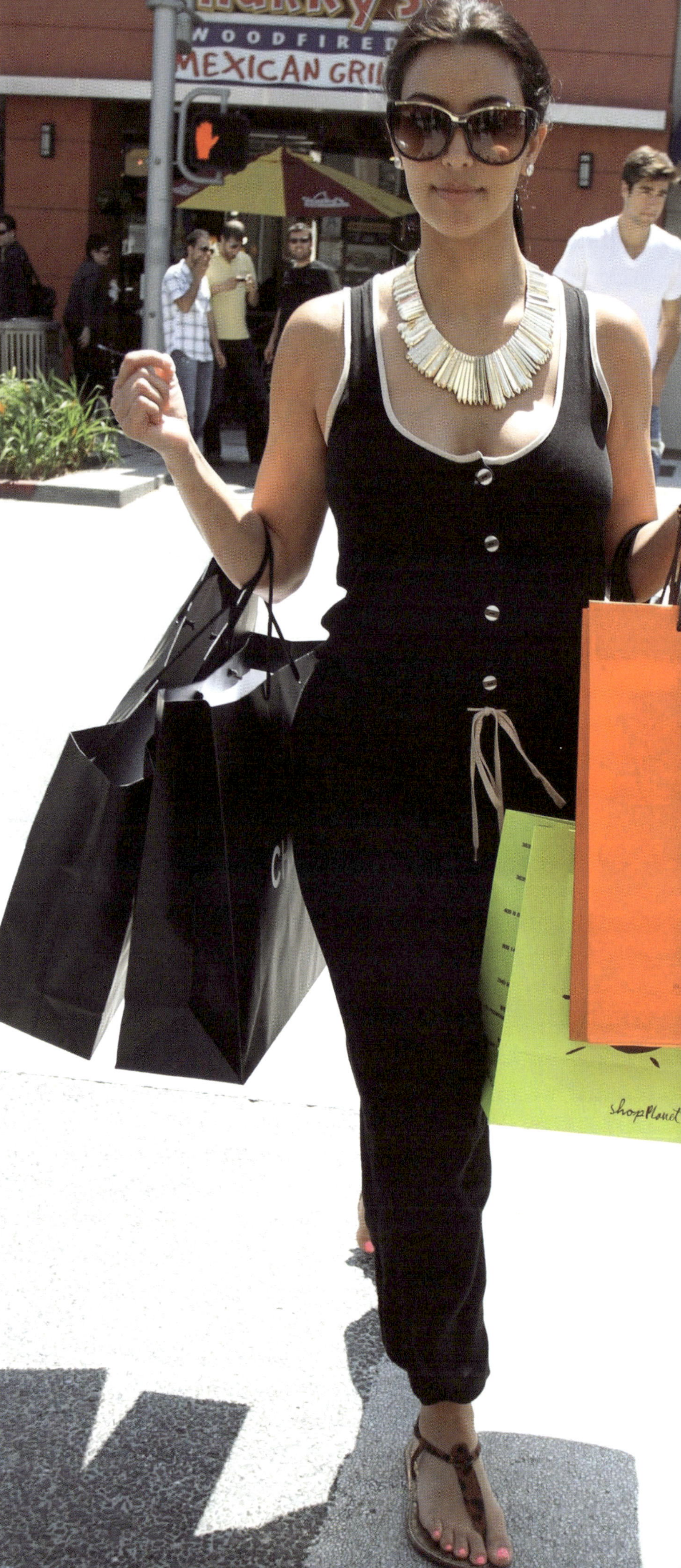

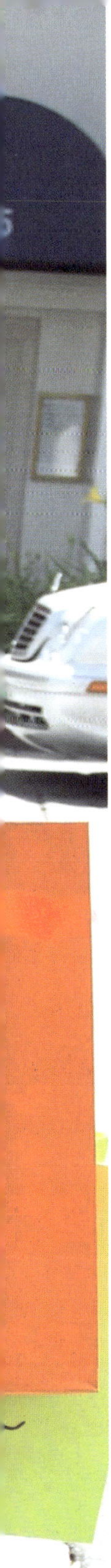

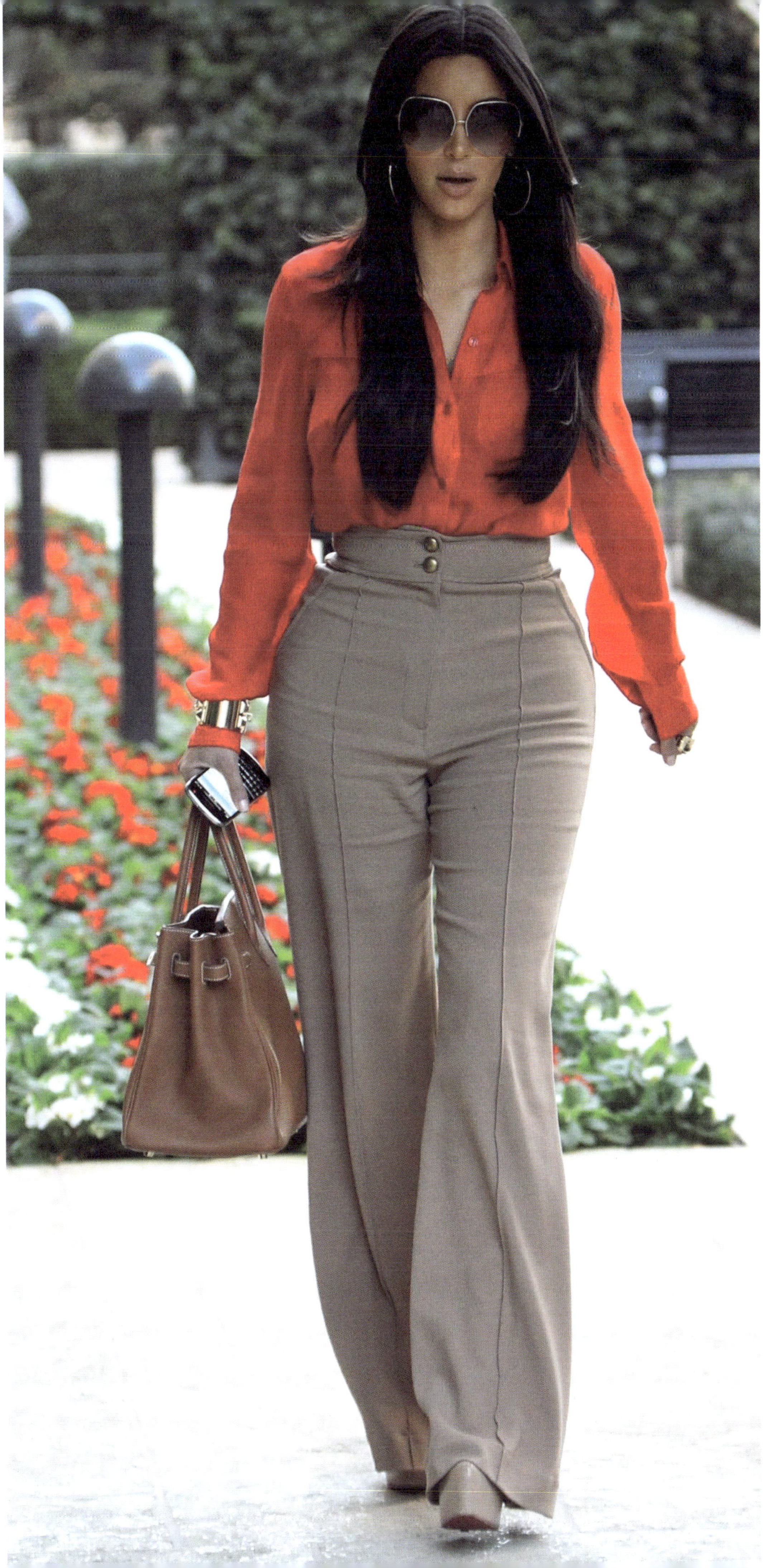

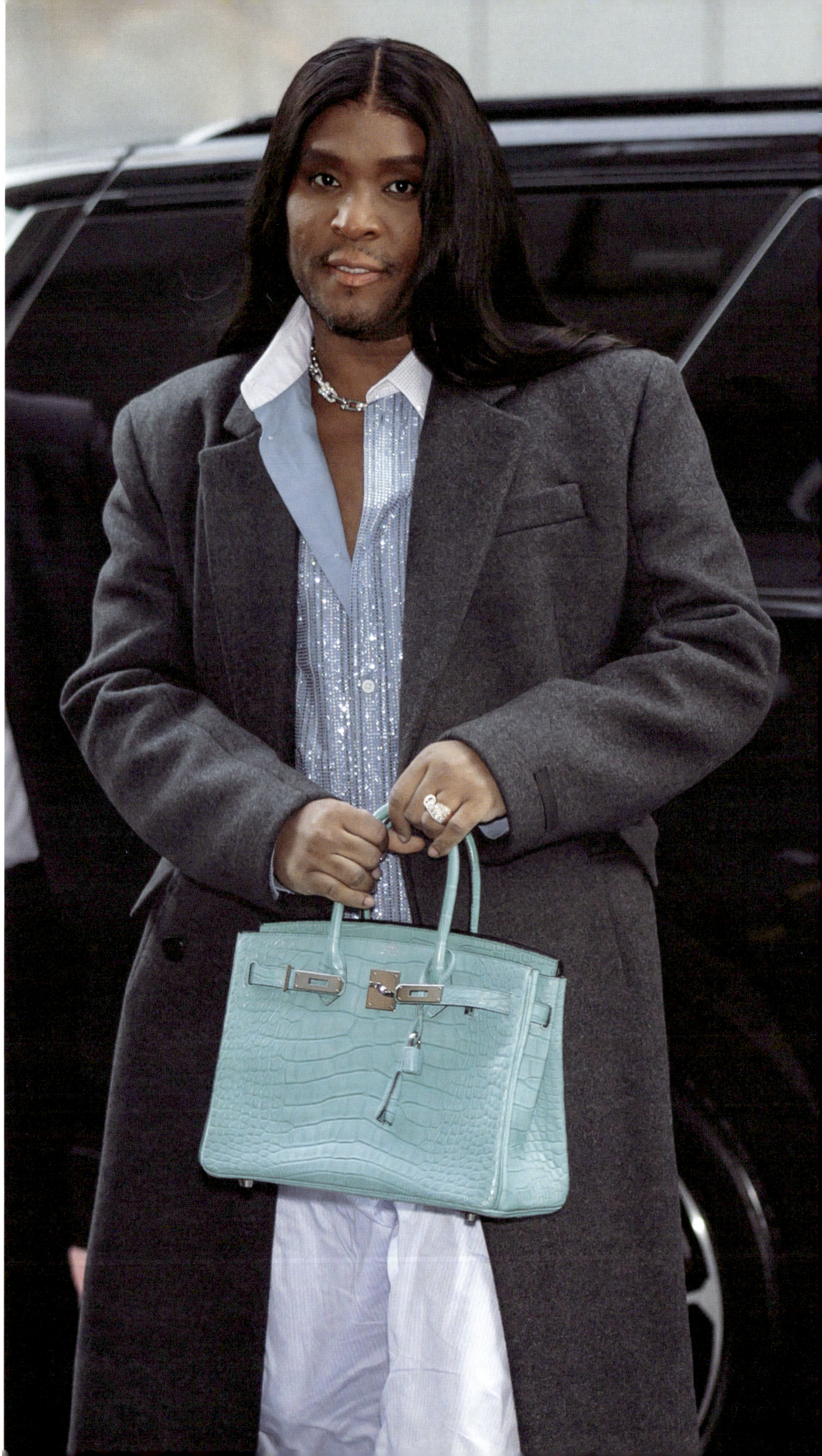

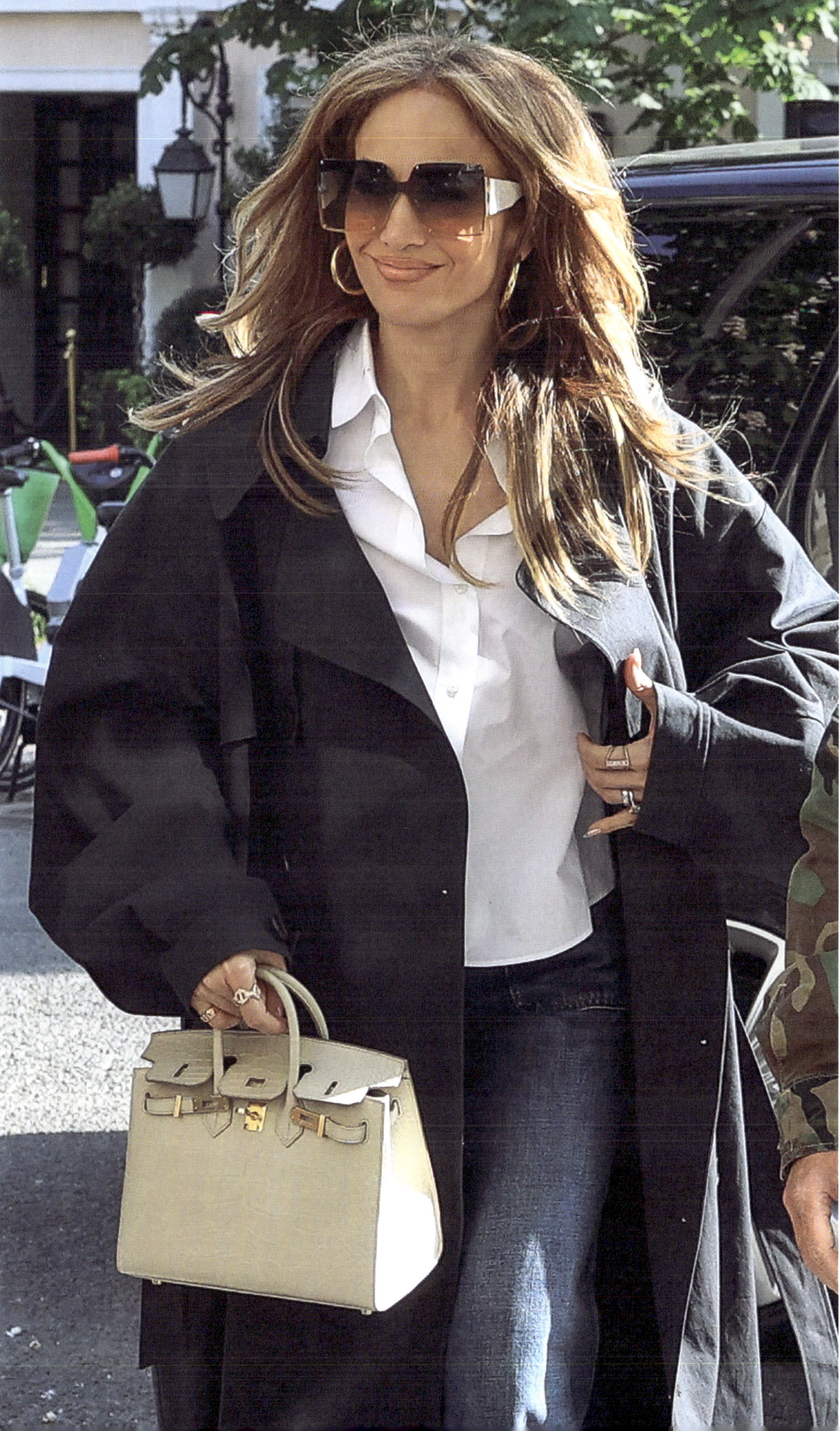

This page: Kesha carried her green Birkin through Midtown, New York City, April 2025

Next page: Diane Kruger wearing a Constance Elan in the East Village, New York City

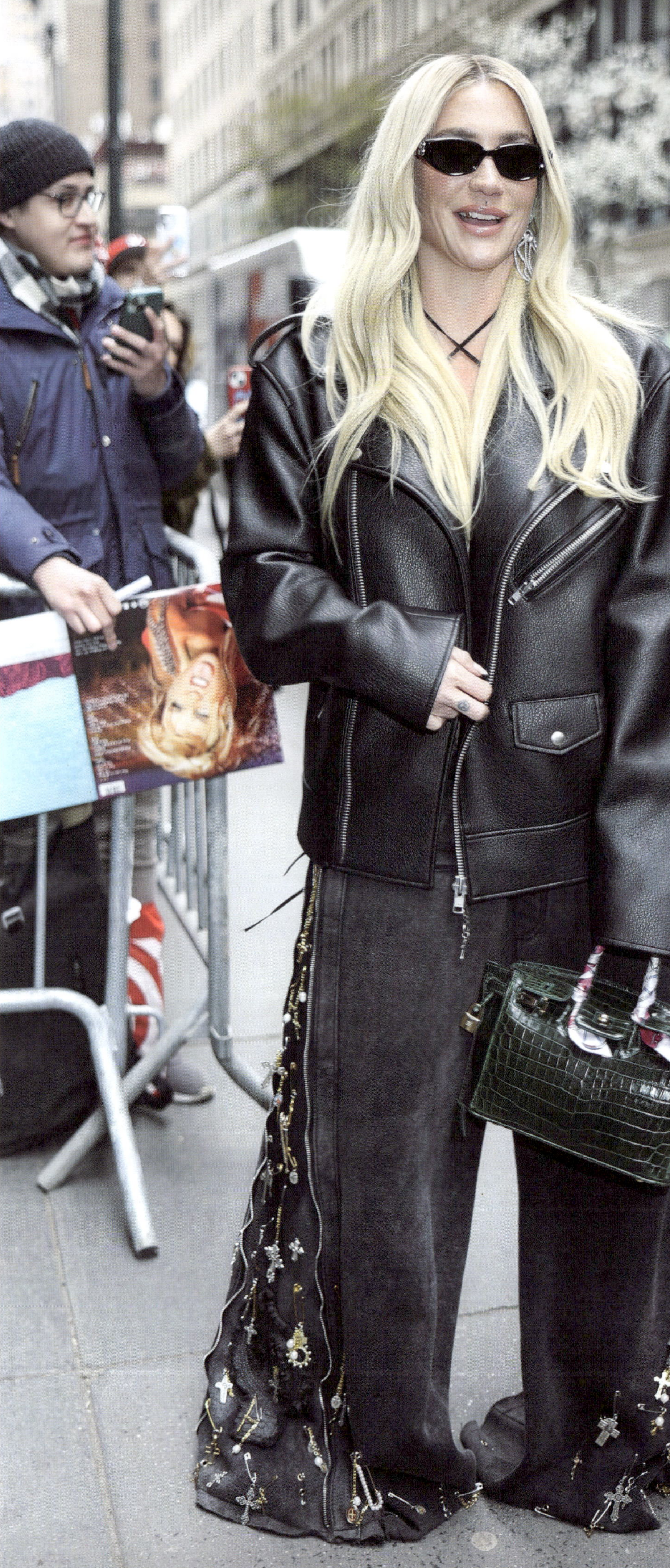

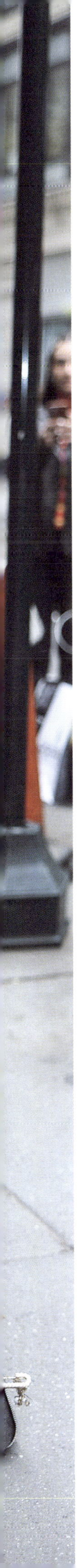

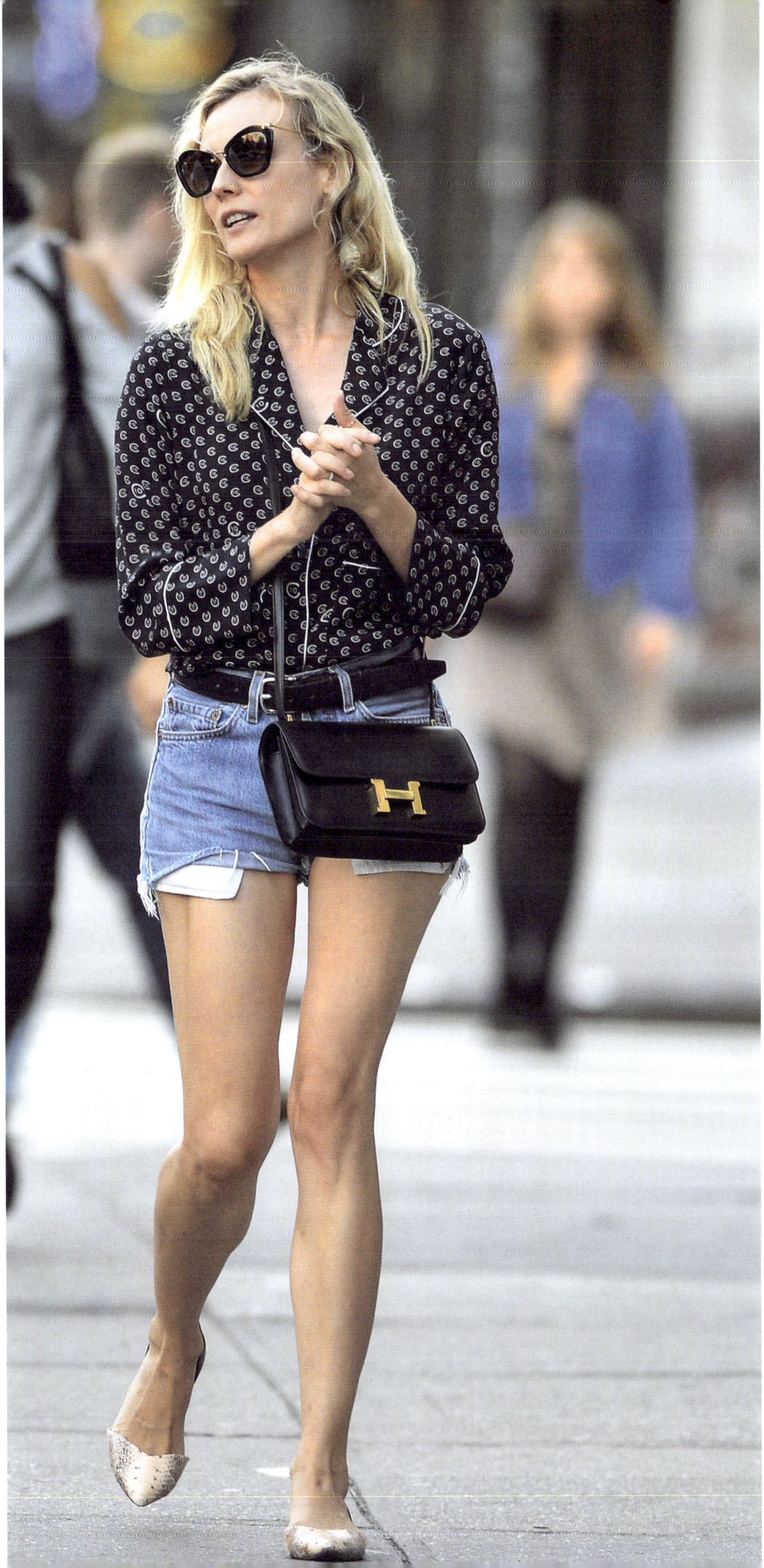

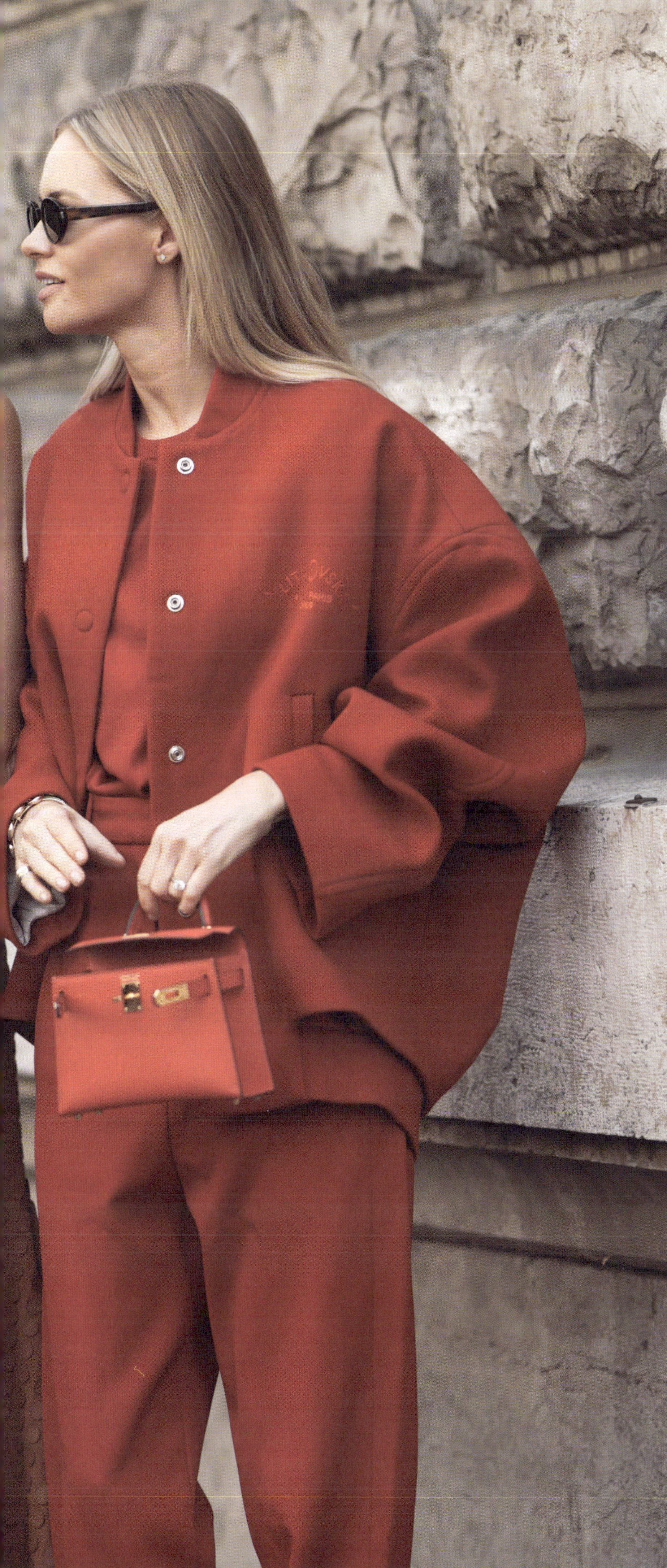

Paula Nata (center) is seen outside the Hermès show wearing a black Médor clutch, Claire Rose (right) carries a red Kelly bag, and another guest wears an orange Constance, Spring/Summer 2024 Paris Fashion Week, 2023

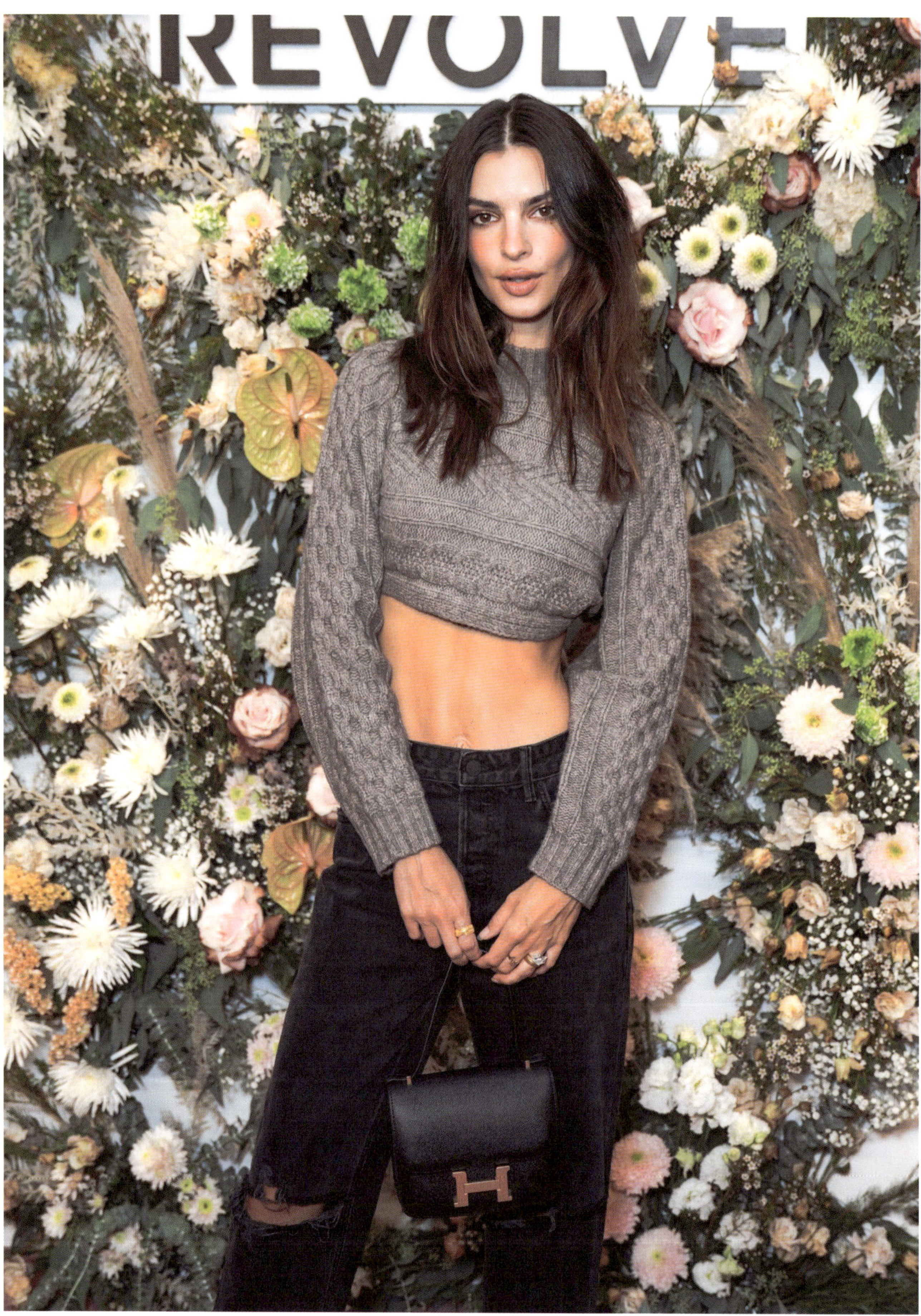

Emily Ratajkowski attends the Revolve Gallery at Hudson Yards carrying a black Constance, 2021

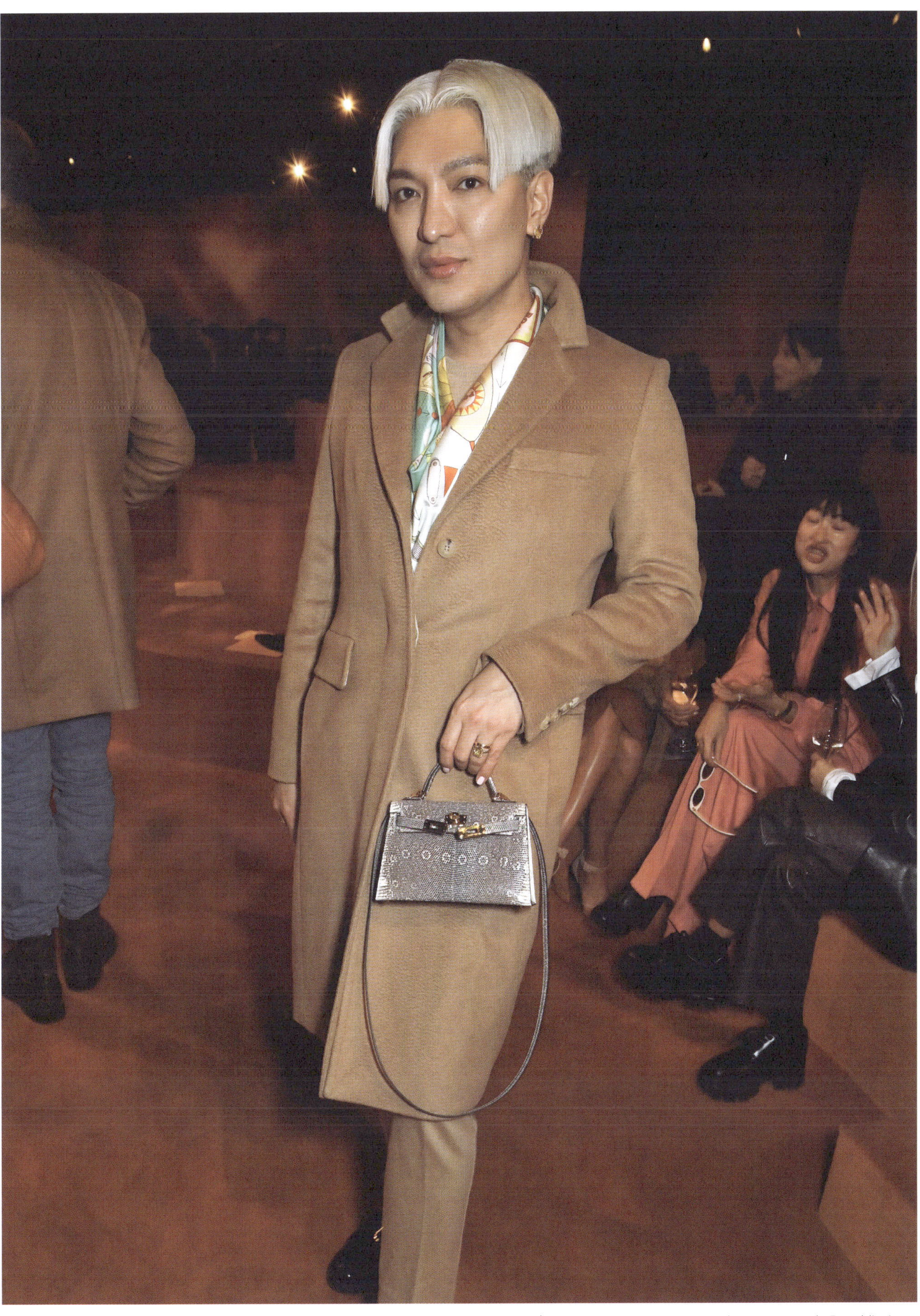

Bryanboy aka Bryan Yambao takes his front row seat, carrying a Mini Kelly at Hermès Fall/Winter 2023 women's runway show at La Garde Republicaine on March 4, 2023, Paris

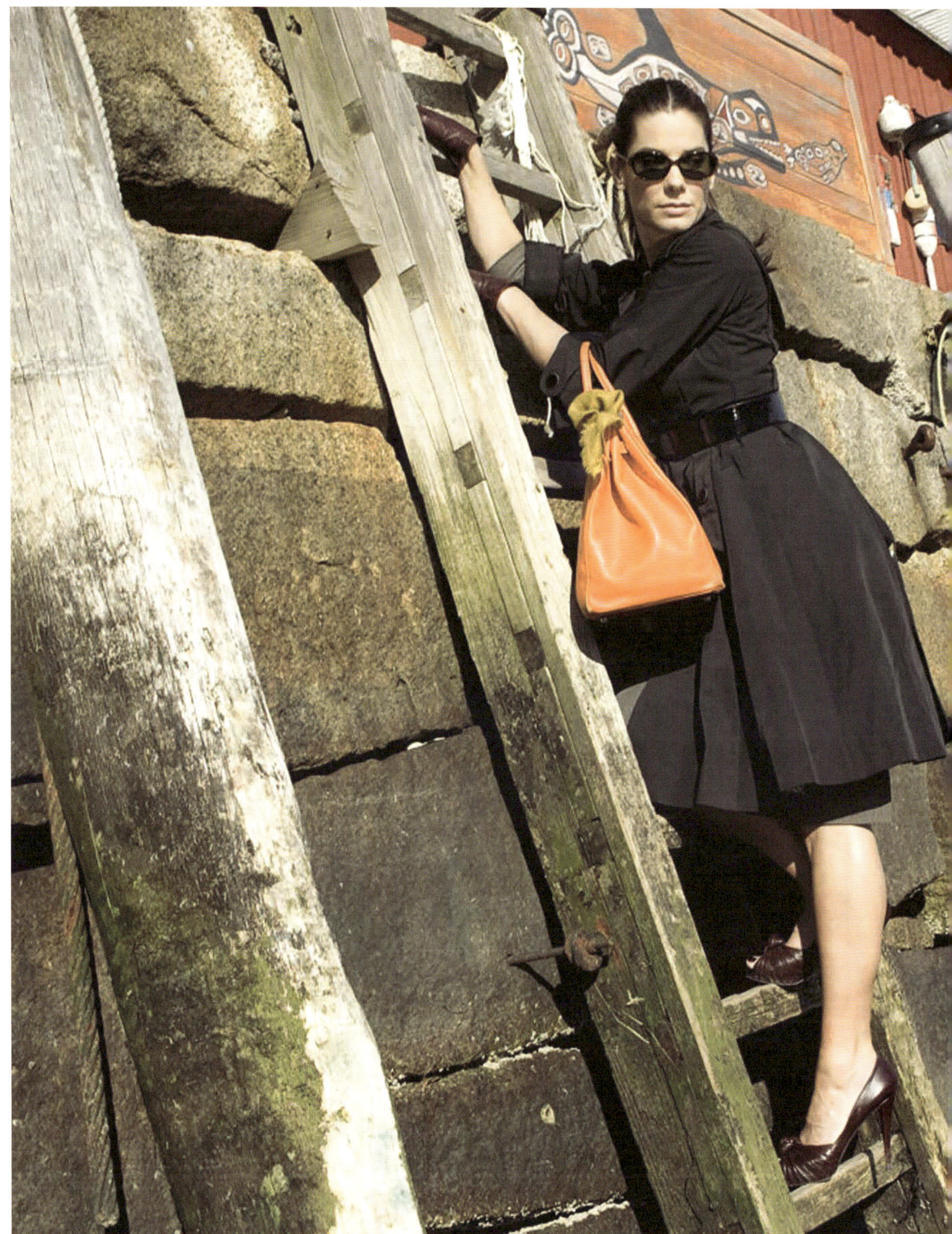

Sandra Bullock carries a Birkin in the 2009 movie *The Proposal* by director Anne Fletcher

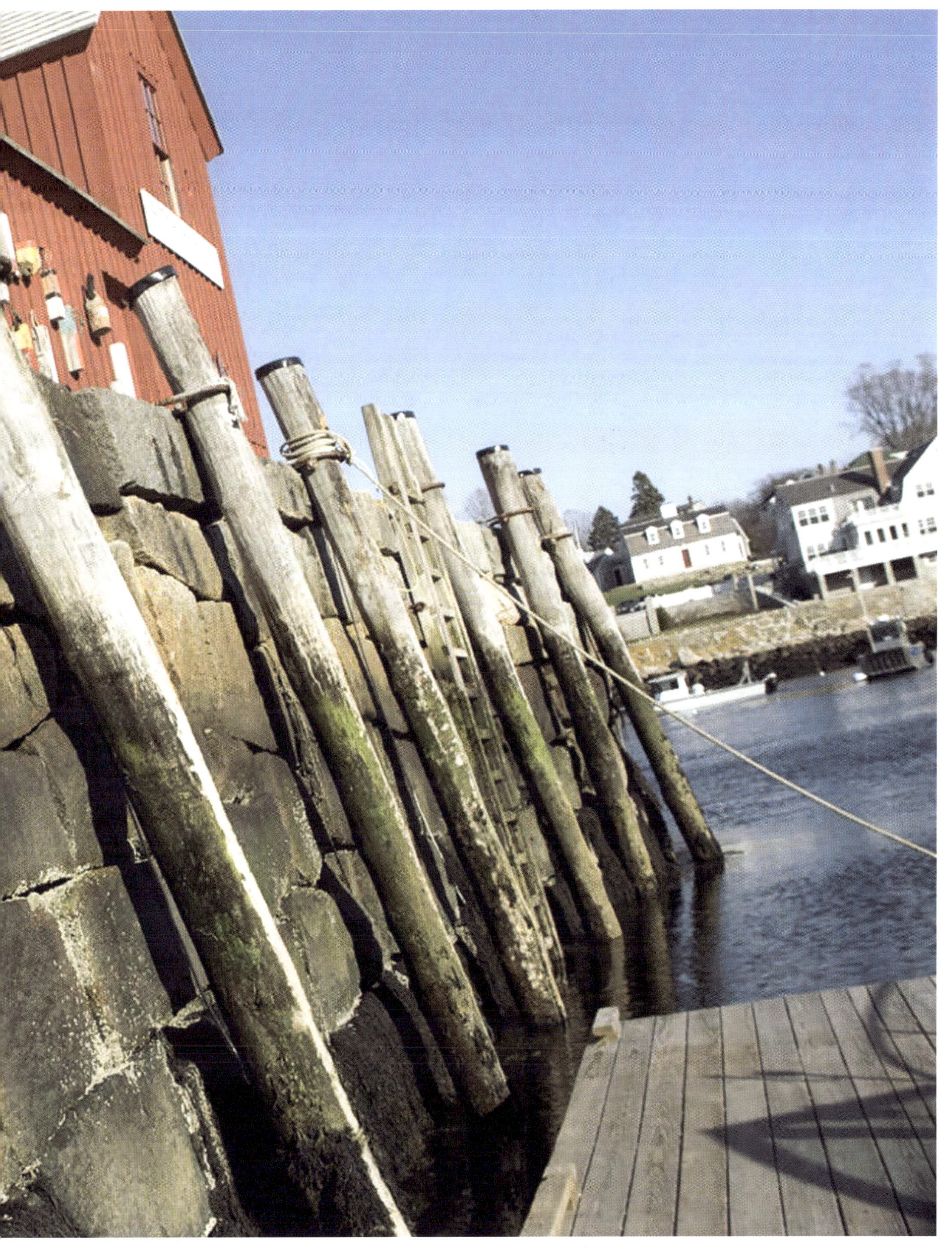

Victoria Beckham carries an ostrich Birkin at Gare du Nord station, Paris, 2019, and a black exotic skin Birkin on January 18, 2020 in Paris

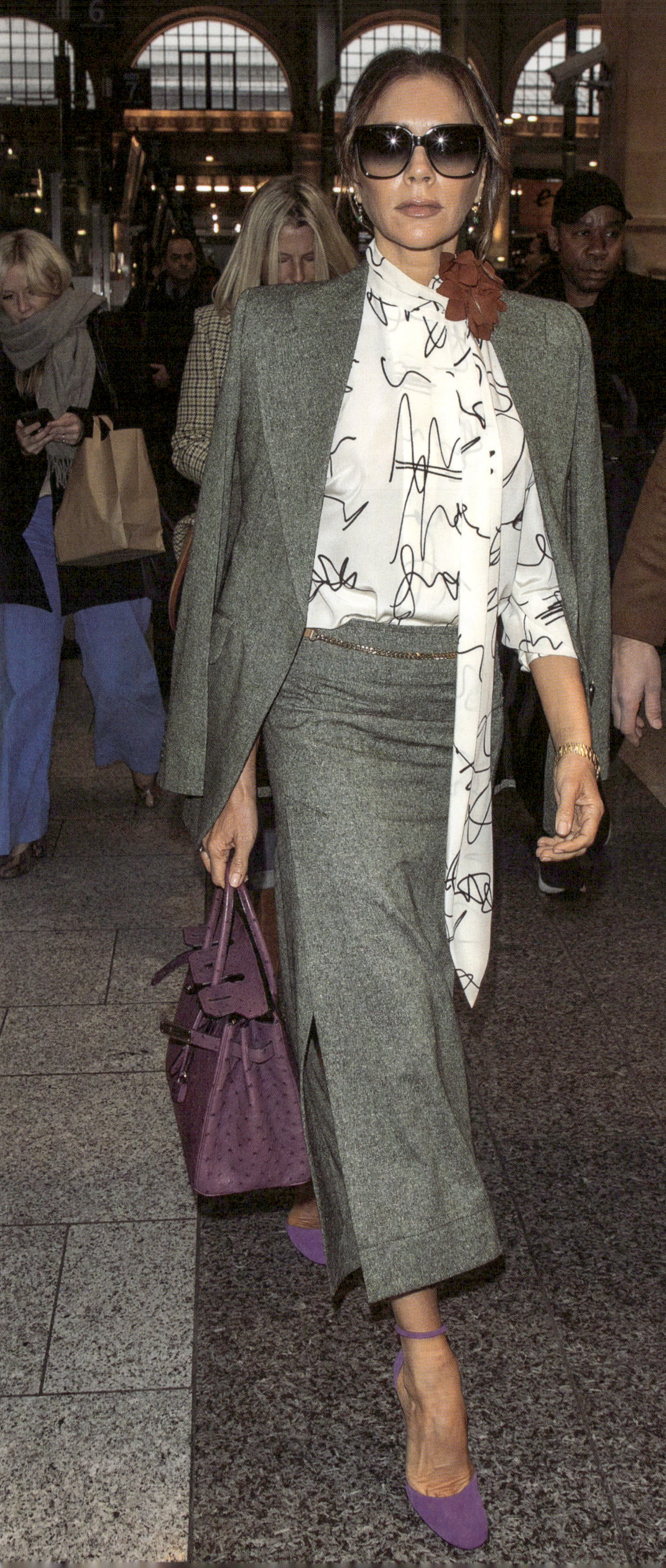

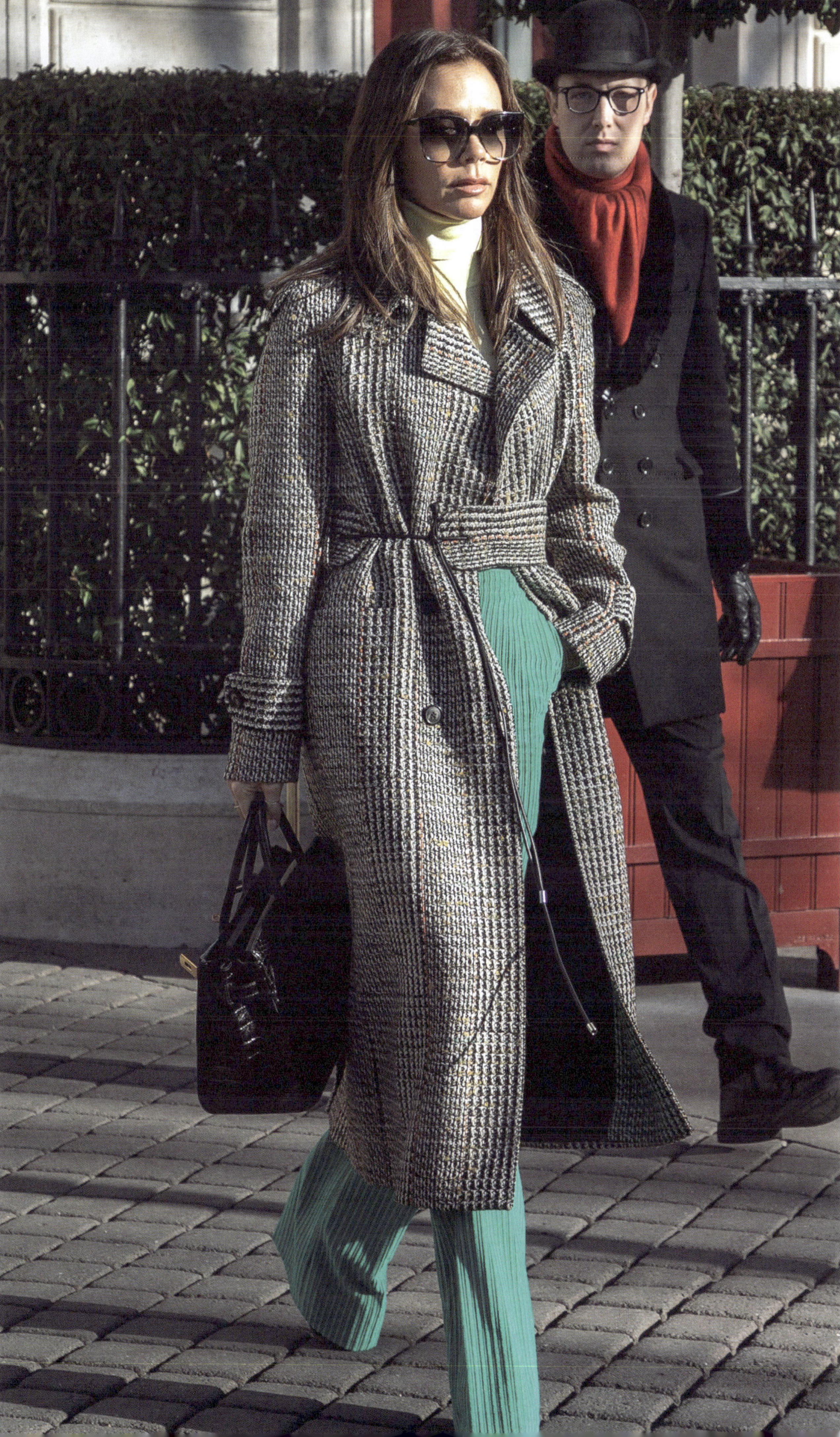

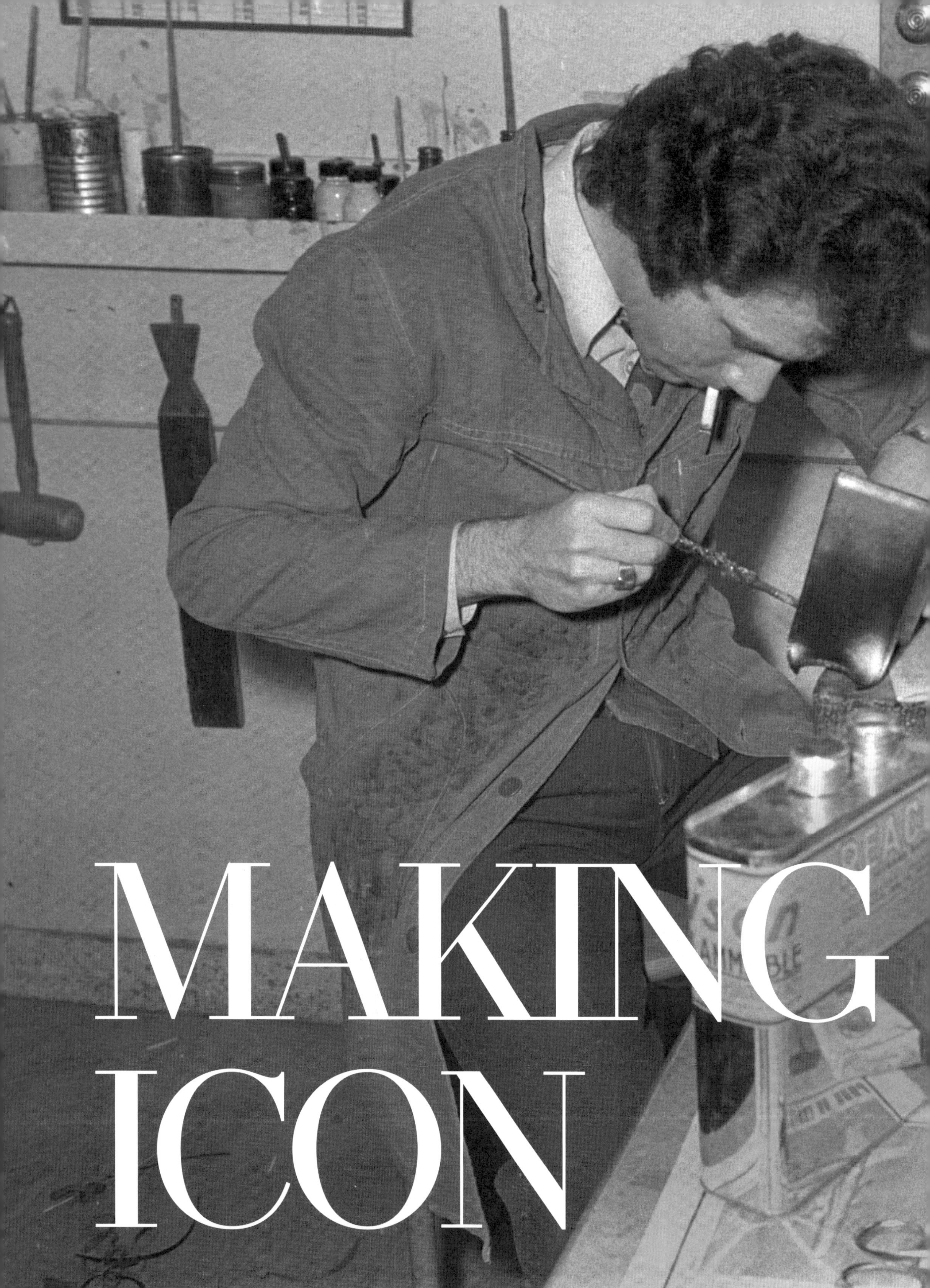

MAKING ICON

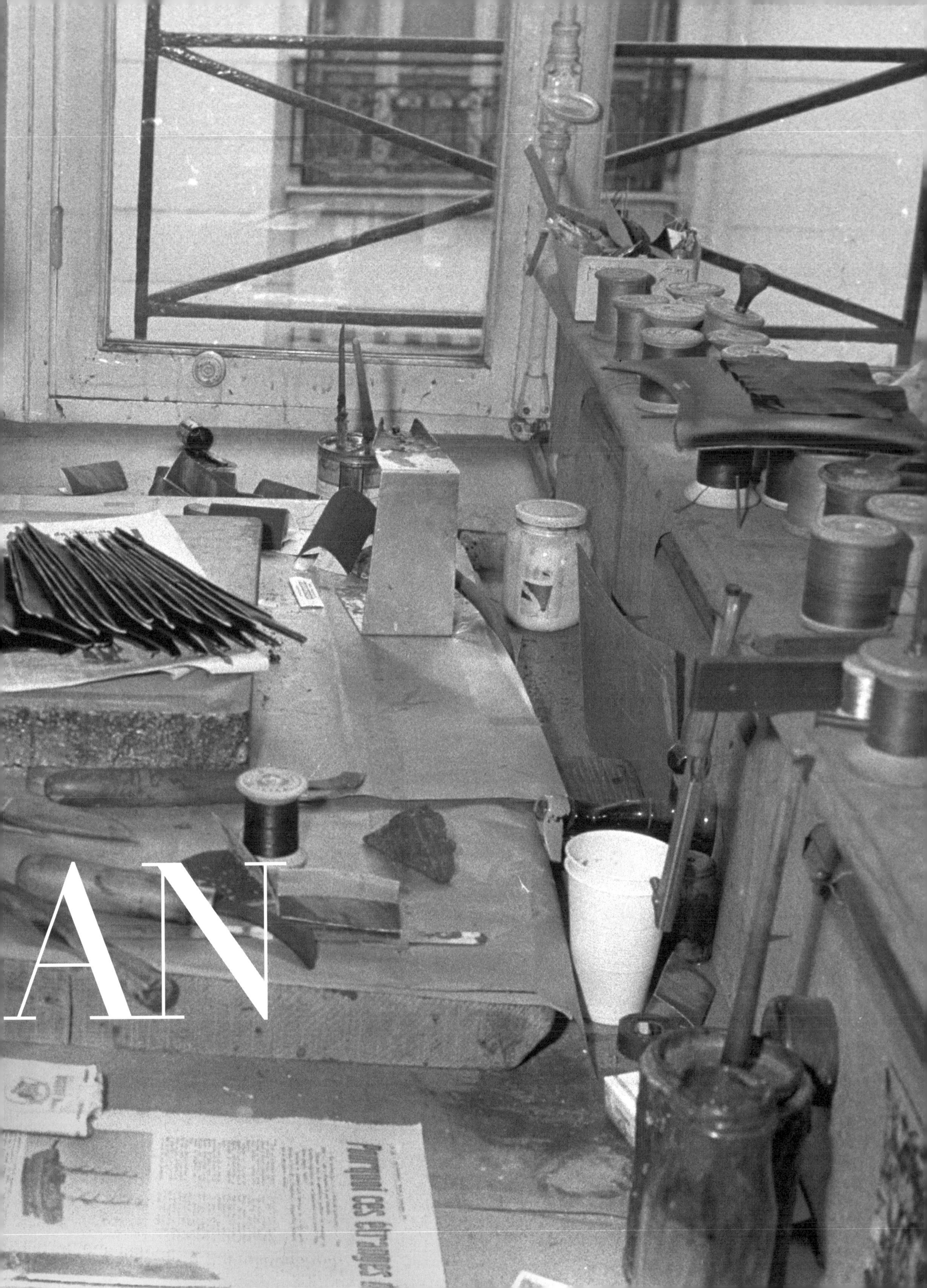
AN

CRAFT AND CREATION

In terrible news for many bank account balances, the rumor that Hermès bags are available as seconds is a myth. While counterfeiters claim to use the same leather and artisan methods as the Hermès workshops, it is a dream that is just too good to be true. In one case, however, a group of thieves that included former Hermès leatherworkers did use stolen Hermès offcuts, tools, zips, faulty bags *and* those iconic orange boxes to create fake Birkin bags and rake in a profit of over €2 million. In 2020, the ten criminals were fined and received sentencing, including jail time, in a French court, following several years of intense investigation.

Beyond this insider criminal ring, fakes smell plastic-y, are floppy and unstructured, feature cheap metal, wonky stitching, misplaced authenticity stamps, spelling mistakes and sometimes even contain dangerous levels of chemicals. Aside from the significant crime of intellectual property theft, the fake bag business is linked to human trafficking, the drug trade and gun smuggling. Under many countries' laws, fake bags are to be destroyed immediately, so if you travel with one, beware. For those even vaguely aware of the real deal, a fake bag should be considered an unforgivable fashion faux pas. In addition to being illegal, fakes are vulgar and embarrassing to be seen with.

The desire to own a piece of Hermès heritage remains strong; combined with the prohibitive price tag of authentic Hermès pieces, it can drive some shoppers to search for fake versions. Dupe culture is particularly widespread on social media, perhaps boosted by the number of influencers flaunting their wealth via their extensive handbag collections and wardrobe tours. In 2024, a Walmart bag that looked similar to the Birkin went viral in TikTok unboxing videos. The tote, sold for \$78-\$102 by third-party sellers, was only available online and was nicknamed the 'Wirkin.' It was a painfully inadequate poor-quality imitation of the real bag, and Walmart discontinued them in 2025. Yet bags not dissimilar to Hermès iconic pieces are still for sale on Amazon and in countless online ads that pop up on social media. The buyer should certainly be wary of deals that seem too good to be true.

As prices across the planet rise on everything from food and fuel to fashion, Hermès have their own annual price hikes in place. Usually European items are the first to be given a larger price tag, with increases of 1% to 4% depending on the model. Introduced at the start of each new year, the new prices then roll out across the globe. However in recent years, prices have been pushed even higher. In 2023, price hikes ranged from 8-21%, with exotic leathers seeing the biggest jump, while 2024 saw the price of a Kelly 25 *Retourné* in Togo climbing 13%. According to CEO Alex Dumas, subsequent price increases will be based on production and material costs, which are also rising across the globe, and have not been adjusted to reflect demand.

Pages 164/165 and next page: Manufacture of a Constance bag

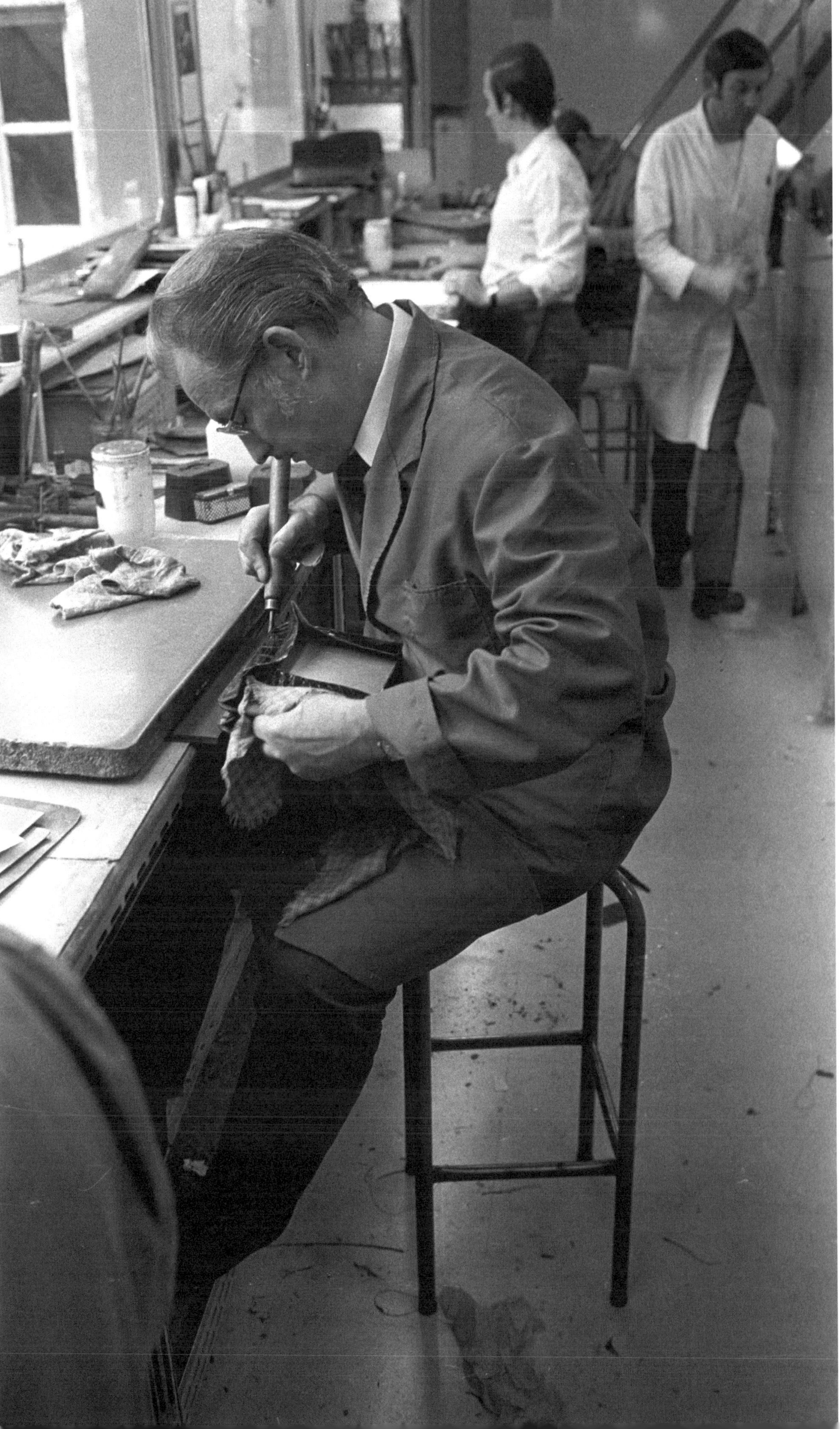

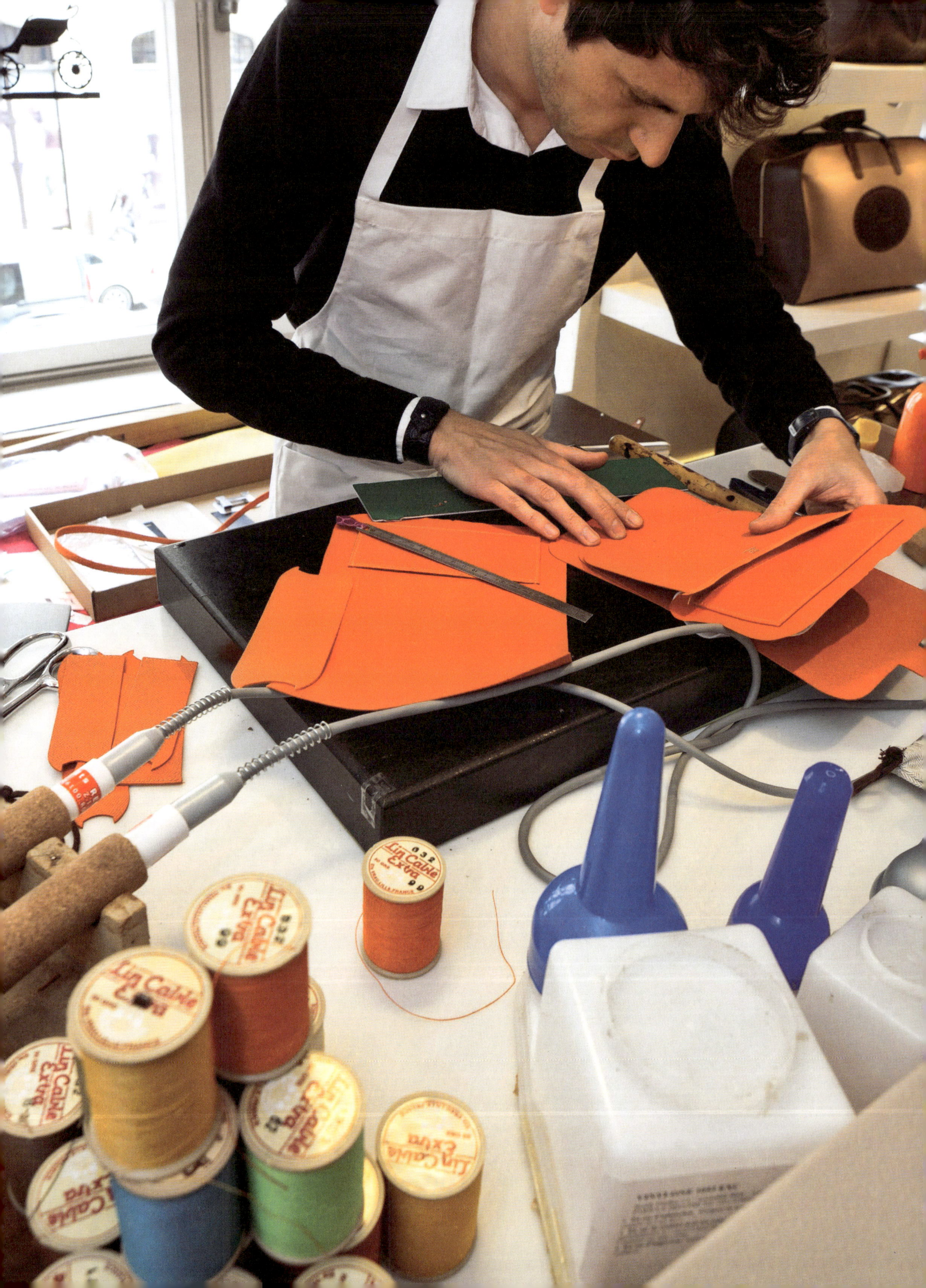
Lin Cable Extra

THE CREATION OF HERMÈS LEGENDARY BAGS AND ACCESSORIES TAKE PLACE IN WORKSHOPS ALL AROUND FRANCE

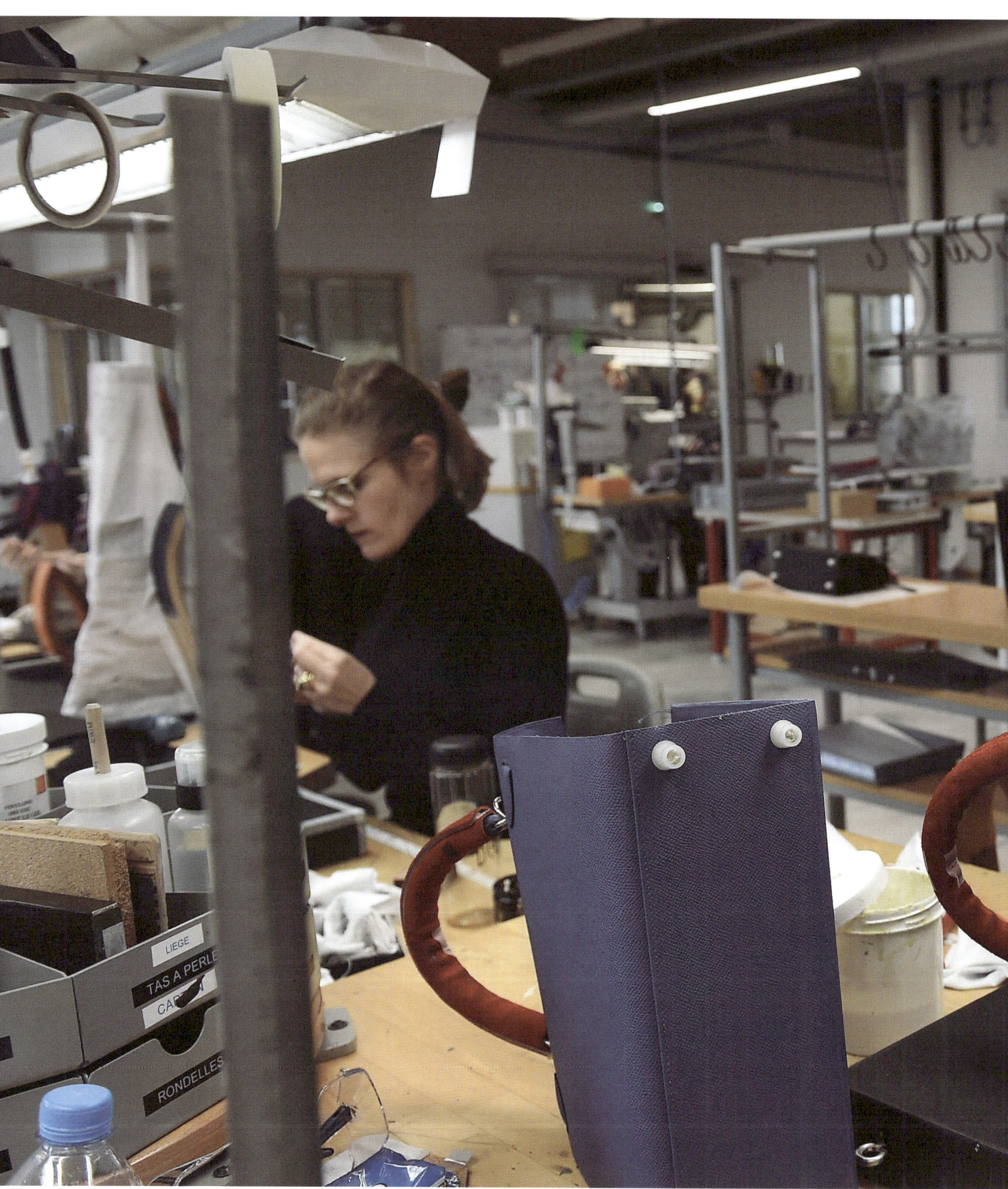

A craftsperson on a training course works on a Kelly bag in the new Hermès leather goods workshop (La Manufacture de l'Allan Hermès), on April 5, 2018 in Allenjoie, France.

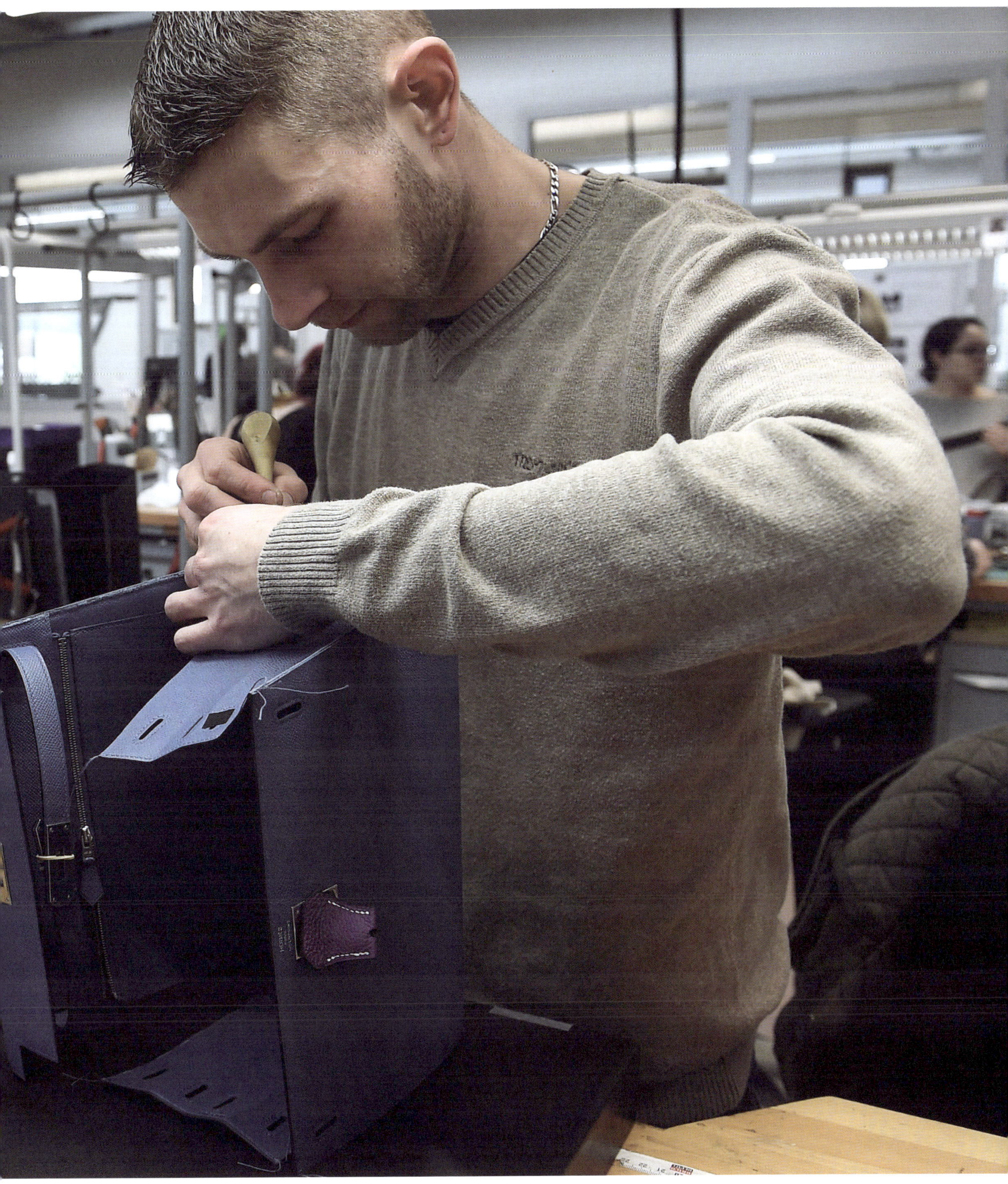

Without courting celebrity endorsements, Hermès has become one of the most coveted brands for the A, B, C *and* Z list. Despite the risk of potential overexposure, their bags remain highly coveted while rising far above the vagaries of fashion. Traditionalists at heart, the Hermès artisans have put their craft above all else. Their recruitment and training processes ensure that their output remains impeccable, and Hermès has never licensed their name for use on other products, unlike other major *maisons*.

Hermès' legendary bags and accessories are made in workshops around France; Hermès has a presence in 11 of the 13 French regions. Seventy-six percent of production takes place in Hermès' home country, although there are twelve global manufacturing hubs in Switzerland, Italy, UK, the USA, Portugal and Australia. Across France, Hermès runs approximately sixty production and study sites; future artisans spend two to five years enrolled in their training programs before becoming apprentices and finally graduating to unsupervised work. In 2024, 62% of the Hermès workforce was based in France, and the business continues to expand. An additional 2,400 new people were welcomed into the Hermés community in 2023, bringing the grand total to 25,000 employees in 2024. Each Hermès worker uses their own set of tools which they get to keep when they retire. Former workers join *Club des Anciens*, joining other 'ancients' for lunches, outings and an outpouring of extreme respect for their knowledge and skills. Hermès is incredibly proud of how the company treats all staff members during their employment—and beyond.

For Birkin and Kelly bags, a single artisan will make the bags from start to finish, responsible for executing every single step by hand. Other brands use machined elements and employ different people to make different parts of their bags in a production line, so the human touch is another unique reason why Hermès pieces are so expensive and prized. Once a Hermès piece is looking a little tired or has sustained some damage, owners can book their bags (or any item) into the Hermès spa, where the dedicated restoration and repair group will return the items good as new. Apparently, over 200,000 items received a glow-up in 2023. Some items reportedly take over a year to come back pristine and refreshed, echoing the time it may have taken to buy that piece in the first place. Good things come to those who wait.

While Hermès keeps the number of items produced in the ateliers a closely guarded secret, annual production estimates range from 12,000 to 70,000 Birkin bags each year. A New York Times analysis suggested that there were over one million bags on the market in 2019. The quality and longevity of Hermès' craftsmanship means that the bags are wildly desirable pieces to find on the resale market. The exquisite materials hold their value. It's also far easier and quicker to buy a used bag rather than a new one due to the wish process and production lead times. The resale market can also offer almost infinite access to old season models, discontinued styles, limited edition colorways and unique details that can't be found in the boutiques.

Pages 168, 170/171, 173, 174, 176: The French bag maker Samuel Lefranc assembles a Constance bag in the Hermès store in Munich, Germany.

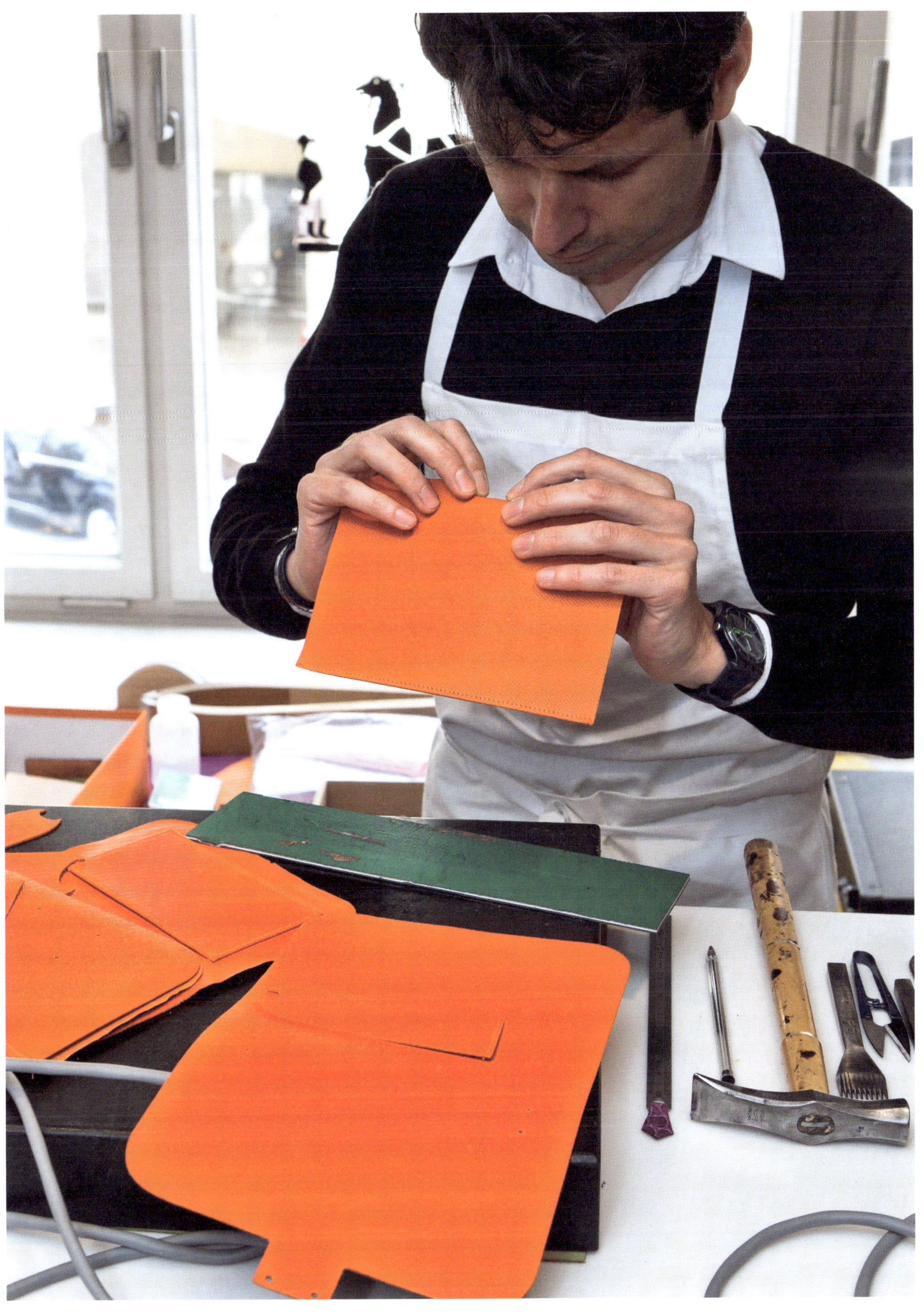

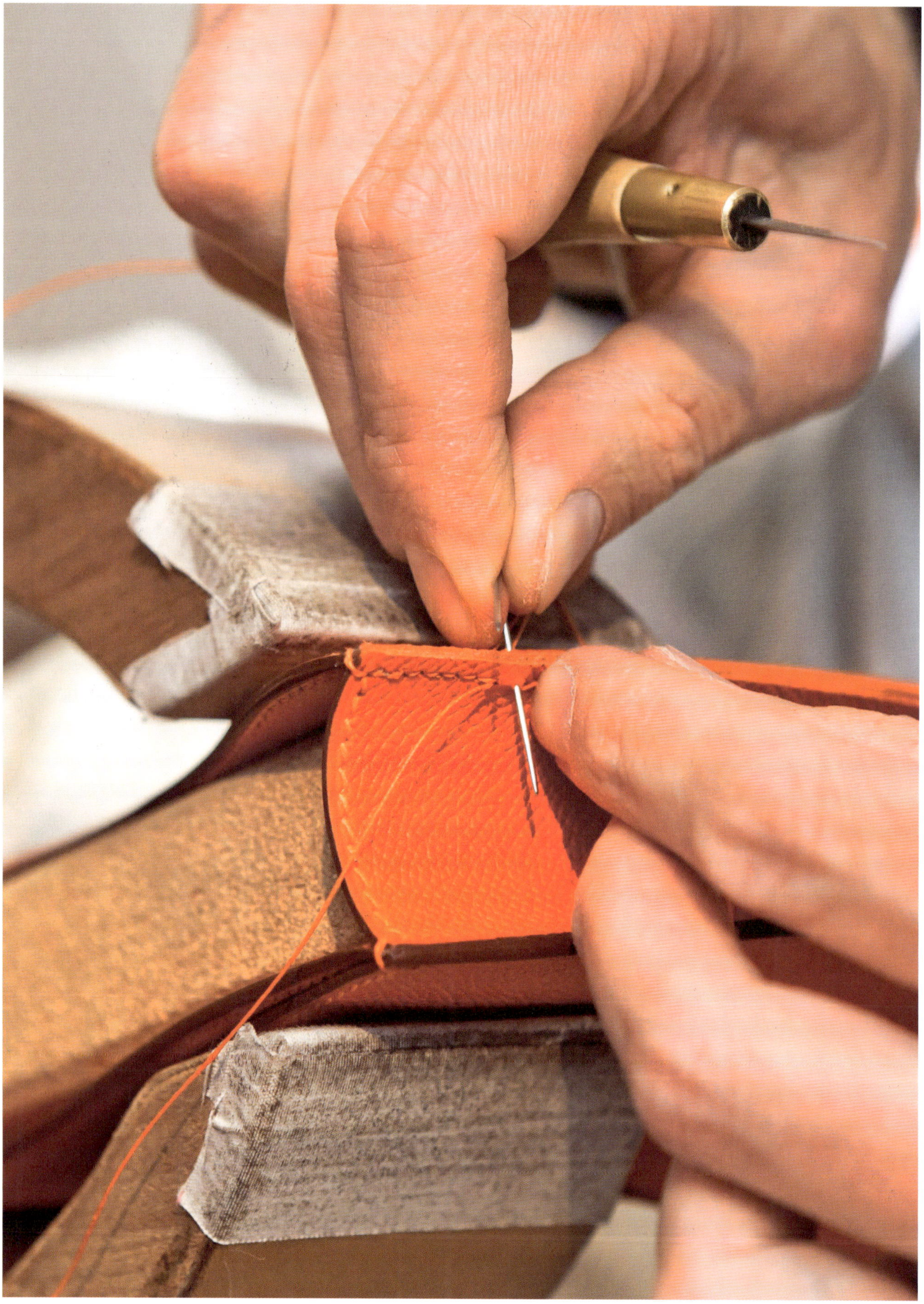

Considering their convoluted purchasing systems, Hermès is very aware of the fast turnaround of some of their customers' bags. Shoppers should remember that their receipts state that they agree not to resell their bags. However, that caveat doesn't stop people keen to recoup their investment immediately. At Love Luxury, a resale boutique with branches in London and Dubai, clients regularly head straight to their shop from the Hermès store, eager to cash in on a successful purchase.

With resale prices sometimes hitting double the in-store purchase price, depending on the leather, hardware, color, usage and availability, one can see why collectors are tempted to turn a quick profit, particularly if they have spent a significant amount of money building a profile in the Hermès store. A relationship with a sales associate, or SA, is key to accessing the upper echelon quota bags, as is the purported practice of spending six-figure sums on other Hermès goods to be offered a bag.

Understandably, these sales practices have drawn the ire of some Hermès clients. In 2024, three California customers brought a lawsuit alleging that Birkin sales violate antitrust laws. Plaintiffs Tina Cavalleri, Mark Glinoga and Mengyao Yang alleged that sales of other items were linked to the offer of a Birkin and that they were told they would need to buy other Hermès accessories to be considered for a Birkin. They believed this constituted a breach of antitrust laws, but U.S. District Judge James Donato agreed with Hermès and dismissed the case, ruling that these alleged sales practices could actually benefit the competition. Hermès was facing intense competition across the luxury market, prompting Donato to write in his verdict, "Hermès can run its business any way it wants. If it chooses to make five Birkin bags a year and charge a million, it can do that." Donato continued, "The fact that a lot of your clients may not be able to get a Birkin bag is not an... antitrust problem."

While physical counterfeits may have been a traditional irritation for Hermès, other problems loom as the world moves into the digital realm. Mason Rothschild is the artistic alias of Sonny Estival, an artist who created a series of 100 brightly colored and patterned MetaBirkin virtual bags as NFTs in 2021. Earning over $1 million on secondary sales sites, Rothschild took 7.5% in royalties—until Hermès placed an injunction on the sales. Rothschild responded that these NFTs were a critique of the fashion world and thus protected speech under his American First Amendment rights, permitting him to create art that "depicts" Birkin bags. U.S. District Judge Jed Rakoff and the jury disagreed, failing to find any artistic expression in the work. According to Rakoff, "Hermès proved that Rothschild intentionally misled consumers into believing that Hermès was backing its products... the jury found that Rothschild was simply a swindler." While NFTs are no longer as desirable as they were when they first appeared on the market, this was a landmark case proving that the importance of trademarks also extends to the virtual world. Rothschild was ordered to pay Hermès $133,000 in damages for copyright infringement.

In a world where fast fashion just keeps getting faster and ever more disposable, the longevity of Hermès, and particularly its *bags*, is a marvel. Pascale Mussard is currently director of the *Petit h* division of Hermès. She recalled asking her uncle Jean-Louis Dumas to describe the company's USP. His response echoed his own father Robert's comment that Hermès was and is different, and why? Because they made a product that could be repaired. "Think that you can repair something because

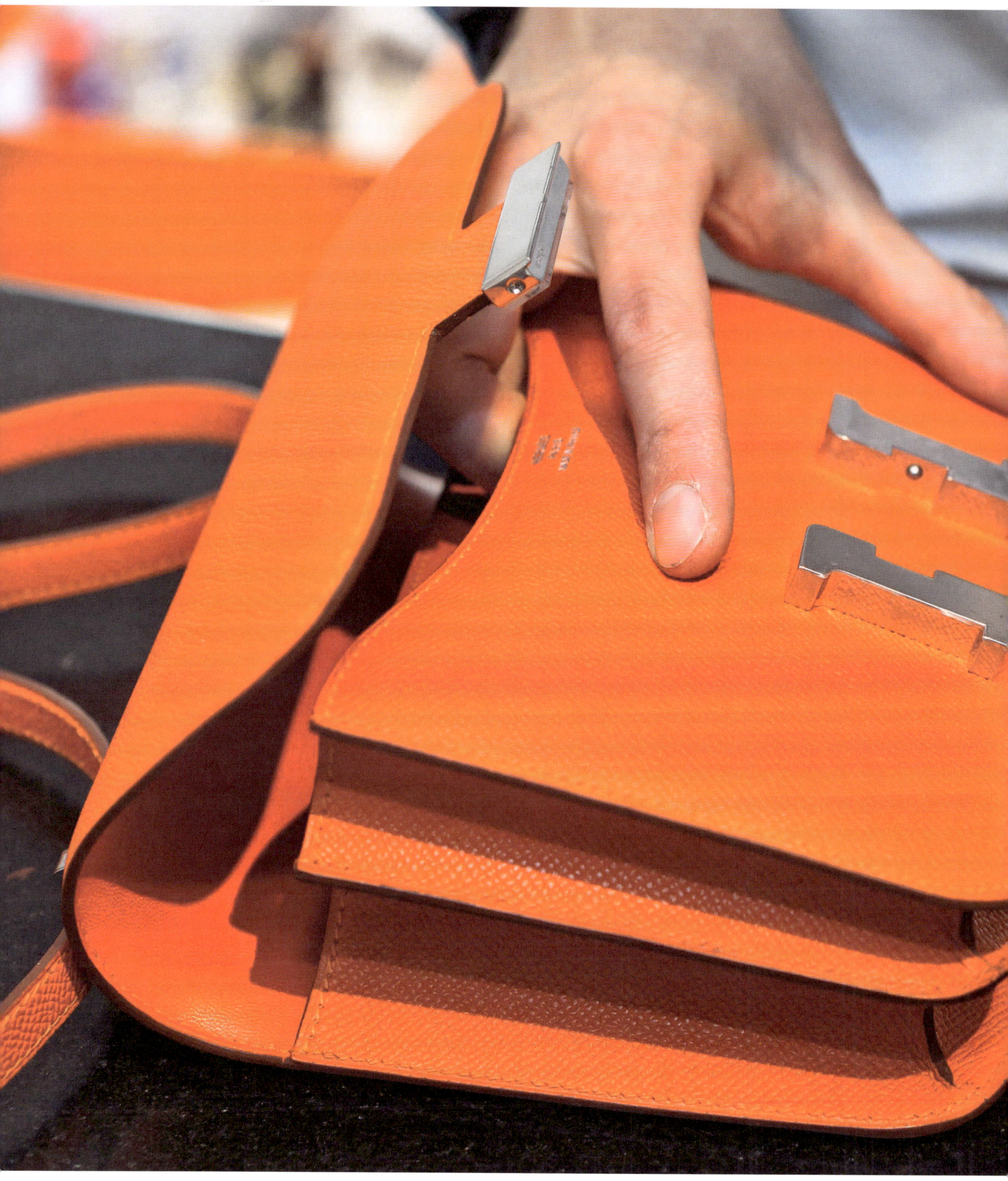

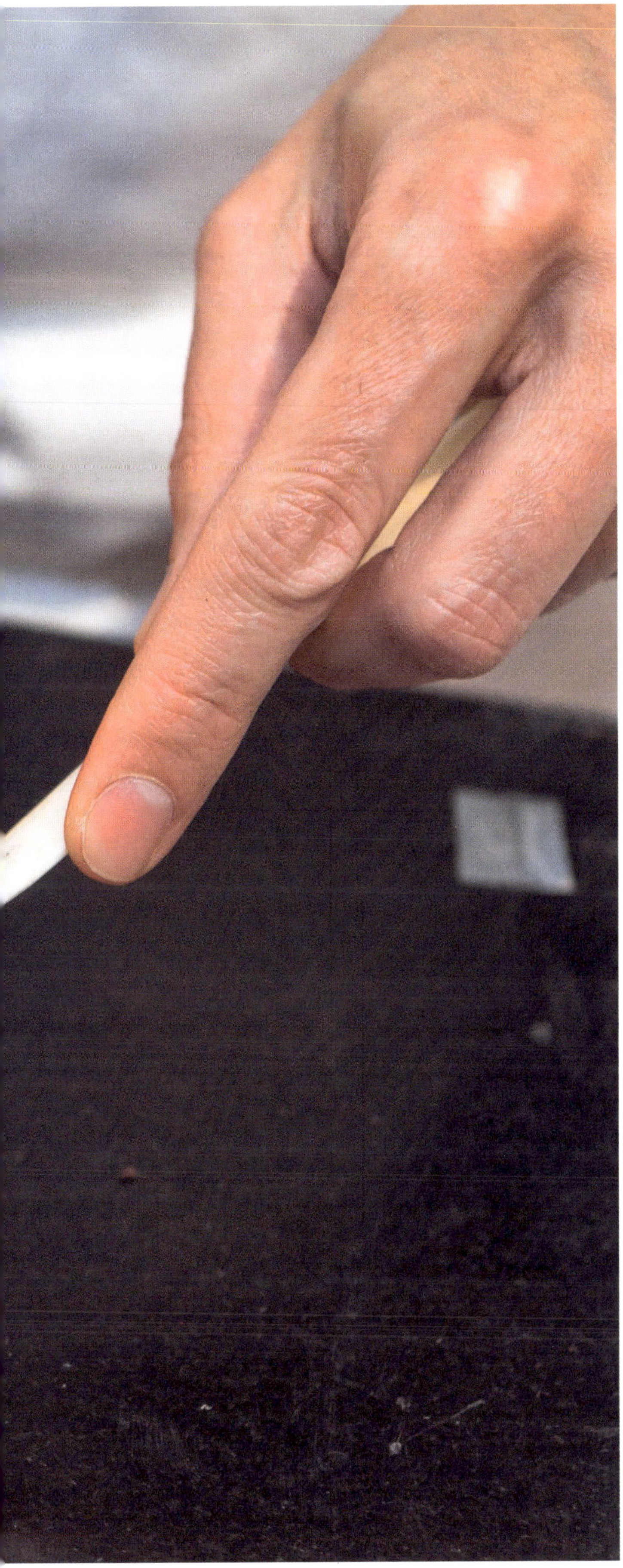

you know how to repair it and why it has been damaged. You have the hands. Think that you can repair it because you want to keep it. And think that you can repair it because you want to give it to someone else." Mussard's role is to oversee the *labo-atelier* (lab/studio) focused on recycling rejected or discarded Hermès production elements—scraps of leather, ceramics and hardware—and using them to create new pieces that are completely unique, meticulously made and unmistakably Hermès. Combining almost two hundred years of heritage with this forward-looking appreciation of the future will ensure that the handcrafted quality and care, time and excellence invested in making the world's most famous handbags will continue well into a third century.

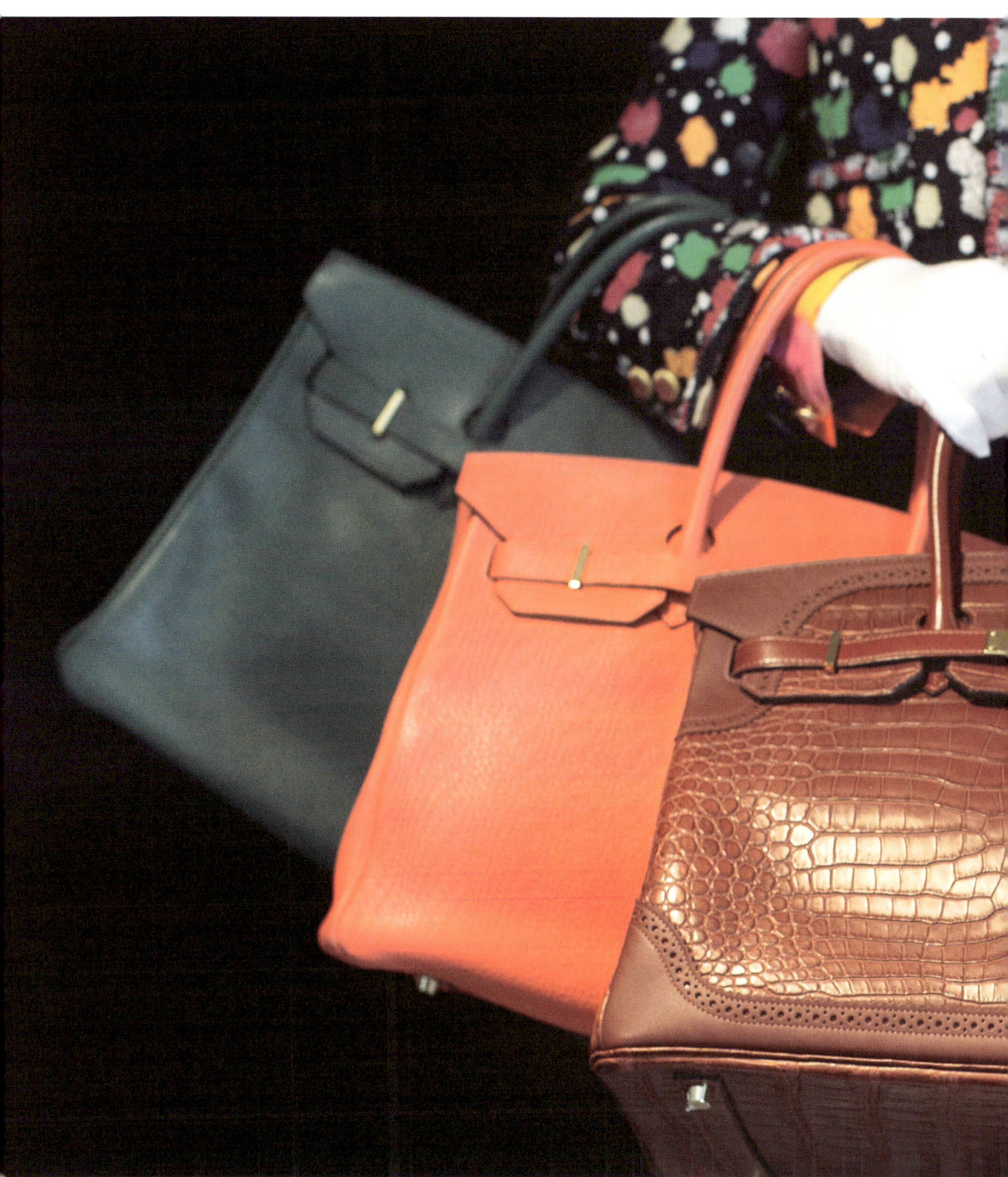

Designer Handbags and Fashion auction at Bonhams London, October 13th, 2020

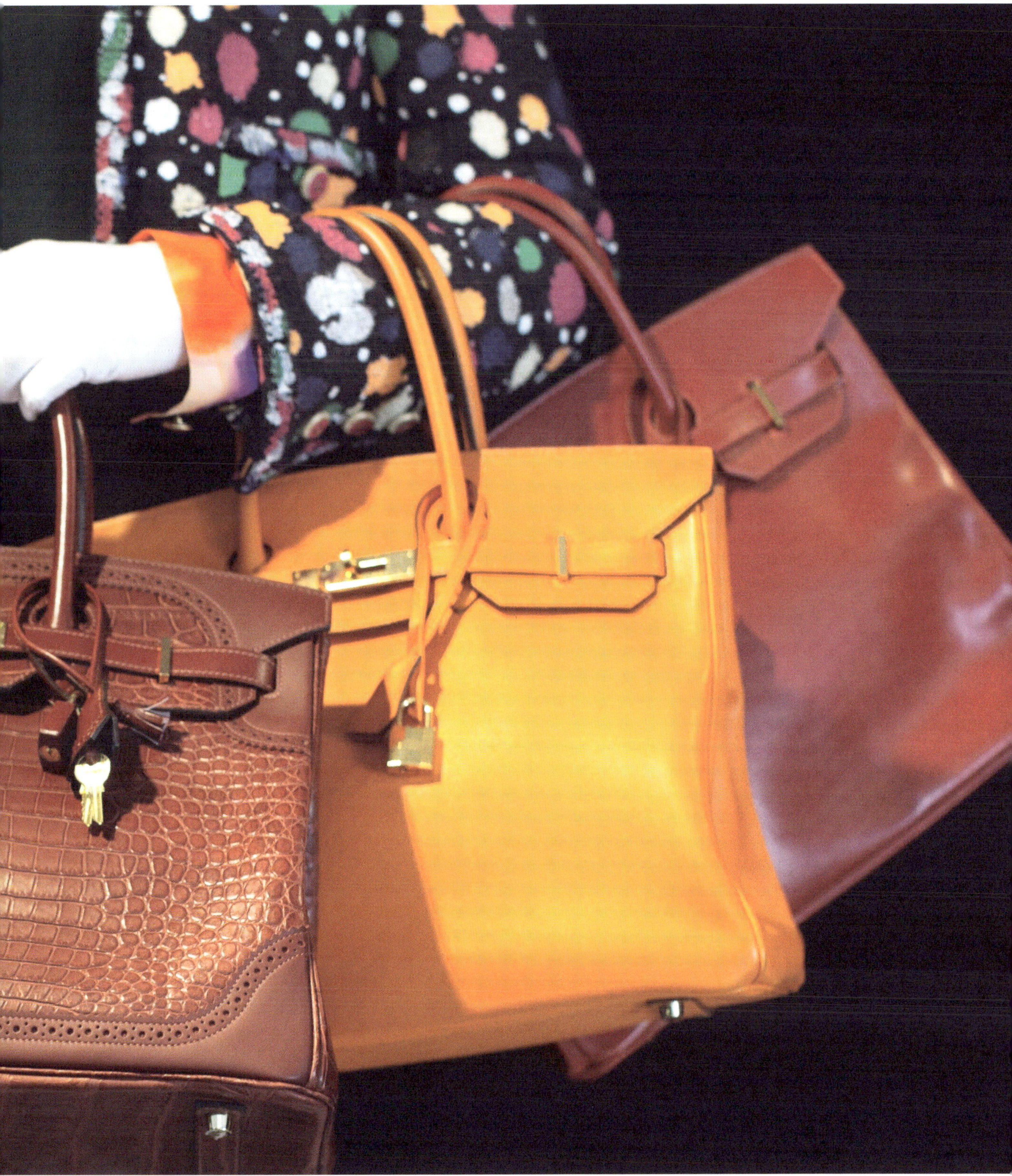

BUYING HERMÈS AT AUCTION

Q&A with Meg Randell, Head of Bonhams Designer Handbags and Fashion Department

How many Hermès bags are up for auction per year?
A typical Bonhams Luxury auction can feature between 40 and 50 Hermès handbags, along with a selection of Hermès accessories and ready-to-wear pieces.

What was the most exceptional (expensive) Hermès bag you've auctioned?
One of the most exceptional Hermès bags Bonhams has auctioned was the Hermès Birkin Faubourg, sold in Paris for €108,350 in 2023. The Faubourg Birkin is one of Hermès' most imaginative and coveted designs, created to resemble the façade of the historic Hermès flagship store at 24 Rue du Faubourg Saint-Honoré in Paris. In the original blue colorway, the miniature Birkin 20 exemplifies Hermès' exceptional craftsmanship, featuring a meticulous combination of leathers and intricate details such as stylized window awnings and a whimsical 'shopping bag' clochette.

What is the story behind the privilege of auctioning the original Birkin bag that was worn by Jane Birkin?
In 2021, we had the pleasure of offering one of Jane Birkin's own Birkin bags. The vendor had originally purchased the bag through an online charity auction in 2014, organised by Anno's Africa, and, remarkably, had left it forgotten at the back of a wardrobe for many years. It was only when a housekeeper asked whether the "beat-up bag" should be thrown away that the vendor remembered it and decided to have its current market value assessed.

Jane Birkin, an enduring cultural icon, famously inspired the creation of one of the world's most sought-after handbags. Since the Birkin bag debuted in 1984, Hermès gifted her several Birkin bags, all of which she later sold to support various charitable causes. This particular bag bore charming signs of per-

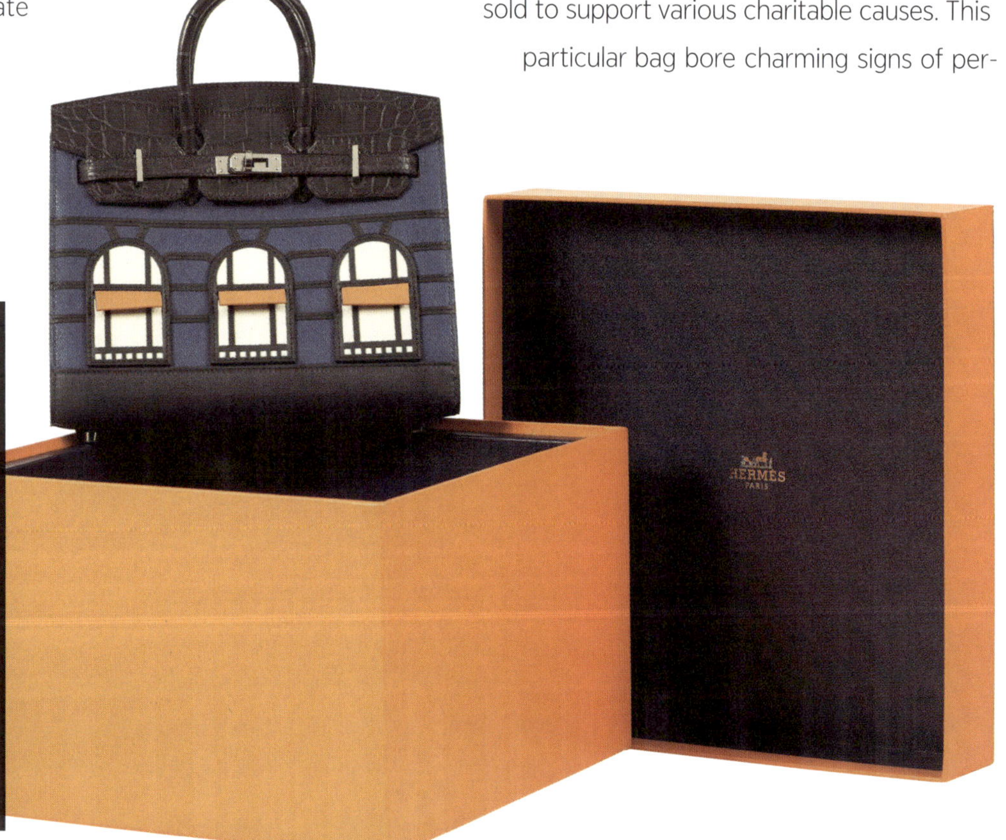

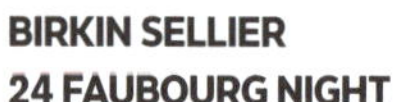

BIRKIN SELLIER
24 FAUBOURG NIGHT

Year: 2020

Material: Madame blue grained calfskin, Alligator Mississippiensis Matte, Swift calfskin inlays, palladium metal fasteners and clasp

Size: 20 cm

Sold at auction at Bonhams in Paris for €108,350 in 2023

sonal use by Jane Birkin herself, including a red cord tied around one of the handles and distinctive bite marks left by her cat. We presented the bag at auction with a pre-sale estimate of £15,000–20,000. Thanks to its remarkable provenance, the bag achieved an outstanding result of £119,000 at auction.

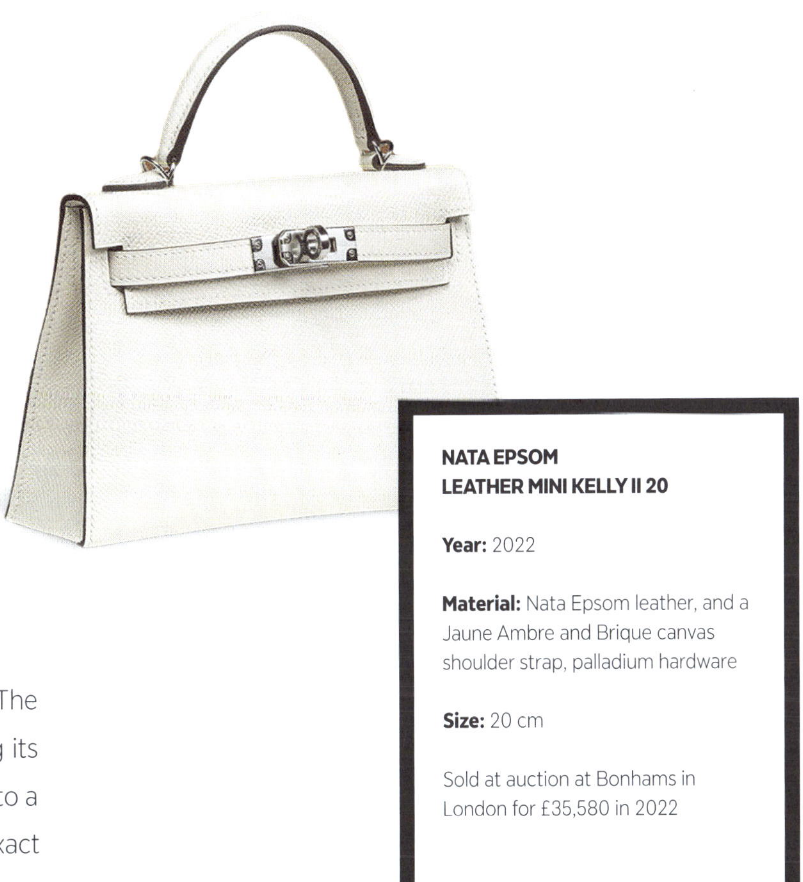

NATA EPSOM LEATHER MINI KELLY II 20

Year: 2022

Material: Nata Epsom leather, and a Jaune Ambre and Brique canvas shoulder strap, palladium hardware

Size: 20 cm

Sold at auction at Bonhams in London for £35,580 in 2022

Are there any interesting anecdotes regarding other auctions of Hermès bags?

In London in 2022, Bonhams sold a brand-new Mini Kelly II 20 in the highly sought-after Nata color. The bag achieved an impressive £35,580, far exceeding its pre-sale estimate of £12,000–22,000, and was sold to a private collector who had been searching for that exact piece to add to their collection. This sale serves as a prime example of how the resale market can be particularly strong when Hermès pieces are brand new and offered in colors and styles that are in high demand. Originally purchased directly from Hermès for approximately £4,500, the bag's resale value of nearly eight times the retail price highlights the extraordinary demand and the intense bidding activity for such coveted items.

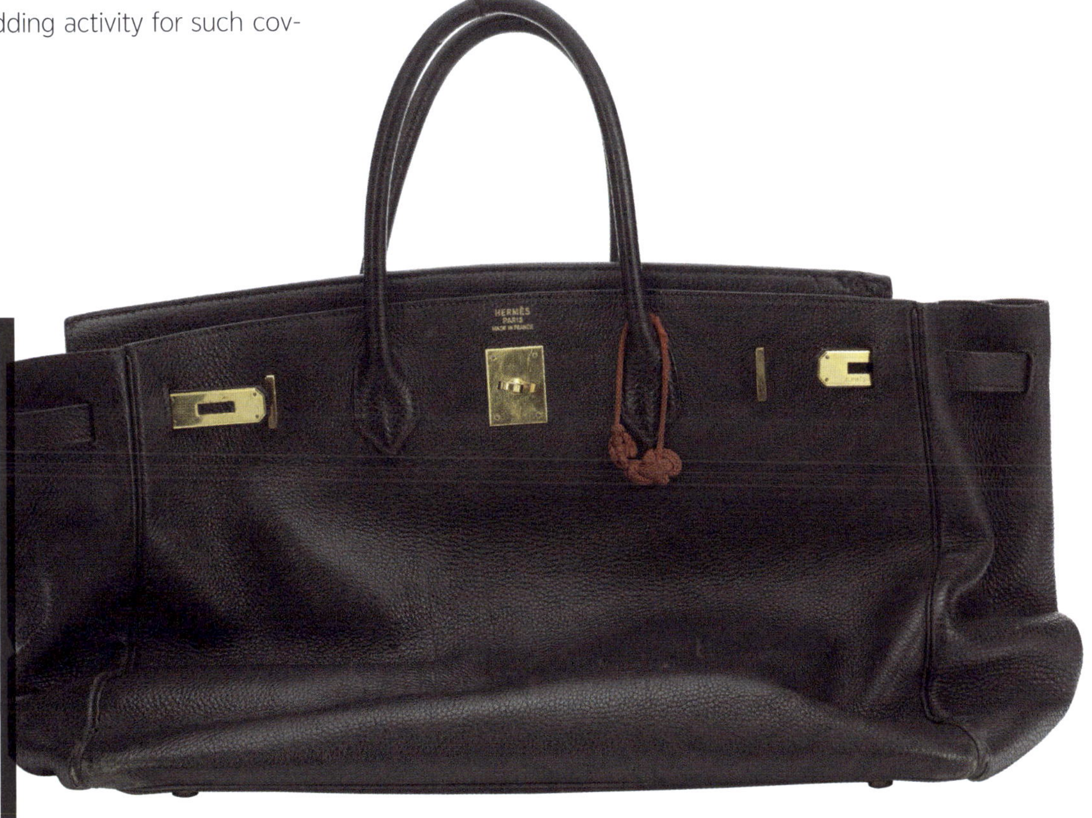

JANE BIRKIN'S BLACK TOGO BIRKIN 35

Year: c. 1999

Material: Togo leather, gold-tone hardware

Size: 35 cm

Sold at auction at Bonhams in London for £119,000 in 2021

What are the specific characteristics of Hermès bags that ensure they are authentic?

The characteristics we look for to ensure the authenticity of Hermès bags are constantly evolving, as counterfeit producers are continually refining their techniques. Nevertheless, there are key elements we consistently examine.

These include the quality and type of leather, the material and precision of the stitching, the color, material, and engraving of the hardware, the overall construction of the bag, and even the smell of the materials used. We also carefully assess the accompanying accessories such as the dust bag and box for additional clues.

Another useful indicator is Hermès' famous practice of producing seasonal colors. By cross-referencing the year of production with the color of the bag, it is sometimes possible to detect inaccuracies that counterfeiters overlook.

Meticulous attention to all these details, combined with a thorough understanding of Hermès' production standards, is crucial when authenticating each piece.

Which Hermès bags sell best?

While trends evolve and client preferences continually shift, unsurprisingly, the classic models remain consistently popular. The Birkin and Kelly bags continue to be the most sought-after pieces at auction. Other models that are often considered to be more accessible, such as the Constance, Garden Party, and Evelyne, also remain in demand among buyers.

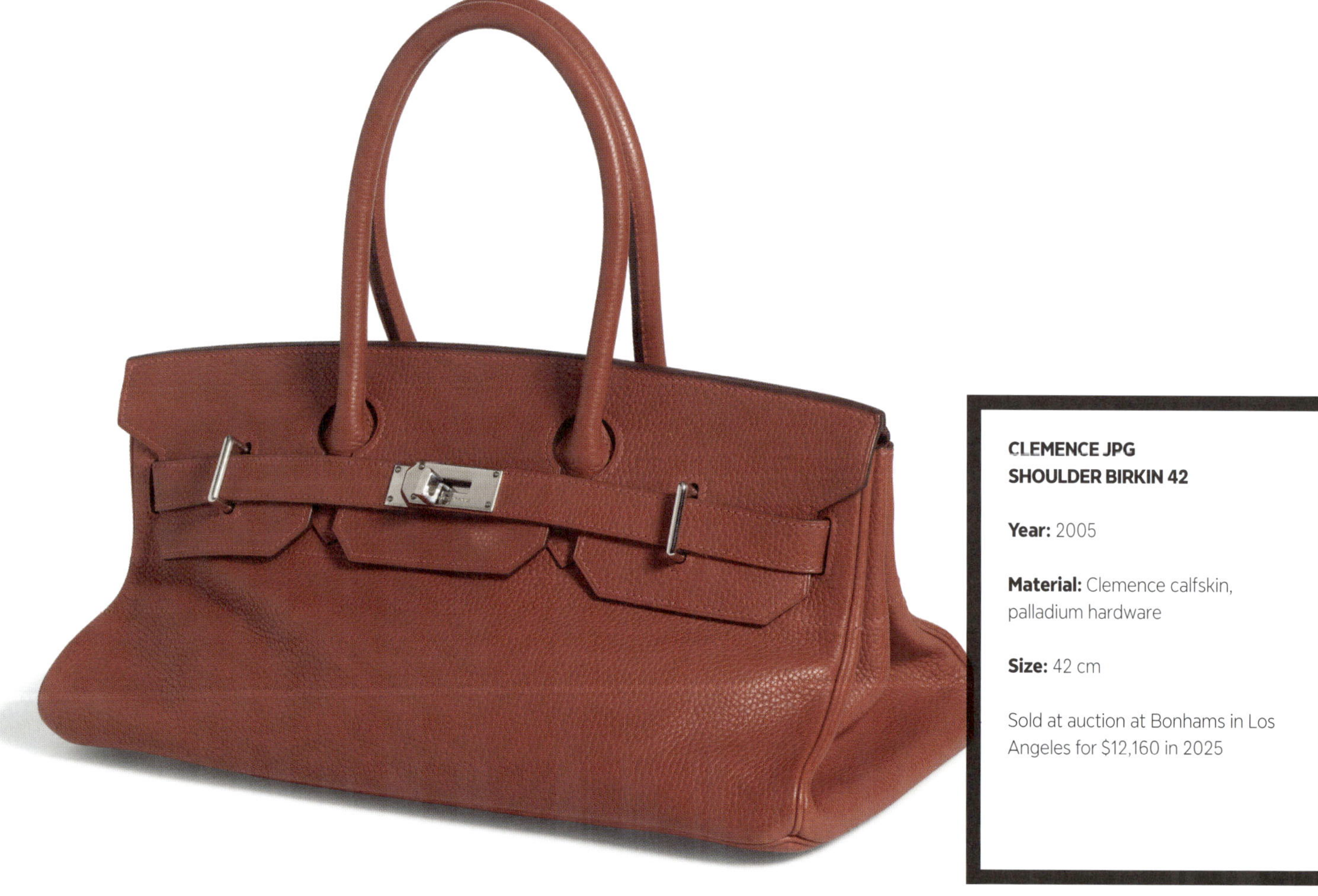

CLEMENCE JPG SHOULDER BIRKIN 42

Year: 2005

Material: Clemence calfskin, palladium hardware

Size: 42 cm

Sold at auction at Bonhams in Los Angeles for $12,160 in 2025

ROSE SAKURA SWIFT LEATHER BIRKIN 25

Year: 2023

Material: Swift leather, palladium hardware

Size: 25 cm

Sold at auction at Bonhams in London for £28,160 in 2024

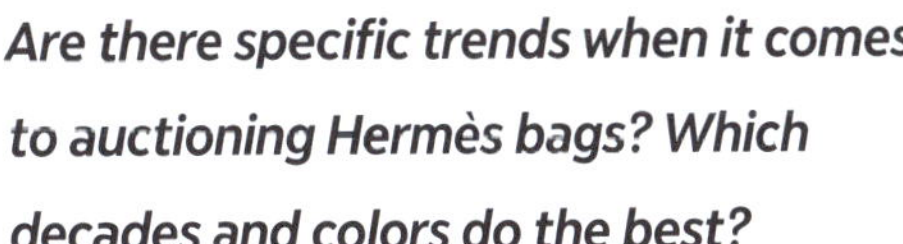

Are there specific trends when it comes to auctioning Hermès bags? Which decades and colors do the best?

Over the past five years, small bags have experienced a significant surge in popularity. Mini sizes consistently achieve outstanding results at auction. Additionally, limited edition models based on the classic Birkin and Kelly designs, such as the 'So Black' designed by Jean Paul Gaultier, Kelly Doll, and Cargo Birkin, are highly coveted and fiercely competed for by collectors. In terms of color, timeless shades such as Etoupe, Gold, and Black remain staples among both seasoned collectors and first-time buyers. However, colors with extremely limited availability such as Rose Scheherazade also generate considerable excitement, often commanding significant premiums due to their rarity.

ROSE SCHEHERAZADE LISSE ALLIGATOR KELLY WALLET

Year: c. 2017

Material: Lisse Alligator, palladium hardware

Size: 20 cm

Sold at auction at Bonhams in London for £6,310 in 2020

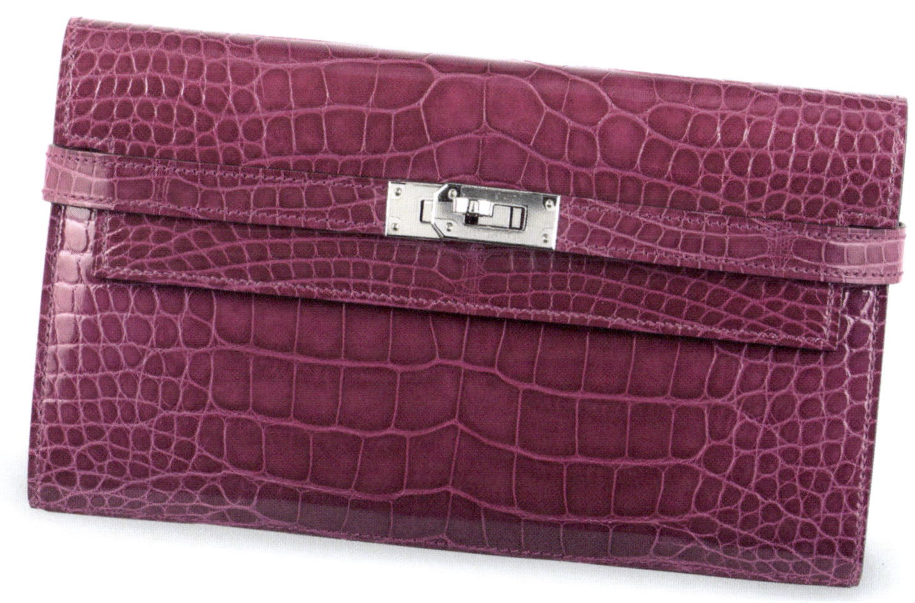

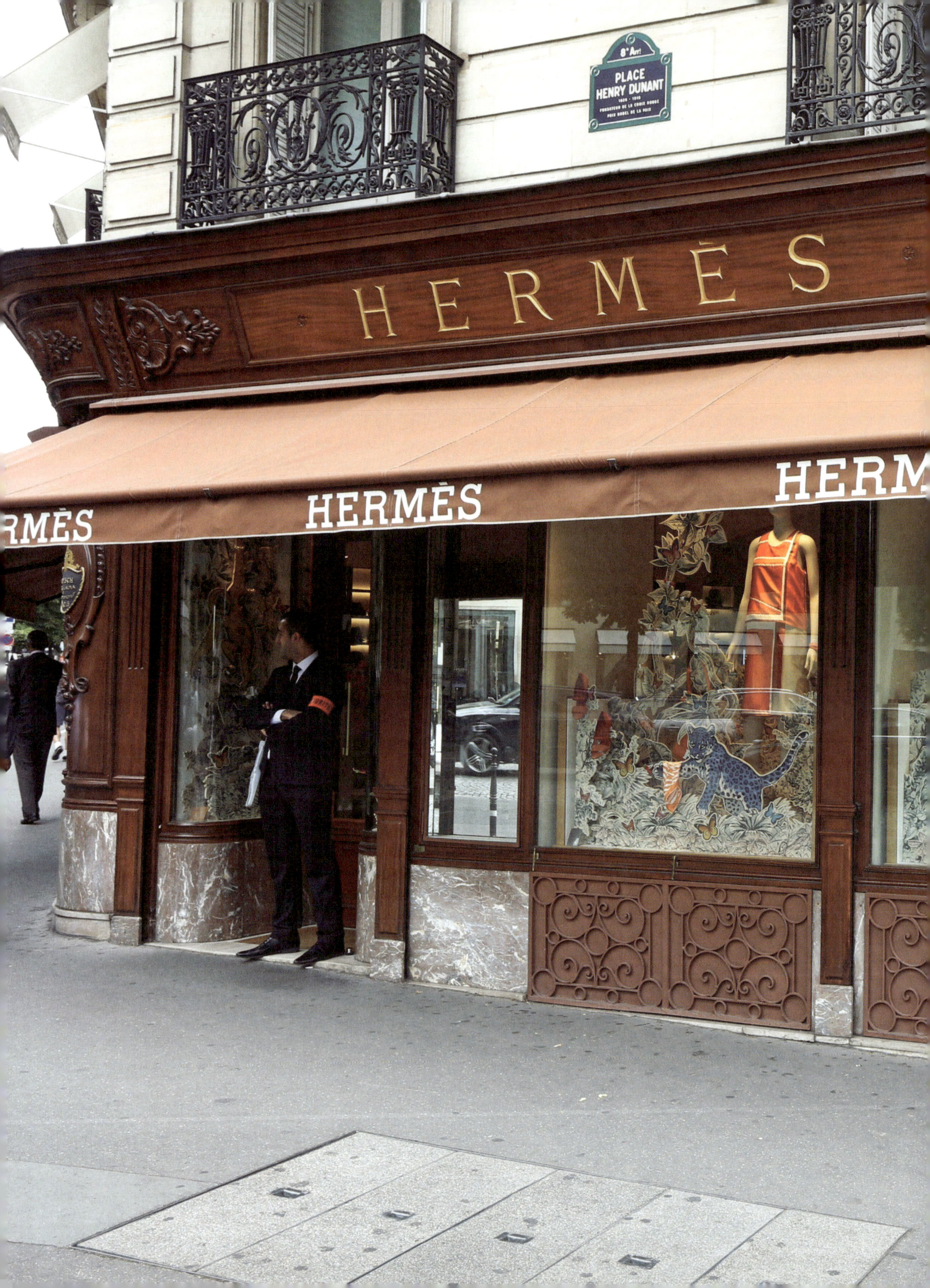
8e Arr.
PLACE
HENRY DUNANT
HERMÈS
HERMÈS

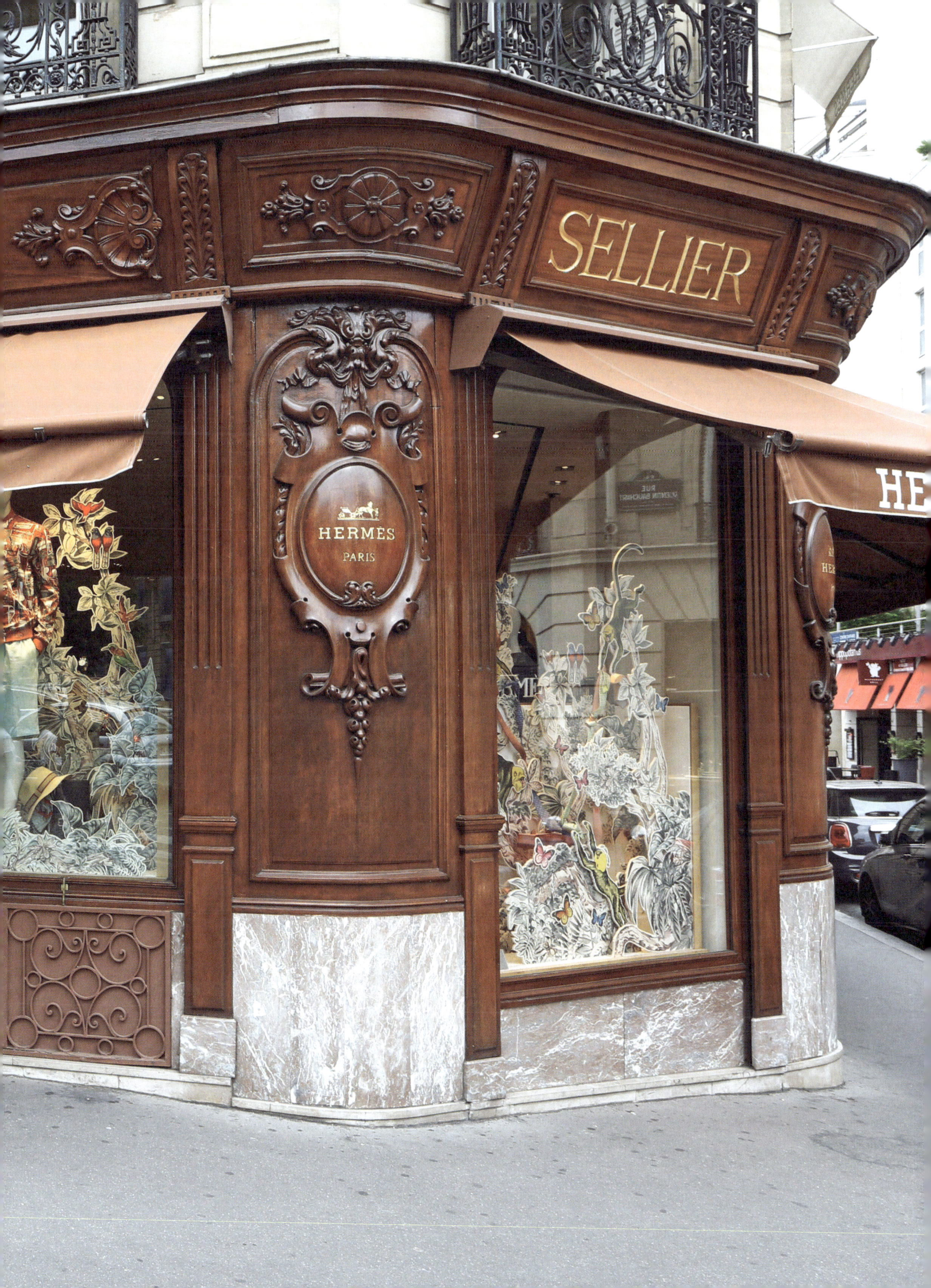
SELLIER
HERMES
PARIS

BIBLIOGRAPHY

- The Fashion Icons Hermes, by Alison James

RETAILERS

- Hermès https://www.hermes.com/uk/en/
- Love Luxury https://loveluxury.ae/
- Sellier https://www.sellierknightsbridge.com/
- 1st Dibs https://www.1stdibs.com/
- Lilac Blue https://lilacblue.com/
- The Handbag Clinic https://www.handbagclinic.co.uk/
- Vestiaire Collective https://www.vestiairecollective.com/
- By Rotation https://byrotation.com/
- Bag Borrow or Steal https://www.bagborroworsteal.com/
- Bonhams www.bonhams.com

RESOURCES

- https://vb.com/
- https://www.independent.co.uk/life-style/fashion/features/handbags-at-dawn-the-battle-at-the-heart-of-french-fashion-house-herm-232-s-2195076.html
- https://www.stanhopeinsurance.co.uk/
- https://www.vanityfair.com/news/2007/09/hermes200709
- https://www.ft.com/content/6fbb0e1f-8ec1-44b1-b2a4-406a9c06aff9
- https://www.nssmag.com/it/fashion/31681/hermes-martin-margiela
- https://www.ft.com/content/ff27f287-ebad-4d31-b1b9-e5b1f05154c8
- https://www.forbes.com/sites/bluecarreon/2017/09/26/what-martin-margiela-brought-to-hermes/
- https://www.pursebop.com/
- https://www.businessoffashion.com/
- https://edition.cnn.com/
- https://www.glamour.com/story/so-you-want-a-walmart-birkin-good-luck
- https://madisonavenuecouture.com/
- https://www.voguescandinavia.com/articles/jane-birkin-on-the-hermes-birkin-how-fashions-most-iconic-handbag-was-first-sketched-on-a-sickbag
- https://www.bbc.co.uk/news/entertainment-arts-39430589
- https://www.ft.com/content/dff3907a-35fa-11e5-bdbb-35e55cbae175
- https://www.telegraph.co.uk/fashion/brands/hermes-respond-to-jane-birkin/

- https://www.reuters.com/legal/government/hermes-shoppers-try-again-birkin-bag-antitrust-lawsuit-2024-10-14/
- https://www.thefashionlaw.com/
- https://news.artnet.com/art-world/mason-rothschild-hermes-metabirkin-banned-in-us-2328232
- https://www.vogue.co.uk/fashion/article/charles-gross-tiktok-hermes-birkin-bags
- https://www.nytimes.com/1986/10/18/style/for-staid-hermes-a-younger-beat.html
- https://www.elle.com.au/fashion/fashion-news/kylie-jenner-birkin-bags-24190/

Page 184: Hermès store, George V, Paris

Page 188: Hermès store window display, Rue du Faubourg Saint-Honoré, Paris

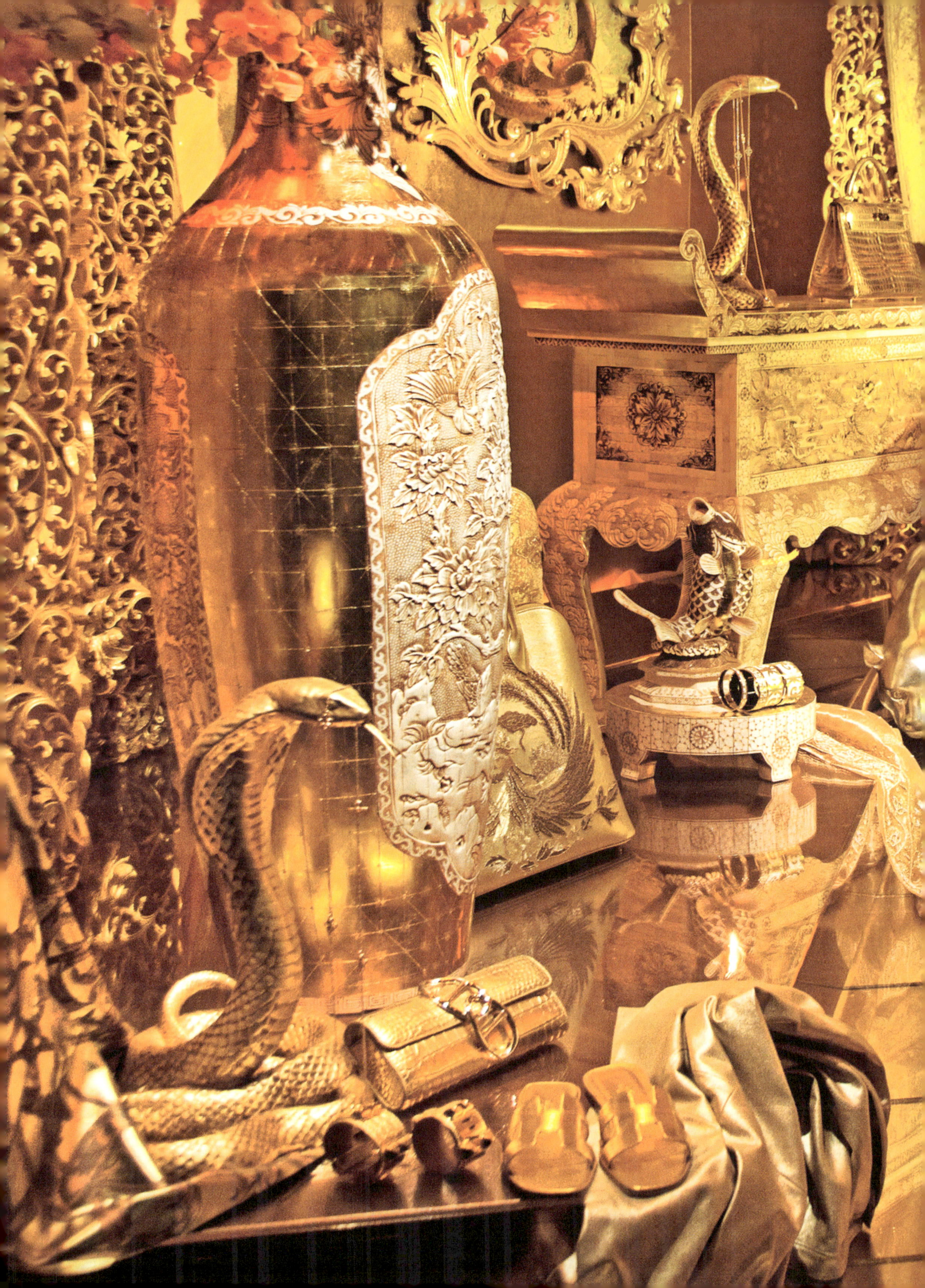

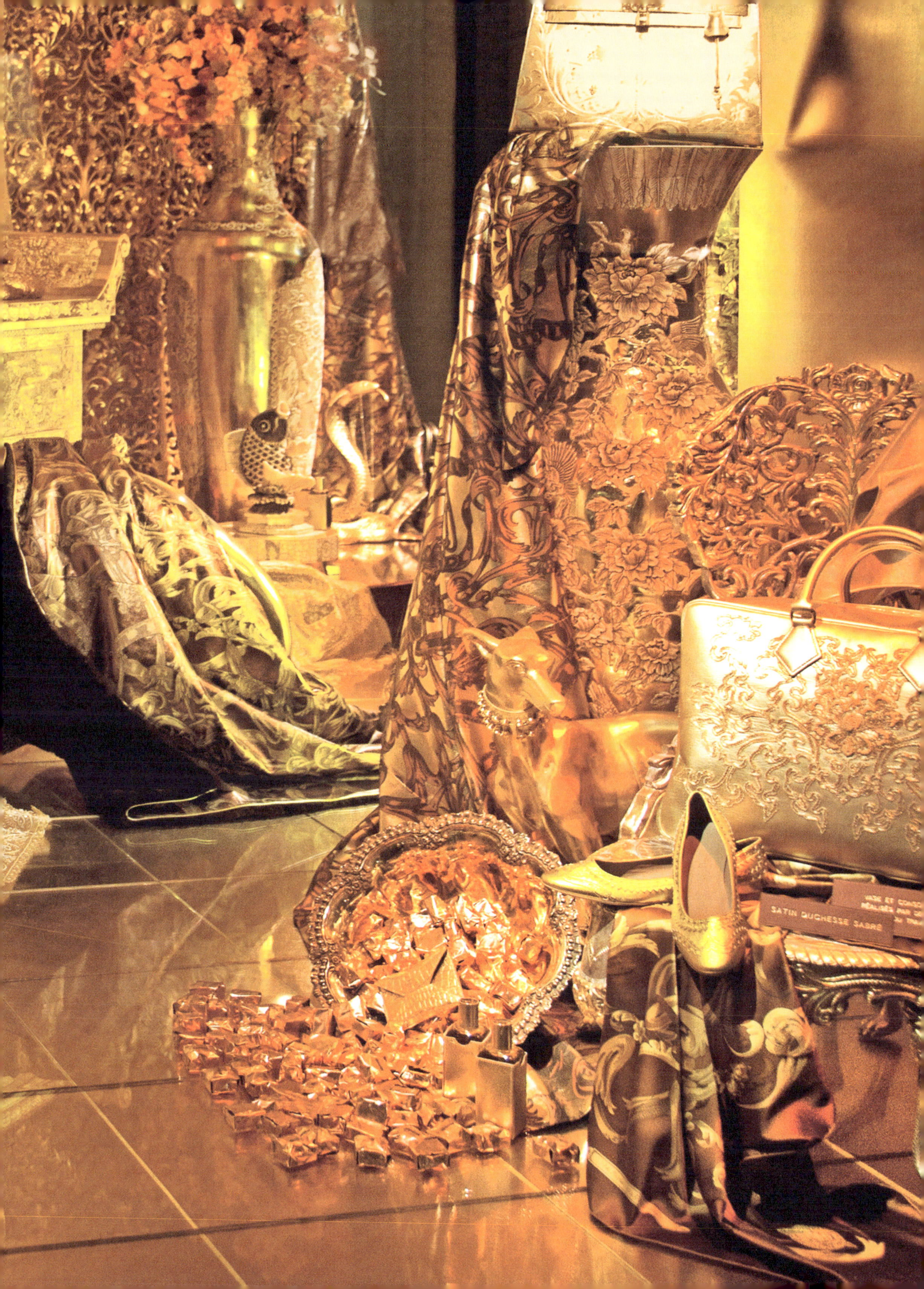
SATIN DUCHESSE SABRÉ

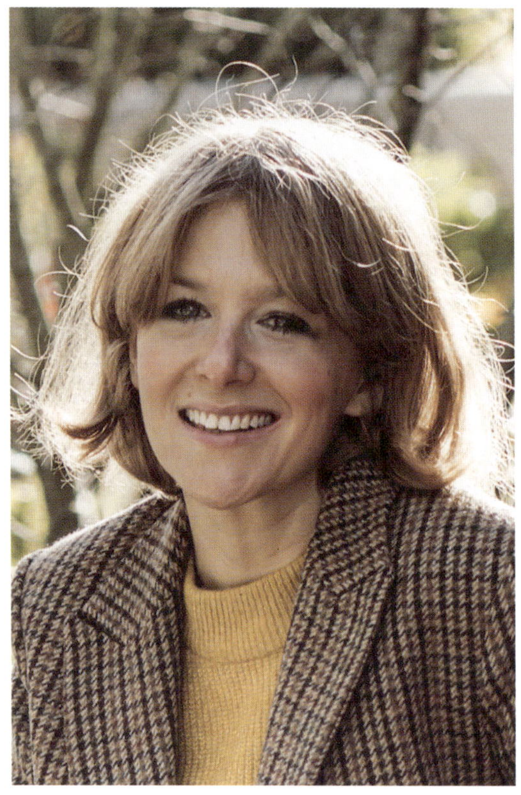

ALEXANDRA FULLERTON

Alexandra Fullerton is an Essex Girl by birth and former Londoner, however she now resides in Norfolk, having done a pandemic pivot towards a more rural life. She lives in a small village with her husband, daughter, long-haired chihuahua Ozzie and Nibbles the rabbit. The majority of Alex's career has been spent on magazines as a fashion director (7.5 years as Fashion director at Stylist magazine, 5 years as fashion director at large of Glamour UK) which meant styling A list actors, musical icons and celebrities (including Kylie Minogue, Rosie Huntington-Whiteley, Sophie Turner, Florence Welch and Kelly Rowland), travelling the world to shoot fashion stories and sitting front row at fashion shows. Now Alex is self-employed and has a portfolio career that combines fashion writing for The Telegraph and Bazaar Arabia, commercial styling (brands she has worked with include Stella McCartney and Marks & Spencer), personal styling, ghostwriting, writing her own books and running a shopping platform My3Words.co. When not working, Alex loves to explore provincial charity shops and dreams of unearthing a stash of Hermès Birkin bags. alexandrafullerton.com / @alexandrafullerton

IMAGE CREDITS

Cover Illustration: Jasmin Taeschner

p. 3: Photo by Jinsoo Choi/unsplash; pp. 4/5: © JP Yim/Getty Images; p. 7: © Grzegorz Czapski /Alamy /Alamy Stock Photos/mauritius images; pp. 8/9: © Bettmann/Getty Images; p. 11: © Georges MERILLON/Gamma-Rapho via Getty Images; p. 12: © VAN DER HILST/Gamma-Rapho via Getty Images; p. 15: © Giovanni Giannoni/WWD/Penske Media via Getty Images; p. 16: © Fairchild Archive/Penske Media via Getty Images; p. 17: © Keystone/Getty Images; p. 18: © Francois Durand/Getty Images; pp. 20/21: © PIERRE VERDY/AFP via Getty Images; pp. 22: © Giovanni Giannoni/WWD via Getty Images; p. 25: © Dave Benett/Getty Images for Hermès; p. 26/27: © Edward Berthelot/Getty Images; p. 29: © picture alliance /ASSOCIATED PRESS | Bill Ingraham; p. 30: © Daniel Zuchnik/Getty Images; p. 31: © Christian Vierig/Getty Images; p. 32: © Edward Berthelot/Getty Images; pp. 34/35: © Jeremy Moeller/Getty Images; p. 37: © Valentina Frugiuele/Getty Images; pp. 38/39 © Edward Berthelot/Getty Images; p. 40: © Edward Berthelot/Getty Images; p. 41: © Kirstin Sinclair/Getty Images; p. 43: © Christian Vierig/Getty Images; pp. 44/45: © Edward Berthelot/Getty Images; p. 47: © Jun Sato/WireImage; pp. 47/48: © Edward Berthelot/Getty Images; p. 50: © Claudio Lavenia/Getty Images; p. 51: © Claudio Lavenia/Getty Images; pp. 52/53: © Edward Berthelot/Getty Images; p. 54: © Ignat/Bauer-Griffin/GC Images; pp. 56/57: © James Devaney/GC Images; p. 58: © Sarah Treacher/WWD via Getty Images; p. 58: © Christian Vierig/Getty Images; pp. 60/61: © Jeremy Moeller/Getty Images; p. 63: © A. Astes /Alamy /Alamy Stock Photos/mauritius images; pp. 64–69: © Jeremy Moeller/Getty Images; pp. 70/71: © Edward Berthelot/Getty Images; pp. 72/73: © Jeremy Moeller/Getty Images; pp. 74/75: © Edward Berthelot/Getty Images; pp. 76/77: © Christian Vierig/Getty Images; p. 78: © Jeremy Moeller/Getty Images; p. 79: © Pascal vandon /Alamy /Alamy Stock Photos/mauritius images; pp. 80/81: © picture alliance /Eibner-Pressefoto | Eibner-Pressefoto/Annika Graf; p. 82: © Giovanni Giannoni/WWD via Getty Images; p. 83: © Victor VIRGILE/Gamma-Rapho via Getty Images; pp. 84/85: © REPORT /Alamy /Alamy Stock Photos/mauritius images; pp. 86/87: © Victor VIRGILE/Gamma-Rapho via Getty Images; p. 88: © picture alliance /ZUMAPRESS.com | www.Fashionpps.com; p. 89: © Daniel Zuchnik/Getty Images; pp. 90/91: © Casimiro PT /Shutterstock.com; pp. 92/93: © Christian Vierig/Getty Images; p. 94: © Mathis Wienand/Getty Images; p. 95: © Jeremy Moeller/Getty Images; pp. 96/97: © Victor VIRGILE/Gamma-Rapho via Getty Images; pp. 98/99: © Edward Berthelot/Getty Images; pp. 100/101: © gpriccardi – stock.adobe.com; p. 102: © Jeremy Moeller/Getty Images; p. 103: © Photolime /Alamy /Alamy Stock Photos/mauritius images; pp. 104/105: © Victor VIRGILE/Gamma-Rapho via Getty Images; pp. 106/107: © Cyril Marcilhacy/Bloomberg via Getty Images; pp. 108/109: © REPORT /Alamy /Alamy Stock Photos/mauritius images; p. 110(bottom): © picture alliance /IK ALDAMA | IK ALDAMA; pp. 110(top) & 111: © Victor VIRGILE/Gamma-Rapho via Getty Images; p. 112(top): © Daniel Zuchnik/Getty Images; p. 112(bottom): © picture alliance /abaca | Bertrand-Hillion Marie-Paola/ABACAPRESS.COM; p. 113: © Edward Berthelot/Getty Images; pp. 114/115: © Photo12 /Alamy Stock Photos/mauritius images; p. 117 © Alexander Tamargo/Getty Images for E11EVEN; p. 119: © Nicolas Khayat/ABACA/ddp images; p. 120: © Bryan Bedder/Getty Images; p. 121: © Dimitrios Kambouris/Getty Images for Hermes; pp. 124/125: © mauritius images/United Archives GmbH/Alamy/Alamy Stock Photos; p. 126: © Headlinephoto Limited / Alamy /Alamy Stock Photos/mauritius images; p. 127: © picture alliance /dpa | P Stevens; p. 128: © Jose Perez/Bauer-Griffin/GC Images via Getty Images; p. 129: © Raymond Hall/GC Images via Getty Images; pp. 130/131: © Arnaldo Magnani/Getty Images; p. 132: © Pierre Suu/GC Images via Getty Images; p. 133: © James Devaney/WireImage via Getty Images; p. 135: © METROPOLIS/Bauer-Griffin/GC Images via Getty Images; p. 136: © GP/Star Max/GC Images via Getty Images; p. 137: © Edward Berthelot/Getty Images; pp. 138/139: © Gotham/GC Images; p. 140: © Prince Williams/GC Images via Getty Images; p. 141: © Prince Williams/WireImage via Getty Images; p. 142: © Rachpoot/Bauer-Griffin/GC Images via Getty Images; pp. 143–145: © Edward Berthelot/Getty Images; p. 146: © GVK/Bauer-Griffin/GC Images via Getty Images; p. 147: © WENN Rights Ltd. /Alamy Stock Photos/mauritius images; pp. 148/149: © Storms Media Group /Alamy /Alamy Stock Photos/mauritius images; p. 150: © GTCRFOTO /Alamy /Alamy Stock Photos/mauritius images; p. 151: © picture alliance /maxppp | P STEVENS; p. 152: © The Hapa Blonde/GC Images via Getty Images; p. 153: © Marc Piasecki/GC Images via Getty Images; p. 154: © Aeon/GC Images via Getty Images; p. 155: © Avalon.re/IMAGO; pp. 156–157: © Jeremy Moeller/Getty Images; p. 158: © Gotham/WireImage/Getty Images; p. 159: © Dave Benett/Getty Images for Hermès; pp. 160/161: © Moviestore Collection Ltd /Alamy /Alamy Stock Photos/mauritius images; pp. 162/163: © Marc Piasecki/GC Images via Getty Images; pp. 164–167: © Reginald Gray/WWD/Penske Media via Getty Images; pp. 168 and 173–177: © HRSchulz/IMAGO; pp. 170/171: © SEBASTIEN BOZON/AFP via Getty Images; pp. 178/179: © Mark Thomas /Alamy /Alamy Stock Photos/mauritius images; pp. 180–183: Courtesy of Bonhams; pp. 184/185: © Igor Prahin /Alamy /Alamy Stock Photos/mauritius images; pp. 188/189: © Peter Horree /Alamy /Alamy Stock Photos/mauritius images; p. 190: © Rekha Damhar

IMPRINT

The Ultimate Guide to Hermès Bags
This book was conceived, edited, and designed by teNeues.

Text by Alexandra Fullerton
Proofreading by Amanda Ennis, Nadine Weinhold, Benine Mayer

Editorial Management by Nadine Weinhold
Design by Marcus Taeschner
Layout by Marcus Taeschner
Picture Editing by Heide Christiansen
Production by Sandra Jansen-Dorn, Nele Jansen
Color Separation and Prepress by Jens Grundei

Printed in the Czech Republic by Finidr
Produced in Europe

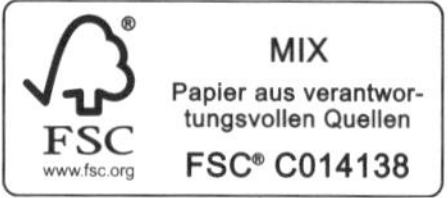

Published by gestalten, Berlin 2025
ISBN 978-3-96171-712-5

2nd printing, 2026

The German edition is available under
ISBN 978-3-96171-730-9.

For more information, and to order books, please visit www.teneues.com and www.gestalten.com

Die Gestalten Verlag GmbH & Co. KG
Mariannenstrasse 9–10, 10999 Berlin, Germany
hello@gestalten.com

Krefeld Office
Uerdinger Str. 265 / Villa Pattberg
47800 Krefeld, Germany
verlag@teneues.com

teNeues Press Department
press@gestalten.com

Bibliographic information published by the Deutsche Nationalbibliothek. The Deutsche Nationalbibliothek lists this publication in the Deutsche Nationalbibliografie; detailed bibliographic data is available online at www.dnb.de

https://instagram.com/teneuespublishing

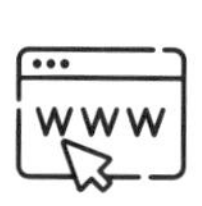

www.teneues.com